Economics

by
Marcel Lewinski

AGS Publishing
Circle Pines, Minnesota 55014-1796
800-328-2560

About the Author

Marcel Lewinski is currently Associate Professor of History Education at Illinois State University. Previously, he was an award-winning high school social studies teacher. He has taught a wide range of subjects, including economics, world history, United States history, geography, political science, sociology, and contemporary problems. Lewinski is professionally active in many organizations and has given presentations at many state, regional, and national conferences. He has conducted numerous workshops for social studies teachers and has traveled all over the world. As author of several books in social studies, Mr. Lewinski acts as a consultant to school systems and has served as a frequent contributor to educational publications.

Photo credits for this textbook can be found on page 474.

Content Reviewers

Lois Barnes
School Improvement Consultant
Brentwood, TN

John McKinnon
Assistant Professor/Clinical Supervisor of Student Teaching
Illinois State University
Normal, IL

The publisher wishes to thank the following educators for their helpful comments during the review process for *Economics*. Their assistance has been invaluable.

Patricia L. Anderson, Resource Teacher, Foothills Adult School, El Cajon, CA; **William R. Daniel,** Social Studies Resource Teacher, Jefferson County Public Schools, Gheen Academy, Louisville, KY; **Sharon H. Duncan,** Curriculum and Transition Coordinator, Elim Christian School, Palos Heights, IL; **Shelly Faust,** Government/Economics Teacher, Southwood Junior/Senior High School, LaFontaine, IN; **Zoe Flatman,** Teacher, Riverdale Collegiate Institute, Toronto, Ontario, Canada; **Kevin Griffin,** Teacher, Algonac High School, Algonac, MI; **Patricia Ann Jordan,** Director of Exceptional Services, Canton Public Schools, Canton, MS; **Lynn E. Pritchett,** Ed.S., Special Education Department Head, Colquitt County High School, Moultrie, GA; **Janet K. Raney,** Inclusion/Consultation Teacher, Southwestern Middle School, Deland, FL; **Christina M. Rivett,** Special Education Teacher, East Jackson High School, Coldwater, MI; **Pamela Russell,** Special Education Teacher, Learning Disabilities, Muscle Shoals High School, Muscle Shoals, AL; **Bill Shaver,** Teacher, Lincoln High School (Alternative), Fort Morgan, CO; **Monica M. Thorpe,** Teacher, Canutillo Middle School, Canutillo, TX; **Diane Tournis,** Special Education Teacher, Crown Point High School, Crown Point, IN

Publisher's Project Staff

Vice President, Product Development: Kathleen T. Williams, Ph.D., NCSP; Associate Director, Product Development: Teri Mathews; Managing Editor: Patrick Keithahn; Assistant Editor: Stephanie Hasselmann; Development Assistant: Bev Johnson; Creative Services Manager: Nancy Condon; Designer: Katie Sonmor; Desktop Production Artist: Peggy Vlahos; Purchasing Agent: Mary Kaye Kuzma; Market Director/Secondary Curriculum: Brian Holl

Printed in the United States of America
ISBN 0-7854-3770-3
Product Number 94000
A 10 V051 12

Contents

Biographies

Economics in Your Life

Economics at Work

Document-Based Readings/ Document-Based Questions

Writing About Economics

Skill Builders

Figures

Figures, continued

How to Use This Book: A Study Guide

Welcome to *Economics*. Consumers, business owners, and government leaders make economic decisions every day. They must decide how best to use money and resources for the things they need and want. *Economics* shows how scarcity, supply and demand, and competition affect these decisions. You will learn the skills needed to spend, save, and invest your money wisely. Other focuses of *Economics* include the history of labor and banking in the United States and the different economic systems. Finally, you will learn about the importance of trade to the world economy.

As you read this book, notice how each lesson is organized. Information is presented in a straightforward manner. Graphs, charts, and photos help to clarify the text. Read the information carefully. If you have trouble with a lesson, try reading it again.

Before you start to read this book, it is important that you understand how to use it. It is also important to know how to be successful in this course. Information in this first section can help you achieve these things.

How to Study

These tips can help you study more effectively:

◆ Plan a regular time to study.

◆ Choose a desk or table in a quiet place where you will not be distracted.
  Find a spot that has good lighting.

◆ Gather all the books, pencils, paper, and other equipment you will need to complete your assignments.

◆ Decide on a goal. For example: "I will finish reading and taking notes on Chapter 1, Lesson 1, by 8:00."

◆ Take a five- to ten-minute break every hour to keep alert.

◆ If you start to feel sleepy, take a break and get some fresh air.

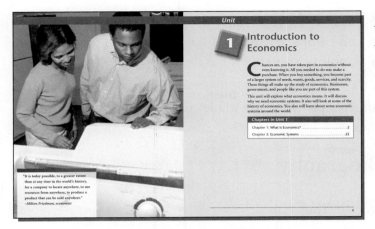

Before Beginning Each Unit

◆ Read the unit title and study the photograph. Do you recognize anything in the photo?

◆ Read the quotation. Try to connect the ideas to the picture.

◆ Read the opening paragraphs.

◆ Read the titles of the chapters in the unit.

◆ Read the Chapter Summary and Unit Summary to help you identify key ideas.

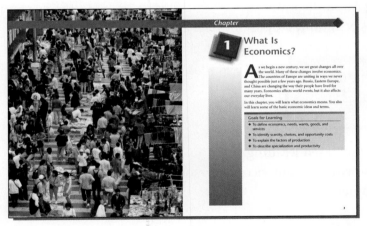

Before Beginning Each Chapter

◆ Read the chapter title and study the photograph. What does the photo tell you about the chapter title?

◆ Read the opening paragraphs.

◆ Study the Goals for Learning. The Chapter Review and tests will ask questions related to these goals.

◆ Look at the Chapter Review. The questions cover the most important information in the chapter.

Note These Features

You can find complete listings of these features in this textbook's table of contents.

Biography

Highlights people who have made contributions to economics or business

Economics in Your Life

Relates economics to the "real world"

Economics at Work

Examines different careers related to economics

Writing About Economics

Provides economics topics to write about in each chapter

Document-Based Reading

Presents primary- and secondary-source documents related to each chapter

Skill Builder

Focuses on economics and social studies skills

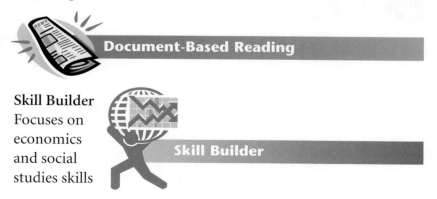

Before Beginning Each Lesson

Read the lesson title and restate it in the form of a question.

For example, write: *What is a market economy?*

Look over the entire lesson, noting the following:
◆ bold words
◆ text organization
◆ photos
◆ graphs and charts
◆ Lesson Review questions

As You Read the Lesson

◆ Read the major headings.
◆ Read the subheads and paragraphs that follow.
◆ Study the graphs and charts.
◆ Before moving on to the next lesson, see if you understand the concepts you read. If you do not, reread the lesson. If you are still unsure, ask for help.
◆ Practice what you have learned by completing the Lesson Reviews.

Using the Bold Words

Bold type

Words seen for the first time will appear in bold type

Glossary

Words listed in this column are also found in the glossary

Knowing the meaning of all the boxed words in the left column will help you understand what you read.

These words appear in **bold type** the first time they appear in the text and are often defined in the paragraph.

A **resource** is anything that people use to make things or do work.

All of the words in the left column are also defined in the **glossary**.

Resource (rē′ sôrs) anything that people use to make things or do work (p. 4)

Word Study Tips

◆ Start a vocabulary file with index cards to use for review.

◆ Write one term on the front of each card. Write the chapter number, lesson number, and definition on the back.

◆ You can use these cards as flash cards by yourself or with a study partner to test your knowledge.

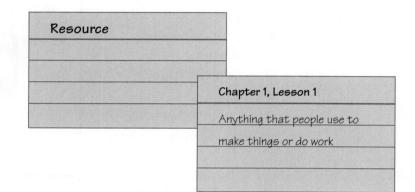

Taking Notes in Class

◆ Outline each lesson using the subheads as the main points.

◆ Always write the main ideas and supporting details.

◆ Keep your notes brief.

◆ Write down important information only.

◆ Use your own words.

◆ Do not be concerned about writing in complete sentences. Use phrases.

◆ Do not try to write everything the teacher says.

◆ Use the same method all the time. Then when you study for a test, you will know where to go to find the information you need to review.

◆ Review your notes to fill in possible gaps as soon as you can after class.

Using the Summaries

◆ Read each Chapter Summary to be sure you understand the chapter's main ideas.

◆ Review your notes and test yourself on vocabulary words and key ideas.

◆ Practice writing about some of the main events from the chapter.

◆ At the end of each unit, read the Unit Summary to be sure you understand the unit's main ideas.

Using the Reviews

◆ Answer the questions in the Lesson Reviews.

◆ In the Chapter Reviews, answer each fill-in-the-blank, multiple choice, and short-answer question.

◆ Review the Test-Taking Tips.

Preparing for Tests

◆ Complete the Lesson Reviews and Chapter Reviews. Make up similar problems to practice what you have learned. You may want to do this with a classmate and share your questions.

◆ Review your answers to Lesson Reviews and Chapter Reviews.

◆ Reread the Chapter Summaries and Unit Summaries.

◆ Test yourself on vocabulary words and key ideas.

"It is today possible, to a greater extent than at any time in the world's history, for a company to locate anywhere, to use resources from anywhere, to produce a product that can be sold anywhere."
–*Milton Friedman, economist*

Introduction to Economics

Chances are, you have taken part in economics without even knowing it. All you needed to do was make a purchase. When you buy something, you become part of a larger system of needs, wants, goods, services, and scarcity. These things all make up the study of economics. Businesses, government, and people like you are part of this system.

This unit will explore what economics means. It will discuss why we need economic systems. It also will look at some of the history of economics. You also will learn about some economic systems around the world.

Chapters in Unit 1

1

What Is Economics?

As we begin a new century, we see great changes all over the world. Many of these changes involve economics. The countries of Europe are uniting in ways we never thought possible just a few years ago. Russia, Eastern Europe, and China are changing the way their people have lived for many years. Economics affects world events, but it also affects our everyday lives.

In this chapter, you will learn what economics means. You also will learn some of the basic economic ideas and terms.

Goals for Learning

- ◆ To define economics, needs, wants, goods, and services
- ◆ To identify scarcity, choices, and opportunity costs
- ◆ To explain the factors of production
- ◆ To describe specialization and productivity

Resource

Anything that people use to make things or to do work

Labor

Work

Capital

Things of worth: machines, buildings, tools, and money

Natural resource

A raw material found on Earth, such as water, minerals, land, and forests

Economics

The study of how people and countries make decisions about how to use their scarce resources in the most efficient way

Choice

The act of deciding on and selecting what is wanted most

Need

Something that is necessary to remain alive

Want

A thing that is not needed to survive but that makes life better

What Is Economics?

Every country and person has **resources** they use to get the things they want. A resource is anything that people use to make things or to do work. You may have a part-time job by which you earn money. The work you do is one type of resource, called **labor.** **Capital** is another type of resource. It refers to all machines, buildings, tools, and money. **Natural resources** are a third type of resource. Natural resources refer to raw materials found on Earth. Some natural resources are water, minerals, land, and forests. **Economics** is the study of how people and countries make decisions about how to use their scarce resources in the most efficient way.

Let's look at economics in another way. It is all about making **choices**. Countries and people use their resources in different ways. A country might like to spend money on improving the lives of its people or on building up its defenses. A person might like to spend money eating out or buying a new CD player. Land can be used for farming, for business, or for housing. However, people and governments cannot do all the things they want. They have to make choices. If they choose to spend money on one thing, they have less to spend on something else.

What Is the Difference Between Needs and Wants?

All people share certain **needs**. A need is something that is necessary to remain alive. To survive, we all need food, water, clothing, and a place to live. Governments also have needs. Many people think that a strong military defense, good schools, and a safe environment are needs. Most of us want more than just the basic needs. Our **wants** are things that we do not need to survive but that make our lives better.

Imagine that you suddenly receive a surprise gift of $10,000. You might buy yourself a car or a television. You might take a trip or save the money for college. These are examples of wants. Just like people, governments also have wants. For example, a government may want to provide free college education for certain students. A government may want to make sure everyone has enough money, or it may want to cure cancer.

What Are Goods and Services?

Goods are the things that people buy. Cars, televisions, and beds are examples of goods. Goods are **manufactured**. Manufacturing is the process of turning materials into products we use every day like soap, radios, TVs, eyeglasses, school buses, and even textbooks. **Services** refer to work done for other people for a fee. Most of the jobs in the United States and Canada are service jobs. For example, your teacher offers a service. Doctors, auto mechanics, and store clerks also provide a service.

Service jobs involve doing work for someone. A window washer provides the service of cleaning windows.

Economics at Work

Economist

Economists give advice about how to use resources. They study the distribution of resources such as land, labor, raw materials, and machinery. They keep records and do research. They make comparisons among businesses and groups. They analyze and predict changes and trends. The information economists gather is often used to determine the need for new goods or services.

Economists analyze ways in which government laws may affect a group. They may propose changes in those laws. These changes may improve the use of the group's resources. If the group is a business, such changes may mean the business earns more money.

Economists often gain information from other social sciences to help with their job. They learn about the effects that politics, sociology, psychology, and geography can have on economics. Most economists have high degrees in business administration or economics.

Word Bank

economics
labor
making choices
need
want

Lesson 1 Review On a separate sheet of paper, write the word from the Word Bank to complete each sentence.

1. The study of how people and countries make decisions about resources is called _____.

2. Economics is all about _____.

3. Work that people do is a resource called _____.

4. Something people use but do not need to survive is a(n) _____.

5. Something necessary to remain alive is a(n) _____.

What do you think ?

6. If you received $10,000, how would you choose to spend it?

7. Why do you think most of the jobs in the United States and Canada are service jobs?

Scarcity

A problem in which wants are greater than what is available

What Is Scarcity?

What does "scarce" mean? It means that people want more than there is. No matter how hard people try, not everyone's wants can be satisfied. Resources are limited, but wants are unlimited. This creates the problem of **scarcity**. Scarcity is the most basic of all economic problems. If scarcity were not a problem, there would be enough of everything to meet everyone's needs and wants. Unfortunately, we do not live in such a world. There are just not enough resources for people to have everything they want.

We all have had scarcity in our own lives. For example, when you want to go see a movie that costs more money than you have, you have experienced scarcity. You probably also have experienced scarcity of time. This happens when you have too little time to do all the things you want to do. Countries have scarcity because their wants are greater than their resources. A country may want to spend more resources on education and health, but it may not be able to because it also has to pay for roads and defense.

Scarcity also is a problem for business. Business owners always have to make decisions about which goods and services to make. They have to decide how much of a product to make. They do not have the resources to do everything they want. A decision might have bad results. For example, maybe a business chooses to make more of Product A than Product B. If Product A does not sell or if too much of it is made, the business loses money. On the other hand, if people like Product A, the business makes money. In either case, choosing to use scarce resources to make Product A may mean that the business cannot make as much of Product B.

Why Do We Have to Make Choices?

We have to make choices because of scarcity. We have to make a choice because our wants and needs are greater than our resources. Economics is about how people and governments make these choices.

What Are Trade-Offs and Opportunity Costs?

We have learned that resources are scarce. A resource can only be used one way at a time. For example, if land is used to grow corn, it cannot be used as a golf course. As another example, say you have $20 in your pocket. If you use it to buy a basketball, you cannot use the same money to take a friend out to dinner. In a **trade-off**, you give up one thing for another. The trade-off for buying the basketball is not being able to take your friend out.

Each possible use of the same resource is an **opportunity**. Every time we make a choice, we give up an opportunity to do something else. When you leave high school, you have a choice. You may go on to college or you may choose to work full-time. There is a cost for giving up the other choice. The cost of this trade-off is called the **opportunity cost**. It is the cost of the next best choice or the choice not taken. Going to college may mean that you delay having enough money to move out on your own. Finding a full-time job may mean more money in your pocket now but less in the future. In general, college graduates earn more money than people whose education ends with high school.

Let's go back to the example of farmland. The farmer decides to grow corn instead of turning the fields into a golf course. The golf course becomes the opportunity cost of farming the land. It is the cost of the choice the farmer made. You decided to use the $20, your limited resource, to buy the basketball. By choosing the basketball, taking your friend out became the opportunity cost. Choosing to go to college makes having a job the opportunity cost.

Going to college is an example of an opportunity. The opportunity cost of not going to college might be making less money on the job.

Production possibilities

All combinations of goods and services that can be produced from a fixed amount of resources in a given period of time

Governments and businesses have opportunity costs too. They have to make choices, and each choice has a cost. A business owner might decide to use floor space to sell furniture. The owner cannot use the same space to sell cars. This is the owner's opportunity cost. A government might decide to spend $20 billion on improved health care. It cannot use the same money to improve roads. Improving roads is the opportunity cost of improved health care.

Another way of looking at trade-offs and opportunity costs is by using a **production possibilities** curve. This is an economic model. It is a simple way to show the real world. Production possibilities are all the combinations of goods and services that can be produced from a fixed amount of resources in a given period of time. First, we assume that all of the resources are used in the most efficient way. Second, the period of time for production is fixed. Third, the amount of resources does not change. Look at Figure 1.1.

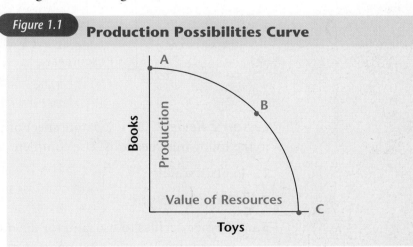

Figure 1.1 Production Possibilities Curve

Let's say that we want to produce both books and toys. If the manufacturer were at Point A, all resources are used to make books. The trade-off is that no toys can be produced because no resources are left. To move to Point B, the manufacturer has to give up half of the resources for making books to make toys. At Point B, the resources are evenly divided between toys and books. At Point C on the graph, the manufacturer uses all of the resources to produce toys. The opportunity cost of making the toys is the whole production possibility for making books.

In the real world, resources do change. New ideas might make workers more efficient. New machines might cost a lot less to operate. These changes may cause the production possibilities curve to shift.

Look at Figure 1.2. The new curve, P2, shows the expanded production that results from changes or new resources. Sometimes resources become scarcer. This also can cause the curve to shift. P3 shows how production is affected.

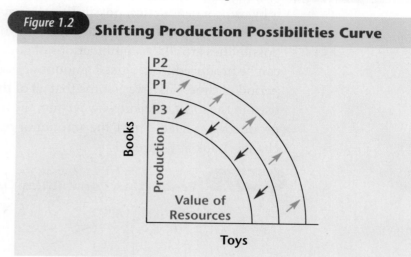

Figure 1.2 **Shifting Production Possibilities Curve**

Lesson 2 Review On a separate sheet of paper, write answers to the following questions. Use complete sentences.

1. Explain scarcity.

2. What is trade-off?

3. A farmer decides to use land for farming instead of building a golf course. What is the opportunity cost of farming?

4. Explain production possibilities.

5. What is an opportunity?

What do you think

6. Would you rather go to college after high school or get a job right away? Why?

7. Write an example of a time you had scarcity in your life.

Factors of production

Resources that are used to make goods and services

What Are the Factors of Production?

Maybe owning a business is your dream. To do this, you would need different resources. The kinds of resources are natural, labor, and capital. Resources that are used to make goods and services are called **factors of production**.

What Are Natural Resources?

Writing About Economics

Natural resources are one of the factors of production. Research what natural resources are in your area. Create a list and write a paragraph describing each resource you find.

All businesses need natural resources. Natural resources are resources found on Earth. Some natural resources are water, minerals, land, and forests. There is not an endless supply of these resources. Natural resources often go to whomever can pay the most for them. This is because they are scarce. For example, it might not be a good idea to start your new business in the middle of Manhattan in New York City. Land there is very expensive because it is scarce. Land with mineral resources like oil, coal, gold, and silver is also expensive because it is scarce. There is only a limited amount of good farmland, so it costs a lot of money too.

What Is Labor?

Labor is a second factor of production. The production of goods and services always involves people. The work people do to provide goods and services is called labor. Some of the work is physical. For example, construction workers use their muscle power to build a building. Labor also includes the people who design the building. They use brainpower instead of muscle power to create things. Whether the work you do involves muscle power or brainpower does not matter. You are part of labor even as a part-time worker.

Sometimes economists call labor human resources. You can tell how scarce labor is by how much you have to pay for it. Doctors and plumbers can be very expensive because they are somewhat scarce and they require special training. Servers at a restaurant or clerks at a department store earn less because they are not scarce.

What Are Capital Resources?

The third factor of production is called capital. Capital resources are all the buildings, tools, equipment, and money used to provide goods and services. Think of a sandwich shop. To open the shop, the owner needs money. This money pays the rent or buys the building. The owner also needs money for a bread oven, tables, chairs, and other equipment. Capital includes all the things the money buys to produce sandwiches.

What Is Entrepreneurship?

Economists sometimes include **entrepreneurship** in the list of production resources. It refers to people's ability to start new businesses or improve old ones. A **manager** is the person who runs a business or some part of it. Managers make important decisions. They decide how to make a product or service. They also might decide how much to charge for it. Managers decide how many workers are needed and how much to pay them.

All businesses have managers who make important decisions and oversee the work.

The entrepreneur combines all the factors of production in a way that will hopefully make money. Entrepreneurs take risks to make new ideas happen. They are successful when they develop a new and better product. They make money when they make a product or process more efficient.

American history is full of stories of successful entrepreneurs. John Deere saw that a steel plow was more effective than one made of iron. The company he started is a big maker of farm equipment. Michael Dell realized that many people could not afford a personal computer. He decided to sell computers through the mail and by telephone. Later, his computers were sold on the Internet. Today, his company is the world's biggest computer maker.

Madame C. J. Walker: 1867–1919

Madame C. J. Walker was the daughter of former slaves who was orphaned at age seven. As a young woman, she wanted to improve the look of her hair. She tried out many kinds of chemicals. She created a shampoo that soothed the scalp. She created an ointment that made hair easier to manage. Madame Walker began selling her hair-care products to other African-American women. She trained others to sell them door-to-door. After a while, she created a way to sell them by mail.

Within a few years, Madame Walker opened a factory to produce large amounts of her products. The business grew quickly. At one point, she had about 3,000 employees. Madame Walker spoke to women's groups all over America. She encouraged them to make the most of their talents. She was among the first American women to become a millionaire from her own efforts.

Lesson 3 Review On a separate sheet of paper, write the letter of the answer that correctly completes each sentence.

1. Resources used to make goods and services are called _____.

   A factors of production **B** people **C** scarcity **D** work

2. Three factors of production are labor, capital, and _____ resources.

   A artificial **B** commodity **C** natural **D** wood

3. All buildings, tools, equipment, and money used to provide goods and services are _____ resources.

   A capital **B** common **C** expensive **D** necessary

4. Starting a new business or improving an old one is an ____.

   A energy **C** engagement
   B entrepreneurship **D** integrity

5. A person who runs a business is _____.

   A capital **B** scarcity **C** a manager **D** wealthy

What do you think ?

6. Whose services cost more, a dentist or a store clerk? Why?

7. If you were given money to start your own business, what business would you choose? Why?

What Is Productivity?

Productivity is the amount of goods and services workers can produce in a given time. Let's say you work at a restaurant. You usually cook 20 hamburgers per hour. The owner buys a new grill. Now you can cook 40 hamburgers in the same time. Your productivity has doubled.

Productivity increases when workers make more of a product in the same time than in the past. As it increases, the real value of goods and services produced goes up. Increased productivity may mean that products or services may cost less. It also may result in workers earning more money for their work.

Henry Ford changed the way cars were made. This change is a good example of how productivity can increase. Long ago, one person built an entire car from start to finish. Only a small number of cars were made. The price was so high that only the rich could afford them.

Ford thought that he could make cars in a better way. He divided up the job of making cars. This idea is called the **division of labor**. Instead of building a whole car, workers performed only one job. They specialized. **Specialization** occurs when a person, country, or region works on making one part of an item.

Ford introduced the **assembly line** to auto manufacturing. The assembly line is a system in which the product moves from worker to worker. Before the assembly line, only a few hundred cars could be made each year. With the assembly line, many thousands could be made in the same time. As productivity increased, the price of a car dropped. More and more people could afford cars. Today, the assembly line makes mass production possible.

Productivity

The amount of goods and services workers can produce in a given time

Division of labor

Dividing up workers so that each worker completes one job, which is one part of a larger job

Specialization

When a person, country, or region works on making one part of an item

Assembly line

A system in which a product moves from worker to worker so it can be put together faster

---

What Are the Advantages of Specialization?

Specialization has several advantages:

1. It raises production.

2. Workers learn their skill better.

3. Workers can be better trained.

4. It makes production more efficient.

What Are the Disadvantages of Specialization?

Among the disadvantages to specialization are:

1. Doing the same thing over and over again can be boring.

2. Workers might take less pride in their work.

3. Workers are trained to do only one thing and may not be able to find other jobs.

What Causes Productivity to Increase?

We have learned that economics is about choices. Decisions have to be made about how best to use scarce resources. Using resources well increases productivity.

Using human resources well is important. Productivity goes up if workers are educated and well trained. Well-educated and trained workers often produce more. The way workers feel about their jobs may also affect productivity. People who like their jobs are often more productive than workers who do not like their jobs.

Capital resources also affect productivity. Workers are more productive when they have the best tools, equipment, and buildings available. A new machine, for example, may allow a worker to produce more than he or she did with the older machine. Workers who work in new, air-conditioned, and well-lighted buildings are more likely to be productive.

Technology is the use of science to create new products or make old ones better. It has a big effect on productivity. Sometimes a single invention can help. The steam engine, telephone, and the airplane changed the way people live. The computer is one example of technology that has had far-reaching importance.

How Have Computers Changed Our Lives?

Computers have affected almost every part of our lives. They have changed medical care. Doctors use them to help find cures for patients. Computers have changed manufacturing. For example, carmakers use computers to design new models. They use computers to reduce costs and increase profits. Computers link **databases**—large collections of information stored on computers. Databases help businesses make decisions on how scarce resources can be used better.

You probably know firsthand how computers have changed education. Many schools today have access to the Internet. Students and teachers use computers for information, for research, and to make learning fun.

Economics in Your Life

Technology and Business

Technology has changed the way business is done. Computers have become essential to both communication and the storage of information. Word processing is fast and simple. Papers may be copied or faxed in just seconds.

The Internet allows people to send messages by e-mail or instant messaging. Files can be sent as attachments to e-mails. Huge files may be sent by file transfer protocol (FTP) from one computer to another. Some companies sell their products through Internet Web sites. Payment services accept credit card payments from buyers. Then they deposit that money into the seller's account.

Cell phones, laptop computers, and personal digital assistants (PDAs) help business on the go. Often called "palm pilots" or "handhelds," PDAs help store data. Many PDAs now can be used with a telephone.

Word Bank

assembly line
capital resources
productivity
specialization
technology

Lesson 4 Review On a separate sheet of paper, write the word from the Word Bank to complete each sentence.

1. To raise the productivity of his auto workers, Henry Ford introduced the _____.

2. In general, if workers are well educated and trained, _____ goes up.

3. The use of science to create new products or make old ones better is _____.

4. When a person, region, or country works on making one part of an item, _____ occurs.

5. _____ increase productivity.

What do you think ?

6. Describe three ways computers have changed your life.

7. Do you think better technology is good or bad? Explain.

The Principles of Economics

Alfred Marshall was an important British economist from the late 1800s until he died in 1924. He studied economics for much of his life. He also taught political economics at the University of Cambridge in England. Two other famous economists, John Keynes and Arthur Pigou, were among Marshall's students.

In 1890, Marshall wrote a book called the Principles of Economics. *His book covered many parts of economics. Many of the economics terms that we use today come from Marshall's ideas. This passage is from a section of the book called* On Wants And Their Satisfaction.

Human wants and desires are countless in number and . . . various in kind: but they are generally limited and capable of being satisfied. The uncivilized man indeed has not many more [wants and desires] than the . . . animal; but every step in his progress upwards increases the variety of his needs together with the variety in his methods of satisfying them. He desires not [only] larger quantities of the things . . . but better qualities of those things; he desires a greater choice of things, and things that will satisfy new wants growing up in him.

. . . As man rises in civilization, as his mind becomes developed . . . his wants become rapidly more subtle and more various. . . .

As a man's riches increase, his food and drink become more various and costly; but his appetite is limited by nature, and when his expenditure on food is extravagant it is more often to gratify the desires of hospitality and display. . . .

(T)herefore, although it is man's wants in the earliest stages of his development that give rise to his activities . . . each new step upwards is to be regarded as the development of new activities giving rise to new wants, rather than of new wants giving rise to new activities.

Document-Based Questions

1. Why is Alfred Marshall important to the study of economics?

2. In your own words, what does the first sentence of the passage say about wants and desires?

3. What does the author say happens to a person's wants as the person becomes more developed?

4. Why do you think very wealthy people may spend a great amount of money on expensive goods?

5. What role could scarcity play as a person's wants increase?

- Economics is the study of making choices about how to use resources. Resources include labor, capital, and natural raw materials found on Earth. People, businesses, and governments make these choices.

- Needs are things necessary to stay alive. Wants are not necessary for life but can make people's lives better.

- Goods are manufactured products people buy. Services include work people do for other people. Most jobs in the United States and Canada are service jobs.

- Scarcity occurs when people have unlimited wants but limited resources. Scarcity is the most basic economic problem.

- Resources can be used only one way at a time. A trade-off occurs when people choose to give up one thing to get another. The cost of the choice not made is the opportunity cost.

- Production possibilities are all combinations of goods and services that can be produced from a fixed amount of resources in a given period of time. A production possibilities curve shows the opportunity costs of using resources one way and not another.

- Factors of production include natural resources, labor resources, and capital resources. Natural resources are scarce raw materials found on Earth. Labor resources are people and the work they do. Labor is sometimes called human resources. Capital resources are all buildings, tools, equipment, and money used to provide goods and services.

- Entrepreneurs take risks to make new ideas happen. A manager is someone who runs a business or part of it.

- Productivity is the amount of goods or services workers can produce in a given time. Productivity may increase with educated and well-trained workers. It also may increase with the availability of the best tools, equipment, and buildings. Technology is the use of science to create new products or make old ones better.

- Henry Ford introduced the assembly line and a division of labor among auto workers. Each worker did only one job. Specialization occurs when a person, country, or region works to make one part of an item.

- One advantage of specialization includes raising production. Another is helping workers learn their jobs better. A third advantage is providing better training to workers. Another is enabling more efficient production. One disadvantage includes boredom from doing the same job. Another is lowered pride among workers. A final disadvantage is workers are trained for only one skill. They may not be able to find other jobs.

Chapter 1 REVIEW

On a separate sheet of paper, write the word from the Word Bank to complete each sentence.

1. The work people do is a resource called _____.

2. Work people do for other people for a fee is called _____.

3. Scarcity is a problem of limited resources but unlimited _____.

4. The cost of trade-offs is called a(n) _____.

5. All the combinations of goods and services that can be produced are referred to as _____.

6. Water and minerals are examples of _____.

7. Splitting a job into parts is called _____.

Word Bank

service

production possibilities

labor

division of labor

needs and wants

opportunity cost

natural resources

On a separate sheet of paper, write the letter of the answer that correctly completes each sentence.

8. Natural resources are _____ found on Earth.

   A never   C raw materials

   B people   D trees

9. Economics is the study of how people and countries make decisions about using _____.

   A people   C water

   B resources   D work

10. Wants are not necessary for survival but can make our lives _____.

    A better   C the same

    B bad   D worse

11. Limited resources but unlimited wants create _____.

    A fear   C opportunity

    B jobs   D scarcity

12. Buying a basketball instead of taking a friend to a movie is an example of a(n) _____.

   A friendship   **C** scarcity

   B opportunity cost   **D** selfishness

13. Production _____ are combinations of goods and services that can be produced from a fixed amount of resources in a given period of time.

   A facilities   **C** mergers

   B goals   **D** possibilities

On a separate sheet of paper, write answers to the following questions. Use complete sentences.

14. What are the resources used to make goods and services called?

15. How can a person tell how scarce labor is?

16. What is an assembly line?

17. What are two advantages of specialization?

On a separate sheet of paper, write your opinion to each question. Use complete sentences.

18. What do you think is the most important technology today? Explain.

19. Do you think the advantages of specialization outweigh the disadvantages of specialization? Why or why not?

20. Do you think a government should spend its limited money on better health care, a better military, or some other government service? Explain.

Test-Taking Tip

When studying for a test, learn the most important points. Practice writing or saying the material out loud. Have a partner listen to check if you are right.

2 Economic Systems

In Chapter 1, you learned about some basic economics concepts. One of the concepts is the problem of scarcity. All countries in the world face scarcity. Each nation forms an economic system to deal with this problem. These economic systems vary by country.

This chapter discusses three questions that each economic system must answer. You will also learn about the economic systems used in most countries, including the United States and Canada.

Goals for Learning

◆ To list the three basic questions all economic systems answer

◆ To describe traditional and command economic systems

◆ To explain a market economy

◆ To understand mixed economic systems

What Three Basic Questions Must All Economic Systems Answer?

In Chapter 1, we learned about scarcity. We know that resources are limited, but our needs and wants are unlimited. This forces us to make hard decisions about how to use our resources. To help make these hard decisions, societies have to ask themselves three basic economic questions.

What Should Be Produced?

The first question is *what*. We need to decide what and how much to produce. Even a rich country like the United States cannot produce everything it wants. People choose the kinds of goods and services to produce. They may decide to use scarce resources to make cars. This means there are fewer resources to spend on other products like dishwashers and stoves. Maybe a country can make both of these things, but how much of each is best?

How Should It Be Produced?

The second question is *how*. Now that we know what we will produce, we have to decide how. For example, there are many ways to farm. We could use a lot of machines or very little. There also are many ways to build a house. They can be built on the site or in a factory. The builders can use wood, bricks, or steel. How are the choices made? If times are good, business owners may want to increase capital resources. If many people are out of work, the owners may decide to spend money on human capital instead.

Who Should Get Goods and Services?

The third question is *who*. Who should get the goods and services produced? We know that not enough can be produced for everyone. Should only those people with enough money to buy the goods and services get them? Should the government decide who receives them?

This question is not answered the same way in each country. In some countries, a small group of very rich families receives most of what is produced. The large number of poor people in these countries get very little. Most rich countries have a large group of people who are neither rich nor poor. Rich countries also have a small number of very rich people and very poor people. Almost all people have a chance to get the goods and services produced. Some countries try to even out the amount of money workers earn. No one is very rich, but no one is very poor. In this way, every person shares in the nation's production.

Societies must think about the "what," "how," and "who" when using resources to make things like a CD player. What will be made? How will it be made? Who will it be made for?

What Is an Economic System?

The choices we make as shoppers, workers, business owners, and government leaders create the economy. An economic system answers the three basic questions of what, how, and who. There are no right answers and no wrong answers. The way people answer these questions describes the kind of economic system they have. It is the way societies try to provide for the wants and needs of their people.

Sam Walton: 1918–1992

Sam Walton delivered newspapers before he got his first job in a variety store. After college, he became the manager of a department store. He learned that knowing how to best satisfy customers was important to a successful retail business. Walton and his brother opened a chain of variety stores in the south in the 1950s. He soon realized that people had become more interested in discount stores. Other discount store chains were locating in big cities.

Walton decided that he should open stores in small towns. Small-town customers were pleased to have one of Walton's large, well-stocked stores within minutes of home. Over three decades, Walton opened more than 1,700 stores. He employed nearly half a million people in those stores. At the time of his death in 1992, Walton had built a personal fortune of more than $20 billion. His business is now the largest in the United States.

Lesson 1 Review On a separate sheet of paper, write answers to the following questions. Use complete sentences.

1. What are three basic questions economic systems answer?

2. Can countries produce everything they want? Explain.

3. Give an example of ways countries answer the question of how to produce something.

4. Do all countries answer the basic questions in the same way? Explain.

5. What is the best way for a country to answer the three questions?

What do you think ?

6. Do you think only people with enough money should get the goods produced in an economic system? Or should a government decide who receives the goods? Explain.

7. Which basic economic question do you think is the most important? Explain.

What Is a Traditional Economy?

Tradition

Something that is passed down from one group to another

Traditional economy

An economy that does things as they were done in the past; custom and tradition determine answers to the three economic questions

Ancestor

A person who lives before your time

Rural

Away from the city

A **tradition** is something that is passed down from one group to another. You probably have many traditions in your own family. Maybe you go to a place of worship with your family on your holy days. Some Americans put out the American flag on the Fourth of July. People do these things because their parents and grandparents did so.

A **traditional economy** does things as they were done in the past. In other words, the three basic economic questions are answered as they were in the past. One of the advantages of a traditional economy is that people know what is expected from them. *What* to produce is based on what was produced in the past. If you are born to a family of hunters, you hunt. If your family was farmers, you farm. The answer to *how* also is simple. You produce the same way as your **ancestors**, or the people who lived before you, did. The answer to *who* should get the goods and services produced is easy. Custom and tradition determine it. All three basic questions are answered directly by the people involved.

Traditional economies exist on almost every continent. They usually are found in **rural** areas of the world, which are places away from cities. In these areas, there is no national economy. The economy is centered on a family or tribal group. One example is the Inuits. Most Inuits live in small coastal villages in northern Canada. The Inuit culture is very old. They have their own language. In the past, many traveled with dogsleds or in small, covered canoes called kayaks. Most Inuits were hunters. They learned how to survive in a harsh climate. Tradition told them where the hunting was good.

Traditional economies are most common in isolated places in Africa and Asia. These are often farming societies. Over the years, custom and tradition told farmers what crops to grow. Farmers also learned how to plant the crops and harvest them. The role that the men, women, and children play often is decided by tradition. In a traditional economy, change occurs very slowly.

What Is a Command Economic System?

In a **command economy**, government leaders give the answers to the three basic economic questions. It is called a command economy because the government gives commands. It gives commands on what, how, and for whom to make goods and services. Usually, the people living in these command economies are not free. They are expected to follow the decisions the government leaders make.

Government leaders usually are a group of planners. For this reason, this type of economy is sometimes called a planned economy. The planners make the decisions about how the resources are used. They control most of the natural resources, labor, and capital. They also decide how the goods and services are distributed. They even may decide what jobs people in the society will do.

The planners may decide to stress **heavy industry**. This is the large-scale production of basic items like steel. This means that the same resources cannot be used to make the everyday products people need.

The former Soviet Union was a good example of a command economy. The government planners were successful in changing the country. In the past, most people worked in **agriculture**, or farming. By shifting resources, the Soviet Union changed to an industrial power in only a few years. During this time, however, there was a shortage of **consumer goods** like soap.

What Is Socialism?

Socialism is the belief that governments rather than individuals should own a country's major industries. The government owns communication systems, transportation systems, oil, and **utilities** such as gas and water. The government also controls services for the people. It provides free health care, education, **welfare** (aid for those in need), and cultural programs. Sometimes it even provides jobs in government-owned businesses.

Command economy

An economy in which government leaders give the answers to the three economic questions

Heavy industry

Large-scale production of basic items

Agriculture

Farming

Consumer goods

Everyday items that people purchase

Socialism

The belief that governments rather than individuals should own a country's major industries

Utilities

Items such as electricity, water, or gas

Welfare

Aid (money or goods) for those in need

Today many socialist countries are **democracies**. Democracies are governments in which citizens take part. In a democracy, citizens elect **representatives** to make and carry out laws. A country where the people have a say in government but in which the government owns the major industries is called **democratic socialism**. Democratic socialism is found in many European countries.

What Is Communism?

Communism is a form of socialism based on the writings of Karl Marx. Under communism, the government owns all property. The government owns all factories and even the land. The idea behind communism is that people work to the best of their abilities. They use only what they need. Communists believe that this system takes care of everyone's needs and wants. Therefore, in time there is no need for a government. No country in the world has pure communism.

Communist countries like the former Soviet Union developed into a **dictatorship**. In a dictatorship, the people have no rights. One person or a small group of people rules the country by force and makes all the laws. The Soviet Union collapsed in 1991 in part because the economy fell apart.

Russia used to be part of the Soviet Union. It is no longer a communist country.

Word Bank

communism
planned
rural
socialist
traditional

Lesson 2 Review On a separate sheet of paper, write the word from the Word Bank to complete each sentence.

1. In a _____ economy, people do things the way things have been done in the past.

2. In many countries, traditional economies are found in _____ areas.

3. Another name for a command economy is a _____ economy because government leaders plan how to use all resources.

4. In a _____ economy, the government owns the utilities, transportation systems, and other major industries.

5. The idea behind _____ is that all people work as well as they can.

What do you think

6. Why do some communist countries become dictatorships?

7. Do you think a country should have a democratic, socialistic, or communistic form of government? Why?

Profit
Money left over after all
the costs of production
have been paid

Competition
A contest between
businesses or
individuals to sell a
product or service

Invisible hand
Adam Smith's idea that
competition acts like an
invisible hand; it pushes
people to do what is best
for themselves

Market
A place where people
come together to buy
and sell

Why Is Adam Smith Called the Father of Modern Economics?

In 1776, Adam Smith wrote one of the most important books on economics. It is called *Wealth of Nations*. Smith thought that people should be free to produce and sell products at a **profit**. Profit is the money left over after all the costs of production have been paid. Smith believed that it is best if people would just take care of themselves. They would work harder, produce more, and grow richer. He said that **competition** was good. Competition is like a contest between businesses or individuals to sell a product or service. Smith thought that competition makes people do what they do best. He believed that this competition acted like an **invisible hand**. This invisible hand pushes us to do what is best for ourselves. He said people would be better off if they used their resources to do what is best for them.

Adam Smith lived from 1723–1790.

Smith believed that governments should not get in the way of this process. He believed that competition would produce the best goods and services at the cheapest prices. Smith thought that an economy works best in a free **market**. A market is a place where people come together to buy and sell.

A good place to see how the "invisible hand" works is the former Soviet Union. The government owned 99 percent of the farmland. Only one percent was privately-owned land. About one-third of the country's food was produced on that one percent! It is clear that the farmers who were working their own land worked a lot harder. They knew that the more they produced, the more profit or money they would make.

What Is Capitalism?

Smith's ideas are called **capitalism**. In this system, people and private businesses own and control production. Unlike communism, the means of production are all privately owned. People and businesses make decisions about how resources can best be used. Another name for capitalism is **market economy**.

Capitalism is a very efficient economic system. People are free to buy whatever goods and services they want. For example, people can buy and own property. The producers use their resources to make what consumers want the most. It is also a very flexible system. For example, a few years ago people were collecting little stuffed beanbag animals. Some were made in limited numbers. The price of these animals was high because so many people wanted them. Their maker hired more workers to make more animals. When the fad ended, prices dropped. Some of the workers lost their jobs. The toy makers chose to use their resources to make other products instead.

Capitalism provides people with an **incentive** to work. An incentive is something that makes a person take an action. The incentive is often profit. If you make a product that people want to buy, you will make money. According to Smith, everyone wants to make money. This is what makes people produce. Communism offers people few incentives. Under communism, the hard worker and the lazy one are both rewarded the same.

Economics at Work

Economic Geographer

Economic geographers study the use of resources in certain places. Those resources may include money, goods, services, or things found in nature. Economic geographers work for governments as well as for companies. They spend a good deal of time doing research. They organize data and make presentations of their findings. Economic geographers working for a country may find ways to improve its quality of life. They may help create plans for better housing, employment, or transportation. They may help create ways to provide better food or a cleaner environment. A major change in one country may have powerful effects on the resources of another country.

Economic geographers working for companies provide advice for changes based on a company's location. They study how location affects distribution of goods or services. Location also may have major effects on the availability of good employees. They may make proposals for changes that will increase the company's profits.

Lesson 3 Review On a separate sheet of paper, write the letter of the answer that correctly completes each sentence.

1. Adam Smith is sometimes called _____.
   A the father of modern economics
   B the invisible hand
   C Karl Marx
   D the man of modern times

2. Adam Smith believed the best economic system has _____.
   A competition
   B democracy
   C government help
   D lots of capital

3. Adam Smith's ideas are called _____.
   A capitalism
   B communism
   C fair play
   D planned economy

4. Unlike communism, capitalism provides people with a work _____.
   A document   B ethic   C incentive   D pass

5. The former Soviet Union is an example of _____ because there was no incentive to work harder.
   A capitalism
   B the invisible hand
   C fair play
   D a market system

What do you think ?

6. Would most people work harder in a capitalist or communist system? Why?

7. What is the "invisible hand"? Do you think it works? Why or why not?

Mixed economy

An economy in which there is a blend of economic systems; individuals and the government share in the decision-making process

Writing About Economics

The economic systems in the world are traditional economy and mixed economy. Write a paragraph describing the similarities and differences of each. Then create a diagram to support your paragraph.

Pure forms of command or market economies do not exist. Only the traditional economic system really exists. All other major economies are **mixed economies**. They are a blend of economic systems. Individuals and the government share in the decision-making process. They combine to answer the basic economic questions.

Many capitalist countries have a mixed economy. The United States is a good example. Americans believe in free markets. However, not all decisions are made by individuals. The government also plays an important role. All levels of government pass laws. Some laws set a minimum amount of money that workers can earn. Others do not allow children to work. Many laws try to ensure good working conditions for workers. The American economy is very efficient in providing its people with what they want. At the same time, the government prevents cheating and abuse of labor.

China also has a mixed economy. However, its economy leans more toward a command economy. Government planners still set goals. They control much of the capital. The government owns much of the land. Many factories are government owned. China also has some features of capitalism. Some people own their own businesses. Today, most goods and services China produces are made by privately owned companies.

Both the United States and China have mixed economies. However, it would be a mistake to think that both economies are the same. No two economies are exactly the same even if they have some things in common.

Figure 2.1 on the next page shows the three types of economic systems: traditional, command, and market. In the world today, economies are either traditional or a mixed economy. (Remember, a mixed economy is a mix between command and market.)

Figure 2.1 Three Types of Economic Systems

	Traditional	Command	Market
Description	Things are done as they were done in the past.	The government controls the economy.	People and businesses control the economy based on market needs.
Effects on the People	Everyone knows what is expected, because things have always been done that way.	Usually, the people are not free. They must follow decisions made by government officials.	People are free to buy goods and services. Businesses are free to provide goods and services people want.
Three Economic Questions: What, How, Who	The three economic questions are answered by custom and tradition.	Government leaders give answers to the three economic questions.	People give answers to the three economic questions.

Word Bank

command
economies
free markets
individuals
market

Lesson 4 Review On a separate sheet of paper, write the word from the Word Bank to complete each sentence.

1. Pure forms of command or _____ economies do not exist.

2. In the United States, both the government and _____ share in making economic decisions.

3. In China, the economy leans more toward a _____ economy.

4. Americans in general believe in _____.

5. Even with some things in common, no two _____ are exactly the same.

What do you think ?

6. Is the United States more like a capitalist or command economy? Explain.

7. Is China more like a capitalist or command economy? Explain.

The Communist Manifesto

Karl Marx and Friedrich Engels were the leaders of a new social movement. They thought it would change history. In 1848, the two men published the Communist Manifesto, *a pamphlet that stated their beliefs. Marx and Engels called themselves Communists. They believed that the bourgeoisie (business owners) were becoming much more powerful than the proletariat (workers). They argued that the proletariat should overthrow the bourgeoisie. Their ideas would become a revolutionary force in the twentieth century. This passage is from the* Communist Manifesto.

The modern bourgeois society [middle class factory owners] that has sprouted from the ruins of the feudal society . . . has but established new classes, new conditions of oppression, new forms of struggle in place of the old ones. . . .

The discovery of America, the rounding of the Cape [of Good Hope in Africa], opened up fresh ground for the rising bourgeoisie. . . .

The feudal system of industry, in which industrial production was monopolized by closed guilds, now no longer (meets) the growing wants of the new markets. . . .

Meantime, the markets kept ever growing, the demand ever rising. . . . The place of manufacture was taken by the giant, MODERN INDUSTRY; the place of the industrial middle class by industrial millionaires, the leaders of the whole industrial armies, the modern bourgeois.

Modern industry has established the world market. . . . This market has given an immense development to commerce, to navigation, to communication by land. . . . (I)n proportion as industry, commerce, navigation, railways extended . . . the bourgeoisie developed, increased its capital, and pushed into the background every class handed down from the Middle Ages.

The bourgeoisie . . . has resolved personal worth into exchange value, and . . . has set up that single, (excessive) freedom—Free Trade. . . .

The need of a constantly expanding market for its products chases the bourgeoisie over the entire surface of the globe. It must nestle everywhere, settle everywhere, establish connections everywhere.

The bourgeoisie has, through its exploitation of the world market, given a cosmopolitan character to production and consumption in every country.

Document-Based Questions

1. Why did Marx and Engels write the *Communist Manifesto*?

2. According to the authors, what is one reason that allowed the bourgeoisie to gain power?

3. List three areas that developed because of the growth in the world economy.

4. What freedom do the authors call "excessive"?

5. Why might people who disagree with Marx think that the bourgeoisie helped the world economy?

- To decide how to use resources, all societies must answer three economic questions. The first question is what and how much to produce. The second question is how to produce it. The final question is who receives what is produced. Not every country answers the questions in the same way.

- The choices of shoppers, workers, businesses, and governments create an economy. The way countries answer the three questions describes a country's economic system.

- In a traditional economic system, people answer the three questions as they have in the past. What to produce is based on what was produced in the past. To answer how, products are produced in the same way as in the past. Custom determines who receives what is produced.

- Traditional economies are found on nearly every continent on Earth. They usually are in rural areas. They are most common in isolated areas of Africa and Asia.

- In a command economy, government leaders answer the three questions. The leaders usually are planners who command how to answer the questions. The leaders control most resources, labor, capital, and distribution.

- In socialism, the government controls a country's major industries and services. Many socialist countries today are democracies. They allow their citizens to take part in the government. These countries have democratic socialist societies.

- Communism is a form of government based on Karl Marx's writings. In communism, the government owns all factories and land. All people are to work to the best of their abilities. They receive only what they need. Some communist governments have developed into dictatorships.

- In 1776, Adam Smith wrote a book called the *Wealth of Nations*. It discusses capitalism as a market economy. People buy and sell products and services at a profit. Competition acts as an invisible hand to push people to work for themselves and use resources wisely. Capitalism is an efficient economic system. It provides an incentive for people to work hard.

- Purely traditional economies do exist. Pure command or market economies do not exist. Major economies are mixed economies. They are a blend of market and command economies. Not all mixed economies are the same even if they have features in common.

Chapter 2 REVIEW

On a separate sheet of paper, write the word from the Word Bank to complete each sentence.

1. Each society has to answer three questions to decide how to use its _____.

Word Bank

capitalism

command economy

free markets

incentive

invisible hand

resources

traditional economy

2. A family that has hunted or farmed for many years often is part of a(n) _____.

3. Often people are not free when they live in a(n) _____.

4. Adam Smith wrote a book about competition and the _____.

5. _____ is a very efficient economic system.

6. Something that encourages people to take an action is a(n) _____.

7. Adam Smith believed governments should not be involved in _____.

On a separate sheet of paper, write the letter of the answer that correctly completes each sentence.

8. The choices _____ create an economy.
  A between planning and commanding
  B everyone makes
  C the government makes
  D individuals make

9. The Inuit society provides an example of a _____.
  A capitalist economy
  B command economy
  C planned economy
  D traditional economy

10. The economic system where people have a say in government but where the government owns major industries is called _____.
  A command economy   **C** dictatorship
  B democratic socialism **D** realism

11. A place where people come together to buy or sell is a(n)
_____.

   A competition   **C** incentive

   B economy   **D** market

12. In a(n) _____, people are free to buy and sell whatever they want.

   A capitalist system   **C** invisible hand

   B communist system   **D** price system

13. The only pure economic system that really exists is a _____ economy.

   A command   **C** profit incentive

   B market   **D** traditional

On a separate sheet of paper, write answers to the following questions. Use complete sentences.

14. List the three questions economic systems answer.

15. Where are most traditional economies found?

16. List two things Adam Smith discussed in his book *Wealth of Nations*.

17. What is another name for market economy?

On a separate sheet of paper, write your opinion to each question. Use complete sentences.

18. Is communism or capitalism more efficient? Explain.

19. Why do you think traditional economies are most common in isolated places in Asia and Africa?

20. Would you rather live in a capitalist, communist, or socialist society? Explain.

Test-Taking Tip

To prepare for a test, study in short sessions rather than one long session. During the week before the test, spend time each evening reviewing your notes.

Unit 1

Graphs and Charts

A graph is a concise visual aid. It helps to show how numbers relate to one another. Line, bar, and circle graphs often are used in this manner. The graph below is a circle graph.

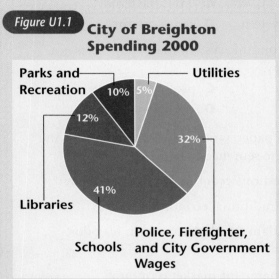

Figure U1.1 **City of Breighton Spending 2000**

A chart is another type of visual used to display information. It is organized in rows that go across and in columns that go up and down. The chart at the right has six columns. The first column names the years represented on the chart. The second column tells the percentage of the city budget that went to schools. The third column provides the percentage of funds spent for the wages of city workers. The fourth column gives the percentage spent for utilities.

The fifth column tells the percentage of the city budget that went to parks and recreation. The last column shows the percentage of funds spent on libraries.

Figure U1.2 **City of Breighton Expenses 1970–2000**

Year	Schools	Wages	Utilities	Parks	Libraries
1970	28%	35%	9%	13%	15%
1980	30%	29%	6%	27%	8%
1990	38%	35%	4%	11%	12%
2000	41%	32%	5%	10%	12%

Study the chart above and answer the following questions:

1. Did Breighton's schools get a larger or smaller percentage in 2000 than they did in 1970?

2. Which row's information is also shown on the circle graph at the left?

3. During which year did the city need the most money for the construction of new parks?

4. Does it appear that the libraries were as important to the city in 2000 as they were in 1990? Explain.

5. What would you say about the percentage paid to city workers in 1970 as compared to 1990?

- Economics is the study of making choices about how to use resources. The three types of resources are labor, capital, and natural resources. Needs are things people must have to stay alive. Wants are things that people do not need for survival but that can make their lives better. Manufacturing turns materials into products called goods. Work people do for other people is called service.

- Having unlimited wants and needs but limited resources creates scarcity. Scarcity causes people to make choices about using resources. Using resources in one way instead of another is a trade-off. The cost of the trade-off is called opportunity cost. Production possibilities are all of the combinations of goods and services that can be produced from a fixed amount of resources in a given period of time.

- Natural resources, labor, and capital are the factors of production. Natural resources include water, minerals, land, and forests. Labor includes the work people do. Capital resources are the tools, buildings, money, and equipment used to provide goods and services. Entrepreneurs take risks to make new ideas happen.

- Productivity is the amount of goods and services workers make in a given time. Productivity may increase when human resources are used well. Productivity also increases when workers have the best tools, equipment, and buildings. Technology has a big effect on productivity.

- Economics attempts to answer three questions. First, what and how many goods and services will be produced? Second, how will they be produced? Finally, who receives them? The way countries answer these questions describes their economic system.

- In a traditional economy, people do things as they have in the past. In a command economy, government leaders decide how to use resources, which they control. Under socialism, the government controls major industries. Many socialist countries are democracies. Under communism, the government owns all the property.

- Economist Adam Smith believed the "invisible hand" of competition pushes people to work efficiently. He believed governments should stay out of the market. Under Smith's capitalist system, individuals and private businesses own production. By working hard, people may earn more money. This is called the profit incentive.

- Only traditional economies exist in a pure form. Other economies blend systems. Economies may share features, but no two economies are exactly alike.

"We hold these truths to be self-evident, that all men are created equal, that they are endowed by their Creator with certain unalienable rights, that among these are life, liberty, and the pursuit of happiness."

–*United States Declaration of Independence, 1776*

2 The Free Enterprise Economy

What do you think of first when you think of the American economy? Is it tall buildings in a large city? Do you think of crops on rolling farmlands? Maybe you think of your favorite place to shop. Whatever you think of, the economy of the United States is much more complex than that. It goes by many names, but most people call it the free enterprise system.

This unit will introduce you to the main ideas of free enterprise. You will learn how the United States started to use this system. You also will learn about key ideas such as supply, demand, price, and competition.

3

Economics in the United States

The American Declaration of Independence was signed on July 4, 1776. It was signed in Independence Hall (the building pictured to the left) in Philadelphia, Pennsylvania. This document stated that the American colonies no longer wanted to be ruled by Great Britain. It was the beginning of the United States.

You may have heard of the Declaration of Independence. You also may have heard of two other American documents: the Constitution and the Bill of Rights. These writings describe the American system of government and ideas that are important to many Americans.

In this chapter, you will learn how these documents relate to economics. You also will learn about the American free enterprise system, profits, and losses.

Goals for Learning

◆ To explain economic ideas in the Declaration of Independence, the Constitution, and the Bill of Rights

◆ To detail practices of the American free enterprise system

◆ To define profits and losses and understand their role in the free enterprise system

What Economic Ideas Exist in the Declaration of Independence?

Declaration of Independence

A document written by American colonists explaining why the American colonies should no longer be ruled by Great Britain

Natural right

A right given by God

Constitution

A plan of government

The **Declaration of Independence** is one of the most important documents in United States history. It was written in 1776. It explained to the world why the American colonies should no longer be ruled by Great Britain. The writer was 33-year-old Thomas Jefferson. He wrote that the British king had taken away the natural rights of the colonists. He believed **natural rights** are rights given by God. These rights cannot be taken away.

The Declaration lists many complaints against the king. An important complaint was that the king had stopped the colonists from trading with other countries. The colonists were angry. They were not free. The king had taken away their freedom to do business with countries Great Britain did not agree with.

Colonists felt they were not free under the British king. The Declaration of Independence listed complaints the colonists had against the king. Some of these complaints were related to economics.

What Economic Ideas Exist in the Constitution?

After America gained independence from Great Britain in 1783, the United States had to set up a working government. During the Revolutionary War, the United States had a very weak government. Many Americans believed that a "more perfect union" was needed. Leaders met in Philadelphia to write a new **constitution**. A constitution is a plan of government. By late 1789, 12 of the 13 states accepted the Constitution as the new law of the land.

The writers of the Constitution believed in the right to private property. One of the signers was John Adams of Massachusetts. He believed "property must be secured or liberty cannot exist." He thought that there was no freedom if people were not allowed to own property. James Madison of Virginia often is called the "father of the Constitution." He believed that governments are set up to protect property.

Article 1 of the Constitution deals with the **legislature**, or lawmaking branch of government. The power to make laws is given to **Congress**, the American lawmaking branch. Two sections of Article 1 deal with the economy. Section 8 gives Congress the right to control trade among the states and with other countries. It also says the states cannot print their own money. Only Congress was given the right to print money. Section 9 limits the powers of government. It says the government cannot get in the way of private contracts. Another part of Section 9 says that no state can tax goods it buys from other states.

What Economic Ideas Exist in the Bill of Rights?

Some people were against the Constitution almost as soon as it was written. They believed it gave too much power to the new government. Those people suggested changes. A formal change to the Constitution is called an **amendment**. The first ten amendments are called the **Bill of Rights**.

Two amendments in the Bill of Rights deal with economic issues. This shows how important property rights are to Americans. Amendment 4 protects citizens. It says that government officials need a good reason before searching citizens or taking their property. Usually, government officials like the police need a **search warrant**. A search warrant is issued by a judge. It says exactly who and what will be searched.

Amendment 5 explains when the government can take private property. Some reasons for this include to build roads or parks. In return, property owners receive payment.

What Does Amendment 14 Say About Citizens?

Amendment 14 is not part of the Bill of Rights. However, many people believe it is one of the most important amendments. It deals with the rights of citizens. Amendment 14 was added to the Constitution in 1868. It defines **citizenship**, or the act of being a member of a country. Amendment 14 states that a person cannot be "deprived of life, liberty, or property, without **due process** of law." Due process means that the government must follow clear rules in court and treat everyone fairly.

Economics in Your Life

Alexander Hamilton's Vision

Alexander Hamilton (1757–1804) was an American statesman at the time of the Revolutionary War. After the war, President George Washington made Hamilton the new nation's first secretary of the treasury. The country had many money problems. Many of the states were in debt from war expenses. Hamilton believed that the United States should pay its debts in full. He also thought that the government should pay the states' debts. He thought this would make the states and their people more loyal to the American government.

Hamilton proposed to Congress the idea of creating a national bank. The bank could manage the country's trade and finances. He believed that the country needed to have good credit. This would attract business at home, as well as from other countries. Hamilton went on to build strong relationships with other countries. Many of these countries did business with the United States.

Word Bank

Bill of Rights
constitution
government
natural rights
property

Lesson 1 Review On a separate sheet of paper, write the word from the Word Bank to complete each sentence.

1. Thomas Jefferson believed no one can take away a person's _____.

2. A plan of government is called a(n) _____.

3. The first ten changes, or amendments, to the U.S. Constitution are called the _____.

4. In the Bill of Rights, two amendments deal with _____.

5. After the U.S. Revolutionary War, the United States had a weak _____.

What do you think ?

6. Why do you think the writers of the Declaration of Independence were so concerned with protecting private property?

7. Do you think the police should have a search warrant to search someone's property? Why or why not?

What Is the Free Enterprise System?

Free enterprise

A name for the American style of economy; same as capitalist or market economy

Consumer

One who buys and uses products

The American economy goes by many names. It sometimes is described as capitalist or as a market economy. Another name is **free enterprise**. In a system of free enterprise, people enjoy many economic freedoms. They can own their own property. They can set up their own businesses. They are free to buy and sell things. **Consumers** are the people who buy and use products. They can choose the best-quality products at the lowest price.

How Do People and Businesses Control Property?

In a free enterprise system, people own and control property. The government plays a much smaller role. Personal property may include things like a car, stereo, CDs, and clothes.

Businesses also own property. Business property might include a shop, machinery, tools, and land. In the United States, privately-owned businesses produce over four-fifths of all goods and services.

People and businesses are free to use their private property any way they please, within the laws. As an individual, you decide how to use your property. For example, you decide what to wear. If you want to buy a new car, you are free to sell your old one. Businesses try to use their private property to make money.

Individuals and businesses have incentives to use their resources wisely. You know that if you do not take care of your things, you pay the cost. For example, if you do not change the oil in your car regularly, the engine will have to be replaced. This will cost you money. Businesses that use their resources wisely make a greater profit. The profit incentive gets businesses to provide goods and services to us.

Why Is Free Choice Important?

People in a free enterprise system enjoy freedom of choice. They can choose how best to use their private property. They are free to make agreements with others to buy and sell goods and services. People can choose the jobs they want. They can change jobs. They generally are free to choose where and when they want to work. Businesses are free to make and sell whatever goods and services they choose. They are also free to hire and fire workers. Consumers are free to buy the goods and services they need and want.

Figure 3.1	Free Enterprise Freedoms	
Freedom...	**What Is the Freedom?**	
To buy and sell	People can choose things to buy and sell. Consumers have the freedom to buy at the lowest price.	
To own property	People and businesses can own land and personal property. They can use their property as they please, and as the law allows.	
To maintain a business	Businesses can own land and property and can operate without much government control.	
To choose	People are free to make agreements with others, to choose where and when to work, and to choose to change jobs.	

What Is the Role of Competition in the Free Enterprise System?

We have learned that resources are scarce. Often, people and businesses want the same resources. To gain use of these resources, people may have to pay more money for them than other people are willing to pay. For example, there is not enough oil for everyone in the world. Countries often compete to buy the limited supply. To gain use of the oil, the buyers have to pay more than buyers in other countries are willing to pay.

When you finish school, you will have to compete with other people for jobs. You will be more likely to get a job than other people if you have a better education. You will also be more likely to get a job if you have better skills than the other people have. Well-trained workers are somewhat scarce. If you have skills, you probably will get paid more than someone without any skills.

There also is competition in markets. Usually, many companies in the same business sell the same goods and services. Sellers compete with each other. They may lower prices to get you to buy from them. They also may improve their product so it is better than the products made by other companies. Competition is good. It encourages producers to make the best products at the least cost.

Producers are not the only ones competing. Consumers also compete in the market. For example, you may want to attend a concert that many other people also want to see. Seats are limited. You may have to pay more to get one of the scarce seats.

What Is the Principle of Voluntary Exchange?

An **exchange** is a transfer. You make an exchange when you give another person something and get something back. If you were not forced to make the exchange, it was a **voluntary exchange**. In free enterprise, buyers and sellers are free to make exchanges. Both benefit from the exchange. Sellers get money for their goods and services. Buyers get products they want. Both buyers and sellers use their economic freedoms to satisfy their needs and wants.

What Is the Role of Government in a Free Enterprise System?

The role of government is very limited in a free enterprise system. Individuals and businesses decide how resources are best used. The government may pass laws to promote competition. It may regulate business. It fights against **discrimination**, or unfair treatment because of a person's race, sex, religion, age, or physical condition. The government watches the way banks do business. It also makes sure workers are working under safe and healthy conditions.

Exchange

The act of giving another person something and getting something back

Voluntary exchange

An exchange someone makes on purpose

Discrimination

Unfair treatment because of a person's race, sex, religion, age, or physical condition

Writing About Economics

The American economy is based on many freedoms. Review each freedom that you read about earlier in this chapter. Decide which freedom you believe is the most important. Write a paragraph explaining why.

Andrew Carnegie: 1835–1919

Andrew Carnegie was the son of poor Scottish immigrants. He began as a worker in a cotton factory. Then he worked as a messenger boy before taking a job as a railroad clerk. During his spare time, he read library books on science and machines. Carnegie continued working for the railroads until he became a manager. As the money he earned increased, he began putting money into iron companies, a train company, and an oil company. By his early thirties, he was making thousands of dollars from these companies.

On a trip to England, Carnegie learned about making steel from iron ore. He started his own steel company. His company became one of the most profitable in the United States. Carnegie's wealth totaled about one-half billion dollars by the time he retired. He gave most of that money away for the building of schools and libraries. He also gave funds to groups that helped promote world peace.

Lesson 2 Review On a separate sheet of paper, write answers to the following questions. Use complete sentences.

1. What are two other names for a market economy?

2. List the four free enterprise freedoms.

3. Why is free choice important in a market economy?

4. What happens when people or businesses want the same resources?

5. What is a voluntary exchange?

 **What do you think**

6. Would you say the U.S. government is heavily or lightly involved in the economy? Why?

7. What are some reasons a government would get involved in a free enterprise system?

Total revenue

All money received by selling something; this amount is reached by multiplying the number of units sold by the average price of a unit

Total cost

All costs involved in making something to sell

Revenue

All the money taken in by a business

Fixed cost

A cost that stays the same no matter how much business is done

Overhead

The costs of doing business

In Chapter 2, you learned that profit is the money a business or person makes after expenses have been paid. Profits are very important to free enterprise. No business can survive without at least some profit. Making a profit is not easy. There is no guarantee that consumers will buy what producers offer. To be successful in business, producers have to work hard to keep their costs down. Producers also have to work hard to satisfy their customers. If they do not, consumers may turn to other businesses.

How Are Profits Measured?

To measure profit, economists look at both **total revenue** and **total cost**. **Revenue** includes all the money taken in by a business. The total revenue is figured by multiplying the number of units sold by the average price of a unit. For example, let's look at a bicycle maker. If the business sells 1,000 bikes for an average cost of $200, the total revenue is $200,000 (1,000 × $200 = $200,000). Total cost is all the costs of running a business. To make the bikes, the business has many costs. Say that the average cost of making a bike is $150. The total cost is the number of bikes sold times $150. Since 1,000 bikes were sold, the total cost is $150,000 ($150 × 1,000 = $150,000).

The difference between the total revenue and the total cost is the profit. In our example, the bicycle maker made a profit of $50,000 ($200,000 − $150,000 = $50,000).

How Are Costs Measured?

Some costs are fixed. A **fixed cost** is a cost that stays the same no matter how much business is done. Sometimes fixed costs are called **overhead**. These are the costs of doing business. The bicycle business needs a factory where the bikes are made. It also needs machinery, tools, and equipment. Capital goods are the most common example of fixed costs. They generally stay the same no matter how much is produced.

A bicycle manufacturer needs to sell a certain number of bikes at a certain price to make a profit. Total revenue and total cost are used to find the profit of something being sold.

Unlike fixed costs, **variable costs** do change. The two most important variable costs are labor and raw materials. The number of workers can change as more or fewer products are made. Hourly wages can change. Insurance rates for workers also change often. Going back to the bicycle example, say the bicycle model is very popular. Many people are buying the bicycles the company is making. The manager decides that hiring more workers can increase production. On the other hand, if fewer people are buying, the company may **lay off** workers. This means that the workers lose their jobs. The price of raw materials also can change quickly. The suppliers of all the parts that go into a bicycle can raise or lower the cost of their parts. The variable costs of doing business also include things like office supplies, property taxes, and much more.

How Does Competition Prevent Profits from Being Too Great?

Competition is supposed to keep profits from becoming too great. Profits may be very high for a new product. When the first DVD players were made, the price was very high. Many people wanted the new product. Because of the high profits, other businesses also decided to produce DVDs. The increased competition increased production. It also reduced the price. The first company to market the DVDs discovered that it now made less profit.

What Are Losses?

Losses are the opposite of profits. If the total cost of doing business is greater than the total revenue, the business suffers a **loss**. Let's say our bicycle maker has to lower the price of the bicycle to $100 in order to sell them. The total cost is the same. The total revenue is now only $100,000 (1,000 × $100 = $100,000). The business has a loss of $50,000.

Why Are Profits Important?

Profits are important because they provide capital. The profits pay for new factories and equipment. This allows the businesses to make new products or improve the old ones. Businesses that cannot compete do not make a profit. If they lose money often, they may be forced out of business.

Economics at Work

Market Researcher

Market researchers work to find out whether a new product or service will sell. They identify the buyers. They learn about the needs and shopping habits of those buyers. They study other products and how those items have been sold. Market researchers gain knowledge by taking surveys of people's needs and wants. They gather information in reports, often using charts and graphs.

In some cases, the market researcher may conduct tests of products or services. This happens before large-scale production begins. Tests help to find out whether there are buyers. In some cases, the tests may provide ideas for change that will help create a better selling product. Market researchers often create sales approaches to help sell the new product or service. They may be involved in advertising or packaging decisions. Most companies require a market researcher to have at least two years of college. Some companies provide on-the-job training.

Lesson 3 Review On a separate sheet of paper, write the letter of the answer that correctly completes each sentence.

1. All the money a business takes in is _____.

    A illegal **B** legal **C** revenue **D** a loss

2. The opposite of profits is _____.

    A costs **B** losses **C** money **D** revenue

3. Fixed costs may be called _____.

    A cheap **B** insurance **C** labor **D** overhead

4. A cost of production that may change is called a(n) _____.

    A consumer cost **B** fixed cost **C** investment **D** variable cost

5. A cost of production that does not change is called a(n) _____.

    A consumer cost **B** fixed cost **C** investment **D** variable cost

What do you think ?

6. Why do you think producers need to satisfy their customers?

7. Do you believe a company could ever make too much profit from producing a product? Explain.

Constitutional Amendments

When the United States won its independence from Great Britain, leaders had to set up a government for the new country. They decided to write the Constitution. This document gives certain rights to United States citizens. It also describes the powers and duties of the government. The writers of the Constitution knew that changes might have to be made from time to time. They included a part about amendments to the Constitution. In over 200 years since the Constitution was written, only 27 changes have been made. Three of these amendments are about a person's rights and responsibilities in a free enterprise economy.

Amendment 4—Search and Arrest Warrants

The right of the people to be secure in their persons, houses, papers, and effects, against unreasonable searches and seizures, shall not be violated, and no warrants shall issue, but upon probable cause, supported by oath or affirmation, and particularly describing the place to be searched, and the persons or things to be seized.

Amendment 5—Rights in Criminal Cases

No person shall be held to answer for a capital, or otherwise infamous crime, unless on a presentment or indictment of a grand jury . . . nor shall any person be subject for the same offense to be twice put in jeopardy of life or limb; nor shall be compelled in any criminal case to be a witness against himself, nor be deprived of life, liberty, or property, without due process of the law; nor shall private property be taken for public use, without just compensation [payment].

Amendment 16—Income Taxes

The Congress shall have power to lay and collect taxes on incomes, from whatever source derived, without apportionment [sharing] among the several States, and without regard to any census or enumeration.

Document-Based Questions

1. Why is the Constitution important to United States' citizens?

2. Based on Amendment 4, what does a police officer need to have in order to search another person's property?

3. List three ways that Amendment 5 protects citizens.

4. According to Amendment 16, is money from a person's job the only source that can be taxed? Explain.

5. Of the three amendments described above, which one do you think is most important in a free enterprise economy? Why?

Chapter 3 SUMMARY

- The founding documents of the United States are the Declaration of Independence, the Constitution, and the Bill of Rights.

- The Declaration of Independence was written in 1776. It states that the British king had stopped the colonists from freely trading with other countries. The colonists were angry and thought they were not free.

- In 1788, the leaders of the United States accepted the U.S. Constitution. Some parts of this plan of government deal with private property.

- Two amendments in the Bill of Rights deal with economic issues. Amendment 4 stops the government from searching and taking private property without a good reason. Amendment 5 explains what those reasons might be.

- Amendment 14 is not part of the Bill of Rights but does address economic issues. It orders that a citizen's property may not be taken without going through the court system.

- The U.S. economy is called the free enterprise system. People, rather than a government, own most of the property. They can buy and sell as they please. The profit incentive helps people use their resources wisely.

- Competition occurs when several people, businesses, or even countries, want to use the same scarce resources. Competition encourages producers to make the best products at the lowest cost.

- In a free market, buyers and sellers make voluntary exchanges. No one tells them what to buy or sell.

- Governments have a limited role in a free market. They may pass laws to promote competition. They may regulate businesses, fight discrimination, or make sure workplaces are safe for workers.

- Profits are the money left after all expenses are paid. Making a profit is not easy.

- Total revenue minus total cost equals profits.

- Costs may be fixed or variable. Fixed costs, or overhead, always stay the same. These costs include equipment, tools, and other capital goods. Variable costs may change. These costs include the price of raw materials or labor.

- Competition keeps prices from becoming too great.

- Losses are the opposite of profits. Losses occur when total cost is greater than total revenue. Profits are important so businesses can make or improve products. Without profits, a company may be forced out of business.

Chapter 3   REVIEW

On a separate sheet of paper, write the word from the Word Bank to complete each sentence.

Word Bank

choice
free enterprise
loss
natural rights
profit
property
voluntary
  exchange

1. Thomas Jefferson called rights given by God _____.

2. Two amendments in the Bill of Rights deal with _____.

3. The U.S. economy is sometimes called a capitalist, market, or _____ system.

4. In a market system, freedom of _____ is important.

5. If two people buy and sell without being forced, they have made a(n) _____.

6. By looking at total revenue and total cost, economists can figure out _____.

7. If total cost is greater than total revenue, a business will have a(n) _____.

On a separate sheet of paper, write the letter of the answer that correctly completes each sentence.

8. A plan of government is called a(n) _____.

  A agenda   **C** election

  B constitution   **D** idea

9. The writers of the U.S. Constitution believed the government should _____ people's property.

  A decrease   **C** protect

  B double   **D** control

10. Consumers buy and use _____.

  A businesses   **C** products

  B natural rights   **D** revenue

11. Businesses and consumers compete in the _____.

  A fixed costs   **C** market

  B profit   **D** government

12. Multiplying the average price of a unit by the number of units sold tells a business its _____.

   A profit   **C** market share

   B competition   **D** total revenue

13. Costs that stay the same regardless of how much business a company does are _____ costs.

   A fixed   **C** vague

   B labor-related   **D** variable

On a separate sheet of paper, write answers to the following questions. Use complete sentences.

14. In the late 1700s, why were people in the American colonies angry at the British king?

15. Give an example of voluntary exchange.

16. List two examples of the government's role in a free enterprise system.

17. List two kinds of variable costs.

On a separate sheet of paper, write your opinion to each question. Use complete sentences.

18. Do you think the government is right to take away someone's property if it pays "just compensation"? Explain.

19. Would you rather live in a free enterprise system or a communist system? Why?

20. Do you think a business should be able to hire and fire its workers anytime it pleases? Why?

Test-Taking Tip

When taking a test where you must write your answer, read the question twice to make sure you understand what is being asked.

4 Demand

Do you like seafood? Lobster, fish, and other seafood often is expensive. Most people buy it only for special meals. Most seafood is more of a want than a need. All things you buy are either a want or a need. The things that you and other consumers want and need affect what goods and services are made available.

This chapter will tell you about these wants and needs. You will learn how they relate to a term called *demand*. You also will find out about the different kinds of demand and the things that can influence it.

Goals for Learning

◆ To define demand

◆ To describe the differences between elastic and inelastic demand

◆ To analyze the factors that influence changes in demand

What Is Demand?

Demand

The amount of a good or service that consumers are willing and able to buy at a given price

Income

The amount of money a person makes

Imagine that you want to set up a business of your own. Before you start, you need to find out whether anyone wants the goods or services you want to produce. It is important to see the difference between people wanting something and their willingness to buy. We all have things that we want. If the price is right, we may buy. If the price is too high, no one will buy.

Economists often use the word **demand**. It is the amount of a good or service that consumers are willing and able to buy at a given price. Demand has two parts. Consumers must be willing to buy. They also must have the ability to pay. Wanting something does not create demand. Suppose you go to an auto show and see a $50,000 sports car you like. You probably do not have $50,000 to pay for it. According to economists, you have not added to demand. Likewise, if you have $50,000 but will not spend it on the sports car, demand is not affected.

Wanting something like a sports car does not create a demand. Demand is only affected when consumers are willing to buy and have the ability to pay.

What Factors Influence Demand?

The amount of a product demanded depends on several factors. The first factor, as we saw in the example of the sports car, is *price*. **Income** of the consumers—how much money they make—is a second factor. A third factor is the *demand for substitute goods* that could be used. For example, you could buy another nice car for much less. *Consumer taste* is a final factor. There will be little demand for a car that no one likes, even if it is cheap.

What Does the Law of Demand Say?

The law of demand is quite simple. It says that when the price of a good goes up, the amount demanded goes down. If the price goes down, demand generally goes up. Producers are very aware of this law. They know that if the price gets too high, consumers will stop buying. This explains why consumers like special sales in which prices are lowered for a short time. Consumers tend to buy more when prices are lowered.

Demand curve

A way to explain the law of demand in a picture; the picture shows prices and units demanded at each price

What Does a Demand Curve Look Like?

A **demand curve** is a way to explain the law of demand in a picture. Look at Figures 4.1 and 4.2. They show how the demand for a soft drink is influenced by price. The demand schedule shows demand at each price. The demand curve shows the same information in graph form. Both figures show that demand for the soft drink is greater when the price is lower. Consumers are more willing to buy a soft drink at 50 cents than they are at $2. The movement of the curve is upward to the left and downward to the right.

Figure 4.1	Demand Schedule

Price of Soft Drink	Quantity Demanded (Number of Units Sold)
$2.00	1
$1.50	2
$1.00	3
$.75	4
$.50	5

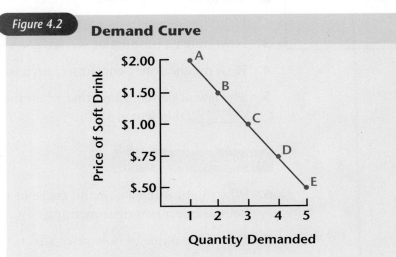

Figure 4.2 — Demand Curve

Economics in Your Life

The Rising Costs of Health Care

A good example of demand in the United States is health care. There are many reasons for the rising costs of health care. People are living longer than ever before. This means that there are more people needing health care. Older people often need more hospital care and treatment than young people. The demand for health care has grown much more rapidly than the supply of services. Increased demand raises the cost of the service.

Many people today do not make direct payment for their health care services. Many pay a fixed amount for insurance. They do not wait to see the doctor because it costs little, if anything, to do so.

Doctors are more concerned with laws about treating patients. As a result, they may use more expensive treatments, just to make sure they have tried every possible cure.

Every year patients benefit from new and better technology. These methods help to cure disease, relieve pain, and allow people to live longer. However, technology is also very costly.

Word Bank

demand

demand curve

income

price

rises

Lesson 1 Review On a separate sheet of paper, write the word from the Word Bank to complete each sentence.

1. A picture that explains the law of demand is a(n) _____.

2. The amount of goods and services people will buy at a given price is _____.

3. How much a product or service costs is its _____.

4. How much money consumers earn is _____.

5. The law of demand says that when the price of a good _____, the demand falls.

What do you think ?

6. Why might using a demand curve or other picture be helpful in explaining something?

7. Give an example of how price affects your life. For example, you might have shopped for the lowest price of a music CD you wanted to buy. What happened?

Elastic demand

The state in which a price increase causes a large change in demand

What Is the Elasticity of Demand?

Let's compare two products, candy bars and milk. Assume that the price of each goes up by 20 percent. A candy bar that used to sell for 75 cents now would sell for 90 cents. Milk that cost $3 a gallon now would cost $3.60. How would these price rises affect demand? Economists would predict that the demand for the candy bars would fall much more than the demand for milk. Why? Some goods have **elastic demand**, while others do not.

Milk does not have elastic demand. An increase or decrease in price would not affect demand very much.

The law of demand tells us that a rise in prices causes demand to go down. It does not tell us by how much demand decreases. Economists use the term elasticity to measure the impact of the price effect. When the price increase causes a large change in demand, the demand is elastic. Even a small change in the price causes a large change, or "stretch," in the amount demanded. In other words, people are less likely to buy the product if the price goes up.

Some food items are good examples of elasticity. For example, let's say strawberries normally sell for $2 a quart. How will the amount of strawberries demanded be affected if the price goes up to $3 a quart? Fewer people are likely to buy at the higher price. Suppose the strawberries go on sale. They are offered at a dollar per quart. Consumers who were not willing to pay the higher price are now more likely to want strawberries.

The demand for lobster is also elastic. Usually lobster is priced higher than beef or chicken. At the regular price, only a certain number of people will buy it. But if the store has a half-price sale, consumers will rush in to buy the lobster. Figure 4.3 shows how price changes affect the demand for lobster.

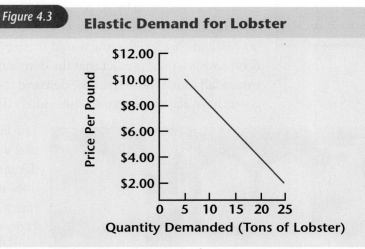

Figure 4.3

Elastic Demand for Lobster

Why Is the Demand for Some Products Called Inelastic?

The demand for some products is inelastic. **Inelastic demand** occurs when a price increase has little effect on demand. Milk is a good example. Raising or lowering the price is not likely to affect demand for milk very much. Even if the price were cut in half, the amount demanded would not go up much. People can only drink so much milk. Likewise, if the price doubled, people would still buy milk. Figure 4.4 shows how price changes affect the demand for milk. Demand is inelastic for some other food items too. Sugar, salt, and bread are examples of items with inelastic demand.

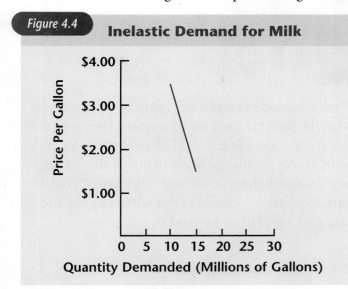

Figure 4.4

Inelastic Demand for Milk

What Three Questions Help Decide Whether Demand Is Elastic or Inelastic?

1. Is the product or service a **luxury** or a **necessity**? Some goods and services are luxuries. Luxuries are things that give us pleasure but that we really do not need. A sports car is a luxury. Decorating your home with fine paintings is a luxury. Milk, on the other hand, is more of a necessity. A necessity is something we need to live. Other necessities are water and medicines.

   Elasticity is greatest in goods and services we consider luxuries. Things we think of as necessary have little elasticity. Most of us do not think of candy bars as something we really need, so candy is a luxury. The demand for candy is elastic. Milk is a necessity, so the demand for it is inelastic.

2. Is a **substitute** available? Substitutes are products that can be used in place of other products. For example, juice, tea, milk, and water are all substitutes for soft drinks. Sometimes consumers have many substitutes to choose from. When this is true, even small price changes can cause consumers to switch from one product to another. Generally demand is more elastic when there are many substitutes available.

   Sometimes, consumers have no substitutes available. This often is true for some medicines. Consumers have to buy the medicine they need even if the price goes up. When few substitutes are available, demand is often inelastic.

3. How much of a person's income does the purchase require? Some products are not very expensive. If you have a job, you have an income. You might not think twice about buying something that costs only a few dollars, even if the price has gone up a lot. The few dollars you spend are only a small part of your total income.

On the other hand, you would spend a large part of your income to buy a new car. Does price affect your decision on which car to buy? Of course it does! Price changes affect demand for more expensive products more than they do for things that cost a little. A 10 percent increase in the price of the car affects you much more than a 10 percent increase in the price of a candy bar. Demand tends to be elastic for products that take up a large part of income. Demand tends to be inelastic for products that take up only a small part of income.

Why Does Elasticity Matter?

Elasticity matters because it affects the **bottom line**, or how much profit a business makes. Sellers may think that they will always make more money if they charge more for their products. However, we have learned that demand may be elastic. A price increase may not make sense if fewer people want the product.

Let's look at it in another way. Suppose a bicycle maker makes 10,000 bicycles a year. The company sells them for an average price of $250. The business's total revenue is $2,500,000 (10,000 × $250 = $2,500,000). The company decides to increase its profits by raising the average price by 10 percent to $275. Demand for bicycles is elastic. The law of demand says that a 10 percent increase in the price will cause demand to fall. Suppose demand falls by 10 percent so the business sells only 9,000 bicycles. The business's total revenue will be only $2,475,000 (9,000 × $275 = $2,475,000). The company actually will have lost money by raising the price. Raising the price when demand is elastic brought about lower total revenue.

Biography

Jerry Yang: 1968–

Jerry Yang was born in Taiwan but raised in San Jose, California. As a college student, he had a strong interest in the World Wide Web. He and his friend David Filo needed a way to organize their personal interests on the Internet. They founded a Web site to do this in 1994.

Within a short time, Yang and Filo turned their site into one for the general public. It became one of the first Internet directories and search engines. It soon developed into a major Internet site. Within four years, it had grown into an $11 billion business. Yang is presently a member of the company's board of directors. He works with the company's leaders to develop future strategies for the company he founded. Today, about 30 million people use Yang's site per month, more visitors than any other site.

Lesson 2 Review On a separate sheet of paper, write answers to the following questions. Use complete sentences.

1. What are products called that can be used in place of other products?

2. What is the money called that a person earns from having a job?

3. What is something called that gives people pleasure but that they do not need?

4. List at least two examples of elastic products. Why did you select these examples?

5. List at least two examples of inelastic products.

What do you think ?

6. Explain why a rise in the price of bread might cause demand to fall less than a similar rise in the price of house paint.

7. Explain how you could decide if a good or service you wanted was a luxury or a necessity.

What Factors Cause Demand to Change?

Demand can change. Several factors influence demand. The factors include:

1. changes in income
2. the number of substitutions
3. changes in the weather or seasons
4. changes in population
5. changes in consumer tastes
6. how satisfied we are as consumers

How Do Changes in Income Affect Demand?

Income can change demand. Clearly, the more money we earn, the more goods and services we can buy. What we may have thought of as luxuries in the past now become needs. Instead of buying a small car, we buy a large truck or van. We vacation in Mexico instead of renting a cabin in the woods. At the same time, if income goes down, consumers buy less.

How Do Substitutes Affect Demand?

A person who is thirsty does not have to drink a soft drink. The person can find substitutes. How does an increase in the price of soft drinks affect the demand for bottled water? (See Figure 4.5.) Demand for all the substitutes, including bottled water, will increase. The reverse also is true. If the price of the substitutes increases, the demand for soft drinks may increase. The prices and demand for the products and the substitutes are related. The demand for a product tends to go up if the price of the substitute goes up. The demand for a product tends to go down if the price of the substitute goes down.

Families can find a lot of substitutes when planning a meal. Suppose you have to decide what your family has for dinner tonight. The choices are chicken or steak. You want to get the most you can for your money. You probably would buy steak if the store has steak on sale. As a result, the demand for chicken, the substitute, goes down. But you might decide to buy chicken if you find that the steak is expensive. This means that if the price of steak stays high or even goes up, the demand for chicken goes up.

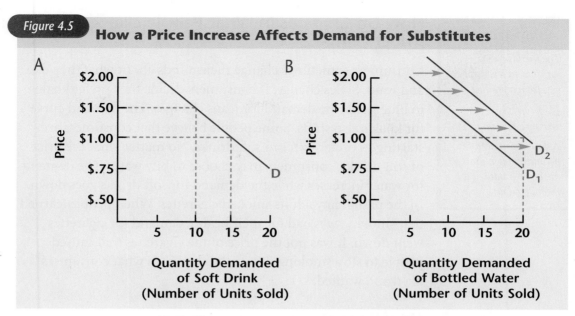

Figure 4.5

How a Price Increase Affects Demand for Substitutes

A

Price

$2.00
$1.50
$1.00
$.75
$.50

5   10   15   20

D

**Quantity Demanded
of Soft Drink
(Number of Units Sold)**

B

Price

$2.00
$1.50
$1.00
$.75
$.50

5   10   15   20

D_2
D_1

**Quantity Demanded
of Bottled Water
(Number of Units Sold)**

Part A shows how an increase in the price affects demand for the soft drink. At $1.00, 15 units were sold. When the price went up to $1.50, only 10 units were sold. Part B shows how the demand for bottled water is affected by the increase in price of the soft drink. If the cost of bottled water stays at $1.00 and the price of the soft drink goes up to $1.50, the original demand curve for bottled water is shown as D1. The demand curve for water will shift to the right (D2) as more people demand bottled water. The graph shows that now 20 units of water will be sold rather than the 15 that were sold before the price of the soft drink went up.

Writing About Economics

List 10 things that are in high demand because of the weather or seasons where you live. Pick one item and explain why you think it is in the highest demand.

How Can Weather Change Demand?

Demand is affected by the weather and season. During the summer, people tend to drink more than during the winter. Demand for soft drinks and all the substitutes is high. Suppose the summer is cool. Demand for all drinks will decrease.

Demand for gasoline changes in different seasons. People go on vacations in summer when school is out. Often they drive. This means that demand for gasoline usually goes up. Consumers have little choice. There are few substitutes for gasoline. They have to pay whatever price is charged for gasoline.

How Do Population Increases Change Demand?

In most areas, population is always growing. As the population increases, so does demand for goods and services.

How Do Changes in What People Like Affect Demand?

Consumers sometimes change their minds about what they like and want. Styles change. If consumers decide they prefer khakis to blue jeans, the demand for jeans changes. The demand curve for khakis also shifts. Some people believe that consumers are starting to prefer water to soft drinks. No matter what the price of soft drinks, consumers may choose to buy water. The demand for water increases while the demand for soft drinks goes down. In the past, many adults smoked cigarettes. When people learned that smoking was bad for their health, demand for cigarettes went down. It was not the price of the cigarettes that caused people to stop smoking. It was the change in what consumers liked and wanted.

How Does Utility Affect Demand?

Utility is the usefulness or satisfaction a consumer gets from a product. Utility varies from person to person. The more utility or satisfaction you get from a product, the more you are willing to pay for it. The less utility you get, the lower the price you are willing to pay. At some point, consumers cannot use any more of a product. There is a limit to how much satisfaction or utility a product gives to consumers. Thus, the demand for a product is limited.

Demand is affected by what economists call **diminishing marginal utility**. Imagine it is a very hot day and you have been working out. You are really thirsty. You are willing to spend one dollar on a bottle of water. In fact, you are so thirsty you would be willing to spend even more than one dollar for the water. You drink the first bottle. You are still thirsty, so you might decide to spend another dollar on a second bottle. The first bottle was really satisfying. How much extra satisfaction does the second bottle bring? The extra satisfaction you get is the marginal utility of the second bottle. At some point, you would be completely satisfied. You would not want to buy any more water, no matter what the price.

Lesson 3 Review On a separate sheet of paper, write the letter of the answer that correctly completes each sentence.

1. Demand for a product tends to go up if the price of the _____ goes up.

   A consumer   **B** elastic   **C** substitute   **D** utility

2. The demand for gasoline changes with the _____.

   A brand of car   **B** price of cars   **C** seasons   **D** time of day

3. Satisfaction consumers get from a product is _____.

   A demand   **B** happiness   **C** sale price   **D** utility

4. The decrease in need because enough units are produced to meet demand is called _____.

   A demand   **B** diminishing marginal utility   **C** income   **D** a substitute

5. The more _____ a person earns, the more goods and services the person can buy.

   A credit   **B** good grades   **C** goodwill   **D** money

What do you think

6. Give an example of how weather might change demand for items used at the beach.

7. Explain why gasoline prices change according to the season.

House on Hold: The Drywall Shortage

The strong economy of the late 1990s brought about rapid growth in home and business building. Although builders enjoyed the increased work, there also were some concerns. For example, in 1999, builders had a difficult time completing projects on time. This happened because there was a shortage of drywall.

Drywall is made from a mineral called gypsum. It usually comes in large white sheets and is used to form the inside walls of a house or building. When there is a shortage of drywall, electrical and plumbing work cannot be finished. A shortage of drywall also means there are no walls to paint. An article in the San Antonio (Texas) Business Journal *described the problems the drywall shortage caused.*

The shortage in the material . . . is causing both suppliers and contractors to quote longer delivery times for both product and project completions.

Industry officials say the shortage of the gypsum-made drywall or wallboard is due to the boom in the economy. . . .

"Generally, residential is high and commercial is low, or vice versa," says Dewitt Churchwell, the division president for local contractor Merek Brothers Systems Inc., "This time, both are high. But it is all a factor of rapid growth across the country." . . .

According to figures released by the Washington, D.C.-based Gypsum Association, an industry trade group, the demand for drywall reached a record level of 27.8 billion square feet (in 1998). Since 1990, the demand for wallboard has increased by 48 percent.

The demand has caused prices to fluctuate in the past year. The price for a single sheet of drywall has risen as much as 36 percent in one year, according to some contractors. . . .

"The gypsum manufacturers are working hard to satisfy customers' demand for gypsum board now and into the future by increasing their production capacity," says Jerry A. Walker, executive director of Gypsum Association. "Many companies are building new plants, as well as upgrading present facilities."

Document-Based Questions

1. What caused a drywall shortage?

2. Why is drywall so important to the building industry?

3. According to the article, why is there not always a shortage of drywall?

4. Describe how the building industry tried to decrease the demand for drywall.

5. List two other examples that you can think of where high demand has caused shortage of a product.

■ Demand is the amount of a product consumers will buy at a given price. Demand has two parts. Consumers must be willing to buy. They also must be able to buy. Price, income, demand for substitute goods, and consumer taste all affect demand.

■ The law of demand says if prices fall, demand generally will rise. If prices rise, demand falls. A demand curve is a picture that explains the law of demand for a product.

■ Elasticity of demand describes the effect of a price increase or decrease. When a small price rise causes a large change in demand, the demand is elastic. People are less likely to continue to buy that product. If a price increase has little effect on demand, the demand is inelastic. The demand for sugar, salt, milk, bread, and other foods is usually inelastic.

■ Three questions help decide if demand is elastic or inelastic. Is the product a luxury or a necessity? Is a substitute available? How much of a person's income does the purchase require?

■ Elasticity of demand affects the bottom line, or how much profit a business can earn.

■ Several factors may cause demand to change. If income rises, consumers usually buy more. If income falls, consumers buy less.

■ If substitutes for a product are available, demand for the product will fall if its price rises.

■ Weather and season may change demand. When school is out, demand for gas usually rises because people use their cars more for vacations.

■ As the population increases, demand also increases.

■ When consumers change their minds about what they like, demand for a product may go up or down.

■ Utility is the usefulness or satisfaction a person receives from a product. The more utility a person receives, the more of the product the person will buy. There is a limit to how much utility a product provides.

■ Diminishing marginal utility is the decrease in need because enough units are being produced to meet demand. Eventually, a person will be completely satisfied and will stop buying the product.

Chapter 4 R E V I E W

On a separate sheet of paper, write the word from the Word Bank to complete each sentence.

Word Bank
bottom line
demand
elasticity
go up
income
summer
utility

1. The amount of goods consumers are willing to buy at a given price is _____.

2. Four factors influencing demand include price, _____, the demand for substitute goods, and consumer tastes.

3. To measure the impact of the price effect, economists use the term _____.

4. Elasticity matters because it affects a business's _____.

5. If the price of a product rises, the demand of a substitute tends to _____.

6. The more _____ a person gets from a product, the more the person will be willing to pay for the product.

7. The demand for gasoline usually increases during the _____.

On a separate sheet of paper, write the letter of the answer that correctly completes each sentence.

8. Demand has two parts: Consumers must be willing to buy, and they must have the _____ to pay.
   A ability   C friends
   B utility   D demand

9. A picture that explains the law of demand is a _____.
   A demand curve   C utility
   B pictograph   D supply curve

10. Water and medicine are examples of a _____.
    A food   C necessity
    B luxury   D utility

11. Juice, water, milk, and tea are _____ for soft drinks.
    A bought   C substitutes
    B demanded   D used

12. A decrease in need because enough units are produced is called _____.

   A advertising   **C** diminishing marginal utility

   B demand   **D** pleasure

13. Consumers affect demand by changing their minds about what they _____.

   A know   **C** see around them

   B like and want   **D** supply others

On a separate sheet of paper, write answers to the following questions. Use complete sentences.

14. What are the two parts of demand?

15. What are luxuries?

16. What is income?

17. How do substitutes affect demand?

On a separate sheet of paper, write your opinion to each question. Use complete sentences.

18. If people buy more of a product at a lower price, why do you think producers have sales instead of keeping prices low all the time?

19. Why do you think buying a more expensive product requires more thought than does a less expensive product?

20. How do you think your demand for clothing is affected by consumer tastes?

Test-Taking Tip

Look over a test before you begin answering questions. See how many parts there are. Know what you are being asked to do on each part.

5 Supply

Businesses always are making choices. They have to decide what products or services to offer consumers. How much of a product or service to offer is another problem. The success of a business depends on making sound choices.

This chapter will introduce you to the term *supply*. The idea of supply is key to business. You will learn how businesses decide what to make, how much to make, and how to make something.

Goals for Learning

◆ To define supply

◆ To explain the law of supply

◆ To analyze the factors that influence changes in supply

◆ To evaluate how production decisions are made

What Is Supply?

Like the word *demand*, the word **supply** has a different meaning in economics than it does in everyday life. It has a very specific meaning. Supply refers to the ability and willingness of sellers to make things available for sale. Ability means that the seller is able to produce and sell a product or service. Willingness means the seller wants to produce or sell. Suppose you decide to make wooden toys to sell. You quickly find out that the job is harder than you thought. You lack the "ability" to produce the toys, so there is no supply. Say you learn that another seller is selling the same toys for less than the cost of the materials you need. Then you may no longer be "willing" to make the toys. Again, this means there is no supply.

You add to demand by being a consumer. You buy products and services. You also add to supply. You are a producer. You supply goods and services. If you bag groceries or make hamburgers in a paid job, you supply your labor to provide a service. If you are an athlete on a school team, you also are a producer. You supply a product that others may pay to see. You are paid not in money but in the good will and school spirit you create.

What Is the Law of Supply?

Suppose you are a farmer. You can grow corn or soybeans. Last year, the price of soybeans went up while the price of corn went down. What crop would you plant this spring? Most farmers would choose soybeans. Whether they knew it or not, they were applying the **law of supply**. The law of supply says that as the price of a good rises, the quantity supplied will rise. As the price of a good goes down, so does the supply of the good. Farmers, like other producers, will not be willing to produce if they do not receive a fair price for their goods. The law of supply, like the law of demand, really is common sense. Suppliers are more willing to supply large quantities of their goods at higher prices than they are at lower prices.

Figure 5.1

A Supply Schedule

Price Per Flower	Quantity of Flowers Supplied
$1.00	50
$2.00	100
$3.00	150
$4.00	200

Supply schedule

A way to show the law of supply using a chart; it shows the quantity of a good offered at each possible market price

Supply curve

A graph showing that suppliers are more willing to sell at higher prices than lower prices

What Is a Supply Schedule?

A **supply schedule** is a way to show the law of supply using a chart. The chart shows the quantity of a good offered at each possible market price. Figure 5.1 is an example of a supply schedule. Suppose that a school club you belong to sells flowers for Mother's Day. The supply schedule shows the quantity of flowers that a flower shop would supply at certain prices. As the price goes from $1.00 to $4.00, the quantity supplied goes from 50 to 200. It is clear that the flower shop wants to sell (supply) flowers at the higher price rather than the lower price.

What Is a Supply Curve?

The information shown on a supply schedule also can be shown as a graph. That graph is called a **supply curve**. The supply curve is the opposite of a demand curve. The demand curve shows that consumers are more willing to buy at lower prices than higher prices. The supply curve shows that suppliers are more willing to sell at higher prices than lower prices. Figure 5.2 shows the same data as Figure 5.1 but uses a graph instead of a chart. Movement along the curve is upward to the right and downward to the left.

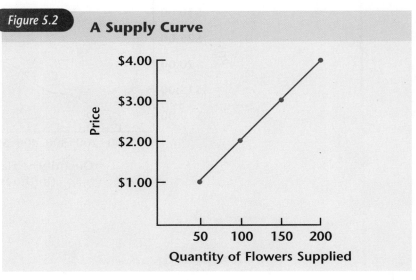

Figure 5.2

A Supply Curve

Elasticity of supply

The measure of how changes in price affect the quantity of supply

Elastic supply

When a change in price has a big effect on the quantity supplied

Inelastic supply

When a change in price has very little effect on the quantity supplied

Just like demand, supply can be either elastic or inelastic. **Elasticity of supply** measures how changes in price affect the quantity of supply. If a change in price has a big effect on the quantity supplied, there is **elastic supply**. However, if a change in price has very little effect on the quantity supplied, there is **inelastic supply**.

Let's look at an example of elastic supply. On September 11, 2001, the World Trade Center in New York City was destroyed. Many people wanted to show their love of the country by buying American flags. Consumers were willing to pay extra to get a flag. Since so many people wanted a flag, demand increased.

How did this affect the supply of flags? Making flags is fairly easy and cheap. They can be made with resources that are common and available. Sewing flags is not hard. They usually are made out of cloth that is not very expensive. Within a few weeks, stores had many flags to sell. The fact that the price for flags went up caused a large increase in supply. Figure 5.3 shows the elastic supply for flags during a two-month period.

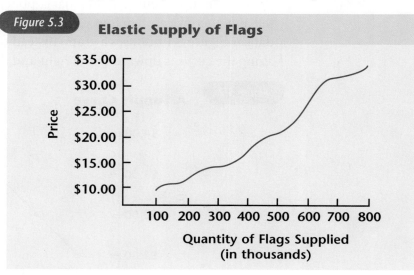

Figure 5.3   **Elastic Supply of Flags**

Other goods may have an inelastic supply. A few products have zero elasticity of supply. For example, only one original of the famous Mona Lisa painting exists. No matter how much anyone is willing to pay, there never will be more than one. Inelastic supply exists when a small increase in price has little effect on the supply demanded. Goods usually have an inelastic supply if their production requires a lot of time and money.

Sometimes the resources used to make a product are rare or hard to find. Suppose you collect rare coins. Coins have a date on them. Their supply is limited. Collectors are very interested in Indian head pennies. A few are always available. The sellers might offer the pennies to buyers at many times what they paid for them. If you really want the coin, you will have to pay whatever price the seller charges because the supply is so limited. Figure 5.4 shows what an inelastic supply curve would look like.

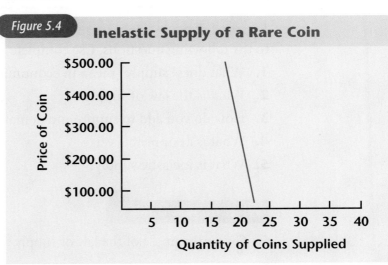

Figure 5.4 **Inelastic Supply of a Rare Coin**

Economics in Your Life

Changes for the Computer Consumer

Those who bought computers in the early 1990s were excited about the new technology. The computers available to them cost much more than today's models.

In the early 1990s, there were mainly two major companies building computers, operating systems, and software. As each year passed, other companies introduced new products. Computers could be used for word processing, accounting, and for playing many different games. As the Internet developed, more people wanted to own a computer to use e-mail and the Internet.

As the number of computer buyers went up, so did the types of computers available from different companies. The supply had increased right along with the demand. Manufacturers during the 1990s developed simpler methods of mass-producing computer parts. This also helped to keep computer costs down. Today's computers are nearly as affordable as TV sets. This means many millions of households have at least one.

Lesson 1 Review On a separate sheet of paper, write answers to the following questions. Use complete sentences.

1. What does "supply" mean in economics?

2. What is the law of supply?

3. How do you add to supply and demand?

4. What is a supply curve?

5. What is inelastic supply?

What do you think

6. Give an example of the law of supply.

7. Why might a rare item have an inelastic supply?

How Does the Cost of Resources Affect Supply?

Tax

Money that people and businesses pay to help pay the cost of government

Subsidy

A government grant

Writing About Economics

What kinds of technology do you think lower the cost of production today? Write a list of five examples. Explain how you think each one lowers costs.

In Chapter 1, we talked about the factors of production. We learned the three types of resources used in production. The three were natural resources, labor resources, and capital resources. Any change in the cost of these resources will affect supply. What happens if the price of the resources goes down? The result is that producers can produce more because it is cheaper to make the goods. Likewise, if the cost of the resources goes up, producers will make less. Why? Because the goods are more expensive to make.

What Effect Does Technology Have on Supply?

New technology tends to lower the cost of production. Today's farmers, for example, are able to produce a great deal more than in the past. New technology in the form of better pest control, better fertilizers (substances that help crops grow), and machines allows the farmer to grow more. The cost of production goes down. Because production costs are less, farmers are more willing and able to produce more.

How Do Taxes and Subsidies Affect Supply?

A **tax** is money that people and businesses pay to help pay the cost of government. Businesses think of taxes as an extra cost of producing goods or services. The effect of an increase in taxes is the same as an increase in the cost of resources. It makes production more expensive. As a result, producers make less.

Governments sometimes identify industries they believe are very important to the country. Many governments believe their countries should not be dependent on other countries for food. To encourage farmers to continue to produce, governments sometimes provide **subsidies**. Subsidies are government grants.

One type of subsidy to farmers is **price supports**. Price supports are government-guaranteed minimum prices farmers receive for their products. These subsidies have the opposite effect of taxes. They encourage businesses to continue production by lowering the cost of production. This increases the supply. What would happen to many farmers if they did not receive a government subsidy? They would have to give up farming and the supply would go down.

Governments provide subsidies to some farmers. Subsidies help farmers increase the supply of farm goods by lowering the costs of farming.

What Effect Does Worker Productivity Have on Supply?

Productivity is affected by how workers feel about their jobs. If they are happy, productivity often increases. Workers make more products at every price. If workers are unhappy, they produce less. Fewer products are offered for sale. The supply decreases.

How Does Competition Affect Supply?

Let's look at the home entertainment industry. The market is changing. A few years ago, many companies made and sold video recorders. Only a few DVD machines were available. Now, more DVD machines are sold than video recorders. What happened?

When the first DVD players went on the market, there were few available, and they cost a lot. But people liked what they saw. Many consumers wanted them. The businesses making and selling DVD players soon had high sales and high profits. Other manufacturers took note of the high profits. They also began making DVD players. Soon the supply of DVD players jumped.

What happened to the supply of video recorders? Their manufacturers noticed that consumers were not buying many recorders anymore. Profits were down. The businesses shifted their resources to making other products. Supply shrank. Competition usually increases supply, as we saw with DVD players. Lack of competition shrinks supply.

How Do the Prices of Related Goods Affect Supply?

Video recorders and DVD players are related goods. Both are part of the home entertainment industry. Being related goods means that changes in the price of one can affect the supply of the other. What happened to the supply of video recorders when the price of DVD players dropped? The supply went down.

Lesson 2 Review On a separate sheet of paper, write the letter of the answer that correctly completes each sentence.

1. _____ may affect supply by lowering the cost of production.

    A Big government   **B** A person   **C** Taxation   **D** New technology

2. Money people pay to help support a government is called _____.

    A income   **B** price supports   **C** taxes   **D** subsidies

3. Government grants of money to produce something are called _____.

    A income   **B** production   **C** subsidies   **D** taxes

4. Unlike taxes, _____ encourage businesses to continue or increase production.

    A incomes   **B** price supports   **C** productivities   **D** workers

5. If workers are happy, their _____ generally increases.

    A price supports   **B** health   **C** subsidy   **D** productivity

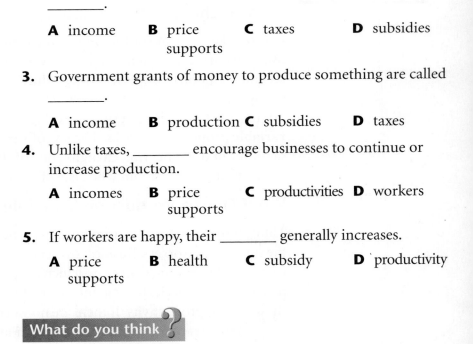

What do you think ?

6. Do you think government subsidies for farmers are good or bad? Why?

7. Should the government give money to a failing business to keep it producing? Explain.

Law of variable proportions

The belief that in the short run, changing one of the inputs changes the output

Production schedule

A table that shows how the number of workers affects productivity and marginal product

We have learned that several factors influence what is produced. The laws of demand and supply affect the amount of goods produced. Elasticity of demand and supply also influence what is produced, as do changes in both demand and supply. Two other factors also are important: productivity and the costs of production.

In Chapter 1, we noted that productivity is the amount of goods and services workers can produce in a given time. When productivity is high, producers know that they are using scarce resources well. They always look for ways to improve productivity. This is because the higher the productivity, the higher the profits.

What Is the Law of Variable Proportions?

Do you like sugar in your iced tea? One teaspoon of sugar improves the taste. You might like it even more if you added a second teaspoon. However, adding a third or fourth teaspoon of sugar might make the tea too sweet. You probably would not like the taste. This is a simple example of how the **law of variable proportions** works. The law of variable proportions says this: in the short run, changing one of the inputs (the sugar) changes the output (the taste of the iced tea).

What Does a Production Schedule Show?

Think about this example from business. One of the inputs is the number of workers. Business owners need to think about whether adding more workers will increase profits. Figure 5.5 is a **production schedule**. Look at just the first two columns. They show worker productivity. If there are no workers, there is no production. As workers are added, production goes up. Workers may be able to specialize and do the job they are best at. At some point, production goes as high as it can. What happened when the ninth and tenth workers were hired? Production went down. Maybe the extra workers got in each other's way. The production schedule shows that adding more workers does not always increase production.

Marginal product

The extra amount produced by adding one resource to production

Figure 5.5 **Production Schedule**

Number of Workers	Productivity of Worker Per Day (Units)	Marginal Product	Stage of Production
0	0	0	Stage 1
1	10	10	
2	25	15	
3	50	25	
4	90	40	
5	150	60	
6	175	25	Stage 2
7	190	15	
8	200	10	
9	193	-7	Stage 3
10	180	-13	

The third column shows **marginal product.** Marginal product tells us how much extra is produced by adding one input, in this case an extra worker. When a fourth worker was hired, 40 more units were produced than when there were only three workers (90 − 50 = 40).

Biography

Mary Kay Ash: 1915–2001

Mary Kay Ash founded one of the largest beauty products firms in the United States. Beginning in her teen years, Ash stressed the value of setting goals. She wanted to help other women succeed in the business world.

As a young woman, Ash sold books door-to-door. She later became a manager and trainer of other sales people. She began her own beauty supply company in 1963 with just $5,000. She sold her products door-to-door and trained other women to do the same thing. The company eventually developed over 200 different products.

Ash became wealthy. She gave her money and time to help cancer research. She helped the American Cancer Society raise funds from other people. She received hundreds of awards and honors. Mary Kay Ash died in 2001, but her company still has more than 475,000 salespeople and earns more than $1.5 billion in sales per year.

What Are the Three Stages of Production?

Figure 5.6 shows that there are three stages of production.

Increasing returns

When adding resources increases production

Diminishing returns

When adding resources is not always a good thing; it can cause production to slow down slightly

Negative returns

When adding resources causes production to be less than before

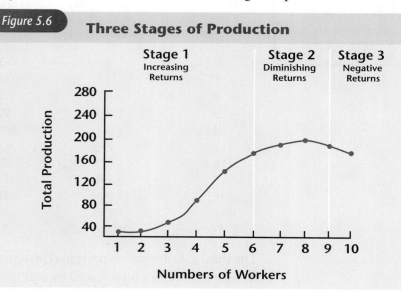

Figure 5.6

Three Stages of Production

The first stage is **increasing returns**. Did the business do well when the first five workers were hired? Yes. Productivity went up dramatically as each new worker was added. In fact, each worker added more to production than the previous worker.

The second stage is **diminishing returns**. The law of diminishing returns says this: adding more resources such as extra workers or machines is not always a good thing. The increase in production eventually diminishes, or becomes smaller. Again, look at Figure 5.5. Hiring the seventh worker added only 15 units. The eighth worker hired added only 10.

The third stage of production is **negative returns**. Adding the ninth and tenth workers actually reduced production. The resource of labor is being wasted.

What does this mean to a business owner? Remember, business owners want to earn the highest profits and use their resources most efficiently. The ideal number of workers hired should be in Stage 2. If labor is not too expensive, eight workers would work out best. Sometimes labor costs are high. The business would then be best off hiring between six and eight workers.

What Are the Costs of Production?

Businesses need to know the cost of production when deciding how much to supply to the market. The cost of production has a big effect on how much profit a business will make. Businesses put their costs into four groups: fixed, variable, total, and marginal.

What Are Fixed Costs?

You learned a little about costs in Chapter 3. A fixed cost is a cost of production. Every business has fixed costs. Fixed costs stay the same no matter how much is produced. Many fixed costs of doing business are obvious. Businesses usually pay rent. They have to pay for insurance. Money has to be set aside for taxes. If loans were taken out to start or expand the business, they have to be paid off. All these are examples of costs that are fixed. Machines and capital goods usually have fixed costs. The cost is the same whether the machine is being used or not. Remember, the cost of doing business sometimes is called overhead.

What Are Variable Costs?

A variable cost also is a cost of production. Variable costs change with the amount of production. The amount the business spends on raw materials can vary, or change, from month to month. Workers' pay also goes up and down. If demand is strong, workers may be asked to work more hours. The business rewards them by paying them more. Labor and the cost of raw materials are the most common examples of variable costs.

Economics at Work

Sales Clerk

Sales clerks help customers in a store or other retail setting. They must know the store's products well to answer customer questions. In many cases, this knowledge may help them to offer advice to customers. Sales clerks may sometimes handle customer complaints and give refunds.

Sales clerks often operate a cash register, receive payments, and make change. They may be asked to balance funds in the cash register against the total recorded within the machine.

A sales clerk should see that there are enough products to sell. He or she may be responsible for reordering products or to report shortages to someone else. A sales clerk may be called upon to help with taking inventory. During this process, the store takes an account of the products on shelves and in storage. Stores do this to complete accounting records.

How Is Total Cost Calculated?

We can figure the total cost of production by adding the fixed costs and the variable costs. It is called total cost because it is the total of all the costs of doing business. Look at Figure 5.7.

Figure 5.7	The Cost of Production		
Output	**Fixed Costs**	**Variable Costs**	**Total Costs**
0	$500	$0	$500
1	$500	$200	$700
2	$500	$350	$850
3	$500	$500	$1,000
4	$500	$700	$1,200

What Is Marginal Cost?

Marginal is another way of saying the extra cost of doing something. **Marginal cost** is the additional cost of producing one more unit. In some businesses, the marginal costs are small.

Here is an example of how marginal cost works. Most of the costs of running a movie theater are fixed. The owner has to pay for the building, the equipment, and the electricity. The cost of the film is a variable cost. If the theater shows first-run films, the cost may be high. Once the owner decides which films to show, the costs are the same whether there are 10 people or 100 people in the theater. Marginal cost is involved if the owner decides to add an extra late night show. Since most of the cost is fixed, the marginal cost of adding the extra show is small.

What if the owner decided to have a live concert by a musical group? Doing so would have high marginal costs. Most of the costs are variable. The group would have to be paid more for an extra concert. The theater would have to be rented for another day. All the people who work at the concert would have to be paid for the extra show. After thinking about all of these factors, the owner might decide to not add the extra concert. Doing so might not increase profits.

Word Bank

diminishing
 returns
fixed cost
marginal cost
marginal product
variable cost

Lesson 3 Review On a separate sheet of paper, write the word from the Word Bank to complete each sentence.

1. _____ tells how much extra is produced by adding one input.

2. The law of _____ says that adding one more resource is not always good.

3. No matter how much is produced, a _____ always stays the same.

4. A _____ changes with the amount of production.

5. The additional cost of producing one more unit is _____.

What do you think ?

6. Why do you think adding extra workers or new equipment might not be a good thing?

7. How do you think a person who runs a business might try to make costs more fixed?

Gold Rush!

On January 24, 1848, gold was discovered in Sutter's Mill near Sacramento, California. Gold has a very limited supply. Word of the discovery spread quickly. In December 1848, President James K. Polk confirmed the rumors of gold in California. Men from all over the United States left their jobs and their families for dreams of finding gold and becoming rich. But the journey to California was long and difficult. Many died from illness or thirst. By the time the others arrived in California, much of the gold was gone.

This excerpt from Captain John Sutter's diary describes the discovery of gold at his mill.

[S]uddenly all my misgivings were put at an end to by his [Sutter's business partner, James Marshall] flinging on the table a handful of scales of pure virgin gold. I was fairly thunderstruck and asked him to explain what all this meant. . . . Mr. Marshall was walking along the left Bank of the stream when he perceived something which he at first took for a piece of opal. . . . He paid not attention to this, but while he was giving directions to the workmen, having observed several similar glittering fragments, . . . he stooped down and picked one of them up. . . .

At the conclusion of Mr. Marshall's account, and when I had convinced myself, . . . I felt as much excited as himself. . . . We agreed not to mention the circumstances to any one, and arranged to set off early the next day for the mill. . . . On our arrival, just before sundown, we poked the sand about in various places, and before long succeeded in collecting between us more than an ounce of gold, mixed up with a good deal of sand. . . . [T]he next day we proceeded some little distance up the south Fork and found that gold existed along the whole course. . . . I think it is more plentiful in these latter places, for I myself, with nothing more than a small knife, picked out from [a] dry gorge, a little way up the mountain, a solid lump of gold which weighted nearly an ounce and a half.

Document-Based Questions

1. What was Sutter's Mill?

2. What do you think was important about President Polk saying there was gold in California?

3. How did Captain Sutter learn of the discovery?

4. Once Captain Sutter learned of the discovery, what did he and Mr. Marshall decide to do?

5. How might history have been different if Mr. Marshall had not picked up one of the "glittering fragments"?

Chapter 5 SUMMARY

- Supply is the ability and willingness of sellers to sell a good or service.

- The law of supply says sellers supply more of a good at higher prices. As the price falls, so does supply.

- The supply of a good is elastic if a small price change causes a large change in supply. If a price change has little effect on supply, the supply is inelastic. Some goods have zero elasticity. No matter how much people are willing to pay for such goods, there is never more than one of the good.

- Technology, taxes and subsidies, worker productivity, competition, the cost of resources, and the price of related goods all affect supply.

- When the costs of natural, labor, or capital resources fall, supply of a product rises. When these costs rise, supply falls.

- New technology raises supply by lowering production costs.

- Increased taxes lower supply by raising the cost of production. Subsidies, or government grants of money, increase supply by lowering the cost of production.

- If workers are happy, productivity and supply increase.

- Competition increases supply as more sellers are willing to produce a product.

- If related goods or services are available, a rise in supply of one product causes a drop in supply of the related good.

- High productivity means scarce resources are being used efficiently. Profits rise.

- The law of variable proportion says that changing a product's input in the short run changes the output.

- A production schedule shows the relation of inputs and outputs. It also shows the marginal product, or the extra amount produced by adding an input.

- In the increasing returns stage of production, productivity rises as inputs or resources are added. In the diminishing returns stage, adding inputs may not increase productivity as much. In the negative returns stage, production falls when more resources or inputs are added.

- Fixed costs, or overhead, remain the same no matter how much is produced. Variable costs change with the amount of production.

- Total cost is the sum of fixed and variable costs. Marginal cost is the additional cost of producing one more unit. Businesses with more fixed than variable costs generally have lower marginal costs than businesses with more variable costs.

Chapter 5 REVIEW

On a separate sheet of paper, write the word from the Word Bank to complete each sentence.

1. Part of the _____ says that as the price of a good rises, the supply of the good rises.

2. A(n) _____ is a table showing the quantity of a good available at every possible price.

3. When a small increase in price has little effect on the supply of a good, a(n) _____ occurs.

4. Money that people and businesses pay to the government is a(n) _____.

5. The way workers feel about their jobs affects their _____.

6. The _____ says that changing one input in the short run changes the output.

7. No matter how much of a good is produced, a(n) _____ always stays the same.

Word Bank

fixed cost

inelastic supply

law of supply

law of variable proportions

productivity

supply schedule

tax

On a separate sheet of paper, write the letter of the answer that correctly completes each sentence.

8. A graph of information from a supply schedule is called a(n) _____.
   A chart   C example curve
   B demand curve   D supply curve

9. Quickly creating extra fireworks in time for the Fourth of July is an example of _____.
   A elastic supply   C inelastic supply
   B diminishing supply   D overhead

10. Any change in the cost of natural, labor, and capital resources will affect a good's _____.
    A looks B materials C overtime D supply

11. A government sometimes gives a subsidy to _____ it believes are very important to the country.
    A industries   C prisoners
    B leaders   D athletes

12. When resources are wasted, thus reducing production, that is called _____.

   A demand   **C** overhead

   B negative returns   **D** supply

13. Rent, insurance, or loan repayments are examples of fixed costs, or _____.

   A overhead   **C** underheating

   B overheating   **D** variable costs

On a separate sheet of paper, write answers to the following questions. Use complete sentences.

14. How do you contribute to supply?

15. How do price supports help businesses?

16. What is marginal product?

17. What are costs of production? Write two kinds of costs of production.

On a separate sheet of paper, write your opinion to each question. Use complete sentences.

18. Imagine you are a farmer and that corn grown in Europe is cheaper than your corn. Should your government give you a subsidy to continue producing corn? Why or why not?

19. New technology lets farmers grow more food more cheaply. Why, then, do you think some consumers are willing to pay more for food grown with old-fashioned farming methods, also called organic farming?

20. If you were to start a business, which three ideas from this chapter would be most important? Why?

Test-Taking Tip

Before starting a test, decide which questions you will do first and last. Limit your time on each question accordingly.

6 Price

L ike most people, you probably like to shop. Usually you find something you like. You may like the style and color. You may think owning it would be useful or fun. How do you decide whether to buy it or not? Most consumers look at prices. Imagine how difficult shopping would be if there were no prices. You would not know whether you could afford to buy or not. Prices are a way that buyers and sellers exchange information.

In this chapter, you will learn about the price system. You will learn how prices are set and how quantity of goods affects prices.

Goals for Learning

◆ To describe the price system

◆ To explain how prices act as a rationing device

◆ To identify how prices are set

Price system

Communication between buyers and sellers through the use of prices

Relative worth

The value that most people would place on a good

Writing About Economics

Think of an item that you really would like to purchase. What things do you consider before making a purchase? Write a letter to a friend explaining your decision-making process.

What Is a Price System?

Prices are important. They give information to both buyers and sellers. This communication between buyers and sellers is called the **price system**.

What Are the Advantages of the Price System?

In Chapter 2, you learned about the three basic questions every economic system answers. Prices help determine the answers to what, how, and who. An economy without prices would not work very well. There are several reasons why prices are so important.

Prices give information. They are important to both buyers and sellers. Prices tell businesses about the values customers put on certain products. They tell buyers the **relative worth** of goods—the value that most people would place on the good. To make good economic choices, buyers need to know how much the things they want cost. Producers base their decisions on prices too. They need to know the price of labor and other resources.

Producers and consumers have many choices available to them. Both can use substitutes for products that are too expensive. The market provides many goods and services in a wide range of prices.

Have you ever wanted to buy something because the price was too good to pass up? The low price was an incentive to you. It caused you to buy. Prices are incentives for producers too. Raising prices for goods that consumers like you want encourages businesses to increase production. Prices also provide incentives in markets for resources such as labor and capital. Increasing workers' pay encourages more people to apply for jobs or switch jobs. Lowering pay has the opposite effect.

Prices encourage resources to be used in the best way. Producers want to make things that consumers want to buy. Prices tell producers what consumers want most. By paying high prices, consumers are telling producers that they are using their resources well. When consumers only pay low prices, they are telling producers that resources are not being used efficiently.

What Are the Limitations of the Price System?

The price system does have some limitations. It works best when buyers and sellers are well informed. Resources must be free to shift from places where they are not used efficiently to industries where they can be better used. The system also works best when prices are set reasonably. This occurs when prices reflect the actual costs of production. Problems sometimes develop when these conditions are not met. This is described as **market failure**.

What Are Externalities?

Economic side effects sometimes are called **externalities**. They can be either helpful or harmful. They affect people other than the buyer and seller. For example, businesses like restaurants may be helped if a new factory is built nearby. This is an example of a **positive externality**. The people living near the new factory may suffer as a result of the extra traffic and pollution caused by the factory. This is an example of **negative externality**.

Externalities are considered market failures. Their costs and benefits are not reflected in the prices the buyers and sellers pay. The restaurant owners near the new factory do not have to share their extra profit with the factory owners. The homeowners near the factory do not receive any extra benefit from the factory owners.

A park is an example of a public good. Taxes pay for parks.

Why Are Public Goods Another Form of Market Failure?

Public goods are products or services available to everyone. They are a kind of market failure. They include parks, schools, highways, police and fire protection, and national defense. Would people be willing to pay for these things by choice? Maybe not. The government usually provides public goods from tax money.

Kenneth Chenault: 1951–

Kenneth Chenault is the chief executive officer of a major credit card company. He joined his company in 1981 as head of strategic planning. In 1989, he was named president of consumer credit cards. Sales of credit card accounts went up steadily. He became head of travel-related services in 1993. He was named vice chairman of the entire company in 1995. In 1997, he was named chief executive officer.

Chenault is on the board of directors of many other companies and nonprofit groups. He has received awards from Phipps House, Wharton University, and the City of New York.

Lesson 1 Review On a separate sheet of paper, write the letter of the answer that correctly completes each sentence.

1. Communication between buyers and sellers is the _____.

   A Internet   **C** phone system
   B market economy   **D** price system

2. Economic side effects are called _____.

   A disasters **B** externalities **C** internalities **D** efficiencies

3. When prices do not reflect the cost of production, a _____ occurs.

   A public good   **C** free choice
   B depression   **D** market failure

4. People pay taxes for the government to provide _____.

   A jobs   **B** public goods **C** subsidies   **D** tax cuts

5. An example of something that is *not* a public good is _____.

   A defense **B** police   **C** schools   **D** taxes

What do you think?

6. What should people do if they disagree with how the government spends tax money?

7. Imagine a factory were built near your home. Would more positive or negative externalities occur? Explain.

Rationing
A system in which the government provides a fixed amount of limited supplies to each person

Crisis
An event that threatens people's well-being

Ration coupon
A piece of paper that can be exchanged for goods during rationing

What Is Rationing?

We have learned that resources are limited. Because resources are limited, goods are limited too. Wants and needs are unlimited. We know that this causes scarcity. Price has an important function in determining who gets what goods and services.

Rationing is a system in which the government provides a fixed amount of limited supplies to each person. Rationing occurs most often during times of **crisis** or war. During World War II, supplies of many everyday things were limited. Much of the world's resources were used to make war material. To make sure that everyone received a fair share, the government issued **ration coupons**. These coupons could be exchanged for meat, butter, bread, and gasoline.

Prices act as a rationing device. Prices treat all consumers the same way. Scarce goods and services go to the people who are willing and able to pay the price. They do not go to those people who are unable or unwilling to pay the price.

Is Using Price as a Rationing Device Fair?

Some people argue that rationing is unfair. Do poor people have the same ability to buy what they want and need as rich people? Clearly, the answer is no. Some people believe it would be better if need rather than price determined who gets what. This also creates problems.

Let's say that the supply of gasoline becomes very limited because of conflict in oil-producing nations. The government then decides to ration gasoline. Everyone receives the same ration. This seems fair. But is it? What if you live in a rural area where you have no choice but to drive? What if your family has two or three cars? What if your newer model car gets better gas mileage than your neighbor's older model? Can you see how difficult it is to create a system of rationing that is fair to everyone?

Black market

An illegal market in which goods and services are sold above their legal price

Economists might agree that using prices as a rationing device is unfair. They might also disagree on what would replace prices in determining who gets what. Would people be willing to work if their wants were given to them only based on need? Using price as a rationing device provides workers with incentives. Workers know that if they earn enough money they will be able to buy the goods and services they want.

In theory, rationing works better than it does in practice. Rationing often is expensive because it requires many people to manage the system. A more serious problem is that it encourages **black markets**. A black market is an illegal market in which goods and services are sold above their legal price. Demand is high despite rationing. For example, during World War II, people wanted and needed more gasoline than was available. The high quantity demanded meant that some people bought gasoline in the black market. People who could get more gasoline than they needed sold their coupons to people who were able and willing to pay high prices for it. This might seem unfair as well.

Some goods were rationed in America during World War II. People only could purchase certain amounts of some goods using coupons.

Word Bank
black market
crisis
incentive
price
rationing
wartime

Lesson 2 Review On a separate sheet of paper, write the word from the Word Bank to complete each sentence.

1. _____ occurs when the government provides fixed amounts of limited supplies to people.

2. As a rationing device, _____ treats all people the same.

3. If people received everything on the basis of need, they might have no _____ to work.

4. An illegal market to sell goods and services above their legal price is a(n) _____.

5. Usually, rationing occurs during _____.

What do you think ?

6. Do you think the government should ration scarce gasoline supplies? Explain.

7. Imagine you are the leader of a country and must ration gasoline, bread, or meat. Which would you choose to ration? What might happen if you did?

What Is the Equilibrium Price?

Equilibrium price

The price that both buyers and sellers will accept

Equilibrium point

The point at which the quantity demanded equals the quantity supplied

Supply and demand work together to set prices. Chapter 4 talked about demand. You learned that consumers buy less if the price goes up. Chapter 5 talked about supply. You learned that producers want to sell more if the price goes up. It might look like buyers and sellers would never agree on a price. There is one price both will accept. This is called the **equilibrium price**. It occurs when the needs of both buyers and sellers are satisfied.

Look at Figure 6.1. It shows a supply and a demand schedule for a video game available in one shop. Figure 6.2 shows both the supply and demand curves for the games on the same graph. Where the two lines cross, the market is balanced. It is balanced between the forces of supply (how many games the seller is willing to sell at a given price) and demand (how many games buyers are willing to buy at the same price). This point is called the **equilibrium point**. It is the point at which the quantity demanded equals the quantity supplied. At $32, the business wants to sell and consumers are willing to buy 13 video games.

Figure 6.1 **A Demand and Supply Schedule for a Video Game**

Price	Quantity Demanded	Quantity Supplied
$50.00	1	30
$45.00	2	28
$40.00	4	24
$35.00	8	17
$30.00	15	10
$25.00	30	2

Figure 6.2 **Supply and Demand Curves for a Video Game**

Price = $32.00 (approximately)
Quantity = 13

What Is a Surplus?

Surplus

Extra goods caused by the difference between what a seller is willing to supply and what buyers are willing to pay at that price

Shortage

When the number of goods needed is greater than the number producers are willing to sell

What if the business owners thought they could sell 24 games at $40? The quantity demanded at that price is only 4. This would result in a **surplus**, or extra amount, of 20 games (24 − 4 = 20). The difference between what the seller is willing to supply and what buyers are willing to pay at that price is the surplus. Surpluses only happen when the price is higher than the equilibrium point. Figure 6.3 shows how a surplus looks on a graph.

Why Do Prices Drop When There Is a Surplus?

A surplus means that the sellers are not able to sell as much as they hoped to sell. They have extra goods. Storing these extra goods costs money. Many businesses try to avoid the extra cost by lowering prices. This is the idea behind clearance and end-of-season sales.

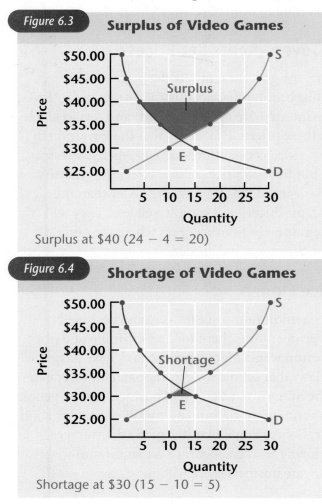

Figure 6.3

Surplus of Video Games

Surplus at $40 (24 − 4 = 20)

Figure 6.4

Shortage of Video Games

Shortage at $30 (15 − 10 = 5)

What Is a Shortage?

What would happen if the business owners decided to lower the price to $30 because of the surplus? At $30, the demand schedule shows that consumers would buy 15 games. This number is greater than the number producers are willing to sell. This causes a **shortage**. The shortage would be 5 games (15 − 10 = 5). Shortages only happen when the price is less than the equilibrium price. Figure 6.4 shows how a shortage looks on a graph.

Why Do Prices Rise When There Are Shortages?

Prices rise when there are shortages. For example, tickets to a concert are often limited. Usually there is a shortage. This means that there are not as many seats as there are buyers who want seats. Some buyers will offer to pay a higher price to get the scarce seats. These buyers are willing to pay more than other buyers.

Why Are Prices Sometimes Fixed?

In a pure market economy, prices change according to supply and demand. There is competition in markets for resources and products. We learned in Chapter 2 that there are no pure market economies. Sometimes governments come between producers and consumers to protect them from big changes in market prices.

Why Might Governments Set Prices?

In some countries, the government sets the price of basic needs of people like bread, milk, heating oil, and housing. **Price ceilings** set a maximum price for some goods and services. The government sets these prices. The idea is that the government is making sure all its citizens can afford basic needs. This seems like a good idea, but how do price ceilings affect the quantity supplied? We have learned that if prices are lower than the equilibrium price, producers will want to sell less. They will move their scarce resources to other areas where they might make more profit. Shortages may occur.

What Is a Price Floor?

A **price floor** sets a minimum price for certain goods and services. The government sets them too. An example of a price floor is the **minimum wage**. Many governments have passed minimum wage laws that set the lowest wage an employer can pay. How does the minimum wage affect business? Some people argue that a minimum wage guarantees unskilled workers a job and a living wage. Others argue that it actually discourages businesses from hiring workers, because the minimum wage is higher than the rate businesses are willing to pay.

Financial Analyst

Financial analysts study the money of a business or other group. To do this, the analyst needs to know accounting. Analysts must review records of costs and the benefits gained from those costs. They compare planned budget amounts to the actual amount received and/or paid out. The analyst may check the financial statements to make sure they are correct.

Financial analysts often use graphs and charts to present their findings to others. The analyst often is called upon to forecast trends. This may include making suggestions for change. Such changes should make the business either make more money or be more efficient.

The financial analyst applies a working knowledge of laws. Many of these may be general business or accounting practices. The analyst checks financial records and makes sure that they meet government guidelines. Large companies may employ several financial analysts. Each may work on a certain area of the company's finances.

Lesson 3 Review On a separate sheet of paper, write answers to the following questions. Use complete sentences.

1. What is the equilibrium price?

2. What is a surplus?

3. What is a shortage?

4. Why are prices sometimes fixed?

5. What is a price ceiling?

What do you think

6. Do you think price floors and price ceilings are good for sellers? Why?

7. Do you think price floors and price ceilings are good for consumers? Why?

Wealth of Nations

Adam Smith is known as the father of modern economics. In 1776, he wrote a book called An Inquiry into the Nature and Causes of the Wealth of Nations. *Smith's book was written over two centuries ago, but many economists still think it is the best statement about capitalism. In this reading, Smith discusses the value of money and the price of labor.*

Every man is rich or poor according to the degree in which he can afford to enjoy the necessaries, conveniences, and amusements of human life. But after the division of labour has once thoroughly taken place, it is but a very small part of these with which a man's own labour can supply him. The far greater part of them he must [gain] from the labour of other people, and he must be rich or poor according to the quantity of that labour which he can command, or which he can afford to purchase. The value of any commodity [good], therefore, to the person who possesses it, and who means not to use or consume it himself, but to exchange it for other commodities, is equal to the quantity of labour which it enables him to purchase or command. Labour, therefore, is the real measure of the exchangeable value of all commodities.

The real price of every thing, what every thing really costs to the man who wants to acquire it, is the toil and trouble of acquiring it. . . . Labour was the first price, the original purchase-money that was paid for all things. It was not by gold or by silver, but by labour, that all the wealth of the world was originally purchased; and its value, to those who possess it, and who want to exchange it for some new productions, is precisely equal to the quantity of labour which it can enable them to purchase or command.

Document-Based Questions

1. According to the reading, what determines a person's wealth?

2. How is labor related to wealth?

3. How does the author define labor in this reading?

4. What does Adam Smith say about price?

5. Based on this reading, why do you think Smith's book is still important today?

Chapter 6 SUMMARY

- The price system communicates the relative worth of goods to buyers and sellers. The market provides many goods and services, plus substitutes, in a wide range of prices.

- Low prices are incentives for consumers to buy goods. High prices are incentives for sellers to produce more.

- The price system works best under several conditions. Buyers and sellers are well informed. Resources can shift easily from one market to another. Prices reflect the actual cost of production. Market failure occurs when these three conditions are not met.

- Externalities, or economic side effects, are market failures. Their cost is not reflected in prices. Parks, schools, highways, police or fire departments, and other public goods are also market failures.

- By supplying a fixed amount of certain goods during a crisis, a government rations the goods. Prices also ration goods to people who are able and willing to pay for them.

- Some people believe need rather than price should determine who gets what. But it is unclear what might replace prices to decide who gets what.

- Prices provide an incentive to workers. By working hard and earning money, workers can buy what they want.

- Rationing requires many people to manage the rationing system. Black markets may arise. In these markets, goods are sold above their legal market price.

- An equilibrium point occurs when sellers and buyers are satisfied about the price of something. All goods produced at that point are sold.

- A surplus occurs when the price of a good is higher than the equilibrium price. People are unwilling to buy all the goods at the higher price. Prices drop for surplus goods because sellers want to sell everything.

- A shortage occurs when prices are lower than the equilibrium price. The demand is greater than the amount produced. Prices for a good rise during a shortage.

- Some governments fix prices for bread, housing, and other basic needs. Price ceilings are the maximum price the government will allow for these goods. A price floor is a minimum price for a good. Minimum wage is an example of a price floor.

Chapter 6 REVIEW

On a separate sheet of paper, write the word from the Word Bank to complete each sentence.

1. Communication between buyers and sellers is the _____.

2. Goods and services available to everyone through the government are _____.

3. A system by which the government provides a certain amount of limited supplies to each person is _____.

4. An illegal market in which goods are sold for more than their legal price is the _____.

5. _____ happen only when a good's price is higher than the equilibrium point.

6. Prices change according to supply and demand for goods in a pure _____.

7. The maximum price for particular goods and services is a _____.

> **Word Bank**
>
> black market
> market economy
> price ceiling
> price system
> public goods
> rationing
> surpluses

On a separate sheet of paper, write the letter of the answer that correctly completes each sentence.

8. Low prices may be a(n) _____ to buy a product.

   A compulsion   **C** incentive

   B exception   **D** expulsion

9. Prices promote _____, or the best way to use resources.

   A efficiency   **C** freedom

   B employees   **D** sales

10. So that everyone gets a fair share of limited resources, a government may use _____.

   A law   **C** reasons

   B rationing   **D** threats

11. Despite rationing, demand for certain goods and services is high in a _____ market.

   A bear   **C** flea

   B black   **D** farmers

12. When sellers do not sell as much as they had hoped, they create a _____.

   A crisis   **C** factory

   B demand   **D** surplus

13. Minimum wage is an example of a _____.

   A black market   **C** surplus

   B public good   **D** price floor

On a separate sheet of paper, write answers to the following questions. Use complete sentences.

14. Why must buyers know how much products cost?

15. Give an example of a positive externality.

16. Why are black markets a problem?

17. What is the equilibrium point?

On a separate sheet of paper, write your opinion to each question. Use complete sentences.

18. What might happen if goods or services had no price? Would the situation be good or bad? Explain.

19. Do you think rationing is fair or unfair? Explain.

20. Should people sell scarce concert tickets for more than they are worth? Why or why not?

Test-Taking Tip

When you read test directions, try to restate them in your own words. Tell yourself what you are expected to do. That way, you can make sure your answer will be complete and correct.

7 Competition

One of the most important parts of the free enterprise system is competition. For example, car companies compete with one another to sell cars. People also compete with each other. Always remember that people have limited resources and unlimited wants. We compete with each other for the scarce resources and products available.

In this chapter, you will learn about economic competition. You also will learn how some parts of competition are controlled.

Goals for Learning

◆ To describe the characteristics of pure competition

◆ To explain how monopolies lessen competition

◆ To compare and contrast monopoly and oligopoly

◆ To identify government policies to ensure competition

What Is Competition?

Schools are places where there is a lot of competition. If you are part of a competition, you are trying to win or gain something that others want. Many students play sports. Your school teams compete against the teams of other schools. Students compete for places on the teams, to be in the school plays, or to become members of the school band. Not everyone can be on a team, in the play, or in the band. There are often more people interested than there are positions available. In the study of economics, competition refers to the economic contest among buyers and sellers. They compete in the purchase and use of resources and products.

What Are the Characteristics of Pure Competition?

Pure competitive markets are rare, if they exist at all. In order for **pure competition** to exist, there must be:

1. many buyers and sellers

2. a **standardized product** (products that are nearly the same)

3. buyers and sellers who are well informed

4. easy entry into and out of the market

5. no control over prices

Many Buyers and Sellers

There must be many buyers and sellers for a product. Otherwise, the actions of any one buyer or seller would affect the entire market. When there are many buyers and sellers, each one has to accept the going market price set by supply and demand. Suppose a seller tries to raise the price even a little bit above the market price. That seller would not be able to sell the product very well. Consumers would buy from other businesses selling the product at the market price.

Pure competition

Competition in which there are many buyers and sellers, there is a standardized product, the buyers and sellers are well informed, there is easy entry into and out of the market, and there is no control over prices

Standardized product

A product group in which competing products are nearly the same

A Standardized Product

The products of all the sellers have to be standardized, or nearly the same. If they are the same, buyers will not prefer the product of one business to that of any other. This means that buyers will be influenced only by the price, not by special features of a product. In other words, there are no brands. Corn grown in one farmer's field is pretty much the same as corn grown in the neighbor's fields.

Buyers and Sellers Are Well Informed

All buyers and sellers in a pure competitive market are well informed. They know all there is to know about the product they are buying or selling. Buyers and sellers need to know such things as who else is selling, at what price they are selling, and how much is being sold.

Easy to Get into and out of the Market

There can be no barriers for new firms to enter or leave the market. If profits can be made, new businesses will want to enter the market. If businesses are losing money, they will want to leave the market. There can be no government rules. This means, for example, that there can be no labor groups or minimum wage laws.

No Control over Prices

Some vegetables are standardized. Some kinds of tomatoes are nearly the same no matter where they are grown.

The workings of supply and demand control prices. Buyers and sellers do not control the prices.

Does a Pure Competitive Market Exist?

Farming probably comes closest to a pure competitive market. There are many farmers and consumers for farm products. The forces of supply and demand largely control farm prices. Farmers are very informed about market conditions. However, farming is a special case. Economists know that a few very large companies control many markets. It is difficult for new firms to enter some markets. Startup costs may be too high. Raw materials necessary to make goods may be hard to get. There are many government rules that tell what businesses can and cannot do.

Economics at Work

Real Estate Agent

Real estate agents sell plots of land, homes, or office buildings. Most real estate agents work on commission. A commission is a part of the sale price of the property. The agent gets paid only if a successful sale is made. Sometimes, a real estate agent may represent someone who wants to sell properties. This may involve holding open houses. At an open house, people who are looking to buy can see the property. They can ask questions of the agent. Buyers rely upon agents to show them several different properties.

A real estate agent has to learn about local real estate laws and loans. The agent also should know about construction and utilities such as plumbing and heating. In most places, real estate agents must be licensed by the local government. Licensing comes after the agent takes classes and passes a test.

Word Bank

buyers and sellers

competition

farming

brands

standardized

Lesson 1 Review On a separate sheet of paper, write the word from the Word Bank to complete each sentence.

1. Buyers will not prefer one product over another if the products are _____.

2. The closest thing to a pure competitive market is in the _____ industry.

3. The contest among buyers and sellers is called _____.

4. One part of a pure competitive market is well-informed _____.

5. Standardized products have no _____.

What do you think ?

6. Have you or has someone you know ever been in a competition? What happened?

7. How might government laws get a business to enter or leave a market?

Monopoly

A market in which there is no competition; one company controls the market

Pure monopoly

A monopoly in which there is only one seller, there are no substitutes for a product or service, getting into and out of the market is difficult, and there is almost complete control over prices

What Is a Monopoly?

We are used to seeing competition in markets. Consumers benefit from competition. It gives consumers many choices. Sellers give consumers a choice of similar products. They know that if products are similar, consumers are likely to buy the best products for the lowest prices. Sometimes, however, there is no competition, and only one company controls the market. This is called a **monopoly**.

What Is a Pure Monopoly?

A **pure monopoly** is the opposite of pure competition. A pure monopoly has four characteristics:

1. There is only one seller.
2. There are no close substitutes.
3. Getting into and out of the market is difficult.
4. There is almost complete control over prices.

There Is Only One Seller

In a pure monopoly, there is only one seller of a good or service. Consumers must buy it from the one producer.

There Is No Close Substitute

Suppose that there were only one carmaker in the world. If you wanted to buy a car, you would have to buy from that carmaker. The carmaker has a monopoly. Anyone who needed a car would have to pay whatever price the one carmaker set.

Getting into and out of the Market Is Difficult

There is only one way to keep a monopoly going. New producers have to be kept out. Think about the example of the carmaker. A new producer might want to enter the market because of the high profits. Starting a new car company is not easy. It requires huge sums of money. New machinery and technology are expensive. Designing, building, and selling cars is not easy. The business with the monopoly has many advantages over the new company.

There Is Almost Complete Control over Prices

Producers can control the prices by controlling the supply available.

What Conditions Are Necessary to Form Monopolies?

Monopolies are formed because they meet three conditions:

1. They control a very important resource.
2. The government approves them.
3. They got there first.

Control of an Important Resource

Think about what is needed to run a professional football team. What is the most important resource? It is the players. Every team owner knows that control over the players is very important. That is why the best athletes are signed to long-term deals. This prevents them from playing for any other team.

Natural monopoly

A monopoly that is allowed to exist because competition is not needed

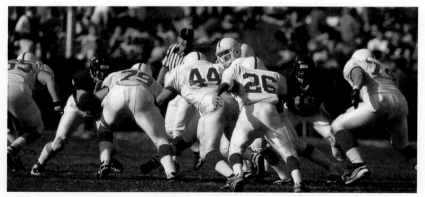

Players on a football team actually are resources. Without the players, there would be no team and no way to make money.

Government Approval

Governments sometimes approve monopolies. For example, local and state governments sometimes limit competition. They give the right to provide electricity, gas, and water to only one company. Why? They believe it is more efficient than many competing companies providing the same services. Some economists call this kind of monopoly a **natural monopoly**.

Patent

Right of sole ownership of an invention given to the inventor of an item

Copyright

The sole right given to writers and artists to sell or make copies of their works

It is an industry where competition is not needed, so the monopoly is allowed to exist. Often these services are utilities. Utilities are businesses that provide a public service such as electricity or water. In exchange for being granted a monopoly, they agree to follow the government rules.

Forming a Monopoly First

Sometimes a company forms a monopoly by getting there first. The companies that came out with the first paper tissues or the first copying machines were very successful. They led their industries for so long that their names became attached to the products they made. The names stuck even after competitors finally entered the market.

How Do Patents and Copyrights Limit Competition?

The government limits competition by granting **patents** and **copyrights**. In a way, a patent is a monopoly. It protects an invention. It gives the inventor sole rights to the invention. In the United States, the patent usually is good for 17 years. Inventors may sell or give away their rights. The patent is their property. A copyright gives writers and artists the sole right to sell or make copies of their works. Today, a copyright in the U.S. is good until 70 years after the author dies.

Why Are Patents and Copyrights Issued?

Suppose you run a company that is trying to find a cure for cancer. You hire many scientists to try to find new drugs. Finally, after many years and great expense, the new drug is ready to market. How would you feel if a competitor copied your new drug and marketed it at lower cost? The competitor did not have to pay the scientists. In fact, that company had almost no costs to make the drug. You would probably feel it is unfair that they benefit from your research without paying any of the costs. A patent issued by the government protects your company from competition for 17 years. It allows your company to make up the money it spent in developing the drug.

The same thing is true for artists and writers. Imagine if you spent several months painting a picture. Everyone tells you it is really beautiful. Several people want to buy it. How would you like it if someone bought your artwork and then made hundreds of copies to sell? Copyrights prevent this from happening without your say.

Economics in Your Life

The First American Monopolies

Andrew Carnegie and John D. Rockefeller were the founders of two of the first American monopolies. As a young man, Andrew Carnegie became interested in the process of making steel from iron ore. He went to England to learn about a new, less expensive way to produce steel. Upon his return to the U.S. in 1873, he was the first American to form a company using this method. As his company grew, he bought coal fields, iron ore mines, and steamships. Carnegie owned all of the components for building his very successful Carnegie Steel.

John D. Rockefeller and a few friends opened an oil refining company in 1870. Like Andrew Carnegie, Rockefeller knew that he would make a fortune only if he could control all parts of production. He developed oil drilling, refining, shipping, and sales departments. He bought up smaller companies. His Standard Oil Company controlled almost all of the oil business in the United States.

Lesson 2 Review On a separate sheet of paper, write answers to the following questions. Use complete sentences.

1. What are two characteristics of a monopoly?

2. What are utilities? Give an example.

3. What does a patent do?

4. What is a copyright?

5. Why might a government approve a monopoly?

What do you think ?

6. Do you think monopolies are good or bad? Why?

7. Why might owning the copyright to an artistic work be helpful?

Oligopoly

A type of market where there only are a few sellers, there is a nearly standardized product, and entry into the market is difficult

Most markets are neither pure competition nor monopolies. They fall somewhere between the two. (See Figure 7.1.) Another type of market is an **oligopoly**. An oligopoly has three main features:

1. There are few sellers.
2. There is a nearly standardized product.
3. Entry into the market is difficult.

There Are Few Sellers

In an oligopoly, a few large businesses control the market for a product. The three to five large companies make up almost all of an industry's sales. A few examples of oligopoly are breakfast cereals, soft drinks, and large appliances.

A Nearly Standardized Product

The products oligopolies sell are almost the same. For example, cereals have almost the same ingredients. Say one maker tries to come out with something new. It usually does not take long before the others offer something similar.

Getting into the Market Is Difficult

The few large companies control the industry for several reasons. Consumers may be used to their products and are loyal to them. Start-up costs may be very high. This discourages new firms from entering the market.

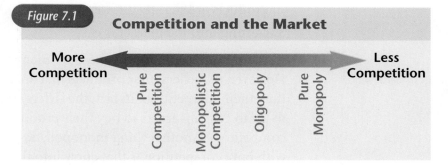

Figure 7.1 **Competition and the Market**

More Competition ← → Less Competition

Pure Competition — Monopolistic Competition — Oligopoly — Pure Monopoly

How Do Oligopolies Control the Market?

Suppose you go shopping for cereal. You might be surprised to find that the major brands sell for almost the same price. This is often true in oligopolies. Raising the price may result in losing sales to a competitor. The price each seller sets is highly dependent on the price the other sellers set. Sometimes one of the sellers tries to lower the price to gain control of more of the market. This sets off a **price war**. In a price war, there usually is a series of price cuts as each company tries to set a price lower than the competition. This has sometimes happened in the airline industry. Consumers benefit from the lower prices. The sellers, in this case the airlines, often lose money. They are selling their services for less than their cost. Profits for the whole industry usually fall.

Sometimes competing firms in an oligopoly break the law to reach high profits. One way is **collusion**. Collusion is a secret agreement between competing firms to cooperate with each other. For example, the competing firms might divide the market by location. This way each firm would be guaranteed a market with little competition. **Price-fixing** is a type of collusion. Price-fixing is an agreement to sell products for the same or similar prices. The price is usually set higher than the price would be in a truly competitive market.

What Is Monopolistic Competition?

Another type of market structure is **monopolistic competition**. Monopolistic competition has three features:

1. There are many buyers and sellers.

2. Products are slightly different.

3. Getting into the market is easy.

Just as in pure competition, there are many buyers and sellers. However, the sellers offer products that are slightly different than their competition. In fact, the sellers stress the differences to try to get consumers to buy their products rather than their competitors'. Another thing monopolistic competition shares with pure competition is that entry into the market is fairly easy.

Differentiate

Differentiate

A way a company attracts buyers by showing the differences between their product and their competitors'

Customer services

A way a company attracts buyers by providing services to those who have bought products

Warranty

A promise to fix something if it does not work

Figure 7.2 — Features of Four Market Structures

Market Structure	# of Sellers	Type of Product	Ease of Entry	Example Industries
Pure competition	Many	Standardized	Very easy	Farming
Monopoly	One	No close substitutes	Very difficult	Utilities
Oligopoly	Few	Nearly standardized	Difficult	Breakfast cereals/soft drinks
Monopolistic competition	Many	Some product differences	Fairly easy	Clothing/restaurants

How Do Businesses Attract Buyers in Monopolistic Competition?

One way to attract buyers is to **differentiate**. This means showing the differences between their product and their competitors'. An example is the tire industry. Car tires are pretty much alike. Each manufacturer tries to make their tires seem better. They may feature a tread that is said to handle water on the road better. They may give their tires a name that makes consumers believe that their tires are stronger or longer lasting.

A second way of attracting buyers is to offer **customer services.** Suppose your car needs new brakes. There are two garages in your area. Both have good mechanics. The price at both is the same. Why would you choose one station over another? Maybe one garage offers to include a free oil change or car wash for every car it fixes. These are examples of customer services. The extras are offered to attract your business.

A third way of attracting business is to offer support services. Computers are expensive. Many companies want to sell you one. The company that offers its customers the best service is likely to attract many customers. Often a **warranty** makes consumers think that the manufacturer stands behind the product. A warranty is a promise to fix something if it does not work.

Another way of getting consumers to buy products is by developing **brand names**. Many companies use a **logo** that is easily recognized. A logo usually is a symbol that everyone knows. It may be a little alligator, a swoosh, or a special set of letters. Companies work hard to get buyers to identify their logo with quality. They spend millions of dollars on advertising. When you buy a pair of popular shoes or jeans, you often buy because of the brand.

Lesson 3 Review On a separate sheet of paper, write the letter of the answer that correctly completes each sentence.

1. By lowering prices to increase market share, a producer may start a _____.

   A collision   **C** price war

   B peace treaty   **D** cold war

2. A secret agreement between competing businesses to cooperate is called _____.

   A price war   **C** collusion

   B warranty   **D** casualty

3. One way businesses can attract buyers is through strong _____.

   A customer services   **C** monopolistic competition

   B price fixing   **D** government regulation

4. One way to develop product recognition is by the use of _____.

   A employees   **C** competition

   B collusion   **D** logos

5. An agreement among competing businesses to sell products for the same or similar prices is called _____.

   A price-fixing   **C** gouging

   B going out of business   **D** marketing

What do you think

6. Why might collusion be an advantage for competing companies? Should it be illegal? Why or why not?

7. Do you think brand names and logos are effective in selling products? Give an example from your life.

Lesson 4 Government Policies to Ensure Competition

Trust
When a few giant companies control important industries

Reform
Change to make things work better

Majority
The quality or state of being greater

What Is a Trust?

The second half of the 1800s in America is often called the era of big business. A few giant companies controlled important industries. These huge monopolies were called **trusts**. They sometimes forced smaller competitors out of business. The trust companies could charge high prices to increase their profits. Trusts were formed in the railroad, steel, copper, coal, and meatpacking industries.

Many people demanded **reform**. Reformers are people who want to make changes to make things work better. They believed that the government has the power to protect and encourage competition.

Figure 7.3 **Top Ten World Economies**

1.	United States
2.	Australia
3.	Canada
4.	Malaysia
5.	Germany
6.	Taiwan
7.	Great Britain
8.	France
9.	Spain
10.	Thailand

How does the American economy rank with the rest of the world? It tops the list for countries that have more than 20 million people. This list shows that the United States is leading the competition.

How Did Congress Try to Limit Trust Companies?

By the 1880s, many members of the U.S. Congress were reformers—they formed a **majority**. Congress passed laws to try to control the problem of trust companies. The Interstate Commerce Act passed in 1887. It created the Interstate Commerce Commission (ICC) to regulate railroads. The ICC continued to regulate the railroads until it was done away with in 1995.

The Sherman Antitrust Act passed in 1890. This law made it illegal for large companies to form monopolies. However, the wording was not clear. Many trusts fought against the government in court and won.

Biography

Bill Gates: 1955–

Bill Gates developed an interest in computers during his teen years. While he was a college student, he got the idea that computers could become an important tool in every home. He began inventing software for the personal computer. He and a friend named Paul Allen began a computer company in 1975.

Gates and his partner created a basic computer operating system. They developed software that would be cheap and easy for the average person to use. They developed new and different types of software as they became aware of what consumers wanted and needed.

Today, Gates is the chief executive officer of the world's leading producer of software for personal computers. He is a successful author and much sought-after speaker. He has given over $800 million to charities, with a special focus on education.

Why Was the Clayton Act Important?

The Clayton Act passed in 1914. It was much more specific than the Sherman Act. It gave the government more power to control monopolies. It banned certain unfair business practices. For example, under the act one company could not control a competing company by buying pieces of the company. One person could not serve on the board of directors of two competing firms at the same time. It outlawed **price discrimination**. This is the practice of selling different buyers the same product for different prices.

What Is the Government's Policy Regarding Monopoly Today?

In 1936, Congress passed the Robinson-Patman Act. It sometimes is called the Antiprice Discrimination Act because it allows more control against price discrimination. Other antitrust laws were passed in the 1970s. They increased the penalties for breaking antitrust laws.

Merger

When one business buys another

The U.S. government seems to want to keep competition. However, some Americans are beginning to doubt this. In recent years, the government has allowed businesses in the same industry to join together. A **merger** results when one business buys another. However, the government has taken some companies to court because it thinks they are monopolies. In several big cases, the judges ruled in favor of the companies.

Word Bank

Congress

era of big business

merger

price discrimination

reformers

Lesson 4 Review On a separate sheet of paper, write the word from the Word Bank to complete each sentence.

1. People who try to change things for the better are called _____.

2. Starting in about 1850, the _____ began.

3. In the 1880s, many reformers were members of _____.

4. Selling the same product for different prices to different people is called _____.

5. When one business buys another, this is a _____.

What do you think ?

6. When large companies merge, how might that limit competition in a market?

7. What is the effect on competition if the same person helped control two competing companies?

The Sherman Antitrust Act

In 1890, the United States Congress passed the Sherman Antitrust Act. The act was created to restore competition and dissolve monopolies. It has been used in court cases for over 100 years. In the late 1990s, the Sherman Act was used against a large U.S. computer software company. The Sherman Act reads, in part, as follows.

Every contract . . . in the form of trust or other-wise, or conspiracy, in restraint of trade or commerce among the several States, or with foreign nations, is hereby declared to be illegal. Every person who shall make any such contract or engage in any such combination or conspiracy, shall be deemed guilty of a misdemeanor, and, on conviction thereof, shall be punished by fine not exceeding five thousand dollars, or by imprisonment not exceeding one year, or by both said punishments, at the discretion of the court.

Every person who shall monopolize, or attempt to monopolize . . . any part of the trade or commerce among the several States, or with foreign nations, shall be deemed [considered] guilty of a misdemeanor. . . .

Every contract, combination in form of trust or otherwise, or conspiracy, in restraint of trade or commerce . . . is hereby declared illegal.

The several circuit courts of the United States are hereby invested with jurisdiction to prevent and restrain violations of this act. . . .

Any property owned under any contract or by any combination . . . mentioned in section one of this act . . . shall be forfeited to the United States. . . .

Any person who shall be injured in his business or property by any other person or corporation by reason of anything forbidden or declared to be unlawful by this act, may sue . . . in any circuit court of the United States in the district in which the defendant resides or is found. . . .

Document-Based Questions

1. What is the purpose of the Sherman Antitrust Act?

2. According to the document, how are people punished if found guilty of creating a monopoly?

3. What happens to property owned under a monopoly if the court finds the business guilty of creating a monopoly?

4. In your own words, explain the last paragraph of the document.

5. Do you think it is important to dissolve monopolies? Explain.

Chapter 7 SUMMARY

- Competition is the economic contest among consumers and sellers to buy and use resources and products.

- For competition to exist, there must be many buyers and sellers. There also must be a standardized product, well-informed buyers and sellers, easy entry into and exit from a market, and no control over prices. The closest thing to pure competition exists in farming.

- A monopoly occurs when there is no competition. Monopolies are the opposite of pure competition. A monopoly has only one seller, no close substitutes, difficult entry into and exit from a market, and almost complete control over prices.

- Monopolies form by controlling an important resource, having government approval, and reaching a market first.

- Government-approved monopolies include utilities, also called natural monopolies. These businesses provide electricity, water, or another public good or service. Utilities agree to follow government rules in return for holding the monopoly.

- A patent allows a product's inventor to be a good's only seller or producer. A copyright gives artists and writers the sole right to sell or copy their work. Patents and copyrights limit competition. They provide incentives to producers to continue production.

- An oligopoly has few sellers, sells a nearly standardized product, and makes entry into a market difficult. In an oligopoly, prices depend on each producer. If one seller lowers prices to increase sales, a price war may occur.

- Collusion occurs when companies in an oligopoly illegally cooperate. They may set prices higher than the equilibrium price. They may divide the market by location to avoid competing with each other.

- Monopolistic competition has many buyers and sellers, some product variation, and easy entry into a market. Sellers in monopolistic competition try to differentiate their product to increase market share. These sellers also may offer customer services, support services, or warranties. The use of logos is a way to increase product recognition.

- During the era of big business, huge monopolies called trusts formed in the railroad, steel, copper, coal, and meatpacking industries. Reformers wanted to limit the trusts and increase competition.

- Congress passed several laws to limit monopolies. The most important laws were the Interstate Commerce Act (1887), the Sherman Antitrust Act (1890), the Clayton Act (1914), and the Robinson-Patman Act (1936).

On a separate sheet of paper, write the word from the Word Bank to complete each sentence.

1. The economic contest among buyers and sellers is _____.

2. The closest example of a pure competitive market occurs in the area of _____.

3. The opposite of pure competition is a(n) _____.

4. A(n) _____ guarantees the right of an inventor to produce or sell an invention.

5. A few large companies control the market in a(n)_____.

6. One way companies try to attract buyers is to _____ between their product and their competitors'.

7. The late 1800s is sometimes called the _____.

Word Bank

competition

differentiate

era of big business

farming

pure monopoly

oligopoly

patent

On a separate sheet of paper, write the letter of the answer that correctly completes each sentence.

8. One part of pure competition is a _____.

   A difficult entry into the market

   B level playing field

   C standardized product

   D unique product

9. The condition of having no competition is called a(n) _____.

   A monarchy

   B monopoly

   C oligarchy

   D oligopoly

10. One way to maintain a monopoly is by keeping out _____.

   A highly paid employees

   B new producers

   C nonunion workers

   D profits

11. In an oligopoly, _____ producers control an industry's market.

   A many

   B no

   C fifteen

   D a few

12. A _____ may occur when sellers lower prices below the competition.

    A price oligopoly   **C** monopoly

    B price war   **D** price collusion

13. Giant monopolies of the late 1800s were called _____.

    A competitors   **B** reformers

    B patents   **D** trusts

On a separate sheet of paper, write answers to the following questions. Use complete sentences.

14. Why must there be many buyers and sellers for pure competition to work?

15. What are two features of a pure monopoly?

16. What are two features of an oligopoly?

17. What are two features of monopolistic competition?

On a separate sheet of paper, write your opinion to each question. Use complete sentences.

18. Why might a monopoly be good?

19. What do you think might happen to small competitors in a price war? Explain whether this is good or bad.

20. Why do companies often want to have a unique logo?

Test-Taking Tip

Always pay special attention to key words in a set of directions—words such as *first, second, third* or *most important, least important, all,* or *none*. These words will tell you how the questions should be answered.

Unit 2

Skill Builder

Analyzing a Political Cartoon

Many newspapers and magazines feature political cartoons. The cartoon may express an opinion about a politician, a political party, a movement, or a trend. It may be designed to amuse. Sometimes it may be expressing a person's opinion. In most cases, a political cartoon causes the viewer to think. It may help viewers to form opinions. It may also help viewers to clarify or identify opinions they had already formed.

Sometimes the creator of a political cartoon may use exaggeration (stretching the truth). Other times the creator may use symbolism (things that represent other things). These can aid in the humor or in creating a mood. Sometimes labels or speech balloons are used to help in the viewer's understanding.

The cartoon below appeared during the 1990s. At the time, the Soviet Union was changing from a communist to a free-market economy. This cartoon has labels reading "Owner's Manual" and "Basic Economics," as well as a speech balloon.

Study the cartoon and answer the following questions. Use complete sentences.

1. What are the people waiting to receive?

2. Why is the little character in the far left corner looking at the owner's manual?

3. What clue did the artist give the viewer about the country being shown?

4. Why do you think the artist made the word SUPPLY larger than DEMAND?

5. How does the artist use comparison to make a point?

- The founding documents of the United States deal with economic issues.

- In the U.S. economy, the people control most of the property and can use it as they wish.

- Profits in a market system provide incentive to producers to work efficiently. Profit is total revenue minus total cost. If total costs are greater than total revenue, the business experiences a loss.

- Demand is the amount of a good buyers will purchase at a given price. Consumers must be able and willing to buy. Several factors affect demand.

- Demand is elastic if price affects demand. Demand is inelastic if price has little effect on demand.

- Factors that affect changes in demand are changes in income, the number of substitutes, changes in weather or season, population increase, changes in consumer tastes, and diminishing marginal utility.

- Supply is the ability and willingness of producers to sell something at a given price. The law of supply says supply rises as price rises.

- Resource costs, new technology, taxes and subsidies, worker productivity, competition, and the price of related goods affect supply.

- The law of variable proportions says changing one input will change the output. The three stages of production are increasing returns, diminishing returns, and negative returns.

- A price system provides information to buyers and sellers about the worth of goods and services. Market failures occur when prices do not reflect the actual cost of production.

- Prices act as a rationing device. Black markets form when goods and services are sold for more than their legal price.

- At the equilibrium price, the needs of buyers and sellers are satisfied. A surplus occurs when prices are above the equilibrium price. A shortage occurs when sellers produce less than consumers want.

- Several other types of markets include pure competitive markets, monopolies, oligopolies, and monopolistic competition.

- Huge monopolies called trusts formed in the late 1800s. To control them and increase competition, reformers in the U.S. Congress passed many laws.

"One should not be assigned one's identity in society by the job slot one happens to fill. If we truly believe in the dignity of labor, any task can be performed with equal pride because none can demean the basic dignity of a human being."
—*Judith Martin, Common Courtesy (1985)*

Unit 2 SUMMARY

3

Free Enterprise at Work

Walk down a busy street anywhere in the world and you will see people at work. Taxi drivers take people to places they need to go. A police officer works to protect people and to enforce laws. Construction workers build houses to sell for a profit. You also will see many different kinds of businesses on your walk. A restaurant provides a place for people to eat. A video store rents videos for people to watch. A factory makes things to sell, such as cars, airplane parts, or electronics.

Workers and businesses are the heart of any economy. There are many kinds of businesses and jobs out there. If you are not already part of the world of work, you will be soon. What job is best for you? This is not an easy thing to decide. Will your job be to provide a service or to make a product? What kind of business will you work for?

This unit will help you think about answers to these questions. It will discuss many kinds of businesses and how they are organized. It will talk about some of the kinds of jobs that are available and how wages work. It also discusses how businesses and workers settle differences.

8

The Role of Businesses

There are more than 16 million businesses in the United States today. Many of them are small businesses that one person owns. The biggest businesses are corporations. Some of them do business in many countries. Businesses provide most of the goods and services produced for and sold to consumers.

In this chapter, you will learn about the three main types of businesses. You also will learn how consumers, businesses, and the government interact.

Goals for Learning

◆ To explain the role of entrepreneurship in the U.S. economy

◆ To describe the three main types of businesses

◆ To explain the circular flow of economic activity

Nationality

The nation one belongs to or comes from

Technical know-how

The knowledge or skill to do something

In Chapter 1, we learned that entrepreneurship is sometimes included among the factors of production. It refers to people's ability to start a new business or improve old ones. Entrepreneurs provide leadership and new ideas for the economy. They are willing to take risks. Often they start out with a new idea. They hope the new idea can turn into a business that makes money.

What Are Some Qualities That Entrepreneurs Have?

Entrepreneurs can be men or women. They can be members of any race, religion, or **nationality**. Some are born in the United States, and some come from other countries. Entrepreneurs can be found in every country in the world. Often entrepreneurs are people who are confident, independent, and have a lot of enthusiasm. They are willing to take risks because they believe that things usually turn out for the best.

What Makes a Successful Entrepreneurship?

The business an entrepreneur starts may be called a small business. It also could be called a family business or a home-based business. Remember, the usual reason for starting a business is to make a profit. The key factors in being a successful entrepreneur are to have:

1. a marketable idea
2. potential customers
3. **technical know-how**
4. financial resources

Before you start a business, you need to know that there are consumers interested in your product. Many new ideas are good, but sometimes putting the idea into action is not easy.

Suppose you have an idea for a new video game. You have to answer many questions before you start a business making the games. Do others like your game? Are they willing to buy it? How will you promote and sell your game? Can you make enough games to meet the demand if many people want it?

Technical know-how means the knowledge or skill to do something. Your game idea may be great. However, if it costs more to make than you can charge for it, it will not make a profit. Your business will fail.

Starting a new business costs money. Creating a new video game requires all sorts of skills. Before you could even start thinking about making the games, you would have to find the money to pay for everything. Sometimes banks loan entrepreneurs money. **Venture capitalists** are investors who back entrepreneurs in return for part of the profits.

What Are the Chances for a Business's Success?

Starting a business is risky. Statistics about new businesses are sometimes confusing. A 1995 poll showed that there were more than 4.5 million new businesses started in the United States that year! Of that number, 3.5 million were new businesses, and 900,000 were bought from previous owners. About 68,000 were taken over by someone else after the owner died.

Sometimes we read that many new businesses fail. The reasons for failure vary. The owners might sell their idea to another company. For example, several large companies develop video games. One of them might buy your new company and the game it produces. You did not fail if your company has been bought. A business owner may move the business to another state or country. Owners sometimes die, become disabled, or retire. The statistics do not reflect these factors. Only one in seven businesses that close down actually fails. Of those entrepreneurs who actually fail, 53 percent become owners of another business. About 73.2 percent say they plan to start a new business in the future.

When a business closes, it does not always mean the business has failed.

Economics at Work

Entrepreneur

Entrepreneurs are people who start and run their own business. They would rather work for themselves than work for someone else. Starting a business most often means taking great risks of both time and money.

People becoming entrepreneurs have a strong belief in what they are doing. They might start a business with a unique idea. They may see a need for a new product or service in the marketplace. They may feel that they have better production methods or a more effective approach than any other business. In some cases, an entrepreneur's idea may be a response to a change in society. This change may have created an interest in (or need for) that new product or service.

Many entrepreneurs believe there is greater security in running their own business. They do not have to depend on an employer whose decisions affect their job. Instead, they are able to directly control their own employment future.

Word Bank

consumers

entrepreneurs

risk

technical
 know-how

venture capitalists

Lesson 1 Review On a separate sheet of paper, write the word from the Word Bank to complete each sentence.

1. _____ start a new business or improve an old one.

2. The knowledge or skill to do something is _____.

3. Starting a business involves _____.

4. Investors who back an entrepreneur are called _____.

5. Before starting a business, it is a good idea to find out if _____ are interested.

What do you think ?

6. Why do you think so many people start their own businesses?

7. What qualities should an entrepreneur have? Why?

Businesses can be organized in different ways. They generally fall into three very different groups.

What Is a Sole Proprietorship?

Sole proprietorship

A business that one person owns

A **sole proprietorship** is a business that one person owns. Far more sole proprietorships exist than any other kind of business. Most are very small. You could probably name dozens of sole proprietorships in your area. They include corner stores, barbershops and hair salons, some restaurants, jewelry stores, and many family farms. They are popular because they are easiest to organize. Usually they require less money to start than do other forms of business.

What Advantages Do Sole Proprietorships Have?

The biggest advantage is that sole proprietorships are easy to form. They can be started with very little money. For example, suppose you wanted to start a dog-walking business. You would not need much equipment or even a shop. Your costs might be limited to a few leashes and the cost of flyers to attract customers. Another big advantage is that the owner gets to keep all the profits. As the owner of the dog-walking business, you get to keep whatever money you make. You can spend your profit any way you like.

A third advantage is that sole proprietors get to be their own boss. They decide what to sell and at what price. They get to make whatever changes they want. The single owner makes all the management decisions. In your dog-walking business, you get to set the hours you want to walk the dogs. You decide what price you will charge your customers. If you want to charge extra for weekends, the decision is up to you.

A fourth advantage is that owning your own business gives you a sense of pride. Many business owners take pride in providing an important product or service to the community.

What Are the Disadvantages of Sole Proprietorship?

One of the drawbacks of owning your own business is **unlimited liability**. This means the owner is responsible for paying all of the money the business owes. Let's go back to the example of a dog-walking business. Suppose you are careless and one of the dogs gets hurt. The dog's owner may take you to court. You are responsible for the debts of the business. You may have to sell your car and other personal belongings to pay your debts. Sometimes a business owner has to sell his or her home to pay the business's debt.

Another disadvantage is **limited capital**. The single owner usually does not have extra funds to grow the business. Let's say there are many people who want you to walk their dogs. You cannot take care of all the business yourself. You might want to hire a worker to help you, but there is not yet enough business for two of you. The amount of money available to the business is limited to what you have in savings or what you can borrow. A third disadvantage is that the business depends totally on the one owner. If the owner becomes sick, disabled, loses interest, or dies, the business ends.

What Is a Partnership?

A **partnership** is a business that two or more people own. Usually, a legal agreement called a **contract** is drawn up to create a partnership. This document is also called a partnership agreement. There are probably many businesses in your area that are partnerships. They may include many of the same types of businesses that a single person owns. Sometimes lawyers, accountants, and doctors form partnerships. Like sole proprietorships, partnerships have advantages and disadvantages.

Many businesses are partnerships. Two or more people own a partnership. The owners' names often are included in the company name.

What Are the Advantages of a Partnership?

A partnership is fairly easy to start. The partnership combines the funds and skills of the partners. The partners have more money to grow the business than each would have alone. Another advantage is that each partner could specialize in what he or she does best. For example, perhaps one partner is better at selling than the other. The second partner may be better at keeping the books. The partners can use their special skills to increase the business's profit.

A third advantage is that business losses are shared. Partnerships generally have more capital, or money, than sole proprietorships. They can survive longer during hard times than can the business owned by a single person.

What Are the Disadvantages of a Partnership?

The main disadvantage is unlimited liability. Like a sole proprietorship, the partners are responsible for all of the company's debt. If one of the partners leaves, the other partners still have to pay all debts. The partners may have to sell things they own to pay what the company owes. A second disadvantage is that decision making and profits also have to be shared. Thirdly, there is a chance that the partners will disagree on how best to run the business. The disagreement may be great enough to cause the business to fail.

A fourth disadvantage is limited funds. The funds available are limited to what the partners together have in savings and their ability to borrow. Finally, partnerships have a limited life. The partnership ends when one of the partners withdraws or dies. A new partnership agreement must be drawn up if the business is to continue.

What Is a Corporation?

A **corporation** is a third form of business organization. It can be made up of many owners, but the law allows it to act like a single person. This means that, in a legal sense, a corporation has most of the same rights as a person. Corporations can own and sell property. They pay taxes. They enter into contracts. They can be sued in court.

How Are Corporations Formed?

State governments give all corporations the right to exist. To form a corporation, a person or group must apply for a **charter**. A charter is an official document issued by state governments that gives the right to create a corporation. After receiving the charter, the corporation is allowed to sell shares of **stock**. Stock is a sign of ownership in a corporation. It is issued in the form of a certificate.

When people buy stock in a business, they are issued **shares**. Suppose the corporation decides to sell 10,000 shares. An investor who buys 1,000 shares owns one-tenth of the business. A person, group, or even another business can buy stock. Everyone holding shares of the corporation is a **stockholder** and part owner of the corporation. Stockholders are also called **investors**. An investor hopes to gain money back.

What Are the Advantages of a Corporation?

Corporations have **limited liability**. Unlike sole proprietorships and partnerships, corporate liability is limited. This means that the investors can only lose as much money as they have invested. The investor who bought 1,000 shares in the new corporation can only lose what the shares cost. A shareholder's private property cannot be taken to pay the corporation's debts. This advantage is so important that corporations often add "Ltd."(for "limited") to their company name.

Corporations can raise capital more easily than a single person or partnership. The corporation's management can decide to raise more money by selling more stock. It also can sell **bonds**. Bonds are a type of loan. You may be familiar with U.S. Savings Bonds. You pay the government $25 now. Every year you own the bond, it becomes more valuable. After several years, the government gives you back $50. Corporate bonds work the same way. Investors buy the bonds and the corporation promises to pay them back their money plus a profit at a later date.

Corporations have **unlimited life**. Businesses owned by one person or a partnership end when their owners die. Corporations go on, even if there is a change in ownership, management, or labor.

Charter

An official document issued by state governments that gives the right to create a corporation

Stock

A sign of ownership in a corporation

Share

A unit of stock in a company

Stockholder

Someone owning shares (or stock) of a company

Investor

One who spends money to buy stock in the hope of gaining money back

Limited liability

When investors can only lose as much money as they have invested

Bond

A type of loan that an investor buys from a company or from the government; the company or government promises to pay the investor back their money plus a profit at a later date

Unlimited life

The ability of a corporation to go on, even if there is a change in ownership, management, or labor

---

A corporation allows easy transfer of ownership. Stockholders can easily enter or leave the corporation. They do this by simply buying or selling their shares in the corporation.

What Are the Disadvantages of a Corporation?

Corporations are fairly expensive to create. Usually, a lawyer needs to get a charter. Investors need to be found and stock sold. The costs are higher than organizing a sole proprietorship or partnership.

Corporations must follow state and federal laws. Corporations must share information about their finances and operations to any interested persons. Governments force businesses to provide detailed records, which are checked over closely.

Corporations are taxed twice. The corporation is taxed once on the money it makes. Often the stockholders receive a share of the profits in **dividends**. Dividends represent the investor's share of the profit. The investors have to pay taxes on their dividends.

Figure 8.1   **Comparing Types of Business Organizations**

Type of Business	Advantages	Disadvantages
Sole Proprietorship	• Easy to organize • Owner keeps all of the profit • Owner is own boss • Gives owner sense of pride and independence	• Unlimited liability • Limited capital • Totally dependent on owner
Partnership	• Easy to organize • Partners can specialize • Losses are shared	• Unlimited liability • Decision making and profits are shared • Limited life
Corporation	• Limited liability • Can raise capital easily • Unlimited life	• Expensive to organize • State and federal laws control • Taxed twice

Economics in Your Life

Entrepreneurial Inventors

When people think of inventors, they often picture a person hidden away in a lab or workshop. Inventors may not appear suited to the business world. However, many inventors have gone on to build companies to market their products. Two famous inventors, Alexander Graham Bell and Thomas Edison, began companies that changed the world during the late nineteenth century. Bell invented the telephone. Edison invented the light bulb and made the mass use of electricity possible.

In 1908, Orville and Wilbur Wright won the first contract for mass production of the airplane they created. Elisha Graves Otis founded the first passenger elevator company after perfecting his invention in 1853. George Eastman's 1888 invention of a camera for the general public led to the development of a huge photography business. Henry Ford completed his first gasoline-driven automobile in 1896. He then went on to found a motor company in 1899. Jacob Schick patented his electric shaver in 1928 and began a major shaving products company. Bill Gates, who developed many types of computer software applications, went on to found a highly successful company in the 1970s.

Lesson 2 Review On a separate sheet of paper, write answers to the following questions. Use complete sentences.

1. List the three types of businesses.

2. List two advantages of sole proprietorships.

3. Why might two people form a partnership?

4. What is limited liability?

5. What is a charter?

What do you think ?

6. If you could open a business, which of the three types would you start? Why?

7. What do you think is the biggest advantage and disadvantage of owning your own business? Explain.

What Is the Circular Flow Model?

Circular flow

A model that shows the process of exchange among consumers (also called households), businesses, and government

Markets are an important part of the free enterprise system. A market is a way goods and services are bought and sold. All markets involve exchanges. An exchange is a voluntary agreement between two sides. Each side gives something to the other and gets something in return. In order to get, one must give. This may mean that people have to work and produce even if they would rather not. In return, they get the goods and services they want.

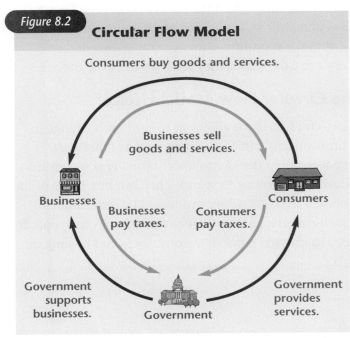

Figure 8.2

Circular Flow Model

Consumers buy goods and services.

Businesses sell goods and services.

Businesses

Businesses pay taxes.

Consumers pay taxes.

Consumers

Government supports businesses.

Government

Government provides services.

The **circular flow** is a model that shows this process of exchanges. There are three key elements: consumers (also called households), businesses, and government. The model tells us that the three elements work together. They work together to make sure that our wants and needs are provided for. (See Figure 8.2.)

This process involves two markets. The first market is the product market. The second is the resource market. The product market involves buying and selling between businesses and consumers. Businesses make products and provide services to consumers. What do consumers give the businesses in exchange? The answer is money. In the resource market, consumers sell resources such as their labor to businesses. They also may sell the products they make to businesses. (For example, farmers sell their crops to businesses.) In return, the businesses pay money to their workers or suppliers.

The third element in the economy is the government. Both businesses and consumers have a relationship with the government. Consumers pay taxes. In return they receive valuable services. The tax money is used to pay for such things as roads, schools, and other services. Businesses pay taxes too. They also receive services from the government. As you can see from Figure 8.2, consumers, businesses, and government rely on each other.

Is the Circular Flow Model Complete?

The model shown in Figure 8.2 does not show every part of a free enterprise economy. It represents a **theory**. A theory is a possible explanation. It does not always give the complete picture. For example, banks are an important part of the economy. They are left out of the circular flow. Trade with other countries also is very important to the economy. Other countries buy and sell goods and services. Like banks, they are left out of the model.

Why Is the Circular Flow Model Useful?

The model is useful because it allows us to see how a change in one part of the economy can cause changes in another part. Suppose the government decides to lower taxes. This means that consumers have more money to spend. They can buy more of the goods and services that businesses produce. The other side of lowering taxes is that the government has less money to spend. It has less money to provide services to consumers and businesses.

 **Biography**

Oprah Winfrey: 1954–

Oprah Winfrey is a very successful entrepreneur. At age 17, Winfrey got a job at a radio station. She became a reporter and news anchor within two years. After college, she began her own talk show. Oprah formed a production company in 1986. She obtained ownership of her show and began producing other television programs and films.

Oprah founded the Angel Network on cable television in 1997. This network has raised over $12 million for scholarships and to build homes and schools. In 2000, it began presenting $100,000 "Use Your Life" awards to people whose groups have improved the lives of others.

Oprah has won countless awards, including the first ever Bob Hope Humanitarian Award. Her Oprah Winfrey Foundation continues to give money to women, children, and families around the world. In 2003, *Forbes* magazine recognized her as the first African-American woman to become a billionaire.

Lesson 3 Review On a separate sheet of paper, write the letter of the answer that correctly completes each sentence.

1. All markets involve _____.

   A cash registers   **C** trade

   B exchanges   **D** transportation

2. _____ are *not* an element of the circular flow model.

   A Businesses   **C** Consumers

   B Churches   **D** Governments

3. A _____ is a possible explanation for something.

   A exchange   **C** theme

   B fact   **D** theory

4. Businesses and consumers have a relationship with the _____.

   A black market   **C** government

   B charter   **D** tax structure

5. The circular flow model is useful for showing how changes in one part of the _____ affect other parts.

   A business   **C** exchange

   B economy   **D** world

What do you think ?

6. An exchange is a voluntary agreement between two sides. To earn money, what might you exchange?

7. What might happen to the circular flow model if government were not involved?

John D. Rockefeller Sr.

John D. Rockefeller Sr. was one of the wealthiest and most successful entrepreneurs in American history. But Rockefeller's family was not wealthy when he was a young boy. Rockefeller used his knowledge of business to create a leading company in the oil industry. The excerpts about Rockefeller's business life are from Titan: The Life of John D. Rockefeller *by Ron Chernow.*

On January 10, 1870, the partnership of Rockefeller, Andrews and Flager was abolished and replaced by a joint-stock firm called the Standard Oil Company (Ohio). . . . With $1 million in capital—$11 million in contemporary [today's] money—the new company became an instant landmark in business history. . . . Already a mini-empire, Standard Oil controlled 10 percent of American petroleum refining. . . . From the outset, Rockefeller's plans had a wide streak of megalomania. . . .

Now, on May 1, 1885, . . . Standard Oil moved into its . . . new fortress, a massive, granite, nine-story building. . . . Twenty-six Broadway soon became the world's most famous business address, shorthand for the oil trust itself, evoking its mystery, power, and efficiency. Standard Oil was now America's premier business, with a reach that ramified [spread] into a labyrinth of railroads, banks, and other businesses. . . .

Rockefeller was a unique hybrid in American business: both the instinctive, first-generation entrepreneur who founds a company and the analytic second-generation manager who extends and develops it. . . .

When Rockefeller receded from the business world in the mid-1890s, the average American was earning less than ten dollars per week. Rockefeller's average income—a stupefying [amazing] $10 million per annum [year] in those glory days before income taxes—defied public comprehension. Of more than $250 million in dividends distributed . . . between 1893 and 1901, over a quarter went straight into Rockefeller's coffers [account]. As Standard Oil shares took flight in the late 1890s, one periodical computed that Rockefeller's wealth had appreciated [increased] by $55 million in nine months.

When Rockefeller retired from business, he used his time to share his fortune with others. Rockefeller gave large amounts of money to churches, colleges and universities, African-American education, and medical research. When he died in 1937, Rockefeller was called by some, "the world's greatest . . . organizer in the science of giving."

Document-Based Questions

1. Who was John D. Rockefeller?

2. How did Rockefeller's company become so powerful?

3. What was Twenty-six Broadway?

4. How was Rockefeller different from other American businessmen?

5. Do you think any companies today are as powerful as Standard Oil was in the late 1800s? Explain.

- Entrepreneurs often are confident, independent, and enthusiastic.

- Successful entrepreneurs have a product idea, potential customers, technical know-how, and financial resources.

- Businesses may disappear when the owner sells them or when the owner moves, retires, or dies.

- A sole proprietorship is a business one person owns.

- Sole proprietorships are easy to form. They need little capital to start. The owners keep all profits and are their own bosses. Owners receive a sense of pride in providing a product or service to the community.

- Sole proprietorships have unlimited liability. The owner may be forced to sell the business or other personal belongings to repay debts. Sole proprietorships have access only to what money the owner has saved and can borrow. Sole proprietorships end if the owners become sick or disabled, lose interest, or die.

- Two or more people own a partnership. Partnerships combine the skills and money of both partners. The partners can use their special skills to increase their profits. Partnerships share losses. Partnerships generally have more money than a sole proprietorship and can better survive hard times. Partnerships have unlimited liability.

- Partners share decision making and profits. Partners may disagree about how to run the business. Partnerships' funds are limited to what partners have saved or can borrow. Partnerships end when one partner withdraws or dies.

- Corporations can be made up of many owners but legally act as a single person. Corporations can own and sell property, pay taxes, enter into contracts, and be sued.

- State governments charter corporations. Corporations can sell stock shares. Everyone who owns shares is part owner of the corporation.

- Corporations have limited liability, can raise capital easily, and have unlimited life. Ownership is easy to transfer.

- Corporations must follow state and federal laws. They are taxed on their earnings and on stockholders' dividends.

- The circular flow model shows the process of exchange among consumers, businesses, and governments.

- The circular flow model does not show a complete picture of an economy. It shows how a change in one part of the economy affects the other parts.

Chapter 8 R E V I E W

On a separate sheet of paper, write the word from the Word Bank to complete each sentence.

1. _____ often is a quality of an entrepreneur.

2. Only one in seven businesses that disappear actually _____.

3. One person owns a _____.

4. One disadvantage of owning your own business is _____.

5. When investors buy stock in a business, they receive _____.

6. The share of profits stockholders receive from a business is called _____.

7. A possible explanation for something is a(n) _____.

Word Bank

dividends
fails
independence
shares
sole proprietorship
theory
unlimited liability

On a separate sheet of paper, write the letter of the answer that correctly completes each sentence.

8. Having the money to start a business is called having _____.

   A capital   **C** taxes

   B stock   **D** stockholders

9. A disadvantage of a sole proprietorship is _____.

   A limited capital   **C** limited liability

   B limited contact   **D** unlimited capital
   with other people

10. Business owners in a partnership are responsible to pay the company's _____.

   A business rivals   **C** debts

   B competitors   **D** labor union

11. Stockholders easily can enter or leave a(n) _____.

   A dividend   **C** investor

   B corporation   **D** market

12. Usually, a _____ must help get a corporation's charter.

   A carpenter   **C** government

   B venture capitalist   **D** lawyer

13. The _____ model shows the exchanges between consumers, businesses, and government.

   A circular flow   **C** charter

   B economic   **D** dividend

On a separate sheet of paper, write answers to the following questions. Use complete sentences.

14. What are the three elements in the circular flow model?

15. What is a corporation? How is one formed?

16. What is unlimited life? Which type of business has unlimited life?

17. What exchange do consumers and businesses make?

On a separate sheet of paper, write your opinion to each question. Use complete sentences.

18. Which of the three kinds of businesses do you think is most valuable to the economy? Explain.

19. Do you think a corporation can ever become too big? Explain.

20. Would you like to become an entrepreneur? Why or why not?

Test-Taking Tip

When studying for a test, use the titles and subtitles in the chapter to help you recall the information.

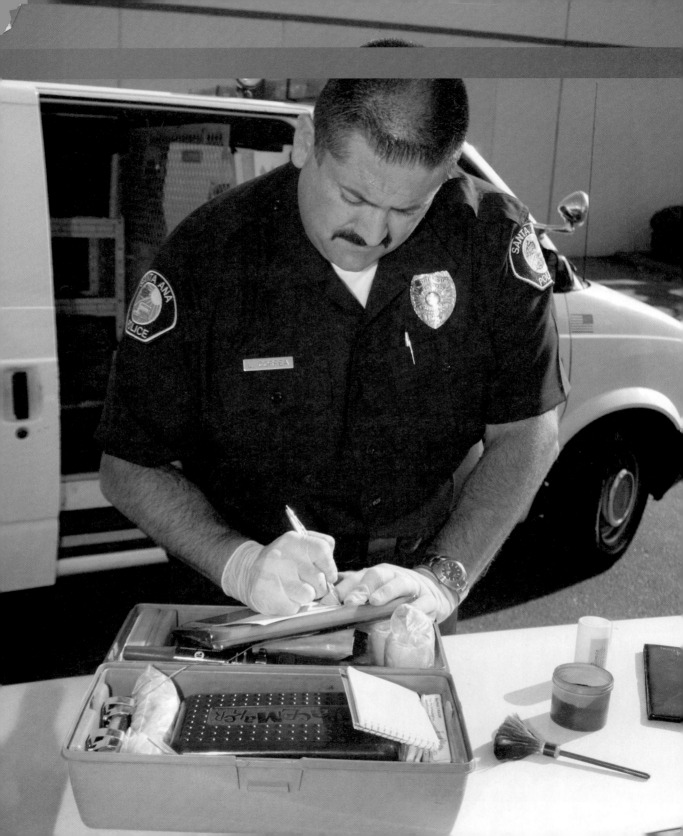

9

Workers and Wages

The production of goods and services always involves people. As you learned in the last chapter, people provide the human resources of this process. In return for their work, they receive money in the form of wages. What makes a police officer earn more money than a restaurant worker? Why does a computer operator make more money than a construction worker? There are many things that determine wages. This chapter discusses some of them.

You will learn many things about the labor force in this chapter. The chapter will describe who makes up the labor force and how wages work. It will also describe the rights workers have.

Goals for Learning

◆ To describe the labor force

◆ To explain the roles women and minorities play in the labor force

◆ To describe wages

◆ To list worker protections and rights

Who Is in the Labor Force and Who Is Not?

Labor force

People who work for pay or who are looking for work

Disabled

Having a physical or mental handicap

Retired

Past the working age

Homemaker

One who takes care of the home and children without pay

People who work for pay are one piece of the **labor force**. Another piece includes people who are looking for work. The United States government defines the labor force very clearly. It says that to be a part of the labor force you must be (1) at least 16 years old, (2) working or looking for work, or (3) in the armed forces. The labor force produces most of a nation's goods and services.

The labor force does not include people who are **disabled** and cannot work. **Retired** persons (those who are past working age) and college students are not part of the labor force either. Some people who work are not counted as part of the labor force. For example, people who are full-time **homemakers** (those who take care of the home and children without pay) are not part of the labor force. Men and women who have stopped looking for work are not part of the labor force either.

Over 140 million people make up the labor force of the United States. American workers are among the most productive workers in the world.

Economics at Work

Law Enforcement Officer

Law enforcement officers keep order in a certain place. They enforce laws that protect the lives and property of people. Many law enforcement officers talk to people about a crime that occurred. They look for clues and facts to solve crimes. They might make reports on the habits of known criminals in order to prevent crimes. Law enforcement officers often are expected to put together reports for trials. They appear in court to talk about their findings.

Law enforcement officers sometimes direct traffic. They may give out tickets and examine accidents. Some work on special projects that are aimed at preventing crimes or accidents. Certain officers may become experts in things like firearms, handwriting analysis, or fingerprint identification. In most cases, law enforcement officers must be able to respond any time their services are needed. They are expected to be in good physical condition, with excellent sight and hearing.

What Are the Three Basic Sectors of the Labor Force?

Economists group workers into three basic types, or **sectors**. The smallest sector in the United States today is the agricultural sector. Until about 100 years ago, it was the largest. In the past, many people earned a living by farming. Today, farmers make up less than 3 percent of all workers. Yet today's farmers produce more goods than ever before. Fewer farmers have been able to produce more. This increase in productivity was made possible by new technology. Better seed, better farming methods, better water systems, and new machines all have helped.

A second sector produces most of a country's goods. This group includes workers in manufacturing and construction. Around 1920 was the first time that the number of jobs in this sector was greater than the number of workers in agriculture. Many people left the farm for better paying jobs in the cities. By the 1930s, the number of jobs in this sector began to level off. In later years, it began to fall.

Since January 2001, the U.S. has lost 2.5 million jobs in manufacturing. There are two main reasons. Technology has increased productivity. Fewer workers can make more goods. Another big reason is that many manufacturing jobs have moved to other countries where the cost of labor is less.

Figure 9.1

Projected Top 15 Fastest Growing Occupations in the U.S. to 2010

Projected Growth

1. Computer software engineers	100%
2. Computer support specialists	97%
3. Computer systems software engineers	90%
4. Network and computer systems administrators	82%
5. Network systems and data communications analysts	77%
6. Desktop publishers	67%
7. Database administrators	66%
8. Personal and home care aides	62%
9. Computer systems analysts	60%
10. Medical assistants	57%
11. Social and human service assistants	54%
12. Physician assistants	53%
13. Medical records and health information technicians	49%
14. Computer and information systems managers	48%
15. Home health aides	47%

Information technology (IT)

A service job that involves the processing of information by computer

Professional

A type of worker who has a college degree and special training

Skilled worker

A type of worker who is well trained and experienced with a certain skill

Experience

Knowledge and skill gained from being on the job

The third sector of the labor force is the largest. It still is growing. It is the service sector. Services refer to work done for other people. People in the service sector include anyone providing a service to other people. This sector includes people who work in restaurants and shops. Other service industries are entertainment, education, and health care. A growing service industry is **information technology (IT)**. It is the processing of information by computer. It includes such things as electronic data processing and management information systems. Many of the jobs in Figure 9.1 on the previous page are IT jobs.

All jobs fit into one of three groups called sectors. Road construction workers belong to the manufacturing and construction sector.

What Are Other Ways of Grouping Workers?

Workers often are grouped according to the skills they have. Some workers are described as **professionals**. Professionals have college degrees and special training. Lawyers, doctors, educators, dentists, and members of the clergy are professionals.

Another category of workers is **skilled workers**. These workers are well trained and have **experience**—knowledge and skill gained from being on the job. Plumbers, electricians, dental assistants, and computer technicians are examples of skilled workers.

Semiskilled workers work in jobs that require some training but not as much training as skilled workers. Cable TV workers, telephone operators, and certain kinds of managers are all semiskilled.

Skilled workers, such as this auto mechanic, have training and experience.

The last category is **unskilled workers**. Being unskilled does not mean these workers have no skills. It means that their jobs require little training. Someone who clears tables or welcomes people in a restaurant may be very skilled. However, that person still is grouped as unskilled. This includes most farmers and factory workers. Working as a store clerk usually does not require much training. Salespersons are therefore thought of as unskilled.

What Are Blue-Collar and White-Collar Jobs?

In the past, many unskilled or semiskilled workers wore uniforms. These workers still are called **blue-collar** workers. Today they may wear street clothes or even suits. **White-collar** jobs include office workers and professionals. They often wear formal clothes like suits and ties.

Lesson 1 Review On a separate sheet of paper, write the letter of the answer that correctly completes each sentence.

1. The work sector in which people produce something is called _____.

   A agriculture   **C** manufacturing

   B information technology **D** service

2. Until about 100 years ago, most workers were in the _____ sector.

   A agricultural   **C** horticultural

   B cultural   **D** services

3. Unskilled or semiskilled workers are _____.

   A blue-collar workers   **C** uniformed

   B highly paid   **D** younger than age 16

4. Processing information by computer is called _____.

   A circuit boards   **C** keyboarding

   B independent technology   **D** information technology

5. Entertainment and health care are included in the _____ sector.

   A labor   **C** service

   B movie   **D** work

What do you think ?

6. Why do you think many American manufacturing jobs have moved to other countries?

7. If you could choose, which labor sector would you enter? Why? What would be the advantages and disadvantages?

<table>
<tr><td>

Minority

A person who belongs to a smaller group of people within a larger group

</td></tr>
</table>

One of the biggest changes in the labor force concerns women and **minorities**. A minority is a person who belongs to a smaller group of people within a larger group. The role of women and minorities in the labor force is becoming more important. They own many businesses. For example, in 1997, there were 3 million minority-owned businesses in the United States. About 4.5 million people worked in these businesses. Together they generated nearly $600 million in revenues.

How Has the Role of Women Changed?

Women were not always viewed as an important part of the labor force. From early days in the history of the United States, some women worked outside the home. Often, these women were unmarried farm girls. They were paid less than men and had few rights. During the Civil War in the 1860s, women replaced men on farms and in factories. By 1930, there were more than 10 million women in the labor force. Women most often worked as secretaries, typists, clerks, or as a servant in someone else's home.

During World War II, women again replaced men who left the farm and factory to go fight. After the war, the number of women workers dropped as the soldiers returned. The 1960s brought big changes. More and more women joined the labor force. Today, women make up nearly half of all workers.

What Are the Trends Affecting Women in the Labor Force?

Most of the growth in the U.S. labor force will come from women. According to one expert, men are leaving jobs faster than they are coming in. At the same time, women are entering faster than they are leaving. Researchers expect that 57 percent of new workers will be women.

Another trend is that women are becoming better educated. Employers generally want workers with the best education. More and more, these workers are women. Women earn over half of all bachelor's degrees and over half of all master's degrees.

In the past, women worked against a **glass ceiling**. They were prevented from rising to a position of leadership in corporations because they were women. Now women are becoming managers. Women fill nearly half of all managerial positions. However, most corporation officers are still men.

What Are the Trends Affecting Minorities in the Labor Force?

Minorities have been helped in many of the same ways as women. The Civil Rights Act of 1964 made discrimination in the workplace against the law. It ended job discrimination against both women and minorities.

The number of African Americans and Hispanics who are not working is at its lowest level ever. More minorities are members of the middle class. There is a growing number of minority students attending colleges and universities.

Minority-owned businesses make up 15 percent of all businesses in the United States. Hispanics own the largest number. African Americans, Asian Americans, and American Indians also own many businesses. About 60 percent of all minority-owned businesses are in five states: California, Texas, New York, Florida, and Illinois. The largest number of these businesses are in California. Most minority-owned businesses are in large cities. Los Angeles, New York, Miami, Chicago, Houston, and Washington, D.C. have the most.

About 44 percent of minority-owned businesses are in the service industry. The next largest group is retail trade industries.

Biography

Walter E. Williams: 1935–

Walter Williams has taught economics at a number of different colleges and universities. At the present time, he is a professor at George Mason University. Dr. Williams has written over 80 articles about economics. These have appeared in journals and magazines. He has written six books. Many have focused on African-American economic issues.

Williams has won many awards. People often call upon his knowledge of economics. He is a board member of many companies. Williams is a popular guest on radio and television programs. He often speaks to educational or business groups in countries all over the world. He also takes part in debates and panel discussions of economics issues. He has appeared before Congressional committees seeking advice about tax and spending issues.

Lesson 2 Review On a separate sheet of paper, write answers to the following questions. Use complete sentences.

1. What is the glass ceiling?

2. Which U.S. minority group owns the most businesses?

3. Why are more women entering the workforce?

4. How did the Civil Rights Act of 1964 affect workers?

5. What are three trends affecting minorities in the labor force?

What do you think

6. Why do you think California has the most minority-owned businesses?

7. Four of the five states with large numbers of minority-owned businesses are on the coasts. Why do you think so many minority-owned businesses are in Illinois?

Volunteer

To choose to do work for no pay

Wage

The money a worker gets in exchange for labor

People work for many reasons. Some people work because they believe they can make a difference. Many people **volunteer** to work for no pay. Most people work to earn money to buy the things they need and want. The money workers get in exchange for their labor is called **wages**.

Why Don't All Workers Earn the Same Wages?

Workers' pay is affected by supply and demand. Employers demand labor; employees supply labor. Just as there is a supply and demand curve for products, there is a supply and demand curve for labor. Figure 9.2 shows an example of the demand for labor. It shows that employers are willing and able to hire more workers at lower pay (B) than at higher pay (A). Figure 9.3 shows that workers are more willing and able to work at higher wages (A) than at lower wages (B).

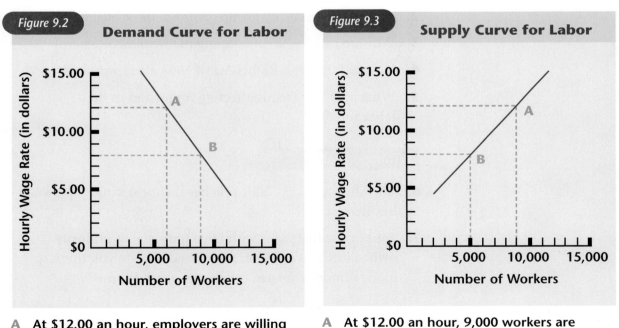

Figure 9.2 — Demand Curve for Labor

Figure 9.3 — Supply Curve for Labor

A   At $12.00 an hour, employers are willing and able to hire 6,000 workers.

B   At $8.00 an hour, employers are willing and able to hire 9,000 workers.

A   At $12.00 an hour, 9,000 workers are willing and able to work.

B   At $8.00 an hour, 5,000 workers are willing and able to work.

Let's combine Figures 9.2 and 9.3. As we can see in Figure 9.4, the two curves cross. The point at which the two lines meet is called the **equilibrium wage rate**. It is the point at which the quantity of labor demanded is equal to the quantity of labor supplied. In other words, at the equilibrium point, employers are willing and able to hire as many workers as are willing and able to work.

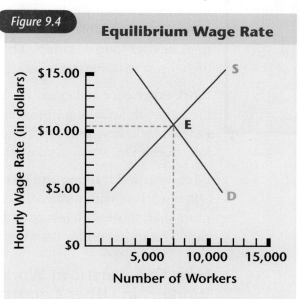

The number of people willing and able to work (S) equals the number of people employers are willing to hire (D). The equilibrium wage rate (E) is $10.25 per hour.

The reason why all workers do not earn the same wage is simple. The supply and demand for different jobs is rarely the same. For example, many pro athletes earn millions of dollars. Why? The supply of star athletes is very small, but the demand is very great. On the other hand, people who work at amusement parks or in big discount stores earn very little. The supply of these kinds of workers is greater than the demand.

There are several other reasons why workers earn different wages. One is difference in ability. Very few people can write songs that others want to hear. Some people type faster than others. Others are good at selling. Some skills are valued more than others. The skills that are most valued receive the best wages.

There are differences in effort and jobs. Some workers are willing to work long hours to earn extra pay. Some jobs are very dangerous. Some jobs demand that the worker be responsible for many things. The work of police officers, firefighters, and construction workers who build high-rise buildings is dangerous. People in these jobs generally make more money than workers with less dangerous jobs. Airline pilots are responsible for moving people safely from place to place over long distances. They are often rewarded with higher pay than most workers.

Work experience makes a difference. Workers who have had the same job for a long time make more money than new hires. Employers believe that experienced workers are better at their jobs than an inexperienced worker.

Education and training also account for differences in pay. Often workers with more education or special training earn more than those with less education. College graduates usually earn a lot more money than high school graduates.

How Can American Workers Compete with Workers in Other Countries?

In Lesson 1, you learned that the United States has lost many manufacturing jobs. Some of these jobs have gone to other countries where workers are paid much less because the cost of living is less. One of the ways Americans can keep these high paying jobs is to keep a high productivity level.

For example, let's compare American automobile workers with automobile workers in Brazil. Let's say that American workers earn an average of $25 an hour while the South American worker earns only $5 an hour. Is it cheaper to make the cars in Brazil? Not always. American workers are much more productive. They can build a car in only three hours. It takes 20 hours to build a car in South America. The total labor cost for building a car in the United States is $75 (3 × $25 = $75). The cost of labor to build the car in South America is $100 (20 × $5 = $100).

Benefits

Anything extra provided to workers besides wages, such as paid vacations, retirement plans, and medical insurance

Word Bank

ability
dangerous
demand
inexperienced
wages

What Are Benefits?

Fifty years ago workers only expected their weekly wages from employers. Now workers expect more. For example, health insurance costs a lot of money. Many workers cannot pay for insurance by themselves. They expect their employers to help pay for the insurance. **Benefits** are anything extra provided to workers besides wages. The most common benefits are paid vacations, retirement plans, and medical insurance. Sometimes people call these fringe benefits.

Lesson 3 Review On a separate sheet of paper, write the word from the Word Bank to complete each sentence.

1. Most people work to earn _____.

2. Labor supply and _____ affect workers' pay.

3. Differences in _____ account for some differences in pay.

4. Workers with more experience generally earn more than _____ workers.

5. Some jobs are more _____ than others and are worth higher pay.

What do you think ?

6. The president of a large corporation has a hard job. Should he or she earn large amounts of money even if the business loses money? Explain.

7. Why should a person applying for a job think about benefits as well as wages? Explain.

The factory system of manufacturing became widespread in the 1880s. Workers were poorly paid. Women and minorities were paid less than white males. Working conditions were very hard. Even children sometimes went to work. To improve conditions for workers, the government passed many laws.

What Were the Progressive Reforms?

In the early 1900s, a group of reformers tried to improve the lives of working people. They were called the **Progressives**. The Progressives wrote books and articles about the problems. They worked to make the workplace safer. They tried to end child labor. They got Congress to pass several reform bills. A child labor act limited the number of hours children could work. The Adamson Act gave railroad workers an eight-hour day. The Seamen's Act improved working conditions on American ships.

How Did the New Deal Help Working People?

In the 1930s, the Unites States economy entered a **depression** (also called the Great Depression.) A depression is a period of economic hard times. Nearly 13 million workers had no jobs in 1933. That year, President Franklin D. Roosevelt began the **New Deal**. The New Deal was the name of Roosevelt's program for getting the United States out of the depression. The New Deal had three goals: relief, recovery, and reform. This plan was intended to provide help to those in need and to get the economy back on track. It also hoped to make sure a depression would not happen again.

Several laws were passed giving workers the right to join **labor unions**. These are groups that make sure workers are treated fairly. Business owners were required to talk with workers to try to reach agreement. They were not allowed to punish workers as they had in the past. The first minimum wage law was passed. Another new law set the maximum workweek at 40 hours. (You will learn more about these laws in the next chapter).

Progressives

Reformers in the 1900s who tried to improve the lives of working people

Depression

A period of economic hard times

New Deal

The name of President Roosevelt's program for getting the United States out of the depression

Labor union

A group that makes sure workers are treated fairly

How Did Workers Benefit from the Civil Rights Act of 1964?

Integration
A process in the 1960s in which African-American students were allowed to attend schools with white students

The Civil Rights Act of 1964 is one of the most important laws ever passed by Congress. It had many parts. One part sped up the process of school **integration**. African-American students were no longer prevented from attending with white students. Another law protected the voting rights of African Americans. The act ended **segregation** in public places like restaurants, theaters, and swimming pools. Segregation is the separation of people of different races. Another part of the law was about discrimination in the workplace. Employers could no longer discriminate on the basis of race, color, religion, national origin, or sex. The law set up an Equal Opportunity Commission to look into any complaints.

Segregation
The separation of people of different races

Occupational Safety and Health Administration (OSHA)
A U.S. government agency that protects workers by setting and enforcing health and safety standards

What Is OSHA?

OSHA is the **Occupational Safety and Health Administration**. It was created by Congress in 1970. It says that workers have a right to a safe and healthy workplace. The agency protects workers by setting and enforcing health and safety standards.

Americans with Disabilities Act (ADA)
A law that outlaws discrimination against persons with physical or mental handicaps

What Protections Do Disabled Workers Have?

In 1990, Congress passed the **Americans with Disabilities Act (ADA)**. It outlaws discrimination against persons with

physical or mental handicaps. Its aim was to allow these people to enter the labor force. There are over 52 million people with disabilities in the United States. Congress passed this law to encourage employers to look at people's abilities rather than their disabilities when hiring workers.

The Americans with Disabilities Act outlaws discrimination against people who have physical or mental handicaps.

What Can Workers Do If Their Rights Are Violated?

Workers who believe their rights have been violated on the job should:

1. Make a record of all memos, e-mails, documents, and letters that help prove the violations.

2. Review the employee handbook. Make a copy of the company policies that apply.

3. Contact the State Department of Labor to learn about state laws that may have been broken.

4. Find out if discrimination laws have been broken by contacting the Equal Employment Opportunity Commission.

Economics in Your Life

The U.S. Minimum Wage

Beginning more than 100 years ago, government leaders fought for a minimum wage to protect American workers. The Fair Labor Standards Act was passed in 1938. It set a minimum wage of 25 cents per hour. The Labor Department's Wages and Hours Commission enforced the law.

Since 1938, the minimum wage has been raised many times. The most recent change, to $5.15 per hour, was made law in 1997. The U.S. House and Senate have introduced the Fair Minimum Wage Act of 2003. This bill calls for a minimum wage change to $5.90 per hour within 60 days of passage into law. The rate would increase to $6.65 per hour after one year. More than 7% of Americans earn minimum wage or less.

Lesson 4 Review On a separate sheet of paper, write the letter of the answer that correctly completes each sentence.

1. A period of economic hard times is a _____.

   A boom   **C** compression

   B burst   **D** depression

2. Reformers who acted to make workplaces safer were called _____.

   A Aggressives   **C** Progressives

   B Liberals   **D** The labor party

3. Franklin Roosevelt's _____ had three goals to get the nation out of the Great Depression.

   A Congress   **C** New Deal

   B National Relief Act   **D** New Horizon

4. _____ protects workers by setting and enforcing safety standards.

   A FDA   **C** FRG

   B FDR   **D** OSHA

5. The Civil Rights Act of 1964 ended _____.

   A segregation   **C** integration

   B the Great Depression   **D** voting rights

What do you think ?

6. Why do you think a national law was passed to end discrimination based on a person's race?

7. What do you think the workplace would be like without laws protecting workers' rights? Provide at least three examples to support your opinion.

"We Will Not Tolerate . . ."

In the late 1800s and early 1900s, industry in the United States grew rapidly. The demand for labor grew too. Many young children were hired to work long hours at dangerous jobs for low wages. Since then laws have been passed to prevent child labor. Children in the United States must attend school until age 16. However, child labor still exists in many poorer countries. On June 15, 1999, President Bill Clinton gave a speech about child labor to the International Labor Organization. Part of that speech follows.

Every single day, tens of millions of children work in conditions that shock the conscience. There are children chained to often risky machines, children handling dangerous chemicals, children forced to work when they should be in school. . . .

. . . We will not tolerate children in slavery or bondage. We will not tolerate children being forcibly recruited to serve in armed conflicts. We will not tolerate young children risking their health and breaking their bodies in hazardous and dangerous working conditions for hours unconscionably long, regardless of country, regardless of circumstance. . . . These are things that happen in too many places today.

Following the President's speech, the United States Senate passed the Convention on the Elimination of the Worst Forms of Child Labor. *President Clinton made the following statement on November 5, 1999, after the approval:*

With this action, the Senate has declared on behalf of the American people that we simply will not tolerate the worst forms of child labor: child slavery, the sale or trafficking of children, child prostitution or pornography, forced or compulsory child labor, and hazardous work that harms the health, safety, and morals of children. With this action, the United States continues as a world leader in the fight to eliminate exploitative and abusive child labor.

Document-Based Questions

1. What happened as industry grew in the United States?

2. Where does most child labor exist today?

3. In your own words, summarize what Clinton says the United States "will not tolerate."

4. According to the document, what are three ways child workers are put in danger?

5. In the United States, employers cannot hire workers who are under age 14. Do you think this is a good idea? Explain.

- The U.S. government defines the labor force as people who are at least 16 years old, are working or looking for work, or are in the armed forces.

- The three basic parts of the labor force are the agricultural, manufacturing/construction, and service sectors.

- Workers may be grouped as professionals, skilled, semiskilled, or unskilled labor. They also may be called blue-collar workers or white-collar workers.

- Women traditionally have been paid less than men and have had fewer rights. Today, nearly half of all workers are women. That number will continue to rise. About half of all managers are women.

- The Civil Rights Act of 1964 ended discrimination in the workplace. More minority group members than ever attend college and own their own businesses.

- Wages vary for different people based on supply and demand. The equilibrium wage rate is the wage at which employers will hire workers and workers will agree to work. Differences in ability, effort, responsibility, danger, experience, education, and training affect wages.

- U.S. wages are generally higher than wages in other countries. One way to keep jobs in the United States is with a high level of productivity. High productivity can reduce the total cost of business.

- Workers often receive paid vacations, a retirement plan, medical insurance, and other benefits.

- As the manufacturing system spread, the U.S. government passed laws to improve working conditions.

- Progressives were reformers who tried to improve working people's lives. They passed several laws to improve working conditions.

- During the Great Depression, Franklin Roosevelt developed a relief program called the New Deal. Congress passed laws affecting labor unions, working conditions, and wages.

- The Civil Rights Act ended segregation. It also protected the voting rights of African Americans. It outlawed discrimination based on a person's sex, age, race, or religion.

- Congress created OSHA to enforce workplace health and safety standards.

- The Americans with Disabilities Act outlawed discrimination based on a person's mental or physical disabilities.

- Workers can take several steps if they believe their rights have been violated at work.

Chapter 9 REVIEW

On a separate sheet of paper, write the word from the Word Bank to complete each sentence.

Word Bank

benefits

depression

handicaps

labor

professionals

sectors

women

1. Workers in the United States are grouped into _____.

2. Lawyers, doctors, and others with college degrees and special training are _____.

3. Today, _____ make up almost half the labor force.

4. At the equilibrium wage rate, the quantity of labor demanded equals the quantity of _____ supplied.

5. Anything extra beyond wages supplied to workers is called _____.

6. In the 1930s, the U.S. economy entered a _____, or economic hard times.

7. The Americans with Disabilities Act of 1990 outlawed discrimination against people with physical or mental _____.

On a separate sheet of paper, write the letter of the answer that correctly completes each sentence.

8. Well-trained and experienced workers are _____ workers.

   A blue-collar   **C** skilled

   B unprofessional   **D** unskilled

9. Today, _____ earn more than half of all bachelor's and master's degrees.

   A Easterners   **C** married men

   B foreigners   **D** women

10. Most minority-owned businesses are in the _____.

    A agricultural sector   **C** northeastern United States

    B downtown sector   **D** service industries

11. The money workers receive in exchange for labor is _____.

    A education   **C** training

    B competition   **D** wages

12. One way Americans can compete with other countries for jobs is to keep a high level of _____.

    A insurance   **C** productivity

    B labor   **D** self-confidence

13. During Franklin Roosevelt's presidency, laws set the maximum workweek at _____ hours.

    A 20   **C** 40

    B 30   **D** 45

On a separate sheet of paper, write answers to the following questions. Use complete sentences.

14. What are benefits? Give two examples.

15. What is segregation?

16. How does the U.S. government define the labor force?

17. To which labor sector does information technology belong?

On a separate sheet of paper, write your opinion to each question. Use complete sentences.

18. Why do you think the service sector is the fastest-growing labor sector?

19. If most people work to earn money, why do you think so many people do volunteer work for no pay?

20. Do you think American workers have enough rights and protections? Explain.

Test-Taking Tip

If you do not know the answer to a question, put a check beside it and go on. Then when you are finished, go back to any checked questions and try to answer them.

10 Organized Labor and the Economy

The way American workers are treated is very important. Labor leaders have tried to organize workers into groups as powerful as the big business corporations. These groups are called labor unions. Labor unions have a long history in the United States. Today, unions are experiencing a major crisis.

In this chapter, you will learn about the history of labor unions, how they work, and the problems they face.

Goals for Learning

◆ To describe the rise of early unions

◆ To describe the AFL-CIO

◆ To describe the major issues in labor-management dealings

◆ To identify federal labor regulations

◆ To explain the issues facing labor unions today

Radical

Something that is extreme

Strike

The act of stopping work to get better pay and working conditions

Between the Civil War and 1900, the United States changed. It had been a nation of farmers. By 1900, it became the greatest industrial power in the world. The new business leaders had almost complete control over work hours and pay. The people who control and direct a business and its workers are management. The people who work for the management in a business are labor.

The workers felt they had to do something to improve their working conditions. They organized into labor unions. A labor union is a group of workers who promote their common good. The first national labor organization was organized in 1866. It was called the National Labor Union (NLU). Its main demand was for the eight-hour workday. The NLU grew to 650,000 workers, including some women and African Americans.

The Knights of Labor was organized in 1869. Unlike the NLU, it was an organization of workers rather than of labor groups. It hoped to unite "men and women of every craft, creed, and color" into one union. The Knights supported the eight-hour workday. They were against using children and prisoners for labor. They wanted laws protecting the safety and health of all workers. They favored "equal pay for equal work" for men and women. At the time, these ideas were **radical**, or extreme. The Knights of Labor grew quickly. By 1880, it had 700,000 members.

Why Were the Knights of Labor Successful at First?

One reason the Knights thrived was its leadership. The leader of the Knights of Labor was Terence V. Powderly. He was a man of great energy. He was a great organizer and speaker. A second reason was a series of successful **strikes**. A strike is stopping work to get better pay and working conditions. The most important strikes were against the railroads. The Knights went on strike against several railroads to fight against pay cuts and won.

What Caused the Downfall of the Knights of Labor?

By 1917, the Knights broke up. There were several reasons for this. One reason was that it tried to unite both skilled and unskilled workers in the same union. This was a mistake. The Knights tried to improve working conditions for unskilled workers by calling for a strike. The skilled workers did not want to risk their jobs. They did not support the union's call to strike. A second reason why the Knights broke up was that many people thought the union was too radical. Some of its leaders even wanted to replace capitalism. The third reason was the Homestead Strike.

What Was the Homestead Strike?

America's largest steel plant was in Homestead, Pennsylvania, near Pittsburgh. Its manager was Henry Clay Frick. Frick refused to listen to the demands of his workers. When the workers went on strike, Frick tried to reopen the plant with nonunion workers, called **strikebreakers**. He hired 300 armed guards to protect these strikebreakers. When the guards arrived in Homestead, a fight broke out. Ten strikers and some guards were killed. Pennsylvania's governor sent in 8,000 state troopers to restore order. When the plant reopened with strikebreakers, the union was defeated.

The Homestead Strike resulted in fighting. The failed strike was one reason why the Knights of Labor broke up.

What Role Did Women Play in the Labor Movement?

In the new industrial age, more and more women entered the labor force. By 1910, about one in five workers was a woman. Most women worked in the **textile** industry making cloth. Other women made clothing or worked in retail sales. A few women were professionals. They worked in the few jobs open to women at that time, like teaching and nursing. Women earned about one-third to one-half as much money as men, even for the same kind of work. Several women became important labor leaders.

Mary Harris Jones, or "Mother Jones," took part in labor protests in the late 1800s and early 1900s.

Mary Harris Jones was known as Mother Jones. She took part in her first labor action in the great railroad strike of 1877. From then on, she devoted her life to the labor movement.

Mother Jones was concerned about child labor. In 1903, she was present at a strike by 75,000 textile workers. About 10,000 were children. She was shocked at how many of the children had lost fingers or hands in machines. She organized a children's march to the home of President Theodore Roosevelt. About 80 children went on the march. They carried signs reading "We want more schools and less hospitals," "We want time to play," and "Prosperity is here. Where is ours?" A lot of people took notice of the march. A year later, Pennsylvania passed a law against child labor for children under age 14.

Pauline Newman went to work at the age of eight. In 1909, at the age of 16, she became the first organizer for the International Ladies' Garment Workers Union (ILGWU). It represented workers in the women's clothing factories.

Also in 1909, thousands of New York City garment workers went on strike. They wanted better working conditions and better pay. About three-fourths of the strikers were young women between the ages of 16 and 25. The strike lasted 13 weeks. Employers agreed to shorten the workweek and improve pay. They also ended fees for the use of the factory machinery. However, the employers refused to do anything to improve safety conditions in the factories.

What Was the U.S. Government's Attitude Toward Early Unions?

At first the government was against unions. It used its powers to support management against the workers. One example was the Pullman strike of 1894. Pullman owned a company that made sleeping cars for the railroads. He also owned all of the town in which all the workers lived. Business was bad. Pullman lowered the wages of his workers but refused to lower the rents the workers paid. The workers went on strike.

Soon the dispute spread to the railroads. Within four days, all rail service between Chicago and the West Coast stopped. Management brought in strikebreakers. The U.S. Attorney General convinced the President to send in troops to ensure delivery of the mail. In fact, the strike was not stopping mail deliveries. It was just an excuse to convince the court to issue an **injunction**. An injunction is a court order preventing some activity. It forbade any work stoppage against the railroads.

The government's use of injunctions against labor unions continued for many years. This made it harder for unions to organize workers. However, the government's attitude slowly began to change. Congress passed new laws protecting the rights of workers. In recent years, the power of unions has again been limited by government actions. Lesson 4 will explain this in greater detail.

The History of Labor Day

The Central Labor Union planned a holiday celebration in 1882 to honor workers. New York celebrated the first Labor Day holiday in September of that year. The year after, a similar event was held. In 1884, it was decided that the first Monday in September would be recognized as the Labor Day holiday. The next year many different cities across the nation held celebrations on this date.

Some states passed laws making Labor Day a legal holiday. In 1894, Congress passed an act making it a national holiday. Early Labor Day activities usually included a huge parade and speeches, presentations, and public amusement. Since the early 1900s, Labor Day activities focus on certain industries in the area. Labor Day also is celebrated in Canada and many other nations of the world.

Word Bank

Homestead Strike

labor union

strike

strikebreaker

textile industry

Lesson 1 Review On a separate sheet of paper, write the word from the Word Bank to complete each sentence.

1. A group of workers organized to promote workers' common good is a _____.

2. Stopping work to get better pay and working conditions is a _____.

3. Workers in the _____ make cloth in factories.

4. The _____ took place at a steel plant in Pennsylvania.

5. A nonunion worker brought in to replace strikers is called a _____.

What do you think ?

6. Why do you think the U.S. government often supported the businesses rather than striking workers?

7. If you were President Theodore Roosevelt, how would you have felt about the children's march that Mother Jones organized?

The **AFL-CIO** is the largest group of independent labor unions. It has members in the United States, Canada, Mexico, Panama, and Puerto Rico. In 2002, it had 16.1 million members, or 13.2 percent of the labor force.

How Was the AFL Different from Earlier Unions?

The leaders of the Knights of Labor believed that all working people shared the same interests. Therefore, the leaders thought there was no need for specialized unions. The American Federation of Labor (AFL) was started in 1886. Its founder was Samuel Gompers. Gompers believed in **bread and butter unionism**. This is the belief that unions should focus on improving working conditions and pay for skilled workers. He did not think the union should stress political reform. The AFL was against the idea of a labor party.

The AFL was made up of a group of **craft unions**. A craft union includes only skilled workers in a certain craft. For example, electricians and plumbers have specialized skills. They belong to their own unions. Their unions are independent and free to do what they can for their members. However, each of the independent unions is a member of the AFL. The AFL worked to reach goals common to all working people. It helped get higher wages, shorter hours, and laws against child labor. It also was successful in passing a **workers' compensation** law. Workers' compensation is payments made to workers who are injured or disabled while working.

What Was the CIO?

Some industries have many specialized crafts. For example, making cars requires engineers, metal workers, and painters. The huge plants also need janitors, assembly line workers, and all sorts of other workers. The different types of workers were represented by different unions. This seemed to make labor weaker rather than stronger. Early in the 1930s, a group within the AFL decided that workers would be better off if they organized into **industrial unions**. Industrial unions bring together all workers in a specific industry. Both skilled and unskilled workers belong to the same union.

AFL-CIO

The largest group of independent labor unions; stands for the American Federation of Labor and Congress of Industrial Organizations

Bread and butter unionism

The belief that unions should focus on improving working conditions and pay for skilled workers rather than political reform

Craft union

A union that represents skilled workers in a certain craft

Workers' compensation

Payments made to workers who are injured or disabled while working

Industrial union

A union that brings together all workers, skilled and unskilled

The Committee for Industrial Organizations, the official name of the CIO, was organized in 1935. It was led by John L. Lewis of the United Mine Workers. It broke away from the AFL in 1938. The CIO was very successful. It organized workers in the automobile, steel, rubber, textile, meatpacking, and mining industries. Many of the members were new, unskilled African-American workers and women. These two groups had not been allowed to join some of the unions in the AFL.

Why Did the AFL and the CIO Merge?

Leaders within the two labor groups saw that labor would be stronger if there was one union group instead of two. In 1955, the two labor groups merged. The new group was called the American Federation of Labor and Congress of Industrial Organizations (AFL-CIO).

Biography

Cesar Chavez: 1927–1993

As a boy, Cesar Chavez worked with his family growing fruits and vegetables in the California farm fields. Most workers, like the Chavez family, were from Mexico. After time in the navy during World War II, Chavez began speaking to groups of field workers. He told them about their rights. Chavez traveled from camp to camp organizing the workers. He helped them register to vote.

Chavez helped workers form a union, demanding fair pay and better working conditions. The growers would not listen to their demands, so the workers left the fields. People across the country began to stop buying grapes and lettuce to protest for workers' rights. By 1978, some demands were met. During the 1980s, Chavez led protests against the use of chemicals on grapes. Strikes and protests ended with agreements for change.

Lesson 2 Review On a separate sheet of paper, write the letter of the answer that correctly completes each sentence.

1. The belief that the focus of unions should be to improve working conditions and pay is _____.

   A bread and butter unionism
   B communistic
   C fundamental
   D striking

2. The first leader of the AFL was _____.

   A John L. Lewis
   B Mother Jones
   C Samuel Gompers
   D Theodore Roosevelt

3. The first leader of the CIO was _____.

   A John L. Lewis
   B Mother Jones
   C Samuel Gompers
   D Theodore Roosevelt

4. Payments made to a worker injured or disabled on the job is _____.

   A contracts
   B injunctions
   C insurance
   D workers' compensation

5. Many members of the CIO were _____.

   A children
   B doctors
   C government leaders
   D women and African Americans

What do you think ?

6. Why do you think a union of skilled and unskilled labor did not work at first?

7. Sometimes industries and unions have not trusted each other. Why do you think this happens?

Collective bargaining

When representatives of labor and management sit down together to try to reach an agreement on something

Compromise

When both sides of a disagreement give and take

Mediator

A neutral third party who listens to arguments from both sides and suggests ways agreements can be reached

Arbitration

When both sides agree to have a mediator who will decide how to solve a disagreement

Labor almost always believes that it should receive better pay and working conditions. Management often is against labor's demands. It is an advantage to both sides if an agreement can be reached. The agreement is called a contract.

What Is Collective Bargaining?

The AFL-CIO tried to improve working conditions and pay for its members by using **collective bargaining**. In collective bargaining, representatives of labor and management sit down together to try to reach an agreement. Both sides give and take, or **compromise**. Sometimes, the talks break down. Third parties are brought in to help.

A **mediator** is a neutral third party. He or she listens to arguments from both sides and suggests ways agreements can be reached. Neither side has to agree to follow the mediator's suggestions. **Arbitration** is like mediation except that both sides agree ahead of time to go along with the arbitrator's decision.

Labor and management must work to compromise on labor issues.

Overtime

Extra money paid to employees for work beyond 40 hours per week or on weekends or holidays

Job security

A guarantee that the workers will not lose their jobs

Grievance

A worker complaint

Committee

A group that gathers regularly for a certain purpose or goal

What Are the Major Issues in Labor-Management Discussions?

A union's first concern usually is wages. The contract spells out the wage scale that workers earn. The pay scale may have a large range since there are usually different types of workers. Experienced and more skilled workers receive better wages than newer, less experienced workers.

Benefits also are important. These are benefits given in addition to wages. They include things like paid holidays, vacations, sick leave, and life and health insurance. Some companies put money toward employees' retirement plans.

Labor always is trying to make its working conditions better. Workers want to work in a safe and clean workplace. They also want job duties clearly spelled out. Contracts usually set the number of hours in the normal workweek. In the contract, management agrees to pay workers **overtime**. This is money paid for working more than 40 hours per week or for working on weekends or holidays.

More and more, labor is calling for **job security**. Job security is a guarantee that the workers will not lose their jobs. This guarantee lasts as long as the contract is in effect. It gives workers freedom from worry that they will lose their jobs. Sometimes, workers are willing to take less pay for increased job security.

Many labor-management contracts now include a way to deal with worker complaints. These complaints are called **grievances**. Usually the contract has a clear way of dealing with grievances. The process includes several steps. A worker can file a grievance if he or she believes management is not following the contract. The process makes clear who will hear the grievance and decide whether the worker has been treated unfairly. Often there is a grievance **committee** that listens to the complaint and tries to work out a solution. The committee has members from both labor and management.

What Tactics Can Labor Use Against Management?

Labor has several **tactics**, or ways it can achieve change, against management. These include strikes, **picketing**, closed shops, and boycotts. A strike is the strongest weapon labor has. It is the refusal to work until its demands are met. Picketing is a way of informing the public. Workers carry signs explaining why their employer is unfair or why they are on strike. The pickets hope that the public will support them by not buying the company's products. They also hope that other workers will support them by not **crossing the picket line**, or taking jobs of striking workers.

Labor favors a **closed shop**. A closed shop is a business that is closed to nonunion workers. Workers must be members of the union before they are hired. Sometimes unions try to put pressure on management to settle a dispute by organizing a **boycott**. A boycott is a refusal to buy. Labor hopes that if consumers do not buy a company's products, it can pressure management to give in to its demands.

What Tactics Can Management Use Against Labor?

Management has several tactics it can use against labor. These include hiring strikebreakers, a **lockout**, injunctions, and an open shop. Workers go on strike hoping that they can stop management from providing goods and services. If management hires replacements for the workers, production can continue. Not surprisingly, strikers dislike the strikebreakers. They call them **scabs**.

Sometimes management closes the doors to the place of work and keeps the workers from entering until an agreement is reached. This is called a lockout. Management hopes that if the workers do not receive any wages, they will be more willing to accept its demands.

Injunctions are court orders. Management often has been successful in getting the courts to issue injunctions ordering strikers back to work. Injunctions have been used against striking teachers, police, or firefighters. Management favors an **open shop** to a closed shop. In an open shop, workers can still work even if they do not join the union.

Tactic

A way to achieve change or a goal

Picketing

A way of informing the public about worker grievances; workers carry signs explaining why their employer is unfair or why they are on strike

Crossing the picket line

When a worker takes the job of another worker who is on strike

Closed shop

A business closed to nonunion workers

Boycott

A refusal to buy something in hopes that it pressures a company to give in to worker demands

Lockout

When management closes the doors to the place of work and keeps the workers from entering until an agreement is reached

Scab

Another name for strikebreakers or replacement workers

Open shop

Workers can work for a company even if they do not join the union

Economics at Work

Labor Relations Consultant

Labor relations consultants work for employers who want to maintain good relations with their employees. They may serve as a link between management and workers to avoid or clear up misunderstandings. They may work with human resources employees to improve working conditions or to pose compromises for change. Labor relations consultants often help employers to resolve worker grievances.

In some cases, labor relations consultants may create programs to improve communication between employers and employees. They may provide training for both employers and employees to ensure an ongoing harmony in the workplace. As changes occur, they can give important advice to both major parties in the workplace. Many labor relations consultants are hired to solve problems. They might not have long-term work with the employer whose need for their services is short-term. Employment or labor groups may hire labor relations consultants for help in putting together employer policies.

Word Bank

arbitrator

boycott

grievance

mediator

scabs

Lesson 3 Review On a separate sheet of paper, write the word from the Word Bank to complete each sentence.

1. A neutral third person who suggests ways to reach agreement is a(n) _____.

2. A neutral third person whose decisions labor and management agree to accept is a(n) _____.

3. A complaint about the treatment of a worker on the job is a(n) _____.

4. Union members sometimes call strikebreakers _____.

5. A refusal to buy a business's products or services is a(n) _____.

What do you think

6. Which labor tactic do you think is most effective in having union demands met?

7. Why do you think management wants to encourage nonunion workers to work in the business?

Yellow dog contract

Contracts some employers forced workers to sign that made the workers promise not to join a union

The United States government has passed many regulations, or laws dealing with labor. Before World War I, the government often sided with management. Federal courts usually supported management. Courts agreed that businesses could fire workers for union activity. They viewed workers banding together in unions in the same way as businesses banding together in monopolies. They thought both were a "restraint of trade." The courts began to apply the Sherman Antitrust Act to both businesses and labor unions.

The 1930s and the Great Depression changed many things. Production fell. There were many people out of work. Many people lost their homes and businesses. To get the economy moving again, Congress passed new laws. Some of the laws helped labor unions. After World War II, some people believed that unions had become too strong. Congress then passed new laws to limit the power of unions.

What 1930s Laws Were Passed to Help Unions?

One of management's strongest tactics was its use of injunctions. The Norris-LaGuardia Act of 1932 cut down on the use of injunctions. It also ended the use of **yellow dog contracts**. These were contracts some employers forced workers to sign before they would hire them. In them, the workers promised not to join the union. If they joined the union later, they would be fired for not following the contract they had signed.

In 1935, Congress passed the National Labor Relations Act. It gave workers the right to join unions. The act reversed the views of the federal government toward collective bargaining. It said that employers had to bargain with their workers. Companies no longer could threaten workers or fire union members. Unions were allowed to talk with workers and encourage them to join the union. The act set up the National Labor Relations Board (NLRB) to hear complaints from workers. Workers who believed they were treated unfairly could file a complaint with the NLRB. The NLRB also hosted elections among workers to find out if they wanted to belong to a union.

Time-and-a-half

Money earned for working more than 40 hours per week; the hourly wage, plus half of the hourly wage

Union shop

A company that allows nonunion workers to be hired if they join the union

Right-to-work law

A law that is against forcing a worker to join a union

In 1938, Congress passed the Fair Labor Standards Act. It set up a minimum wage of 25 cents per hour. Workers who worked more than 40 hours per week were paid **time-and-a-half**. This means they were paid their hourly wage, plus half of their hourly wage. The minimum wage has been increased over the years. In 2003, the minimum wage was $5.15 per hour.

How Has Congress Tried to Limit the Power of Unions Since World War II?

About 4.6 million American workers went on strike in 1946. The public was scared. Congress responded by passing the Taft-Hartley Act of 1947. It prevented employees from taking part in unfair labor practices. It outlawed the closed shop. The act did allow the **union shop**. A union shop allows nonunion workers to be hired if they join the union. A key part of the law gives the president special powers. The president can delay strikes for 80 days if "national health or safety" is threatened. Another part of the law allows states to pass **right-to-work laws**. These laws exist in 22 states. (Indiana also has this law, but it is for school workers only.) Right-to-work laws make it against the law to require a worker to join a union. Figure 10.1 shows in which states these laws exist.

Figure 10.1 **States with Right-to-Work Laws**

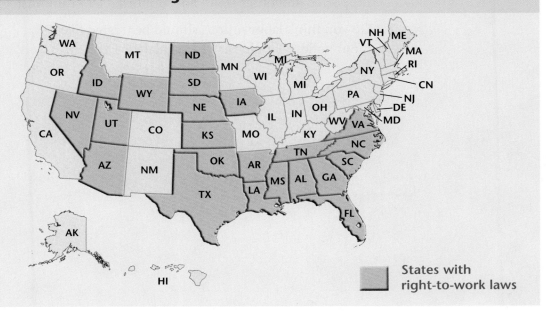

States with right-to-work laws

In 1959, Congress passed a law to make unions more democratic and to reduce illegal acts. This law is called the Landrum-Griffin Act. It required unions to hold regular elections. Union leaders were forced to show financial records to their members. They were not allowed to borrow large sums of money from the union. Ex-prisoners and communists were not allowed to be union leaders.

Lesson 4 Review On a separate sheet of paper, write the word from the Word Bank to complete each sentence.

Word Bank

Great Depression

minimum wage

National Labor
Relations Act

right-to-work law

yellow dog
contract

1. A contract forcing workers to promise not to join a union was a _____.

2. Production fell during the _____ of the 1930s.

3. The _____ of 1935 gave workers the right to join unions.

4. The Fair Labor Standards Act of 1938 set up a _____.

5. A law that makes it illegal to require a worker to join a union is a _____.

What do you think

6. Why do you think the U.S. government has sometimes supported and other times not supported labor unions?

7. Do you think labor unions should be treated like monopolies? Should they be regulated? Explain.

Outsource

Sending work to an outside source, such as another country, to cut costs

Writing About Economics

Many workers belong to labor unions. Find someone you know who belongs to one. Then ask the person about the advantages and disadvantages of belonging to a union. Write a paragraph about what you learned.

Why Is Union Membership Dropping?

Union membership is falling. Unions lost 280,000 members in 2002. As late as 1983, 20.7 percent of the labor force were union members. By 2002, the percentage had dropped to 13.2. Several reasons explain the decline.

Labor leaders cite job losses in manufacturing, construction, hotels, restaurants, and the airlines. These are all jobs that are heavily unionized. Since 2001, the United States has lost 1.85 million manufacturing jobs. This really has impacted union membership. In 1991, there were 4 million union members in manufacturing. Now there are fewer than 2.5 million. New technology, such as computers and robots, has replaced some workers. Young people today need to learn the skills to work with the new technology if they want to have high-paying jobs.

Another reason for the decline is the changing labor market. There is a growing number of workers who work part-time jobs. There are more women workers and teenage workers. These workers often have a negative view of unions and are less likely to join. The service sector of the economy is growing while the manufacturing section is shrinking. Office workers and service people are less likely to join a union.

Management has fought unions by offering employees wages and working conditions similar to union shops. The companies offer workers benefits. They sometimes allow representatives of labor to take part in the decision-making process.

The shift in jobs to other countries is another reason for the decline in union membership. Many large corporations **outsource** work to cheaper labor markets in other countries. Outsourcing is sending work to an outside source to cut costs. Financial services companies say they plan to send 500,000 U.S. jobs to foreign countries in the next five years.

U.S. technology firms are also sending a lot of their work overseas. They now pay foreign companies $10 billion a year to handle data entry, analysis, customer service, and computer programming. Overseas workers generally are paid far less than Americans. For example, a call center employee in the United States makes about $20,000. A person doing the same work in India earns only $2,700.

Figure 10.2	Average Computer Programmer Salaries Across Countries
United States	$63,331
Canada	$28,174
Ireland	$23,000 to $34,000
Israel	$15,000 to $38,000
China	$8,952
Malaysia	$7,200
Philippines	$6,564
India	$5,880
Russian Federation	$5,000 to $7,500
Poland and Hungary	$4,800 to $8,000

Lesson 5 Review On a separate sheet of paper, write the letter of the answer that correctly completes each sentence.

1. Sending work to an outside source is _____.

   A contracting

   B expensive

   C illegal

   D outsourcing

2. Many union jobs in _____ have been lost.

   A manufacturing

   B nonunion shops

   C open shops

   D politics

3. Women and teens often have a _____ view of unions and are less likely to join them.

   A favorable

   B negative

   C neutral

   D positive

4. Office workers and _____ are less likely than factory workers to join a union.

   A athletes

   B manufacturing workers

   C miners

   D service workers

5. Overseas workers often are paid _____ Americans doing the same work.

   A exactly the same as

   B far less than

   C far more than

   D slightly more than

What do you think ?

6. Do you think you will join a union when you enter the labor force? Explain.

7. Why might an increasing number of part-time workers decrease the number of union members?

Uniting America's Workforce—The Music of Joe Hill

In the early 1900s, Joe Hill joined the Industrial Workers of the World (IWW), a group of labor activists. He supported their belief to give business profits to the workers and not to the wealthy business owners. Hill had worked in the dangerous jobs the IWW was fighting against. He used his experiences to write songs to boost the spirits of workers. He wrote lyrics to the music of popular tunes so that people would easily remember his songs. Hill's songs became anthems for struggling workers everywhere. The following song is an example of his lyrics.

Workers of the World, Awaken!

Workers of the world, awaken!
Break your chains, demand your rights.
All the wealth you make is taken
By exploiting parasites.
Shall you kneel in deep submission
From your cradles to your graves?
Is the height of your ambition
To be good and willing slaves?

Arise, ye prisoners of starvation!
Fight for your own emancipation;
Arise, ye slaves of ev'ry nation,
in One Union Grand.

Our little ones for bread are crying;
And millions are from hunger dying;
The end the means is justifying,
'Tis the final stand.

If the workers take a notion,
They can stop all speeding trains;
Every ship upon the ocean
They can tie with mighty chains;
Every wheel in the creation,
Every mine and every mill,
Fleets and armies of the nation,
Will at their command stand still.

Join the union, fellow workers,
Men and women, side by side;
We will crush the greedy shirkers
Like a sweeping, surging tide;
For united we are standing,
But divided we will fall;
Let this be our understanding—
"All for one and one for all."

Document-Based Questions

1. Who was Joe Hill?

2. What is the main idea of "Workers of the World, Awaken!"?

3. In paragraph three of the song, what does Hill say the workers can achieve?

4. Why do you think workers liked Joe Hill's music?

5. Do you think songs are still a good way to spread a message? Explain.

- Around 1900, workers began to organize labor unions to improve working conditions and raise wages.

- The first labor organization was the National Labor Union, founded in 1866. The Knights of Labor was organized in 1869.

- Terence V. Powderly's leadership was one reason for the early success of the Knights of Labor. Another reason was a series of successful strikes against railroad pay cuts. By 1917, the goals of skilled and unskilled workers were too different, and the Knights broke up.

- The Homestead Strike in Pennsylvania resulted in the first major union defeat.

- Mother Jones organized a labor march in 1903. Pauline Newman helped organize the ILGWU.

- The U.S. government was against early labor unions. Later, the government supported unions. Recently, the government has limited the power of unions.

- In 1886, Samuel Gompers organized the AFL. It gathered independent craft unions into a larger group. It helped achieve higher wages, shorter hours, and laws against child labor.

- The CIO broke away from the AFL in 1938. It represented autoworkers, meatpackers, miners, and other industrial unions.

- The AFL and CIO merged in 1955. The AFL-CIO uses collective bargaining. During contract talks, management and labor must compromise. A mediator may suggest solutions, or an arbitrator may order a decision.

- Contract issues include wages, benefits, working conditions, and clear job duties. Job security and a grievance process are also important.

- Labor can use strikes, picketing, closed shops, and boycotts against management. Management can use strikebreakers, lockouts, injunctions, open shops, and other tactics against labor.

- Before the Great Depression, government sided with businesses. After the depression, the government supported unions. Congress passed labor laws including the Norris-LaGuardia Act, the National Labor Relations Act, and the Fair Labor Standards Act.

- After World War II, closed shops were outlawed. Congress passed other laws to reduce illegal acts in unions and make them more democratic.

- Currently, union membership has been dropping. Job losses and new technology have eliminated some jobs. Outsourcing also has added to the loss of union jobs.

Chapter 10 REVIEW

On a separate sheet of paper, write the word from the Word Bank to complete each sentence.

1. In 1903, _____ led a parade of children who had been injured by mill machinery.

2. In 1909, _____ became an organizer for the ILGWU, representing workers in women's clothing factories.

3. In 1869, _____ organized the Knights of Labor to "unite men and women of every craft, creed, and color."

4. In 1886, _____ organized the AFL.

5. Representatives of labor and management try to reach contract agreement during _____.

6. A way for workers to inform the public about their issues is by _____.

7. Court orders stopping strikes are called _____.

Word Bank

collective bargaining

injunctions

Mother Jones

Pauline Newman

picketing

Samuel Gompers

Terence V. Powderly

On a separate sheet of paper, write the letter of the answer that correctly completes each sentence.

8. In the 1860s, "equal pay for equal work" for men and women was a(n) _____ idea.

A accepted   **C** popular

B happy   **D** radical

9. By 1910, one in five factory workers was a(n) _____.

A African-American teenager   **C** man

B child   **D** woman

10. Samuel Gompers believed in improving _____, not in political reform.

A electrical connections   **C** working conditions

B machines   **D** workers' speech

11. In reaching an agreement, labor and management must
_____.

   A argue   **C** compromise

   B picket   **D** get an injunction

12. Labor favors a(n) _____, which is a factory closed to
nonunion workers.

   A closed shop   **C** lockout

   B contract   **D** open shop

13. The first _____, set in 1938, was 25 cents per hour.

   A maximum wage   **C** pay raise

   B minimum wage   **D** pay schedule

On a separate sheet of paper, write answers to the following
questions. Use complete sentences.

14. Before World War I, how did federal courts support
businesses against labor?

15. Explain why union membership has dropped.

16. What is the purpose of strikebreakers?

17. List two tactics management can use against labor.

On a separate sheet of paper, write your opinion to each
question. Use complete sentences.

18. Do you think labor unions are good or bad? Why?

19. Which rights would be most important to you as a
worker? Explain.

20. How do you think declining union membership affects
the economy?

Test-Taking Tip

If you do not know the meaning of a word in a question, read the
question to yourself, leaving out the word. Then see if you can
figure out the meaning of the word from its use in the sentence.

Unit 3

Understanding Payroll Deductions

Employees have money taken out of their paycheck for taxes, insurance, and other fees. These are called deductions. Gross pay is the actual amount that the person is paid. For example, if the worker earns $10 an hour and works a 40 hour week, that worker's gross pay is $400 a week. Net pay is often called "take-home pay." This is the amount received after deductions.

Think about the pay and deductions for working in a beginning position at Highline Manufacturing. For each of the percentages shown in Figure U3.1 below, the worker can figure out the amount in advance. For example, the figure for State Income Tax can be found by multiplying pay times 0.05 for 5 percent ($500 $\times$ 0.05 = $25).

The worker can figure out each of the percentages by multiplying that percentage times the amount of gross pay.

Study Figure U3.1 on this page, then answer the following questions.

1. The first deduction taken, before taxes are computed, is for health insurance. What is the amount of the remaining pay?

2. What is the amount of money deducted for Medicare?

3. What is the amount of money deducted for Social Security?

4. What is the employee's weekly net pay?

5. If the Highline employee received a $50 weekly raise, which of the deductions would remain the same cash amount?

Figure U3.1

Average Gross Wage Per Week at Highline Manufacturing: $500

Employee Health Insurance	$35
Federal Income Tax Deduction	15%
Medicare	1.5%
Social Security	6.5%
State Income Tax	5%

Unit 3 SUMMARY

- Entrepreneurs start many businesses each year. Entrepreneurs need a product idea, technical know-how, potential customers, and money.

- The three categories of businesses are sole proprietorships, partnerships, and corporations.

- The circular flow model shows how businesses, consumers, and governments work together. The model helps show how a change in one part of the economy affects the other parts.

- The U.S. labor force includes people who are at least 16 years old, are working or looking for work, or belong to the armed forces.

- The agricultural, manufacturing/construction, and service sectors make up the labor force.

- Currently, nearly half the labor force consists of women. More minorities have entered the workforce and own their own businesses.

- Labor supply and demand and other factors affect wages. Along with wages, modern workers expect benefits.

- Working conditions were poor as manufacturing spread in the 1880s. These conditions led to efforts to improve workers' lives.

- The Progressives favored laws to improve working people's lives.

- Franklin Roosevelt's New Deal had three goals: relief, recovery, reform.

- The Civil Rights Act helped workers by ending job discrimination. ADA outlaws discrimination based on physical or mental handicaps.

- Congress created OSHA to enforce workplace health and safety laws.

- Early labor unions included the National Labor Union (NLU) and the Knights of Labor. Women were important early labor leaders.

- The U.S. government was against early labor unions and supported businesses.

- The AFL was a craft union. The CIO was an industrial union. It broke away from the AFL. The unions merged in 1955, forming the AFL-CIO.

- To reach a contract, labor and management use collective bargaining.

- Labor may use strikes, picketing, closed shops, and boycotts against management.

- Management may use strikebreakers, lockouts, injunctions, and open shops against labor.

- After the Great Depression, Congress passed laws that helped unions.

- Current union membership is falling because of technology, a shift to service jobs, outsourcing, and other reasons.

"A free market economy works well only when the participants—producers, consumers, savers, investors—have the information they need to make intelligent decisions. People need to understand what banks do and how to deal with them; . . . why saving is important and what instruments are available for saving; . . . Most important, participants in the economy need to know how to think about the economic choices they face and how to get the information they need. . . ."

–Alice M. Rivlin, Vice Chair, Board of Governors of the Federal Reserve System (*Rivlin delivered this keynote speech on May 13, 1999, at the Federal Reserve Bank of Minneapolis.*)

4 Money and Banking

Ask yourself this question: How is money important? You might answer that money buys the basics of life: food, clothing, and a place to live. You also might answer that it buys things that make people happy: a trip to the movie theater, a good book, or maybe a nice meal at a restaurant.

Money is all of these things and much more. Since money is so important, it has to be managed. A bank is one way. Have you ever opened a savings or checking account? If so, the photo to the left might look familiar to you. This is just one of the many services banks provide. In fact, banking in the United States is fairly complex. Many groups, including the government, work hard to keep the money system working.

This unit begins by discussing banking in the United States. Then it discusses the facts you need to know about being a good consumer and keeping track of your money. All of these are important as you begin to think about how you fit into the economic system.

11 The United States Banking System

The modern banking system began in the Middle Ages. This was about a 1,000-year period between 500 and 1500. In those days, people used mostly gold and silver coins for money. These were heavy and hard to handle. They were easily stolen. Businesses found it easier to leave their coins with the local goldsmiths. Businesses were given written receipts in exchange for the coins. Other businesses accepted the receipts for goods. They knew they could go to the goldsmiths who would buy back the receipts and give them coins. In this way, a goldsmith gave services like those of a bank today.

You may have seen a bank vault like the one shown on the opposite page. Banking today involves a lot more than just putting money into a vault. This chapter will talk about the system of money, the history of banks in the United States, and the banking system today.

Goals for Learning

◆ To explain the functions of money

◆ To identify characteristics of money

◆ To trace the history of banking in the United States

◆ To describe the United States banking system today

What Were the Earliest Forms of Money?

Barter

The trading of goods and services

Medium of exchange

The way that money serves as something that both buyers and sellers will accept

Store of value

The way that money serves as something that can be exchanged for the value of something else

Measure of prices

The way that money helps to determine how much something is worth

Long ago people did not need money. They built their own houses. They hunted for food and grew their own crops. Then people began to work in what they did best. The best farmers grew more so they could provide food for those who did not farm. The best fishers caught more fish than they needed. They provided fish for those who did not fish.

Soon people began to trade goods and services. This exchange is called **barter**. Bartering worked well only when people agreed on the value of what was traded. It was difficult to barter when the items to be traded were very different from each other. For example, the traders had to agree on how many furs might equal a metal knife. Each person had to want exactly what the other person had to offer.

To make trading easier, people began to use certain items for money. Anything could be used for money if people agreed on its value. In some parts of Africa, salt was used as money. It was valuable for keeping food fresh and for flavoring. It was hard to find salt if you lived far from the sea. American Indians used beaded belts made from purple and white clamshells for money. In some Mexican villages, people used cocoa beans as money. Tea leaves, feathers, animal teeth, and tobacco also have been used as money.

What Are the Three Functions of Money?

No matter what form money takes, it tends to play three major roles: a **medium of exchange**, **store of value**, and **measure of prices**.

For a barter economy to work well, a person must find someone who wants what that person has. The person who wants the item must be willing to trade something for it. In a money economy, people exchange goods and services for money. For example, if you work, you exchange your labor for money.

As a medium of exchange, money is something that both buyers and sellers will accept. Everyone accepts money. Businesses and other people accept money in exchange for goods and services. You can use it to buy whatever you want. Money makes exchanges much easier.

Money serves as a store of value. Suppose you are a baker. You have lots of cakes to sell. Your cakes will grow stale and spoil if they are not sold. They do not grow more valuable as they get older. You sell your cakes for cash. Unless you spend the money right away, you store the value of the cakes you sold. You are storing the cake's buying power until you need it.

Money is used as a measure of prices. Prices in the United States are set in dollars and cents. All Americans understand them. This allows people to compare the value of things. A $10 watch is cheap. A $500 coat is expensive. Imagine how difficult it would be if the prices of goods were not given in dollars and cents.

Word Bank

barter

measure of prices

medium of exchange

money

value

Lesson 1 Review On a separate sheet of paper, write the word from the Word Bank to complete each sentence.

1. An exchange of goods and services is called _____.

2. To exchange goods and services in a money economy, a _____ is needed.

3. In a money economy, the medium of exchange is _____.

4. To compare the value of things, money serves as a _____.

5. Anything might be used for money if people can agree on its _____.

What do you think

6. Why would a barter system not work well today?

7. Do you think people have the same ideas about what is cheap and what is expensive? Explain.

As we have seen, money can be anything that is accepted to pay for goods and services. To work well, money has to meet certain standards.

Why Must Money Be Stable?

Money needs to be **stable**. By stability we mean that the value of money should be about the same tomorrow as it is today. In some countries, the value of money is not stable. It changes very quickly. In these places, people quickly spend their money because they know that tomorrow it will be worth less. People have no incentive to save. This is harmful to the economy.

What Does Portability Mean?

Think how difficult it would be if money was as large and heavy as a bowling ball! Modern money is small and light. It is **portable**, or easy to carry.

Why Must Money Be Uniform?

Athletes at your school wear uniforms when playing a game. Everyone's uniform is the same. Money also is **uniform**. One $10 bill is just as valuable as another. Imagine how confusing it would be if some dollar bills were worth more than others. All money is made very carefully to make sure that bills and coins of the same amount are uniform. They always are exactly the same size, weight, and appearance.

Why Is Divisibility Important?

Divisibility means able to be divided. Not everything costs an even amount like $1.25 or 25 cents. When you buy something, you almost never need to worry about having exact change. You know that when you pay with a larger bill, you will get change back. Making change is easy because of divisibility.

Stable

The ability of money to maintain a certain value over a period of time

Portable

The ability of money to be small, light, and easy to carry

Uniform

The ability of money to have the same size, weight, appearance, and value as money of the same kind

Divisibility

The ability of money to be divided up evenly into exact change

Why Must Money Have Durability?

Durable

The ability of money to last a long time and withstand wear and decay

Imagine how difficult life would be if our money was made of a liquid. We want money to be **durable**, to be able to last a long time. Money should withstand wear and decay. Money is printed on high quality paper. Eventually it wears out. When it does, new bills replace the old ones.

Economics at Work

Bank Teller

Bank tellers handle large sums of money as they help customers with deposits and withdrawals. Tellers should be good at paying attention to details. They should have strong math skills and the ability to keep good records. Bank tellers must learn banking rules, including security and safety. It is very important that bank tellers keep customer information private.

Good bank tellers have strong people skills, including the ability to give clear instructions about bank practices. When cashing checks, tellers verify amounts, dates, and customer account balances. They are expected to balance bills, coins, and checks at the end of a work shift. They do this with the help of a calculator or computer. A growing number of inner city banks are seeking tellers who can speak Spanish.

Some bank tellers must work with foreign currency exchange rates. These tellers use daily rate sheets or a computer display. They must give information to customers about foreign exchange rules. They compute an exchange value for transactions and charge the correct fee.

Lesson 2 Review On a separate sheet of paper, write answers to the following questions. Use complete sentences.

1. What is meant by money's stability?

2. What is portability of money?

3. Why must money be uniform?

4. Why should money be divisible?

5. What is meant by money's durability?

What do you think ?

6. According to the text, money should be stable, portable, uniform, divisible, and durable. What might happen if one of these were missing from money?

7. All American bills are the same size and color, but other countries use different sizes and colors for their bills. Which system would you prefer? Why?

What Money Was Used in the Early History of America?

Explorer
One who searches around a new place

Mint
A place that makes coins

In the early 1500s, **explorers** from many countries sailed to the Americas. An explorer's goal is to search around a new place. By 1650, Spain, France, the Netherlands, and England had set up colonies in the New World. The early settlers traded fish, furs, and lumber for European goods or money. European coins then could be used to buy colonial goods.

Besides coins, the settlers used other forms of payment. The early colonists used tobacco and animal skins to pay their bills and taxes. Each of the 13 colonies printed their own paper money. Trading became difficult because there were so many different types of money being used. The money system lacked many of the things listed in Lesson 2. That system was not stable or uniform.

When Did the United States First Begin to Use Dollars?

In 1789, George Washington was elected the first president of the United States. In 1792, Washington and Congress set up a new money system for the country. Congress agreed that all of the states would use the new money system. This new system would have the dollar as the basic unit. Each dollar had 100 cents.

A **mint** opened in Philadelphia in 1792. A mint is a place that makes coins. This mint made coins of gold, silver, and copper. The value of the coins was based on their weight.

When Did the First Banks Begin in the United States?

Before the United States won its independence, there were only four banks. By 1811, there were about 100 banks. All but one were state banks. State banks are given the right to organize by the states, not by the federal government. They all were privately owned.

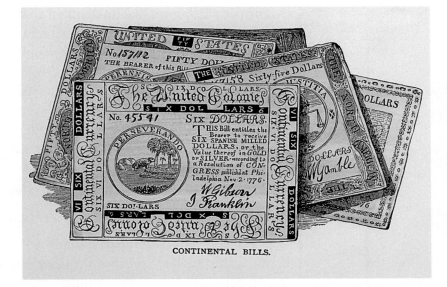

CONTINENTAL BILLS.

Early American money came in many forms. This paper money was in use during the American Revolution.

The state banks printed their own paper money. This caused many problems. Money issued by one bank might not be accepted by other banks. The money was supposed to be backed by silver and gold coins. This means that someone could exchange the money for gold or silver. However, many banks printed so much money that there was not enough gold and silver to back it. When people tried to turn in their money for gold, some of the banks did not have enough gold to cover it. Many banks failed. Thousands of people were stuck with worthless paper money.

In 1791, the U.S. government organized the First Bank of the United States. It was the largest and most powerful bank in the United States. The bank collected fees and made payments for the government in Washington, D.C. But there still was no official national paper money. The charter was renewed for the Bank of the United States in 1816.

Many people did not like the Bank of the U.S. Some people believed it was too large and powerful. President Andrew Jackson thought that a few wealthy people controlled the Bank. He thought it favored rich and powerful people. To weaken it, he spoke out against the bank and refused to renew its charter in 1832. He removed all government money from it and **deposited**, or put, the money into smaller state-chartered banks. Many of these banks were careless and made loans to people who never paid them back. This led to an economic depression called the Panic of 1837.

What Banking Problems Developed in the 1860s?

The United States broke apart in the 1860s. The two sides fought a war against each other called the Civil War. When the Civil War broke out in 1861, both sides printed paper money to pay their bills. The northern states were called the Union. The southern states were called the Confederacy. Union money was black on one side and green on the other. It quickly became known as **greenbacks**. Although the money was not backed by gold or silver, it was **legal tender**. This means it was legal **currency**, or money, that had to be accepted in payment of a debt. People were worried because they were not sure the greenbacks had any value.

The Confederacy did not have good banks and was soon unable to borrow money from Europe to pay for the war. The only way to solve the problem was to begin printing paper money. The Confederacy printed so many Confederate dollars that the dollars began to lose value. Soon they were worth almost nothing. Today, their only value is to collectors.

How Did Congress Try to Reform Banking?

In 1863, Congress passed the National Banking Act. This act set up a system of national banks. The government inspected each bank to make sure each was stable. The government hoped that by setting high standards for the banks, people would feel good about using the banks. The national banks were allowed to print official money, which was good anywhere in the country. The government promised to allow the printing of no more money than it had gold or silver to back it.

What Is Meant by the Gold Standard?

In 1900, Congress passed the Gold Standard Act. It set the value of the dollar to a certain amount of gold. A person could go to the U.S. Treasury and exchange their dollars for gold. It made people feel safer because they knew they could cash in their paper money for gold. It also limited the government from printing more paper money than it had gold or silver to back it.

A gold standard also has disadvantages. Because gold is scarce, the amount of money in use is limited. This slows growth in the economy. In 1934, the United States started to go off the gold standard. Today, U.S. Treasury **securities** back all American money. Securities are things that show ownership of something or proof of debt. Examples are bonds, gold certificates, notes, drafts, and bills of exchange.

 **Biography**

A. P. Giannini: 1870–1949

Amadeo Peter Giannini was born in California. He left school at age 13 to join his father's food business. In 1904, he started the Bank of Italy in San Francisco, lending funds from his father-in-law's estate. A great earthquake shook the city in 1906. On the morning of the quake, Giannini pulled a fruit cart through the streets, under which he had hidden $2 million rescued from his bank. Using an old waterfront shed, he set up the only bank in the wrecked city.

Giannini set up the Bank of America National Trust and Savings Association in 1930. His bank made loans to California fruit growers and filmmakers. By the time of Giannini's death, the Bank of America was the largest unincorporated bank in the world. It was worth more than $6 billion. Giannini gave large amounts of money to medical research and education.

Lesson 3 Review On a separate sheet of paper, write the letter of the answer that correctly completes each sentence.

1. The _____ was organized in 1791 as the largest and most powerful bank.

   A Bank America   **C** First Federal Bank

   B First Bank of the   **D** First National Bank
   United States

2. Each of the 13 American colonies originally printed their own _____.

   A coins   **C** shirts

   B money   **D** stickers

3. President _____ refused to renew the charter of the Bank of the United States.

   A Andrew Jackson   **C** Abraham Lincoln

   B Andrew Johnson   **D** Alexander Hamilton

4. Legal currency that must be accepted to pay a debt is called _____ tender.

   A fake   **C** golden

   B forged   **D** legal

5. The _____ Act set the dollar's value as a certain amount of gold.

   A Golden Rule   **C** Money

   B Gold Standard   **D** Silver Currency

What do you think ?

6. What might happen if every state still printed its own money? How might that affect the economy?

7. Why might the gold standard limit the growth of an economy?

Commercial bank

A bank whose main function is to receive deposits and make short-term loans

Thrift institution

A loan company, mutual savings bank, or credit union

Savings and loan company

A company that allows people to put money in an account and to borrow money, often to buy a home

Mutual savings bank

A bank that accepts smaller deposits than commercial banks

Credit union

A company that provides low-cost loans and savings accounts; members own and run the credit union

Government law defines what a bank is. Banks are "financial institutions that accept deposits and make commercial loans." The term "bank" really refers to a **commercial bank**. A commercial bank is a bank whose main business is to take in deposits and give out short-term loans. However, today when people talk about banks, they may mean any business that provides financial services.

There are some businesses that provide some of the same services as banks. These are called **thrift institutions**. Examples are **savings and loan companies**, **mutual savings banks**, and **credit unions**. Savings and loan companies began in the 1800s. They allow people to put money in an account and to borrow money. When savings and loan companies first began, they often were used to get loans to build a home. Mutual savings banks also began in the 1800s. They accept smaller deposits than commercial banks. Credit unions provide low-cost loans and savings accounts. Members actually own and run the credit unions. Often credit union members are part of a large business or labor union.

What Are the Main Services Banks Provide?

Banks accept and hold deposits. People know that putting money in the bank is safer than keeping it in their homes. The bank protects against theft and fire. The government insures deposits up to $100,000.

Banks collect and transfer funds. Banks offer checking accounts to both businesses and individuals. The purpose of a checking account is convenience. Most people use checks instead of cash to pay their bills. When you write a check to a store, the store deposits it in its own checking account. It is then sent to your bank. Your bank subtracts the amount of the check from your account.

Banks usually send monthly **statements** to all of their customers. These statements show the checks that have been written and subtracted from the account. It is important to keep track of how much money is in the account. If there is not enough money to cover the check, this is called an **overdraft**. Some people also refer to this as "bouncing" a check. The check is returned to the bank and the customer has to pay a fee. Persons who write bad checks will hurt their **credit rating** and may have to go to jail. A credit rating shows how well someone can manage their money and pay off debts and bills.

Banks make loans. When people and businesses need money, banks lend it to them. Banks cannot lend out all the money deposited with them. Depositors know that they have the right to take out their money at any time. Most of the time, people prefer to keep the money in the bank. Banks can lend out almost all of their deposits and still meet the demands of depositors who want to withdraw their money.

One of the main services banks provide is checking accounts. Writing a check is one of the most common ways to pay for things, especially for paying bills.

Figure 11.1 **Other Bank Services**

Brokerage	This is the selling of stocks and bonds. Only a small number of banks are brokers.
Consulting	Banks have many experts when it comes to money issues. Some banks give advice about money matters to other businesses.
Foreign currency exchange	Most countries and some larger regions of the world have their own system of money. For example, many European countries use the euro. The yen is used in Japan. The pound is used in the United Kingdom. Businesses that buy and sell goods among other countries need foreign currency. People traveling to another country also may need some local currency to pay for goods and services. As a service to customers, some banks exchange local money for foreign currency.
Insurance	In some states, banks can sell life insurance to customers. Life insurance is a plan where a person pays money to a company. When the person dies, the person's family receives money.
Investments	Banks can buy government bonds. They can sell these bonds to customers for a profit.
Letters of credit	For a fee, some banks will provide this service to businesses. The letter states that the bank will promise payment of money on behalf of the business when certain conditions are met. This often is used when a company deals with a company in another country.
Safe-deposit boxes	Often banks offer safe-deposit boxes in their vault. People can use these boxes to keep things of value safe.
Trusts	A trust is when a bank keeps and manages funds for people or businesses. The bank provides this service for a fee.
Underwriting	Companies or government groups can raise money from selling shares of stocks or bonds. Underwriting is when experts at a bank help with this task.

Reserve

A percentage of money from deposits that a bank must keep around in case the money is needed

Internet banking

Banking by computer

Banks must keep a part of their deposits on hand in case the money is needed. This money is called the bank's **reserves**. The reserves the bank needs are always stated as a percentage of a bank's total deposits. Suppose a bank had deposits of $1 million and the reserve is set at 15 percent. This means that the bank could loan out up to $850,000. The bank must hold onto the remaining $150,000.

What Is Internet Banking?

Internet banking is banking by computer. The computer is connected to a bank Web site on the Internet. People can have their paychecks added electronically to their checking accounts. As a consumer, you can use Internet banking to see how much money is in your account. You can see if a check has cleared. You can see when bills are due and pay them. You can transfer funds and you can apply for a loan.

Many banks sell securities and insurance online. No actual money changes hands. Everything is recorded by computer. Banks can transfer electronic money anywhere in the world. The main benefit is that you can do these things anytime you want to. Home computers allow people to do their banking without leaving their homes.

Economics in Your Life

On the Money

Paper money in the United States today comes in seven different bills: $1, $2, $5, $10, $20, $50, and $100. Before 1946, there were four other bills: $500, $1,000, $5,000, and $10,000. Before 1929, several other types of paper money were in use. Some examples include National Bank notes, gold certificates, and silver certificates. The largest note ever printed was the $100,000 Gold Certificate, Series 1934.

The $2 and $100 notes are probably less familiar to most people. Here are some facts about each:

• President Thomas Jefferson is pictured on the front of the $2 bill. The first $2 note came to be on June 25, 1776, upon approval of the American Continental Congress. The $2 bill has since had many new designs, with the latest coming in 1996.

• Pictured on the front of the $100 bill is American statesman and inventor Benjamin Franklin. As of 2003, of the over $659 billion total currency in use around the world, over $469 billion was in $100 bills.

Word Bank

commercial bank

computer

deposit

reserves

thrift institutions

Lesson 4 Review On a separate sheet of paper, write the word from the Word Bank to complete each sentence.

1. The amount of money a bank must keep on hand is called its _____.

2. Banking by _____ uses the Internet.

3. Putting money in a bank for safekeeping is called a _____.

4. The main function of a _____ is to receive deposits and make short-term loans.

5. Savings and loan associations, credit unions, and mutual savings banks are _____.

What do you think ?

6. What do you think is the main advantage of Internet banking? the main disadvantage?

7. Why do you think having the government insure bank deposits is important?

Franklin D. Roosevelt's 1933 Inaugural Speech

When United States President Franklin D. Roosevelt gave his inaugural speech on March 4, 1933, the world was in the middle of the Great Depression. People were out of money. Jobs were scarce. Banks were in crisis. The outlook was grim, but Roosevelt urged Americans to think positive. He gave a plan for recovery in his speech.

We face our common difficulties. They concern . . . only material things. Values have shrunken to fantastic levels; taxes have risen; our ability to pay has fallen; government of all kinds is faced by serious curtailment [decrease] of income; the means of exchange are frozen in the currents of trade; . . . farmers find no markets for their produce; the savings of many years in thousands of families are gone.

More important, a host of unemployed citizens face the grim problem of existence, and an equally great number toil with little return. Only a foolish optimist can deny the dark realities of the moment. . . .

Our greatest primary task is to put people to work. . . . It can be [done] in part by . . . accomplishing greatly needed projects to stimulate and reorganize the use of our natural resources. . . .

We must act and act quickly. . . .

. . . [T]here must be a strict supervision of all banking and credit and investments; there must be an end to speculation with other people's money, and there must be provision for an adequate but sound currency. . . .

I am prepared under my constitutional duty to recommend the measures that a stricken nation in the midst of a stricken world may require. . . .

But in the event that the Congress shall fail, . . . and in the event that the national emergency is still critical, . . . I shall ask the Congress for . . . broad executive power to wage a war against the emergency. . . .

Document-Based Questions

1. Describe the situation of the world in 1933.

2. What were five common difficulties Americans were facing, according to Roosevelt's speech?

3. What did Roosevelt say was the government's greatest task?

4. How did Roosevelt want to change the banking system?

5. Do you think the words of this speech were important to the American people? Explain.

- People first used barter to get goods and services. The modern banking system began during the Middle Ages. People first used silver and gold coins as money. Other forms of money included salt, beaded belts, and other valuable items.

- Money is a medium of exchange, a store of value, and a measure of prices. Money must be stable, portable, uniform, divisible, and durable.

- Early settlers in North America used coins and other goods for trade. However, no standard money system existed.

- In 1791, the First Bank of the United States opened. The Bank's charter was renewed in 1816. In 1792, President Washington and the U.S. Congress set up a money system using dollars and cents. That same year, a mint opened in Philadelphia to make coins.

- Most early U.S. banks were privately-owned state banks. Each bank issued its own money, causing problems for trade.

- President Andrew Jackson refused to renew the charter for the Bank of the United States in 1832. He believed it favored rich and powerful people. His removal of government money from the bank led to the Panic of 1837.

- During the U.S. Civil War, the Union and Confederacy had their own banks. When the Confederacy became unable to borrow money, it printed more paper money. The money lost value.

- Congress tried to reform banking during the Civil War by passing the National Banking Act. The act set up a system of national banks.

- The gold standard set the value of dollars to a certain amount of gold. The United States started to go off the gold standard in 1934.

- A bank really is a commercial bank. It receives deposits and makes short-term loans. Savings and loan companies, mutual savings banks, and credit unions are thrift institutions.

- The U.S. government insures bank deposits up to $100,000. Checking accounts often are used instead of cash to pay bills. If a checking account does not have enough money to cover a check, the check is returned to the bank.

- Banks cannot loan out all of their money. They must keep a certain percentage of their deposits in reserve.

- Banking by computer is Internet banking. Internet banking's main benefit is that people can do their banking at home.

Chapter 11 REVIEW

On a separate sheet of paper, write the word from the Word Bank to complete each sentence.

Word Bank

check

divisible

Gold Standard Act

greenbacks

Middle Ages

silver and gold coins

stable

1. The banking system began during the _____.

2. _____ were originally used for money, but they were heavy and hard to handle.

3. _____ were so called because they were green on one side and black on the other.

4. _____ means able to be divided.

5. _____ means having about the same value today as tomorrow.

6. The _____ set the value of a dollar based on an amount of gold.

7. An overdraft occurs if an account does not have enough money to pay for a _____.

On a separate sheet of paper, write the letter of the answer that correctly completes each sentence.

8. In a _____ economy, people trade one item for another.
   A barter
   B capitalist
   C weak
   D strong

9. In a _____ economy, people exchange goods and services for money.
   A barter
   B communist
   C money
   D traditional

10. One way to give money _____ is to print it on high-quality paper.
    A durability
    B compatibility
    C possibility
    D suitability

11. The U.S. government opened the first _____ in 1792, in Pennsylvania.

   A economy   **C** mint

   B gold mine   **D** session of Congress

12. When early U.S. banks failed, many people were stuck with worthless _____.

   A silver   **C** paper money

   B gold   **D** food

13. One service that banks provide is to _____ funds.

   A collect and transfer   **C** improve and correct

   B design   **D** transmit and continue

On a separate sheet of paper, write answers to the following questions. Use complete sentences.

14. Describe what happens when you write a check to a store.

15. Describe one way money acts as a store of value.

16. List three characteristics of money.

17. Describe how the National Banking Act of 1863 reformed banking.

On a separate sheet of paper, write your opinion to each question. Use complete sentences.

18. Why might a strong banking system be necessary for an economy?

19. Do you think the world will ever stop using cash and move to another money system? Explain.

20. Is it better for the economy if people spend their money or save it? Explain.

Test-Taking Tip

You may have to choose the correct ending to a sentence on a test. If so, combine the first part of the sentence with each ending. Then choose the one that best completes the statement.

12

The Federal Reserve System

The United States government created the Federal Reserve System to manage the nation's money. By managing the money well, the Federal Reserve helps to protect the value of the dollar. Nicknamed the "Fed," the Federal Reserve is the nation's central bank. The photo to the left shows the Federal Reserve building in Washington, D.C.

This chapter will discuss why the Fed was created, how it works, and what it does.

Goals for Learning

◆ To explain why the Federal Reserve System was created

◆ To describe the organization of the Federal Reserve System

◆ To identify the main functions of the Federal Reserve System

◆ To describe how the Federal Reserve System regulates the money supply

Panic

A widespread fear of financial loss

By the early 1900s, the American banking system was outdated. Bankers, business people, and leaders agreed that the system needed reform. They all wanted to make the banking system more stable. However, they could not agree on how. Some people wanted a central bank that bankers controlled. The Progressive reformers wanted government control over banking. President Woodrow Wilson sided with the Progressives. On December 23, 1913, the Federal Reserve Act was passed.

How Did the Panic of 1907 Help Create the Federal Reserve System?

In 1907, the United States experienced a **panic**. In banking terms, a panic is a widespread fear of financial loss. Serious banking problems caused the Panic of 1907. Many banks made bad loans and gave too much credit. People lost trust in banks. Many people demanded their money at the same time. The banks did not have enough cash to cover the depositors' demands. Some banks were forced to close.

The pressure on the banks caused more panic and fear. Many businesses failed. Some depositors lost all their savings. A depression followed. Remember, a depression is a period of economic hard times for the entire country.

The Panic of 1907 caused a run on banks. People wanted to withdraw their money for fear of losing it.

After the Panic of 1907, Congress created a National Monetary Commission. Its job was to find ways to prevent panics from happening again. It recommended ways to improve the banking system. People wanted to know that their banks were healthy and safe. They wanted the government to manage bank activities. The Commission's proposals led to the creation of the Federal Reserve System.

Why Is There More Than One Federal Reserve Bank?

Many countries have one central bank. At the time the Federal Reserve System was created, many people were worried about the national government having too much power. They believed that one central bank was a bad idea. For this reason, the Federal Reserve Act created a **decentralized** system. This means power was spread out. There are 12 district banks that make up the Federal Reserve System. (See Figure 12.1.)

Figure 12.1 **The 12 Federal Reserve Districts**

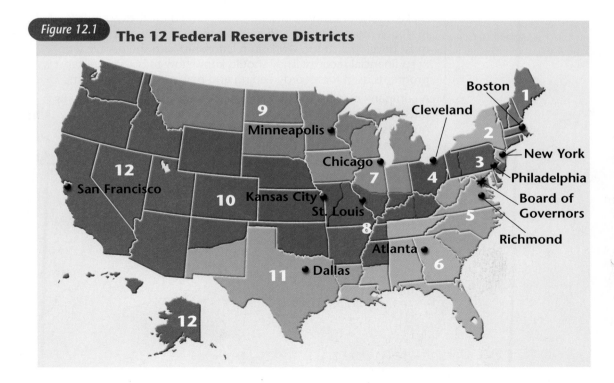

Why Is the Fed Called a "Bankers' Bank"?

The Fed is a bank for banks. It serves all banks that are members of the system. It does not serve businesses or people directly. Even though a federal law created the Fed, the government does not own it. In fact, no one really owns it. The Fed is a part of the government system. Banks in each of the 12 districts use the Fed in much the same way as people use their own banks.

Economics at Work

Auditor

Auditors review financial and accounting records for companies. An auditor's most important task is checking those records to make sure they are correct. This requires knowledge of the Generally Accepted Accounting Principles (GAAP). Auditors also make sure that accounting methods meet with federal, state, and local laws.

Good business practices usually include controls on spending. Auditors must review those controls to see whether they are being followed. Auditors may have suggestions for change to make businesses more efficient. These should make accounting methods more accurate and controls more manageable. Auditors must develop a strong working relationship with the people who keep financial records. They should know how to use computer programs used for record-keeping and making financial reports.

A company may have a staff auditor, or it may use one who works outside of the company for a number of different companies. Auditors must have accounting education and experience. In some cases, they are expected to be Certified Public Accountants.

Lesson 1 Review On a separate sheet of paper, write the letter of the answer that correctly completes each sentence.

1. A period of economic hard times for an entire country is a(n) _____.

    A depression   **C** Fed

    B panic   **D** commission

2. A widespread fear of financial loss is a _____.

    A federal system   **C** reserve

    B panic   **D** terror

3. The Federal Reserve Bank is sometimes called a _____.

    A bankers' bank   **C** panic

    B reformer   **D** district

4. President _____ and the Progressives helped pass the Federal Reserve Act of 1913.

    A Franklin Roosevelt **C** Ronald Reagan

    B George W. Bush   **D** Woodrow Wilson

5. _____ district banks make up the Federal Reserve System.

    A Four   **C** Fifty

    B Twelve   **D** Sixty-eight

What do you think ?

6. What might happen today if a panic occurred?

7. Do you think a system of bankers' banks like the Fed is needed? Why or why not?

The Federal Reserve Act created a banking system of 12 district banks across the country. The act required all national banks to become members. State banks could choose to become members. However, all banks must meet the requirements set by the Federal Reserve System. As of 2003, the Fed had about 6,000 member banks.

How Is the Federal Reserve System Set Up?

Figure 12.2 shows how the Fed is organized. A board of governors controls the system. The board makes the key decisions for the nation's banking system. There are seven people on the board of governors. They are appointed by the president of the United States but must be approved by Congress. The president also chooses two of the seven members to serve as chair and vice chair. They are appointed for a four-year term, but can be reappointed.

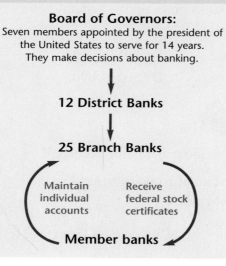

Figure 12.2

The Federal Reserve System

Board of Governors:
Seven members appointed by the president of the United States to serve for 14 years. They make decisions about banking.

↓

12 District Banks

↓

25 Branch Banks

Maintain individual accounts

Receive federal stock certificates

Member banks

To make the seven governors as independent as possible, they serve for 14 years. Normally, only one new member is chosen every other year. This allows the board to make necessary but maybe unpopular decisions. The Fed's headquarters is in Washington, D.C. This is where the board of governors meets.

The Fed has 12 regional districts. Each district has a district Federal Reserve Bank. Each district bank has its own president. The district bank carries out the Fed's policies. The larger districts also have branch banks. As of 2003, there were 25 branch banks. Although each district Federal Reserve Bank is quite independent, they all work together as a team. All share a common goal of keeping the economy stable and healthy.

Biography

Alan Greenspan: 1926–

Alan Greenspan has had many years of experience working on American economic issues. He worked on Richard Nixon's successful campaign for the presidency in 1967. In the 1970s and 1980s, he was chairman of the Council of Economic Advisers and the National Commission on Social Security Reform. He became chairman of the seven-member Federal Reserve Board in 1987.

Greenspan earned praise for his policies in the 1990s. In the late 1990s, unemployment reached a 24-year low, while inflation hit a 34-year low. Consumer confidence was the highest it had been in 30 years. Greenspan is known for the wisdom of his decisions. In his speeches and interviews, he chooses his words carefully to maintain public trust. Greenspan has worked successfully under four U.S. presidents.

Lesson 2 Review On a separate sheet of paper, write answers to the following questions. Use complete sentences.

1. As of 2003, about how many banks were members of the Federal Reserve System?

2. How many people make up the board of governors?

3. How long do the governors of the Fed serve?

4. Why do the Fed's governors serve so long?

5. What is the common goal of all the district banks in the Federal Reserve Bank?

What do you think ?

6. Do you think 14 years is too short, too long, or the right length of time for the Fed's governors to serve? Explain.

7. What do you think the text means by saying the Fed's governors may "make necessary but unpopular decisions" about the economy?

The Fed is the central bank of the United States. It brings order to the nation's banking system. The Fed manages the American money supply. It has a great impact on the daily lives of all Americans.

How Does the Fed Serve Its Member Banks?

The Fed was formed to provide services to banks. As the bankers' bank, it provides the same services consumers get from their banks. It supplies cash, and it lends money.

The Fed manages the flow of money between the district banks and member banks. Each day the Fed processes millions of payments. Some of these are paper checks. Many others are **electronic money transfers**. In these electronic transfers, money changes hands through the use of computers. The Fed keeps track of all these payments through a service called **check clearing**. Together, the 12 banks process more than one-third of the $12 trillion in checks written per year in the U.S. The value of all the electronic transfers handled by the Fed is nearly $200 trillion!

Just as you sometimes may have to borrow money, banks sometimes borrow money. Suppose a large number of a bank's customers suddenly wanted their money. The bank might be forced to borrow money. It contacts the Federal Reserve Bank in its district. The Fed will loan the member bank the money it needs. Banks may find themselves short on cash on paydays, and during vacation time and the holiday season. People spend a lot of money during these times, so banks are forced to borrow.

Just as your bank charges you for services, the Fed earns money by charging service fees to its members. It collects a service fee for each check it processes. It collects **interest** on loans it makes. Interest is a percentage of money paid to get a loan.

Electronic money transfer

The process in which money changes hands through the use of computers

Check clearing

The act of processing a check that transfers money

Interest

A percentage of money paid for a loan or debt

How Is the Fed the "Government's Bank"?

The Federal Reserve System's biggest customer is the U.S. government. The Fed handles the Treasury Department's "checking account." The Treasury deposits government funds in the Fed, including all tax deposits. The Treasury also handles all outgoing government payments. These include Social Security checks, pension checks, and other benefits.

The Treasury also sells and buys back U.S. government securities. These include savings bonds and treasury notes and bonds. These bonds are part of the government's debt. The U.S. Treasury sells bonds to get the money it needs to pay for services. These services include defense, help for poor people, highways, and medical care for the aged and poor.

The Fed also issues the nation's currency. The Bureau of Engraving and Printing in Washington, D.C., produces the money. The district banks distribute the money to their member banks. Take a look at the money you have in your wallet or purse. Notice that each bill is labeled "Federal Reserve Note." Each bill has a symbol and code showing which of the district banks issued it.

The Fed controls the banking system of the United States. All of the 12 district banks have teams of bank examiners. Their job is to check to make sure the banks are following the rules. They check bank records and look carefully at the loans and investments the banks have made. The examiners can pressure banks that are not following the rules to change the way they do business.

The Bureau of Engraving and Printing in Washington, D.C., prints paper American currency.

Economics in Your Life

Where Does Money Come From?

The U.S. Mint produces coins at Philadelphia, Denver, San Francisco, and West Point, New York. Coins made at each branch are identified with a small letter or "mint mark." This shows where the coin was made. Congress approved the mint in 1792. The Philadelphia mint began striking gold coins in 1795. In later years, silver, copper, and nickel coins were also minted.

The Bureau of Engraving and Printing, located in Washington D.C., has been printing paper currency since 1877. Nearly 95 percent of all bills printed are used to replace worn or damaged currency. The paper of U.S. currency is 75 percent cotton and 25 percent linen. There are 65 steps in the production process. Many of these are designed to try to prevent the printing of fake money. The amount of currency printed is based on public demand. The Federal Reserve oversees both the U.S. Mint and the Bureau of Engraving and Printing. The currency is distributed through the network of Federal Reserve Banks.

Word Bank

bonds

borrow

check-clearing service

Engraving and Printing

fees

Lesson 3 Review On a separate sheet of paper, write the word from the Word Bank to complete each sentence.

1. The Fed keeps track of payments through its _____.

2. Vacation seasons and holidays are times when banks may be forced to _____ from the Fed.

3. The Bureau of _____ produces U.S. money.

4. The Fed earns money by charging its members _____.

5. To get needed money for government programs, the U.S. government sells _____.

What do you think ?

6. Why do you think only one place, the Bureau of Engraving and Printing, produces American paper money?

7. Why do you think banks need their own bank like the Fed?

The most important job of the Fed is controlling the money supply of the United States. The Fed acts as the nation's money manager. It tries to balance the flow of money and credit with the needs of the economy.

Why Does the Fed Need to Regulate the Money Supply?

The Fed wants to promote economic growth while keeping prices stable. Too much money in the economy can lead to **inflation**. Inflation is a steady rise in the price of goods and services. As prices go up, the value of money goes down. For example, a book that cost $7.99 in 1990 may now cost $12.99. Too little money in the economy can slow down growth of the economy. The Fed tries to balance money flow.

What Is Monetary Policy?

The decisions the Fed makes about money and banking is called **monetary policy**. The Fed carries out its monetary policy in three main ways:

1. **Open-market operations**
2. Adjusting the reserve requirements
3. Raising or lowering the discount rate

The term open-market operations refers to the Fed's buying and selling of U.S. government securities. These securities are **treasury bills**, notes, and bonds. A treasury bill is a security in which buyers pay money to the U.S. Treasury for the bill. Then the buyers receive more money in return later. Through its open-market operations, the Fed adjusts the amount of money in use.

Eight times a year, a committee called the **Federal Open Market Committee (FOMC)** meets to review the state of the economy. The committee decides whether to speed up or slow down the economy. The committee's decisions are based on research by the staff of the Federal Reserve Board.

How Does the Fed Speed Up the Economy?

If the committee decides the economy needs to speed up, the Fed will increase the amount of money in use. It does this by buying government securities from investment companies. When it buys government bonds and other securities, it pays for them by depositing money into banks and other financial companies. Then the banks have more money to lend. As more money and credit become available, companies are more likely to grow. The effect is to create economic growth. The hope is that people will spend more money. Trade will increase, and so will the number of jobs. This process is sometimes called "loose" money.

Why Might the Fed Want to Slow Down Economic Growth?

Sometimes the economy grows too fast. There is too much money in use, causing inflation. The Fed tries to "cool off" the economy by cutting back on the money supply. It does this by selling government securities to investment companies. When the Fed sells bonds, consumers pay for the bonds by taking money out of their banks. The Fed gives the bonds to consumers in exchange for money. The money goes to the Fed. This means that the banks have less money and credit to offer their customers. Borrowing becomes more expensive. Money becomes "tight." Businesses are less likely to expand. Reducing the money supply may decrease inflation. It also may cause a drop in trade, slow economic growth, and put more people out of work.

The Federal Reserve Board meets regularly to discuss business.

How Does Adjusting Reserve Requirements Affect the Economy?

Earlier we learned that banks must keep a certain amount of money in reserve. The reserve is held in an account with the Fed. The amount depends on how large the bank is and the types of deposits it has. For example, checking accounts require a high level of reserves. Other kinds of savings plans require a smaller level of reserves.

The Fed influences the flow of money and credit by raising or lowering the reserve requirements. The Fed might increase reserve requirements when it decides that prices are rising too quickly. When reserve requirements go up, the cost of borrowing money increases. Banks have less money to lend. Fewer consumers and businesses can afford to borrow money. Money becomes scarce. The price borrowers have to pay, or the **interest rate** (a percentage of the loan), will be high. The higher the cost of credit, the fewer people there are who are willing to pay for it.

On the other hand, if the Fed wants to increase economic growth, it can lower the reserve requirements. The Fed might decide to do this because it believes the economy is slowing down and more people are out of work. When the Fed lowers reserve requirements, the interest rate goes down. Banks have more money to lend. Money becomes "easy." More consumers are willing to borrow money at lower interest rates. They borrow money to buy new cars, build new homes, or expand factories. This increases the need for labor and creates more jobs.

How Does the Discount Rate Affect the Money Supply?

A third way in which the Fed can affect the money supply is by changing the **discount rate**. The discount rate is another name for interest. It is the price that banks must pay to borrow money from the Federal Reserve. Borrowing from the Fed is often referred to as "going to the discount window." The phrase comes from an earlier time when bankers came to the Federal Reserve Bank and borrowed money from a clerk. The clerk stood behind protective glass. Now, all borrowing is done through electronic transfers.

By raising or lowering the discount rate, the Fed influences the banks' ability to lend. If the discount rate is high, banks think twice before making loans. When the discount rate rises, the **prime rate** rises too. The prime rate is the interest rate banks charge their best customers. Smaller and less important borrowers find loans even harder to get. The Fed tends to raise the discount rate if it wants to slow down the economy.

Lowering the discount rate is a sign that the Fed thinks the economy is slowing down. Lowering the rate encourages banks to borrow more. This gives them more money to make loans to customers. It has the same effect as lowering the reserve requirements.

How Is the Money Supply Measured?

Before deciding monetary policy, the Fed must find out how big the money supply is. Economists have several different ways of measuring the money supply.

The easiest measure of the money supply is **M1**. M1 measures only the money actually in use. This includes all currency, all checking accounts, and all **traveler's checks**. These are checks that people purchase from banks and often use on trips.

Other economists believe that a broader measure of the money supply is needed. They use **M2**. M2 includes all M1 money, as well as other monies. These other monies include money such as money market accounts and savings accounts worth less than $100,000.

Still other economists use **M3** to measure the money supply. M3 includes all the money in M1 and M2 as well as large time deposits worth more than $100,000.

Lesson 4 Review On a separate sheet of paper, write the letter of the answer that correctly completes each sentence.

1. The value of money goes down as prices rise when _____ occurs.

   A deflation   **C** a recession

   B inflation   **D** a sale

2. The Federal Open Market Committee meets to decide whether to speed up or slow down the _____.

   A economy   **C** inflation

   B prime rate   **D** printing of money

3. To slow inflation, the Fed may cut back on _____.

   A checking accounts   **C** the jobless rate

   B imports   **D** the money supply

4. The interest rate that banks charge their best customers is the _____ rate.

   A permanent   **C** inflation

   B economic   **D** prime

5. _____ measures only the money in use.

   A M1   **C** M3

   B M2   **D** The Fed

What do you think ?

6. Why are so many people afraid when the economy slows down? How might a slow economy affect you?

7. Why is the money supply so important to the economy?

The New Currency—Combating Counterfeit Money

On May 13, 2003, the United States Bureau of Engraving and Printing announced a new design for the $20 bill. The government is always looking for ways to stop the production of counterfeit, or fake, money. Other bills may be redesigned in the future, but the $1 and $2 bills will not be changed.

"U.S. currency is a worldwide symbol of security and integrity. This new design will help us keep it that way, by protecting against counterfeiting and making it easier for people to confirm the authenticity of their hard-earned money," U.S. Treasury Secretary John W. Snow said. . . .

"This is *The New Color of Money*; it is safer because it is harder to fake and easier to check, smarter to stay ahead of tech-savvy counterfeiters, and more secure than ever," said the Bureau of Engraving and Printing's [Tom] Ferguson. . . .

The most noticeable difference in the notes is the subtle green, peach, and blue colors featured in the background. Different colors will be used for different denominations, which will help everyone—particularly those who are visually impaired—to tell denominations apart. . . .

The new bills will remain the same size and use the same, but enhanced portraits and historical images of Andrew Jackson on the face of the note and the White House on the back. The redesign also features symbols of freedom—a blue eagle in the background, and a metallic green eagle and shield to the right of the portrait in the case of the $20 note.

The new $20 design retains three important security features that were first introduced in the late 1990s and are easy for consumers and merchants alike to check. These features are the watermark, security thread, and color-shifting ink.

The new $20 bill was put into circulation on October 9, 2003.

Document-Based Questions

1. What part of the United States government designs new currency?

2. Why was the $20 bill redesigned?

3. What changes were made to the $20 bill?

4. What three security features of American money should consumers and merchants check for?

5. Do you think the new currency design will protect against counterfeiting? Explain.

Chapter 12 SUMMARY

- The Panic of 1907 and a national depression caused Congress to create the National Monetary Commission. The commission's recommendations led to the Federal Reserve System, or the Fed. The Fed has 12 district banks.

- The Fed acts as a bank for member banks in the Federal Reserve System.

- All national banks had to join the Fed. State banks could choose to join. As of 2003, about 6,000 banks were members.

- The U.S. president appoints seven governors and a chair and vice chair to run the Fed. The governors serve 14-year terms. The chair and vice chair serve four years. The 12 regional banks carry out the Fed's policies.

- The Fed processes millions of checks every day. It tracks them through a check-clearing service. It processes $200 trillion in electronic transfers every year.

- Banks can borrow money from the Fed. The U.S. government is the Fed's largest customer.

- The Fed issues U.S. currency through the Bureau of Engraving and Printing in Washington, D.C.

- Bank examiners make sure the Fed's member banks follow all the rules.

- The Fed tries to control the amount of money in the economy. The Fed's decisions are called monetary policy. It carries out open-market operations, adjusts the reserve requirements, or raises or lowers the discount rate.

- The Federal Open Market Committee meets eight times a year. It decides whether to speed up or slow down the economy.

- To speed up the economy, the Fed increases the amount of money in use. To slow the economy, the Fed cuts back the money supply.

- Increasing or decreasing banks' reserve requirements adds money to or removes it from the economy. These actions either speed up or slow the economy.

- The Fed charges its member banks a discount interest rate. Banks charge their best customers a prime rate. Lowering the discount rate shows the Fed thinks the economy is slowing.

- M1 measures only the money in use. M2 measures M1 and all other monies worth less than $100,000. M3 measures M1 and M2 plus large time deposits worth more than $100,000.

Chapter 12 REVIEW

On a separate sheet of paper, write the word from the Word Bank to complete each sentence.

Word Bank

discount rate

economy

monetary policy

National Monetary
  Commission

reserve

team of bank
  examiners

Washington, D.C.

1. After the Panic of 1907, the U.S. Congress created the
_____.

2. The headquarters of the Federal Reserve System is in
_____.

3. A(n) _____ makes sure banks follow the Fed's rules.

4. The Fed's decisions about money and banking are its
_____.

5. The amount of money that banks are required to keep
is its _____.

6. The price banks pay to borrow money from the Fed is the
_____.

7. When the Fed thinks the _____ is slowing, it may lower
the discount rate.

On a separate sheet of paper, write the letter of the answer that correctly completes each sentence.

8. Instead of one central bank, the Federal Reserve System
has _____ district banks.

   A 12   **C** 8

   B 10   **D** 6

9. The larger district banks of the Fed may have _____.

   A branch banks   **C** smaller offices

   B a discount rate   **D** three presidents

10. The Fed lends _____ to other banks.

    A credibility   **C** money

    B treasury bills   **D** support

11. The biggest customer of the Fed is _____.

   A a major fast-food restaurant   **C** the states

   B the New York Stock Exchange   **D** the U.S. government

12. Treasury bills, notes, and bonds are types of U.S. government _____.

   A money   **C** securities

   B pledges   **D** stock certificates

13. By reducing the money supply, the Fed tries to _____ the economy.

   A cool off   **C** speed up

   B overload   **D** undercut

On a separate sheet of paper, write answers to the following questions. Use complete sentences.

14. How is the Fed organized?

15. What is the common goal of the district banks of the Fed?

16. What is the purpose of the Bureau of Engraving and Printing?

17. What is inflation?

On a separate sheet of paper, write your opinion to each question. Use complete sentences.

18. Do you think the United States needs the Federal Reserve System? Why or why not?

19. Do you think the United States could have another panic like the one that led to the creation of the Fed? Why or why not?

20. Do you think it is important for the Fed's governors to be politically independent? Explain.

Test-Taking Tip

Read test questions carefully to identify those questions that require more than one answer.

13 The Role of Consumers

Every time you buy something you are a consumer. Consumers influence production by buying goods and services. When you spend money, you are taking part in the market for goods and services. You are sending a message. You are saying, "This is a good product. Keep on making it." Being a smart consumer is very important. Knowing how to make a budget will prevent your spending from spinning out of control. If you comparison shop, you will get the most for your money. You need to know how the law protects consumers.

In this chapter, you will learn about budgeting, comparison shopping, and consumer protection.

Goals for Learning

◆ To explain why a budget is important

◆ To learn the steps in making a budget

◆ To describe the benefits of comparison shopping

◆ To identify the rights you have as a consumer

◆ To learn about some of the laws that help protect consumers

What Is a Budget?

Budget
A plan for spending and saving money
Expense
A good or service that costs money
Mortgage
A home loan

A **budget** is a plan for spending and saving money. People who manage their money wisely find budgets useful. Each month, they set aside a certain amount of money for **expenses**, or goods or services that cost money. Examples are rent or **mortgage** (home loan) payments, groceries, entertainment, and gifts.

What Are the Qualities of a Good Budget?

A good budget has several key qualities. It has to be flexible, ongoing, and clearly stated.

A flexible budget changes as needs change. For example, your budget may set aside a certain amount of money for clothes. If your favorite jeans rip, you may have to buy another pair. You may not be able to wait to replace them. This means that you have to adjust your budget. You may be able to buy the new jeans. Buying them means that you may not be able to go to the movies with friends during the month as you planned.

An ongoing budget means it is not just a one-time event. To be effective, consumers have to make the budget part of everyday life. It is good for the budget to be flexible, but not so flexible that the budget does not help manage your money.

A good budget is clear and easy to follow. It should reflect real life. Saying that you are going to save half of all the money you make is probably not realistic. If you have many things to pay for, it may not be possible to save that much.

A budget can help plan for things you need such as clothing.

What Are the Steps to Making a Personal Budget?

The first step in making a budget for yourself is to figure out how much money you make. Remember, this is called income. Most of the income you will earn in your life comes from working. You will receive wages in exchange for your labor. How much you will earn depends on your job, your skills, how well you work with others, and several other factors.

Some of your income may come from **investments**. Investments are things you buy for future financial benefit. Some examples of investments include real estate, savings bonds, and stocks and bonds. By investing your money, you are putting your money to work. For example, if you put your money in a bank, the bank will pay you for letting them use your money. The money you earn this way is called **interest**. (In the next chapter, you will learn more about managing your money.)

Economics at Work

Loan Officer

Loan officers help people who want to borrow money. Most often, loan officers' clients want to borrow money for a home or car. Loan officers work for banks, mortgage companies, or other lending companies.

People borrowing money depend on the loan officer to find the best loan for them. The loan officer should explain borrowing options. This includes interest rates, the term of a loan, and the other terms of repayment. People who apply for loans usually need help from the officer when filling out the forms needed for processing the loan.

Loan officers must make sure that the person applying for the loan has the ability to repay it. Loan officers must research the person's job status, including the salary and length of employment. The person applying for the loan must agree to a credit search. This will show the loan officer whether the person has made regular payments on debts. Loan officers succeed when customers repay their loans as agreed.

Suppose you begin your first full-time job. The job pays $20,000 a year. You may think this is a lot of money. You may start dreaming about all of the things you can buy with the money you will earn. Don't be too quick! The $20,000 refers to **gross income**, the money you earn before taxes and other expenses are taken out. Taxes and expenses like **Social Security** and health insurance have to be subtracted from your gross income. (Social Security is a government program of retirement and disability benefits.) The money left over after all these expenses is your **net income**.

A second step is to look at how you spend your money. It is a little like going on a diet. To make good diet decisions, you need to make a list of everything that you eat. Then you can decide where you can make changes. An important step in making a budget is keeping a record of how you spend your money over a normal month or two.

Expenses are of three types: fixed, variable, and discretionary. **Fixed expenses** occur regularly. They do not change from month to month. These include things like car payments and insurance costs. **Variable expenses** occur regularly but do change from month to month. Groceries, gas, and telephone bills are examples of variable expenses. **Discretionary expenses** are expenses people control themselves. You have the freedom to decide whether you want to spend money or not. These expenses include things like going to concerts or the movies, eating out, and going on a trip.

In budgeting, it may help to categorize your spending. For example, many teenagers spend much of their money on things like clothing, transportation (the cost of owning a car or taking a bus or train), telephone calls, going out, and entertainment.

Next, try to foresee expenses you may have in the future. For example, you may be planning for college or to move out on your own. To achieve these goals, you have to begin saving. You will have to set money aside in your budget.

Figure 13.1

A Sample Monthly Budget

Personal Budget	
Income	January
Wages	$1,620
Investments	$23
Miscellaneous	$0
Total income	**$1,643**
Expenses	
Home	
Mortgage/rent	$720
Electric	$45
Telephone	$43
Water	$30
Home totals	**$838**
Daily living	
Food	$275
Health insurance	$77
Credit card	$20
Entertainment	$75
Savings	$50
Other	$40
Daily living totals	**$537**
Transportation	
Car payment	$140
Car insurance	$80
Gas	$48
Home totals	**$268**

The final step in budgeting is to look at your income and spending. Try to figure out where you can make changes. You may learn that you are spending 20 percent of your income eating out. You might decide to spend this money on other things or to save for the future by eating at home more often. Looking at the numbers may help you realize that you cannot make your dreams come true unless you increase your income. You may have to work more hours. You may have to find a better paying job if you want to reach your goals.

Today, technology makes keeping a budget much easier. Computer programs can help consumers manage their finances and organize investments. They produce summaries of how money is spent. Figure 13.1 shows what a simple budget looks like.

Lesson 1 Review On a separate sheet of paper, write the letter of the answer that correctly completes each sentence.

1. Mortgage payments, groceries, and gifts are examples of _____.

   A income   **C** discretionary expenses

   B expenses   **D** investments

2. People control their _____ expenses.

   A discretionary   **C** net

   B fixed   **D** gross

3. _____ expenses occur regularly and do not change from month to month.

   A Discretionary   **C** Net

   B Fixed   **D** Variable

4. The money left over after taxes and other expenses are removed is _____ income.

   A discretionary   **C** net

   B fixed   **D** variable

5. The money people earn before taxes is _____ income.

   A fixed   **C** illegal

   B gross   **D** variable

What do you think ?

6. Have you ever used a budget? If so, describe how it was helpful. If you have not used a budget, explain how you think a budget would be helpful to you.

7. If you wanted to save money for future expenses, where could you spend less now?

Why Do You Need to Shop Carefully?

You buy many things. You have hobbies and interests. You might attend sporting events, movies, and concerts. You spend money. To make sure you are getting good value for your money, you need to shop carefully.

What Is Comparison Shopping?

Comparison shopping is looking at many brands of the same item to find the best buy. Let's say you received money for your birthday. You would like to buy a digital camera. Do not buy the first camera you look at. Go to several stores and check out the dozens of cameras available. To get the most for your money, it pays to compare.

You need to look at each camera and compare features. Digital cameras vary a lot. They range in price from under $100 to $1,000 or more. Besides the price, you will want to compare the features. Ask yourself which camera is most reliable and easiest to service. It is best to research before buying. Visit different camera stores. Get information about the different brands. Talk to experts about which product is most reliable and requires the least repair. Look at the newspaper ads to see who might offer the best price on the camera you like best. The same process you used to pick a camera works well no matter what product you are buying.

There are several consumer magazines that make comparison shopping easier. They buy and test competing products. They often rate the items they tested and identify good buys. Internet sites often offer the same service. They list stores selling the same product and the price they are charging.

Sometimes store-brand products, also called **generic**, are the best buy. Be sure to include them in your comparison shopping. The same companies that make the heavily advertised brands might make many of the generic products.

Why Should Consumers Avoid Impulse Shopping?

Impulse shopping

Buying something you did not intend to buy

Consumer fraud

When an uninformed consumer is tricked into buying something that falls short of what the seller claimed

Bait and switch

The illegal act of advertising a product at a low price and then discouraging customers to buy the item in order to get them to buy a more expensive item

Have you ever gone into a store for one thing and then bought something you did not intend to buy? This is called **impulse shopping**. We all do it. We get hungry and decide to buy something to eat. We see a good sale on an item and buy it because of the great deal. We go to a music store and hear a CD by a new group and decide to buy it. This is part of our discretionary spending.

Some merchants like grocery stores, bookstores, and music stores know that impulse shopping increases profits. They sometimes offer special deals on a few products. This is to get customers into the store. They expect that once the customers are in the store, they will buy something. Too much impulse shopping can lead to poor money management.

What Is Consumer Fraud?

You may have heard the expression "buyer beware." It means that consumers have to be informed and careful. Uninformed consumers can be tricked into buying something that falls short of what the seller claims. This is called **consumer fraud**. There are many forms of consumer fraud. All consumer fraud involves cheating, lying, and stealing.

Bait and switch is an example of fraud. Generally businesses have to sell products at the price they advertise. In a bait and switch strategy, a business will advertise a product at a low price to lure customers in. This is the bait. They really do not want to sell the product at that price. When consumers come in to buy the bargains, they are discouraged from buying the sale item. They might be told that the sale item is out of stock. They might be told that the sale item is not as good as a more expensive item. The seller tries to switch the consumer's attention to a higher-priced model. This model often costs much more than the customer intended to spend.

Telemarketing

The business of selling things over the telephone

Telemarketing fraud

Any attempt over the phone to cheat consumers

Spam

E-mail messages offering goods or services to purchase

Another kind of consumer fraud is the phony going-out-of-business sale. A company announces that it is going out of business. It says it will sell remaining products at a big discount. It then stocks up on more items. These new products are usually of poorer quality than the normal products. The idea is to keep customers coming and increase profits. Sometimes the going-out-of-business sales last for many months.

What Is Telemarketing Fraud?

Have you ever received telephone calls at your home from someone trying to sell you a product or service? **Telemarketing** is the business of selling things over the telephone. Many businesses use telephone calls to try to make sales. Most of these telephone offers are valid, but some are not. **Telemarketing fraud** refers to any attempt over the phone to cheat consumers. The Federal Bureau of Investigation (FBI) estimates that telemarketing fraud costs American consumers $40 billion each year. The Federal Trade Commission (FTC) estimates that more than 14,000 telemarketing businesses taking part in fraud currently operate in North America. Most fraud involves phony investment ideas, prize promotions, or fake charities.

What Kinds of Fraud Happen on the Internet?

Randy Bish, reprinted by permission of United Feature Syndicate, Inc.

Spam can be like getting junk mail on your computer. Spam is e-mail messages offering goods or services to purchase.

Many of the worst frauds take place on the Internet. Most computer owners receive hundreds of e-mails a year offering deals on different products. These offers are called **spam**.

The Internet Fraud Watch, a project of the National Consumers League, made a list of the most common complaints. The biggest complaint was that items ordered were never delivered or were not what was advertised. Business deals that promised to make the investor lots of money turned out to be much less profitable than promised.

Another common complaint involves **pyramid schemes**. In a pyramid scheme, people are asked to pay money to others with the promise that future investors will send them money in return. Usually the deal falls apart, and most of the investors lose all of their money.

Many people also are taken in by "work at home" offers. These promise big returns if the consumer buys materials or pays for leads. Usually, the buyer ends up the big loser. The Internet also lures consumers by telling them they have won a contest or valuable prize. There have been many complaints that when people tried to claim their awards, they were told they had to buy something first. Usually, these are very expensive items.

What Can You Do to Shop Safely on the Internet?

Before you buy anything on the Internet, it is good to follow these rules:

1. **Research the seller.** Does the Web site provide the name, address, and telephone number of the business? Are all the costs clearly stated? Is there a return policy if you are not satisfied and want to return the item?

2. **Choose your password carefully.** Some Web sites want you to choose a password before ordering. Try to use a mix of numbers and letters that no one will guess. Do not give your password to anyone who contacts you.

3. **Pay by credit card.** This is the safest way to pay. The law protects you from having to pay for things that were never ordered or received.

4. **Keep a record.** Be sure to print and keep a copy of your order. This will help you make sure you are getting what you ordered. The record tells you how much the product or service costs. This will prevent you from being overcharged.

Economics in Your Life

Automated Teller Machines

Automated teller machines (ATMs) were invented to make it easier for bank customers to get service. The first automated teller machines allowed customers to take out cash from an account. Within a few years, they were made to do much more. Today, ATMs take deposits, transfer money, make cash advances to credit cards, and accept payments.

Customers of ATMs use a plastic card that has a magnetic stripe. After the user enters a code (a personal identification number, or PIN), this stripe sends account information to a computer system. Most large banks are connected to this system. Customers can take money from their accounts even when an ATM is owned and operated by a different bank.

People have been using ATMs for more than 30 years. ATMs can be found in stores, shopping malls, hotels, and many other sites in most countries of the world. Many are available to customers 24 hours a day. In different countries, ATMs are known as cash dispensers, robotic tellers, cashpoints, and bancomats.

Lesson 2 Review On a separate sheet of paper, write answers to the following questions. Use complete sentences.

1. What is impulse shopping?

2. What is bait and switch?

3. What is a pyramid scheme?

4. Describe two ways to shop safely on the Internet.

5. What are some ways to comparison shop?

What do you think ?

6. Why do you think the worst frauds are committed over the Internet?

7. Do you think there should be more laws in place to control telemarketers? Why or why not?

In 1962, United States President John F. Kennedy made a speech to Congress. He urged the Congress to pass a "bill of rights" for consumers. Since then, the American government has passed many laws to protect the rights of consumers in the United States.

What Rights Does a Consumer Have?

The basic rights of consumers outlined by President Kennedy were the right to safety, the right to be informed, the right to choose, and the right to be heard.

What Laws Protect the Safety of Consumers?

Consumers have a right to be protected from unsafe products. Products that are sold should not harm consumers. For example, if you buy a toy for a child, you expect that playing with it will not harm the child. When you buy a car, you expect that it is free of flaws.

In 1972, Congress passed a law that created the Consumer Product Safety Commission (CPSC). The commission has many goals. One is "to protect the public from unreasonable risks or injury from consumer products." Another is to help consumers in comparison shopping. A third goal is to develop safety standards that are always the same. Finally, the commission conducts research on what causes accidents and illnesses and how they can be prevented.

The CPSC has the power to enforce laws protecting consumers. For example, one law requires the cloth used in children's sleepwear to be fire-resistant. Another law bans the use of certain poisons and other dangerous items in consumer products.

The Food and Drug Administration (FDA) makes sure that the food and drugs we buy are safe. It has the power to seize unsafe products. It also has the power to take court action against businesses that break the safety laws. The FDA inspects plants where food is processed to be sure the food is safe. It must approve all new medicines before they can be sold. After the FDA has approved them, consumers can be sure that the medicines are safe and work as promised.

The National Highway Traffic Safety Administration (NHTSA) sets highway safety standards. It looks into any reported problems in cars. NHTSA can require the **recall** of defective cars and car parts. A recall is when a company asks consumers to return a product for repair because the product has a safety problem. Since 1966, NHTSA has forced car manufacturers to recall more than 118 million cars.

The FDA approves medicines before they are sold. You can also ask your doctor or pharmacist about a medicine if you are not sure it will be safe for you.

Why Is the Right to Be Informed Important?

In a market economy, consumers are offered many competing products and services. Ads can be misleading. To make smart choices, the consumer needs a lot of information. Consumers have the right to know exactly what they are buying. They should be told all the terms of the sale and any guarantees given. Buyers should be told of all the dangers involved in using the products they buy.

Congress passed the Fair Packaging and Labeling Act in 1966. It requires businesses to tell the truth about how a product is made. For example, a company cannot label a drink as lemonade if it is not made of lemons. Another law requires that consumers be told in clear terms how much it costs them to borrow money. Many state governments also have passed laws requiring companies to give buyers more information.

The Federal Trade Commission makes sure that advertising and labeling are true. Advertisers who make totally false claims can be forced to change their ads.

The right to be informed is important to consumers. Some states have passed laws requiring schools to offer consumer education to their students. In some states, students must take a consumer education class to graduate.

What Is Meant by the Right to Choose?

In Chapter 7, we learned that the American economy is based on competition. The federal and state governments have passed laws making it against the law to restrict competition. The right to choose means that there is more than one seller for consumers to choose from. As we have learned, competition usually results in better products at the lower prices.

Biography

Ralph Nader: 1934–

American consumers have gained many protections from the work of Ralph Nader. His many actions have gone far in keeping businesses and the government honest. Nader started as a lawyer in Connecticut in 1959. Since then, he has grown to become a well-known author and consumer rights advocate.

Nader's first consumer rights success came after he wrote a book about car safety in 1965. Many safety changes occurred in the car industry as a result of his book. Nader has since written or helped produce dozens of books on other consumer topics. He has also founded groups that work for consumer rights. Some include the Public Interest Research Group (PIRG), the Center for Auto Safety, Clean Water Action Project, the Disability Rights Center, and the Project for Corporate Responsibility. He has also helped form several federal regulatory agencies such as the Occupational Safety and Health Administration (OSHA), Environmental Protection Agency (EPA), and the Consumer Product Safety Administration (CPSA).

How Do Consumers Make Themselves Heard?

Consumers who have a complaint against a seller have the right to be heard. Suppose you buy a product and find out it is not the same or as good as advertised. You have the right to ask for your money back or a different item. If you are not satisfied, you can complain. Some laws give consumers the right to sue a business they believe is breaking the law.

Some levels of government have offices to try to settle differences between buyers and sellers. Local businesses sponsor the Better Business Bureaus (BBB). They keep records of complaints with different local companies. If you have a complaint against a business, you should contact the local BBB. It also is good to check with the local BBB before buying a product or service from a local business. That way, you can see if there have been any complaints about that business.

Word Bank

Better Business
  Bureau

Federal Trade
  Commission

Food and Drug
  Administration

John F. Kennedy

National Highway
  Traffic Safety
  Administration

Lesson 3 Review On a separate sheet of paper, write the word from the Word Bank to complete each sentence.

1. President _____ first asked Congress to pass a consumers' bill of rights.

2. The _____ makes sure the food and drugs consumers buy and use are safe.

3. The _____ makes sure labeling and advertising are true.

4. The _____ keeps records of complaints against local companies.

5. The _____ sets highway safety standards.

What do you think ?

6. Do consumers need as many protections as mentioned in this lesson? Why or why not?

7. If you had a question about the safety of a toy, how could you get answers?

Buying a New Car

Buying a car is a large investment. The price of the car is not the only thing to think about. Besides that, the car has to be licensed, insured, and must have gas to run. All of these things cost a lot of money. The reading below from Saving Money *gives some important car-buying advice.*

If you really want to save, buy or lease a solid used car that's two or three years old. With a used car, the down payment, monthly payments, and insurance are less than for a new car. . . .

Be sure to shop around to find the best car at the best price. And when you finally decide to buy a car, remember the following:

• Find out the going interest rates on new- and used-car loans. . . .

• [A]sk for the lowest interest rate, not the lowest monthly payment.

• Try to get a loan pre-approved before you go car shopping so you know how much you can afford. . . .

Another important step in buying a car is the insurance. [Y]ou pay the premiums and . . . the insurance company will pay to fix or replace your damaged car, as well as expenses related to . . . anyone hurt by your car. Without this insurance, . . . you would be liable for sizable damages that could be a burden for the rest of your life.

[Y]ou might want to consider the following options to lower your premium:

• The type of car you drive: Choose a car that costs less to repair. Also avoid cars that are favorites among thieves.

• Your driving record: Drivers who have fewer traffic violations pay less.

• Your age: Younger drivers tend to have more accidents, so their insurance comes at a higher price. . . . Insurance companies sometimes give discounts to students who earn good grades in school.

• Your smoking habits: If you light up, your car insurance premium goes up.

Document-Based Questions

1. Why is buying a new car such a large investment?

2. What is one thing a person should remember when buying a new car?

3. Why is car insurance important?

4. Identify three things that could lower a person's insurance premium.

5. Do you think insurance companies are correct to charge young drivers more for insurance premiums? Explain.

Chapter 13 SUMMARY

- A budget is a plan for saving money. It should be flexible, ongoing, and clearly stated.

- To make a budget, people need to know their income. Income includes wages and interest earned from investments. Gross income is earned before taxes. Money left after taxes and expenses is net income. Budgets should include fixed, variable, and discretionary expenses.

- Comparison shopping is looking at many brands of the same item to find the best buy.

- Generic, or store-brand, items may be cheaper than heavily advertised brands. Consumer magazines often rate competing products.

- Impulse shopping occurs when people buy something they do not intend to buy. Too much impulse shopping leads to poor money management.

- Being informed helps consumers get what they paid for.

- Examples of consumer fraud include bait and switch or the false going-out-of-business sale.

- Telemarketing fraud is an attempt to cheat consumers over the telephone. The worst frauds are committed on the Internet. Spam and pyramid schemes are examples of Internet fraud.

- To shop safely on the Internet, consumers should research the seller, choose a password carefully, and pay by credit card.

- In 1972, Congress created the Consumer Product Safety Commission (CPSC). The CPSC protects consumers from unreasonable risks. It also helps consumers comparison shop. It promotes research into preventing accidents and illnesses. It can enforce consumer-protection laws.

- The Food and Drug Administration (FDA) inspects all foods and drugs Americans buy. The National Highway Traffic Safety Administration (NHTSA) sets highway safety standards.

- Consumers have a right to know what they are buying. They have the right to know all of the terms of sale, guarantees, and dangers of products they purchase.

- The Federal Trade Commission (FTC) makes sure advertising and labeling are true.

- If consumers have a complaint, they should contact the local Better Business Bureau.

Chapter 13 REVIEW

On a separate sheet of paper, write the word from the Word Bank to complete each sentence.

1. A good _____ must be flexible, ongoing, and clearly stated.

2. Property or things bought for future financial benefit are _____.

3. A store brand, or _____, product often is as good as a name brand item.

4. Consumer magazines and Internet sites make _____ shopping easier.

5. Buying something you did not intend to buy is called _____ shopping.

6. Unwanted e-mail offerings are called _____.

7. The _____ says buyers have the right to be safe, to be informed, to be heard, and to choose.

Word Bank

budget
comparison
consumers' bill
   of rights
generic
impulse
investments
spam

On a separate sheet of paper, write the letter of the answer that correctly completes each sentence.

8. The _____ inspects food processing plants to be sure the food is safe.

   A Better Business Bureau

   B Chamber of Commerce

   C Food and Drug Administration

   D Federal Trade Commission

9. States and the federal government have _____ calling for producers to give consumers more information.

   A passed laws

   B stopped

   C set no limits

   D taken back laws

10. A good budget should reflect _____.

   A impulse shopping

   B bait and switch

   C real life

   D interest

11. To create a budget, _____ your spending.

   A categorize   **C** impulse buy

   B disregard   **D** make up

12. The expression _____ means consumers have to be informed and careful about what they buy.

   A "bill of rights"   **C** "spam"

   B "buyer beware"   **D** "generic"

13. The FBI estimates that _____ fraud costs American consumers more than $40 billion per year.

   A Internet   **C** telemarketing

   B shopping   **D** television

On a separate sheet of paper, write answers to the following questions. Use complete sentences.

14. Write the three qualities of a good budget.

15. What are the three kinds of expenses the chapter mentions?

16. What is the biggest complaint about business conducted over the Internet?

17. Why is being an informed consumer important?

On a separate sheet of paper, write your opinion to each question. Use complete sentences.

18. Do you think the U.S. government should be more involved or less involved in protecting consumers? Explain.

19. You have learned about the three qualities of a good budget. Which quality do you think would be the most important for your own budget? Explain.

20. Describe how you could comparison shop for a pair of jeans, a music CD, or another item you wanted.

Test-Taking Tip

Try to answer all questions as completely as possible. When asked to explain your answer, do so in complete sentences.

14 Managing Money

In Chapter 13, you learned that budgeting and comparison shopping are keys to managing your money wisely. In this chapter, you will learn how to make your money work for you. The New York Stock Exchange is pictured on the opposite page. It is part of the stock market in which millions of Americans invest some of their money. This chapter will discuss the stock market. It also will discuss saving, investing, and using credit.

Goals for Learning

◆ To explain the benefits of saving

◆ To describe ways in which money can be invested

◆ To describe how the stock market works

◆ To summarize the advantages and disadvantages of using credit

What Is the Key to Saving Money?

Saving money is not easy. Everywhere we go we see ads urging us to buy. Most of us have many things we want to buy. The problem usually is that we do not have enough money to satisfy our wants. The key to saving is to set goals. Some of your goals are short-term. You might be saving money to go to the prom. Other goals are more long-term. College can be very expensive, so saving for education is a long-term goal.

What Are Some Steps to Starting a Savings Program?

The first step is to pay yourself first! Most experts tell people to save at least 10 percent of their take-home pay. This is not easy for people who never have saved before. Begin with a set percentage. Then try to slowly increase the amount to at least 10 percent. Once you start paying yourself first, you will notice how quickly your savings grows.

A second step is to break costly habits. Maybe you are used to buying a snack each morning before school. At $3 a day, this habit might cost you as much as $15 per week. Breaking this daily habit would save you $780 per year.

A third step is to put in the bank any money that you did not expect to receive. Since you were not planning on getting it, it is money you will not miss. By putting the money into your savings, you can put it to work.

Where Can People Put Their Savings?

Most people think that saving means opening a bank account. You can open a savings account in a bank, savings and loan firm, or credit union. Banks and savings and loans are for-profit groups. They are open to everyone. Credit unions are not for profit. They are owned by people who have something in common. For example, all the members may be pilots working for one airline or they may be union plumbers.

What Are the Different Types of Savings Accounts?

Liquidity

The ability to withdraw funds from a savings account

Annual percentage rate (APR)

The amount of money earned if left deposited in a savings account for one year

Money market account

A type of savings account that usually requires a minimum deposit of $500 or $1,000 but that earns a higher interest rate than a simple savings account

The most common type of account is a simple savings account. Usually you can open an account with only a small deposit. The biggest advantage of a savings account is **liquidity**. This means a saver can take out his or her money at any time. The disadvantage of a savings account is that it earns little interest. Interest is money you earn for allowing the bank to use your money. Interest usually is expressed as an **annual percentage rate (APR)**. This is the amount your money would earn if left on deposit for one year. Many experts say that money for short-term goals should be kept in a savings account. There is little risk of losing the money in a savings account. It also is easily available when you need it.

A second type of savings account is a **money market account**. A money market account usually requires a minimum deposit of $500 or $1,000. However, sometimes less is required. The interest rate your money earns usually is higher than for a simple savings account. One big difference is that the rate varies. Money market deposits can be withdrawn at any time. However, there may be limits on the number of withdrawals a saver can make per month. Some, but not all, money market accounts are insured.

How do you save your money right now? If you save by keeping around lots of cash, it might be better to open a savings account.

Certificate of deposit (CD)

A certificate stating that a person has made a deposit for a fixed period of time at a fixed interest rate

Time deposit

A type of savings account that requires money to be kept in the account for a certain period of time

Certificates of deposit (CDs) are certificates stating that a person has made a deposit for a fixed period of time at a fixed interest rate. CDs are **time deposits**. These require savers to keep their money in the account for a certain period of time. CDs are offered for as short as a few months or as long as 10 years. Firms are willing to pay a higher interest rate on CDs. They know they can use your money for a given period of time. The longer the time period, the higher the interest rate. You usually have to pay a penalty to withdraw your money before the time period is over.

What Does It Mean If a Bank Is a Member of FDIC?

The Federal Deposit Insurance Corporation (FDIC) is an agency of the federal government. It insures money deposited in banks. During the Great Depression of the 1930s, many businesses and factories closed down. People lost their jobs, and many banks failed. Congress saw the need to protect people's savings. As a result, it set up the FDIC in 1933. If the bank fails, the government will give depositors their money back, up to $100,000. People can put their money in a bank or savings firm and know it is safe.

Figure 14.1 **Savings Plans**

Savings Account	Money Market	Certificate of Deposit (CD)
• Minimum first deposit: Usually about $25–$100	• Minimum first deposit: As low as $250	• Minimum first deposit: Usually at least $500
• Interest earned: Usually 1–2 percent	• Interest earned: About 1.2 percent	• Interest earned: Usually 2–4 percent
• Safety: FDIC-insured	• Safety: Not FDIC-insured	• Safety: FDIC-insured
• Access to funds: At any time	• Access to funds: At any time	• Access to funds: At any time, but penalties apply
• Where to get one: At any bank, savings and loan, or credit union	• Where to get one: Set up a money market fund through a financial firm	• Where to get one: At any bank or credit union
• How to get one: Go to a bank or credit union in person	• How to get one: By phone with mailed check or wire transfer from checking account	• How to get one: Go to a bank or credit union in person or send in by mail
• How to make deposits: Through bank tellers, ATMs, or automatic money transfer	• How to make deposits: By check or wire transfer of funds from checking account	• Other: Make sure to be told when the CD will mature
• Other: Some banks charge fees if the account goes below a certain amount	• Other: Many funds allow many transfers per month	

Lesson 1 Review On a separate sheet of paper, write the letter of the answer that correctly completes each sentence.

1. Some experts tell people to save at least _____ percent of their net income.

   A 2   **C** 10

   B 5   **D** 50

2. A saver can withdraw money at any time from a(n) _____ account.

   A closed   **C** savings

   B interest   **D** time deposit

3. _____ is usually expressed as an annual percentage rate.

   A A deposit   **C** Liquidity

   B Interest   **D** Money

4. Financial groups may offer higher interest rates for _____ than for simple savings accounts.

   A budgeted accounts   **C** composite certificates

   B certificates of deposit   **D** stock certificates

5. The Federal Deposit Insurance Corporation _____ bank deposits up to $100,000.

   A insures   **C** matches

   B loses   **D** withdraws

What do you think ?

6. If you had $500, would you put it into a savings account, a money market account, or a certificate of deposit? Why?

7. Describe two ways you might start saving money for short-term and long-term money goals.

Return

The amount investors receive as a payment for use of their money

An investment is the use of money to create more money. There are many different kinds of investments. Before investing, there are many things to think about.

What Factors Should You Consider Before Investing?

There are three key factors each investor should consider:

- **Return**

- Risk

- Liquidity

The amount investors receive as payment for use of their money is called the return. Before you invest, you should ask what the rate of return is. As you have learned, savings accounts often have a fixed rate of return. Many investments do not.

Before you invest your money, decide how much of a risk-taker you are. Risk refers to the chance of loss. Some investments have little risk of losing your investment but offer a small return. Savings accounts are almost risk free. Savers can take out their money whenever they choose. Other investments involve high risk of losing the money you have invested. An example might be buying stock in a new company. If the investment turns out well, the investor makes a lot of money. If the investment turns out poorly, much of the money may be lost.

Liquidity measures how quickly you can change your savings into cash. The easier it is to withdraw your funds, the more liquid the investment. Most investments are not very liquid.

Most experts believe that a person should have an emergency fund before investing. That fund should be equal to two to six months of take-home pay. You also need to learn about all the different types of investments available. Be realistic. Very few investors "get rich quick."

Common stock

A share in the ownership of a corporation

Mutual fund

A special fund in which people pool their money to buy a variety of investments

Diversify

To purchase stock in several companies to reduce the risk of loss

Real estate

A type of investment that includes land and the buildings on it

Buying stocks is one way of investing. Stocks are shares owned in a company. Most stock is **common stock**. A share of common stock is a share in the ownership of a corporation. When a corporation makes a profit, its management may decide to share the profits with the shareholders. This is called a dividend. The prices of stocks go up and down. This means that owning stocks can be risky. There is no guarantee that investors will make money in the stock market.

To lessen the risk, some investors prefer **mutual funds**. Mutual funds are special investment funds in which people pool their money to buy many investments. A mutual fund might invest in hundreds of companies. You can become part owner of many companies by buying shares of a mutual fund. In this way, you can **diversify** your holdings. By diversifying, you reduce the risk of loss. You buy different kinds of investments instead of investing too much in any one investment.

Bonds are IOUs. The federal government, cities and towns, and corporations sell bonds. When you buy a bond, you are lending money. In return for the loan, the seller promises to pay you back your money plus interest. People invest in bonds because they have little risk. You can keep and increase your savings if you hold the bond until it matures, or comes due.

This may take several months or many years. Like stock prices, bond prices can go up and down. Investors can gain or lose money if they sell before the bond matures. U.S. savings bonds are one of the safest investments you can make. The U.S. government guarantees them.

Buying **real estate** is another kind of investment. Real estate is land and the buildings on it. For many people, buying a home is the biggest investment they ever make. Most houses cost well over $100,000. Few people invest more money than they invest in their homes.

Real estate of any kind can be an investment.

Lesson 2 Review On a separate sheet of paper, write answers to the following questions. Use complete sentences.

1. What is a return?

2. Why do some companies pay dividends?

3. What is a mutual fund?

4. What does it mean to diversify?

5. Why are savings bonds a safe investment?

What do you think **?**

6. If the stock market is risky, why do you think so many people want to invest in stocks?

7. What does the text mean when it says buying a home is the biggest investment many people will ever make?

Stock market

The activity of buying and selling stocks

New York Stock Exchange (NYSE)

The largest stock exchange in the world, located on Wall Street in New York City

As the 21st century began, over half of the households in America owned stock. Stocks are bought and sold in a **stock market**. The stock market is not a place but an activity. It refers to the buying and selling of stocks. In the last ten years, the stock market has boomed. Millions of people today are living well because of the investments they made in the market.

The stock market is very important today. It influences people's confidence about the future even if they do not own stock themselves. When the stock market is doing well, people feel good about the economy. When they feel good, they are willing to spend more money. The more they spend, the more the economy grows.

Shares of most large companies in the United States are listed on one of three stock exchanges. The **New York Stock Exchange (NYSE)** is the largest stock exchange in the world. It is located on Wall Street in New York City. Many people refer to Wall Street when they are talking about the stock market. Today, nearly 3,000 companies trade their stock on the NYSE. Millions of shares of stock are exchanged every day. The American Stock Exchange (AMEX) is the second largest exchange in the United States. The NASDAQ exchange is the newest large exchange. Both the AMEX and NASDAQ exchanges are completely computer driven. They are networks of computers instead of people.

Why Do Companies Issue Stock?

Companies need money to grow. Maybe they want to expand or develop new products. They could borrow money from a bank, but they would have to pay it back. They can sell bonds to raise money. A company can raise money without going into debt by selling common stock. Investors who buy the stock are giving the company the money it needs to grow. Not every company can issue stock. Only a business corporation can issue stock.

How Do Investors Buy and Sell Stocks?

To buy and sell stock, investors must open an account with a **stockbroker**. A stockbroker is licensed to buy and sell stocks. Stockbrokers are paid a percentage of the earnings when stock is sold. You must be at least 18 years old to open an account. Parents or guardians can open accounts for younger investors. Of course, there are forms to be filled out and money must be deposited in the account.

The New York Stock Exchange is the largest stock exchange in the world.

Why Do People Invest in the Stock Market?

Most people who buy stocks are interested in a good return on their money. Investors can profit from stock in two ways, from income or from growth. They can earn income by collecting dividends. Usually older, well-established companies pay higher dividends. Newer firms tend to use profits to develop new products or to grow. They rarely pay dividends.

Economics at Work

Stockbroker

Stockbrokers invest in the stock market for clients. These clients may include single investors or large companies. Stockbrokers offer investment advice based on current knowledge of the stock market. They gain much of their information through reading newspapers, magazines, and financial journals.

Stockbrokers often explain to new clients how the stock market works. They find out how much money the client wants to invest and for how long. The stockbroker uses good judgment to figure out which purchases are best for each client. Stockbrokers usually work for financial companies, brokerage firms, or investment companies.

Stockbrokers do not need to have a college degree, but most do. They must be licensed, however. In order to get a license, the stockbroker must pass the General Securities Registered Representative Examination. Many states also require candidates to take another test. In most investment companies, new stockbrokers train for up to two years.

Investors can profit if the price of the stock goes higher than what they paid. This is called growth. Suppose you had $100. You bought 10 shares of a business. You paid $10 a share. The share price goes up to $15. You could sell the stock. Your profit would be $5 a share, or a total of $50. Of course, stock prices go down too. Let's say the price of the stock drops to $5 and you decide to sell. Your loss is $5 a share, or a total of $50.

Why Do Stock Prices Change?

Most newspapers list stocks and bonds and their prices. The opening price and the high, low, and closing prices are listed for stocks. Sometimes the high and low price for the last 52 weeks (one running year) is also included. The value of every stock always changes. When the price of a stock rises, that stock is "up." When the price drops, that stock is "down."

All stock exchanges in the United States trade their stocks in dollars and cents. For example, the price of a stock may go up $1.40. This means that the value of the stock has increased by $1.40. If the stock was selling for $10 yesterday, today it would be worth $11.40.

Generally, the value of stock goes up if the company makes money. If investors think a company will do better in the future, its value may also go up. Another factor affecting stock prices is how confident people feel about the U.S. economy and the world economy. Stock prices cannot be predicted. A good rule to remember is that companies with growing profits are most likely to be the best investments.

What Is the Dow Jones Industrial Average?

One of the most popular measures of stock market performance is the **Dow Jones Industrial Average (DJIA)**. People often just call it the Dow. It is the average selling price of 30 of the top stocks. The DJIA goes up and down all the time. By checking the changes in the DJIA, investors get a fair picture of how the stock market is doing.

What Are Bearish and Bullish Investors?

Bears are cautious animals. They usually do not move too fast. They attack downward with their claws. Bulls are bold animals. They sometimes charge right ahead. They attack upward with their horns. Investors who believe the stock market will go down are called bears. Bearish investors buy stock cautiously. Investors who believe the stock market will go up are called bulls. Bullish investors charge ahead and put more money in the market. In a **bear market**, the prices of most stocks are falling. In a **bull market**, the prices of most stocks are going up.

 Biography

Warren Buffet: 1930–

Warren Buffet began making money at an early age. He spent his childhood as a paperboy, serving many delivery routes. He started playing the stock market with his sister when he was 11 years old. When Buffet was in high school, he started a pinball machine business. By the time he graduated from college, he had earned enough money to buy 40 acres of Nebraska farmland.

By playing the stock market, Buffet learned that it is wise to look for stocks of undervalued companies. At age 25, he started his own investment company and began to purchase stocks. He used $5,000 of his own money and $100,000 from friends and family members to get started. In 1963, Buffet bought stock in a major credit card company. Because of a scandal, many on Wall Street thought this company was near the end. But Buffet thought differently. As the company survived the crisis and grew, he made a lot of money.

Some people have called Buffet "the greatest investor of all time." Currently, he is chairman of a long-term investment and insurance company. The company has more than $2 billion in holdings. Buffet himself is worth over $36 billion. Even so, he still lives in the same house he bought for $31,500 over 40 years ago.

Lesson 3 Review On a separate sheet of paper, write the word from the Word Bank to complete each sentence.

1. To raise money without going into debt, companies may sell _____.

2. To buy and sell stocks, a person must open an account with a licensed _____.

3. One measure of the performance of the stock market is the _____.

4. A person who charges ahead and puts money in the stock market is _____.

5. A person who is cautious in the stock market is _____.

What do you think

6. Why do you think you must buy or sell stocks only through licensed stockbrokers?

7. The Dow Jones Industrial Average measures only 30 of the many hundreds of stocks available. Why, then, do you think people put so much trust in it?

Why Do Some People and Businesses Have to Borrow Money?

Some consumers can and do pay cash for everything they buy. Many people and businesses do not have enough money to buy what they need. They have to borrow money or use **credit**.

Credit is a loan of money to be paid back over a period of time. Credit allows us to buy now and pay later. When businesses offer credit, they are saying they trust that the borrower can and will pay them back.

We all have borrowed things from friends or relatives. When we borrow something, we promise to return it. We borrow things we do not have. It might be a piece of clothing, a tool, or even a car. Sometimes people and businesses borrow money to buy things that they want. When people and businesses borrow money, they promise to pay the money back. The amount of money borrowed is called the **principal**. The fee charged for borrowing the money is called interest. When the loan is repaid, the borrower must pay both the principal and the interest.

What Are Credit Cards?

Many businesses issue credit cards. A credit card is a form of borrowing. Stores that issue credit cards are loaning you the money to buy the things you want. You will have to pay them back more money than you borrowed because of interest. Interest can be thought of as the price of borrowing money.

What Is the Cost of Using Credit?

The amount of interest you pay for a credit card is figured as a percentage of the amount you borrowed. This **annual percentage rate** (APR) is the cost of credit expressed as a yearly percentage. The higher the interest rate, the more money you have to pay back. How long you take to pay back the loan is important too. The longer you take to pay back the money, the more money you will have to pay in interest.

Credit

A loan of money to be paid back over a period of time

Principal

The amount of money borrowed

Annual percentage rate (APR)

The yearly percentage paid for money borrowed on credit

Suppose you bought an entertainment center for your room. It cost over $1,000. The store gave you credit, and you agreed to pay back $100 each month. The store will charge you a **finance charge** until you pay all the money back. The finance charge includes the interest, service charges, and other fees.

Is Using Credit Always a Good Idea?

Suppose you decide to buy yourself a new portable DVD player. You did comparison shopping and picked out the kind you want. The cost of the one you want is $400. The store offers you three choices. You could rent it with the option to buy. You could buy it on credit, or you could pay for it in cash.

What is the cost of each option? If you rented the unit, you would pay about $14 per week for 78 weeks. This would make the total cost $1,092. The store also is willing to give you credit. It offers 18 percent interest and 18 months to pay the money back. Your monthly payments would be about $25. Then the total cost of the DVD player is $459.36. If you saved up for the unit, you could pay cash for it. Let's say you saved $56 per month, the same cost as if you rented it. In eight months, you would have enough money to pay for the DVD player in full. Renting would cost you $692 more and using credit $59.36 more. Saving seems to be the best option.

Can Anyone Get Credit?

Suppose a stranger came up to you. He wanted to borrow $500 to fix his car. You might feel sorry for him, but you probably would not loan him the money. You have no way of knowing if he is able to pay you back. Banks and stores want to make sure they will get their money back too. When you apply for a loan or credit card, you must fill out an application. Before they loan you money, they want to know if you are **creditworthy**. To determine if you are creditworthy, the lender looks at three factors: **capacity**, **capital**, and **character**.

Capacity is your ability to pay the loan back. Lenders will ask if you have a job. They will want to know how long you have worked there. They also will ask about any other debts you have.

Capital is your savings and other assets. Sometimes lenders will ask for **collateral**. Collateral is something of value that the borrower offers as a guarantee of repayment. For example, in an automobile loan, the car is the collateral. If the loan is not repaid, the lender can take the car away. Creditors prefer to loan money to people who have other assets than just their income from their job.

Character is how trustworthy you are. Lenders will want to know how prompt you are in paying your bills. Is your credit record good? Is it likely that you will repay the loan? Lenders must look at these things before giving a loan.

What Are Debit Cards?

Debit cards are different from credit cards. Credit cards are a form of borrowing. Debit cards work a lot like cash, but cash never changes hands. Banks give debit cards to people who have checking accounts. Consumers present the debit card to the cashier instead of cash. The purchase price is electronically subtracted from the cardholder's checking account. Debit cards also can be used at **automated teller machines (ATMs)**. ATMs are electronic terminals where customers can do their banking. They allow you to perform certain banking tasks, such as taking out money from an account, at any time of day.

Economics in Your Life

History of Credit Cards

Credit actually goes back many hundreds of years. People first used credit in ancient Assyria, Babylon, and Egypt. Beginning in the 18th century, vendors began accepting small monthly payments on household goods and clothing. Some large U.S. businesses introduced a system of "buy now, pay later" in the early 1900s. These companies offered metal cards to special customers for delayed payments on goods. The cards could be used only at the businesses that issued them.

Then in the early 1950s, two companies offered a new kind of credit card. These cards could be used at many restaurants and retail businesses. Within a decade, other companies began to offer credit cards. Soon, some national credit card networks began. Customers were given the option of "revolving credit." They could pay off credit card debt all at once or in smaller monthly amounts. The magnetic strip was added to the back of credit cards in the 1970s. This provided for faster processing of credit card purchases. Today, more than 84 million American households have at least one credit card.

Lesson 4 Review On a separate sheet of paper, write the letter of the answer that correctly completes each sentence.

1. The amount of money a person borrows is the _____.

   A collateral   **C** principal

   B interest   **D** rate

2. To receive a loan from a bank, a borrower must prove to be _____.

   A creditworthy   **C** poor

   B debt-free   **D** wealthy

3. The cost of credit expressed as a yearly percentage is the annual _____.

   A payback   **C** collateral

   B percentage rate   **D** principal

4. The type of card that works most like cash is a(n) _____.

   A ATM   **C** credit card

   B checkbook   **D** debit card

5. Lenders may ask borrowers for _____ as a guarantee of repayment.

   A collateral   **C** money

   B credit   **D** cash

What do you think ?

6. Sometimes using a credit card is a better idea than using cash. Give some examples and explain your thinking.

7. Which do you think is a smarter way to pay for things, using a credit card or a debit card? Explain.

October 29, 1929—Black Tuesday

In late October 1929, the American stock market was losing money. Finally, on October 29, the market crashed. Historians call this day Black Tuesday. The stock market crash affected people all over the world. It started the Great Depression, which lasted through the 1930s. The New York Times *reported the crash in its October 30 edition.*

Stock prices virtually collapsed yesterday, swept downward with gigantic losses in the most disastrous trading day in the stock market's history. Billions of dollars in open market values were wiped out as prices crumbled under the pressure of liquidation of securities which had to be sold at any price. . . .

From every point of view, in the extent of losses sustained, in total turnover, in the number of speculators wiped out, the day was the most disastrous in Wall Street's history. . . .

[I]t was estimated that 880 issues, on the New York Stock Exchange, lost between $8,000,000,000 and $9,000,000,000 yesterday. . . .

There were two cheerful notes, however. . . . One was the brisk rally of stocks at the close. . . . The other was that the liquidation has been so violent, as well as widespread, that many bankers, brokers and industrial leaders expressed the belief last night that it now has run its course. . . .

The market on the rampage is no respecter of persons. It washed fortune after fortune away yesterday and financially crippled thousands of individuals in all parts of the world. It was not until after the market had closed that the financial district began to realize that a good-sized rally had taken place and that there was a stopping place on the downgrade for good stocks.

The market has now passed through three days of collapse, and so violent has it been that most authorities believe that the end is not far away.

(Excerpt from *The New York Times* taken from www.nytimes.com. Copyright 1929 by The New York Times Co. Reprinted with permission.)

Document-Based Questions

1. What was Black Tuesday?

2. What historical time period began because of the stock market crash?

3. How much money was estimated to have been lost on the New York Stock Exchange?

4. Name one positive outcome of Black Tuesday.

5. How were people all over the world affected by the stock market crash?

Chapter 14 SUMMARY

- People should try to save at least 10 percent of their take-home pay, break costly habits, and put in the bank any unexpected money.

- Banks, savings and loan companies, and credit unions offer different savings accounts. Accounts include simple savings accounts, money market accounts, or certificates of deposit.

- The FDIC insures savings up to $100,000.

- Before investing, people must decide how much return, risk, and liquidity to accept.

- Stocks provide an investment dividend. Mutual funds allow people to pool their money to buy shares of several companies. Governments and corporations may issue bonds, which are IOUs. Real estate is another investment.

- The New York Stock Exchange (NYSE) is the largest in the world. Other U.S. stock exchanges include the AMEX and NASDAQ.

- Instead of borrowing money from a bank to expand or develop new products, companies may issue common stock.

- People invest in stocks to earn a better return than from other investments. People profit when the price of stocks increases from the price paid. In the United States, stocks are traded in dollars and cents.

- The Dow Jones Industrial Average (DJIA) measures the performance of 30 top stocks.

- People or businesses may borrow money to buy things they need or want. The amount of money borrowed is called the principal. The fee for borrowing is interest. Borrowers must repay the principal and interest.

- Credit is a loan allowing people to buy now and pay later.

- Many businesses issue credit cards. The interest and finance charges people pay is the price of borrowing money.

- Credit cards charge an annual interest rate. The higher this yearly rate, the more money that must be repaid.

- To decide whether to use credit, people must determine the cost of using credit, renting to buy, or using cash.

- Before issuing credit, banks and stores make sure borrowers are creditworthy. Lenders look at three factors: capacity, capital, and character.

- Debit cards work like cash. The price of an item purchased is electronically removed from the buyer's checking account.

- Automated teller machines are terminals where customers can do their banking at any time.

Chapter 14 REVIEW

On a separate sheet of paper, write the word from the Word Bank to complete each sentence.

Word Bank

bonds

borrow

credit union

creditworthy

interest

stock

stockbroker

1. When people do not have enough money to pay cash, they may have to _____ money.

2. When repaying a loan, a borrower repays both the principal and the _____.

3. To decide if a person is _____, lenders look at the person's capacity, capital, and character.

4. A(n) _____ is a not-for-profit financial company owned by people with something in common.

5. Governments, towns, and corporations sell _____, which are IOUs.

6. Corporations may raise money by selling common _____.

7. To open an account with a(n) _____, a person must be at least 18 years old.

On a separate sheet of paper, write the letter of the answer that correctly completes each sentence.

8. The largest stock exchange in the world is the _____.

   A DAG

   B NASDAQ

   C AMEX

   D NYSE

9. The _____ Industrial Average follows the selling prices of the 30 top stocks.

   A FDIC

   B Dow Jones

   C NYSE

   D Liquidity

10. _____ include interest, service charges, and other fees on money a person borrows.

   A Annual percentage rates

   B ATMs

   C Credit cards

   D Finance charges

11. _____ may range from a few months to as long as 10 years.

   A Banking deposits   **C** Contact deposits

   B Certificates of deposit   **D** Liquid deposits

12. Something that is _not_ a key factor in deciding whether to borrow is _____.

   A adventure   **C** return

   B liquidity   **D** risk

13. Land and the buildings on it are called _____.

   A collateral   **C** investments

   B houses   **D** real estate

On a separate sheet of paper, write answers to the following questions. Use complete sentences.

14. List two ways investors can profit from the stock market.

15. What is a good rule to remember about investing in a company?

16. What is credit?

17. What do experts believe a person should have before investing?

On a separate sheet of paper, write your opinion to each question. Use complete sentences.

18. Why is investing in the stock market more of a risk than investing in a savings account?

19. Why might real estate be a good investment? Why might it be a bad investment?

20. Why might investors be bearish at some times and bullish at other times?

Test-Taking Tip

When taking a multiple-choice test, read every choice before you answer a question. Put a line through choices you know are wrong. Then choose the best answer from the remaining choices.

Using Reference Materials

When you need to write a report or learn more about a topic, there are many sources available for your research. You may look in an encyclopedia for many types of subjects. A general information almanac gives recent historical facts of all kinds. Atlases and gazetteers are good sources for information about countries. For the most current information, magazines and newspapers may be the best places to look. The *Readers' Guide to Periodical Literature* provides a directory of the subjects covered in magazine articles.

The development of the Internet has given researchers a new and easy means of gathering information. Researchers can use a number of different search engines to find all sorts of information. Because there is so much information available on the Internet, it is important to explore many different ways of finding just the right data.

Imagine that you want to learn more about the kinds of schools young people attend in Bulgaria. You could do a search using the words "Bulgaria" and "schools." The search brings up 30,000 sources. You need to narrow your search. You add the words "elementary" and "high school" to your search. This narrows the search. Then you decide to check out elementary schools first with a set of even more specific search words.

The line graph above shows the average yearly interest rates of home loans in the United States for the years 1984–1999. This is not current. Imagine that you have been asked to use the Internet to gather

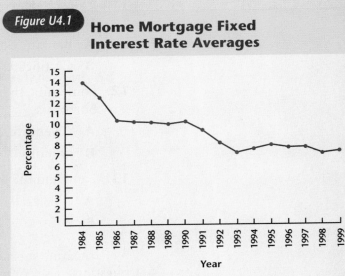

Figure U4.1 **Home Mortgage Fixed Interest Rate Averages**

information to update this graph. Take a good look at the graph, then answer the questions below.

1. What search words or phrases would you use to find out about interest rates for the years 2000–2004?

2. What search words would you use to show some predictions for the years 2005–2009?

3. Say that you must do a search without the use of the Internet. What sources would you use to find out about projected interest rates for 2005?

4. Home mortgage interest rates were very high in the early 1980s. What sources or search words would you use to find out why they became so high?

5. What sources or search words would you use to find out about interest rates in the 1950s and 1960s?

Unit 4 SUMMARY

- Money is a medium of exchange, store of value, and measure of prices. It must be stable, portable, uniform, divisible, and durable.

- After the American Revolutionary War, the government set up the first national bank in Washington, D.C. At the same time, the government created a mint in Philadelphia.

- Serious problems occurred in U.S. banking during the 1830s and 1860s. To reform banking, the U.S. Congress passed several laws. In 1900, Congress passed the Gold Standard Act. In 1934, the United States started to go off the gold standard.

- Banks accept deposits, make commercial loans, and collect and transfer funds. Banks must maintain part of their deposits as reserves.

- Congress created the Federal Reserve System after the Panic of 1907 and a following depression. Twelve district banks make up the Fed. It acts as a bankers' bank.

- Seven governors, a chair, and a vice chair make decisions for the Fed.

- The U.S. government is the Fed's largest customer. The Fed handles the Treasury department's checking account. The Fed issues U.S. currency and controls the U.S. banking system. The Fed also makes monetary policy through open-market operations, adjusting reserve requirements, and adjusting the discount rate.

- A budget must be flexible, ongoing, and clearly stated. To make a budget, a person needs to figure out income and expenses.

- Comparison shopping compares prices and features of a desired product.

- Consumers need to be aware of consumer fraud. To protect consumers, Congress has passed laws about food, medicines, highway safety, labeling, and packaging. If consumers have a complaint, they have a right to be heard.

- Saving at least 10 percent of take-home pay is a good idea. Banks and other financial groups offer several kinds of savings accounts.

- Key factors to consider before investing are return, risk, and liquidity. Common investments include stocks, bonds, and real estate.

- People buy and sell stocks in a stock market in hopes of making a profit. The NYSE is the world's largest stock exchange.

- When businesses and people borrow money, they repay the principal and interest. Credit cards let consumers buy now and pay later. Credit card companies earn money through charging interest and finance charges. Before issuing credit cards, lenders decide whether a consumer has the capacity, capital, and character to repay the loan.

"An economic policy which does not consider the well-being of all will not serve the purposes of peace and the growth of well-being among the people of all nations."
—*Eleanor Roosevelt, February 14, 1945*

5 Government and Free Enterprise

Washington, D.C., is the center of the United States government. All of the major national government offices are located there. The photo on the opposite page shows the tall Washington Monument. The United States Capitol building is just behind it. This is where Congress meets.

Why do we need to talk about government in an economics textbook? In earlier chapters, you learned some ways that government affects the economy. This unit continues to explore this topic. The unit will discuss the many systems and laws that the government uses to control the economy. This unit also describes the process of the United States budget and how the government pays for certain services for its citizens. The unit explains how an economic system is measured to determine its growth. Finally, this unit discusses certain economic problems that the American government is trying to control.

Chapters in Unit 5

15 The Role of Government

Depending on what actions it takes, the United States government can strengthen or weaken the health of the economy. Many government decisions affect economic growth. How much money will the government spend? On what will it spend the money? Where will the money come from? The answers to all of these questions are important to economic health.

If you ever have had to file a tax return, you know firsthand that people pay taxes. This chapter will talk about the many different kinds of taxes. It also will talk about the role of the American government in the economy.

Goals for Learning

◆ To explain how and why the role of government in the economy has grown

◆ To identify the parts of the government bureaucracy that affect the economy

◆ To summarize how fiscal policy is used to manage the economy

◆ To explain the differences between proportional, progressive, and regressive income taxes

◆ To identify the other types of taxes Americans pay

What Does "Laissez-Faire" Mean?

Laissez-faire
The French phrase that means "leave us alone;" it refers to the belief that the government should not get involved in economic matters

In the late 17th century, France had a king. The king's finance minister asked a merchant how the government could help business. The merchant answered "laissez nous faire," which means, "leave us alone." Ever since, **laissez-faire** has become a motto for the free enterprise system. According to laissez-faire, the government should not get involved in economic matters. Business decisions should be left to businesses.

What Gives the Government the Right to Be Involved in the Economy?

The United States Constitution gives the government the power to control trade within the country and with foreign countries. It also gives it the power to coin money and charge taxes. Taxes, as we will see later in this chapter, have a great effect on the economy. The United States government spends a lot of money. You use government goods and services every day. For example, the government provides funds for highways and national defense. About one-third of all money spent in the United States is from government spending.

When Did the Government's Role in the Economy Begin to Grow?

The government's role in the economy grew as the nation expanded westward. Roads and canals had to be built to make it easier for settlers to move west. Once built, roads and canals made it easier to ship goods to markets in the east. Already

The government helped to build the first railroad connecting the east and west coasts in the 1860s.

in the early 1800s, the U.S. government sold public land to help pay for the needed roads. In the 1860s, the first railroads connecting the two coasts were built with help from the government.

Interstate trade

Trade among the states

Public policy

The process of government decision making that addresses problems affecting many people

The American economy grew a lot during the late 1800s and early 1900s. Congress used its power to control the large businesses that developed. Over time, several government agencies were created. They tried to protect the interests of the common people.

For example, after the Civil War, farmers complained about the high rates they were being charged to ship their crops to market. State governments tried to set railroad rates. The Supreme Court ruled that only the federal government had the right to control **interstate trade**. This is trade among the states. This decision led to the creation of the Interstate Commerce Commission (ICC) in 1887. It set the pattern for government control. In the last 100 years, Congress passed other laws controlling business and protecting consumers.

Until the 1930s, the government's role in the economy was limited. This changed in the 1930s. During the Great Depression, the economy was in such bad shape that the U.S. government had to act. Since then, the role of government in the economy has grown. Today, government is involved in the economy in many ways. It plays a very important role in keeping the economy strong and growing.

What Is Public Policy?

Sometimes, government agencies try to solve problems or deal with issues that affect a large number of people. The name for the process of government decision making is **public policy**.

There are policies that keep the national economy running well. There are policies providing health care for the poor and elderly. There are policies about the treatment of disabled Americans. Other policies are in place to make sure that every American gets a good education. Public policy is created when all of the rules and laws about what persons can and cannot do are brought together.

Economics at Work

Accountant

Accountants keep records of a company's finances. They follow the Generally Accepted Accounting Principles (GAAP). Accountants watch revenue and expenses. They are expected to control company spending. Their tasks often include preparing reports and schedules for company leaders. In some cases, accountants are expected to train others in their area.

Many accountants are involved in yearly budgeting of spending and forecasting of income. They look for financial trends. They prepare information for the Internal Revenue Service and other government agencies, as required by law. Accountants may be asked to prepare a regular schedule for auditors who will review their work.

Today's accountants may help design or build computer systems for recording financial information.

Word Bank

Constitution

Great Depression

interstate trade

laissez-faire

public policy

Lesson 1 Review On a separate sheet of paper, write the word from the Word Bank to complete each sentence.

1. The motto for the free enterprise system is _____.

2. The government's power to trade inside and outside the country, to coin money, and to raise taxes comes from the _____.

3. The Supreme Court ruled that the central government could control _____.

4. During the _____, the U.S. government took a much greater role in the economy.

5. Government decision making is called _____.

What do you think ?

6. What might happen if all of the states could set rates for trade among the states?

7. Why do you think the role of government in the economy grew so much during the Great Depression?

What Are the Three Branches of Government?

Legislative branch

The branch of the U.S. government that makes the laws; Congress

Judicial branch

The branch of the U.S. government that interprets the laws; the courts

Executive branch

The branch of the U.S. government that makes sure the laws are carried out; the president and the federal bureaucracy

Federal bureaucracy

The large group of people who work for the federal government, mostly for the executive branch

Cabinet

A group of executive department leaders who advise the president

Executive agencies

Agencies within the executive branch of government under the direct control of the president

Regulatory commissions

Government agencies that watch over some part of the U.S. economy

There are three branches of government in the United States. They are the **legislative branch**, the **judicial branch**, and the **executive branch**. The Congress is the legislative branch. It makes the laws. The courts are the judicial branch. It interprets the laws. The executive branch makes sure that the laws are carried out. The president is the chief executive.

Over three million other federal government workers form the **federal bureaucracy**. Some of the bureaucracy is part of the legislative branch, but most of it belongs to the executive branch. The bureaucracy sometimes is called the fourth branch of government because it has grown so large and important.

How Is the Federal Bureaucracy Organized?

The federal bureaucracy has three main parts:

• **Cabinet** departments and independent **executive agencies**

• Independent **regulatory commissions**

• Government corporations

The Cabinet is not mentioned in the Constitution. It developed almost as soon as George Washington was elected the first president of the United States. The Cabinet is a group of executive department leaders who advise the president. The number of Cabinet members can change. The leader of the newest department, the Department of Homeland Security, became a member of the Cabinet in 2002.

Cabinet departments are large. They include many separate agencies. Many people work within each department. Each department is made up of smaller units called bureaus, offices, services, or divisions. These offices are scattered around the country wherever they are needed to serve the people. Almost every Cabinet department affects the economy in some way. Several Cabinet departments have great power to affect the economy.

The Department of Agriculture has offices in every state. It oversees farmers to make sure food production meets demand. It inspects meat, poultry, and dairy products to make sure they are safe to eat. It tries to help farmers and consumers through its many food services. Its Food and Nutrition Service provides food stamps and runs school lunch programs. Its Natural Resource Conservation Service teaches farmers about the soil and growing crops.

In the late 1800s, Congress passed laws against unfair labor practices. The Department of Labor was set up in 1913 to enforce these laws. Today, it sees that all federal laws concerning labor are carried out. It enforces child labor and minimum wage laws. Its Employment Standards Administration enforces fair hiring practices. It stops discrimination against minorities, women, veterans, and disabled people.

One of the most important parts of the Department of Labor is the Occupational Safety and Health Administration (OSHA). It sets health and safety standards for the workplace. The Department of Labor also includes the Unemployment Insurance Services. This provides money to workers who have lost their jobs through no fault of their own.

The Department of Commerce began in 1903. It was created to encourage the growth of American business. It oversees business and trade in the United States and in foreign countries. It collects information about the health of the U.S. economy. The department is made up of several agencies. For example, the U.S. Patent Office issues patents to people who invent new products or ideas.

What Are Independent Executive Agencies?

Independent executive agencies are not part of the Cabinet. They are agencies within the executive branch of government under the direct control of the president. The size and duties of each agency differ greatly. The General Services Administration (GSA), for example, is very large and important. It manages federal government property and records. The Small Business Administration (SBA) is another large agency. It helps people start new businesses. It gives them advice about setting up and operating a business. It provides low-cost loans to help the businesses get off the ground.

The Social Security Administration (SSA) became an independent agency in 1994. More than 65,000 people work for the agency. The SSA spends more money than any of the other independent agencies. Most of the money is paid to retired or disabled workers. Children and the husbands and wives of workers who have died receive benefits too. The SSA also handles health care for people over 65. The program that provides medical care for the elderly is called **Medicare**.

What Are Independent Regulatory Commissions?

An independent regulatory commission is a government agency that watches over some part of the U.S. economy. Some regulatory commissions look after transportation and communication. Other regulatory commissions control banking, labor unions, public utilities, and corporations. They make and enforce rules. The rules that these regulatory commissions make affect many parts of our everyday lives.

What Are Some of the Most Important Regulatory Commissions?

The Federal Trade Commission (FTC) enforces laws that protect the public. It protects us from such things as price fixing, false labeling, and advertising that makes untrue claims. The FTC also makes sure that products put on the market are safe. It makes sure that labels on products are truthful so that buyers know what they are getting.

The Federal Communications Commission (FCC) controls who can have a license to broadcast over radio and television. It watches over interstate and international communications by radio, television, wire, satellite, and cable. The FCC has several bureaus and offices that have a direct effect on business. For example, the Office of Communications Business Opportunities gives advice to small and minority-owned communication businesses.

The National Labor Relations Board (NLRB) has two main purposes. The first is to see that workers are treated fairly by their employers and by labor groups. The second is to hold secret ballot elections when employees vote on whether they wish to be represented by a labor union. Workers may file complaints and lawsuits against employers and unions through this agency.

The Federal Communications Commission (FCC) controls the many kinds of media such as radio and television.

What Is a Government Corporation?

A government corporation is like a private corporation. The big difference is that the government owns it rather than shareholders. The president of the United States chooses a board of directors and a general manager to run each government corporation. Congress must approve these choices. Government corporations are supposed to be more flexible than regular government agencies. They are free from certain controls that affect other agencies.

Today, there are over 50 government corporations in the executive branch. The best known of these is the United States Postal Service (USPS). It became a government corporation in 1971. It operates and protects the nation's mail service. Only the Postal Service can deliver first-class mail. It delivers over 630 million pieces of mail every day. The USPS employs nearly 800,000 workers.

Another government corporation is the Federal Deposit Insurance Corporation (FDIC). It was created to protect the savings of Americans. The FDIC will repay a person's money, up to $100,000, if a bank fails.

Lesson 2 Review On a separate sheet of paper, write answers to the following questions. Use complete sentences.

1. What are the three branches of the United States government?

2. What is the name of the agency that pays money to retired or disabled workers?

3. What is the purpose of the Federal Communications Commission?

4. List the two purposes of the National Labor Relations Board.

5. What is the name of the best-known government corporation?

What do you think ?

6. Why do you think only the United States Postal Service can deliver first-class mail?

7. Do you think the U.S. government needs a bureaucracy? Explain.

What Is Fiscal Policy?

Economists agree on some things. They agree that steady economic growth is good. They all want employment for every person who wants to work. They also believe that high productivity and stable prices are good goals. Earlier we learned that the Federal Reserve System uses monetary policy to influence the economy. **Fiscal policy** is the government's use of spending and taxes to achieve a strong, stable economy.

How Does the Government Use Fiscal Policy to Encourage Economic Growth?

In Chapter 8, we learned about the circular flow of money in the economy. The circular flow model is important because it shows how a change in one part of the economy can cause changes in another. It is important to keep this idea in mind when we talk about fiscal policy.

Suppose the government increases its spending. For example, it decides to add to the highway system or to build a new weapons system. The effect is to create more jobs. More working people means more total spending in the economy. This kind of policy is called **expansionary fiscal policy**. The hope is that as a result of the policy, the economy will expand, or grow. The government might use an expansionary fiscal policy if the economy is not growing fast enough and there are not enough jobs.

Another way the government tries to get the economy to grow is through tax cuts. Suppose the government decides to lower taxes. This means that consumers and businesses have more money to spend. People have more money for groceries, clothes, and new cars. Businesses have more money to spend on new equipment, factories, and raw materials. If they spend the extra money, it creates a demand for more production. By increasing spending, the economy expands. When people and businesses save the extra money instead of spending it, the economy will not grow.

How Does the Government Use Fiscal Policy to Slow Down the Economy?

Fiscal policy can be used to slow down and expand the economy. The president and Congress might use fiscal policy to slow down spending if they feel that prices are rising too fast. Government might spend less. It could raise taxes. The effect of both actions is to reduce the amount of money available to buy goods and services. There is less total spending. The government might take these actions to lower inflation. The goal is to contract, or make the economy smaller. This kind of policy is called **contractionary fiscal policy**.

How Did President Bush Try to Increase Economic Growth?

In 2003, President Bush got Congress to pass a $330 billion dollar tax cut. Some people believed it was risky. The supporters said the tax cut would create a huge investment boom. Bush and his backers in Congress believed that the tax cut would push businesses to expand. New workers would be hired and the economy would begin to grow again. Some supporters said the tax cut would create as many as one million new jobs.

Those against the tax cut said it would cause a huge jump in the federal **deficit**. The deficit is the difference between how much money the government takes in and how much it spends.

Biography

W. Arthur Lewis: 1915–1991

British economist W. Arthur Lewis published an article detailing his idea of the "dual economy" in 1954. He felt that a poor country's economy could be viewed as having two very different parts. One was a small capitalist sector while the other was a very large farming sector. Employers in the capitalist sector cut down on overhead, often through efficient hiring. Those in the agricultural sector often hire too many people, so the productivity is low.

Lewis thought that more workers should be directed to jobs in the capitalist sector, especially in manufacturing. Increased staffing and profit would mean a growth in industry. He argued that a poor country's increase in farm product exports just brings down the market value of those products. Lewis and another man, Theodore Schultz, were awarded the Nobel Prize in 1979 for research in economic development.

To make up the difference, the government has to borrow money. We know that the supply of money for loans is limited. Government will be in competition with businesses that need money to expand. This will cause interest rates to rise.

One of the problems with fiscal policy is that it works slowly. It takes a long time for the government to make decisions. By the time it does, the economy may have changed. Some economists believe that the government can never get it right. They believe it is best for the government to leave the economy alone.

What Is Supply-Side Economics?

The debate over fiscal policy points out that not all economists agree. They have two very different points of view. **Supply-side economics** is the belief that the best way to keep an economy stable and growing is to increase the supply of goods and services. Supply-side economists believe in laissez-faire. They do not want the government to play a big role in the economy. They believe government control makes it hard for businesses to operate well. Reducing control will give businesses incentives to increase production. Prices will drop because the supply of goods and services increases. Businesses will hire more workers as their production goes up. Supply-side economists favor tax cuts. They believe the tax cuts encourage people and businesses to spend and invest more. This increases demand and causes the economy to grow.

What Is Demand-Side Economics?

Demand-side economics focuses on the role of demand. Demand-side economists believe the government's policies can increase the total amount of goods and services consumers want to buy. They believe that government control of the economy is necessary. They believe that the government should be involved to create jobs. For example, suppose the government decides to spend billions of dollars on new roads. Many new construction jobs would be created. The new workers would spend the money they earned. This would increase total demand. More people would have jobs, and the economy would begin to grow.

Figure 15.1 summarizes the points of view of supply-side and demand-side economics.

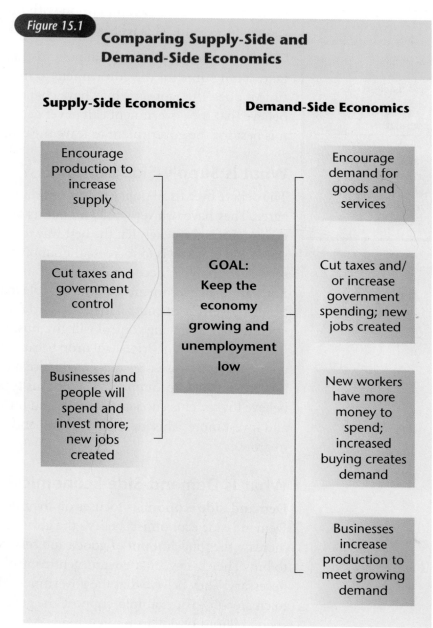

Figure 15.1

Comparing Supply-Side and Demand-Side Economics

Supply-Side Economics

Demand-Side Economics

Encourage production to increase supply

Encourage demand for goods and services

GOAL: Keep the economy growing and unemployment low

Cut taxes and government control

Cut taxes and/or increase government spending; new jobs created

Businesses and people will spend and invest more; new jobs created

New workers have more money to spend; increased buying creates demand

Businesses increase production to meet growing demand

Lesson 3 Review On a separate sheet of paper, write the letter of the answer that correctly completes each sentence.

1. Increased government spending that leads to more total spending is _____.

   A contractionary fiscal policy

   B expansionary fiscal policy

   C laissez-faire

   D legislative fiscal policy

2. By spending less or raising taxes, the government follows a(n) _____ policy.

   A contractionary fiscal

   B expansionary fiscal

   C laissez-faire

   D executive fiscal

3. The difference between what the government spends and what it takes in is _____.

   A laissez-faire

   B the deficit

   C the economy

   D a depression

4. _____ economics is the belief that the best way to make the economy grow is to increase the supply of goods and services.

   A Demand-side

   B Regulated

   C Supply-side

   D Unregulated

5. _____ economics is the belief that one way to make the economy grow is to have more government involvement in the economy.

   A Demand-side

   B Regulated

   C Supply-side

   D Unregulated

What do you think ?

6. Do you think it is fair for the government to raise taxes to slow down the economy? Explain.

7. Do you agree more with supply-side or demand-side economists? Why?

Protective tariff

A tax used to protect certain businesses; it is a tax on imports

Import

A good entering the country from another country

Sin tax

A tax that can be used to get people to stop doing certain things that the government finds harmful

Income tax

A tax people pay on money earned

Progressive tax

A tax in which the more money a person makes, the greater the percentage paid in taxes

In 1789, Benjamin Franklin joked that nothing in life is certain except death and taxes. Taxes are payments to the government. Taxes can be paid to a city, a state, or the federal government. They are as old as civilization. Taxpayers' dislike of taxes goes back as far.

How Are Taxes Used?

The main purpose of taxes is to pay for the cost of government. Taxes also have several other uses. They can be used to protect certain businesses. Such a tax is called a **protective tariff**. It is a tax on **imports**, or goods entering the country from another country. The tax increases the cost of the imported goods. Consumers are more likely to buy goods made in their own country if those goods are cheaper than imported ones.

Taxes can be used to get people to stop doing certain things that the government finds harmful. This type of tax sometimes is called a **sin tax**. For example, governments try to discourage people from drinking alcohol and smoking. To do this, they raise taxes on cigarettes and liquor. The high costs sometimes stop people from drinking and smoking.

Taxes also can be used to encourage certain activities. In the 1970s, the government wanted businesses and people to lower their energy costs. The government offered lower taxes to businesses and people who bought equipment that used less energy. This gave businesses an incentive to build factories and install machines that saved energy. Some homeowners replaced their old windows with new ones that lowered their energy needs.

What Is a Progressive Tax?

The federal **income tax** (a tax people pay on money earned) is an example of a **progressive tax**. The more money a person makes, the greater the percentage paid in taxes. For example, suppose we look at two workers. The first earns $100,000 a year. The second worker makes $20,000. The tax rate for the lower income worker is 15 percent. The person making $100,000 pays 35 percent. The higher income person pays a tax of $35,000. The lower income person pays $3,000.

Proportional tax

A tax that is stated as a percentage; also called flat tax

Regressive tax

A tax in which the higher the income, the smaller the percentage of income paid as taxes

🗒️ **Writing About Economics**

You have learned about progressive, proportional, and regressive taxes. Select the tax that you think is best. Write a speech as if you were a member of Congress. Explain why you think the tax you chose is best.

Some people think that a progressive tax is a good idea. They believe that people making more money should pay a higher rate. Other people argue that this is unfair to people who earn a lot of money.

What Is a Proportional Tax?

A **proportional tax** sometimes is called a flat tax. It is stated as a percentage. Suppose the United States had a flat tax. The tax rate would be the same no matter what a person's income was.

Suppose we look at the two workers in the example in the last paragraph on page 306 again. A proportional tax of 20 percent would take $20,000 from the higher income worker. The lower income worker would pay $4,000. The proportion of money taken out for taxes stays the same as income rises. Some people like this kind of tax because it treats everyone equally. They believe that proportional taxes are more fair than the progressive taxes the United States has.

What Is a Regressive Tax?

Most taxes, other than income taxes, are regressive. With a **regressive tax**, the higher the income, the smaller the percentage of income paid as taxes. For example, let's say that the two workers above both decide to buy a computer. The cost of the computers they buy is $1,000 with an 8 percent sales tax. They both pay an extra $80. The $80 the lower-income person pays is a higher percentage of that person's income than the $80 the higher-income person pays.

What Are the Most Common Types of Federal Taxes?

Figure 15.2 on page 308 shows from where the U.S. government gets its money. Individual income tax provides the biggest share. This tax sometimes is called "personal income tax." Most people in the United States must pay income tax. It is a progressive tax. What people pay depends on how much money they earn. The earnings include money they earn from jobs. It also includes money earned from investments.

Corporate income tax

The amount of money a corporation pays the government on money it earns each year

Deduction

An expense like a medical expense or interest on a loan that can be subtracted from income taxes

Adjustment

A part of income that is not taxed, such as all or part of Social Security benefits

Exemption

An exact dollar amount that is not taxed, such as a claim for each child who depends on his or her parents

Figure 15.2

Where the United States Government Gets Its Money

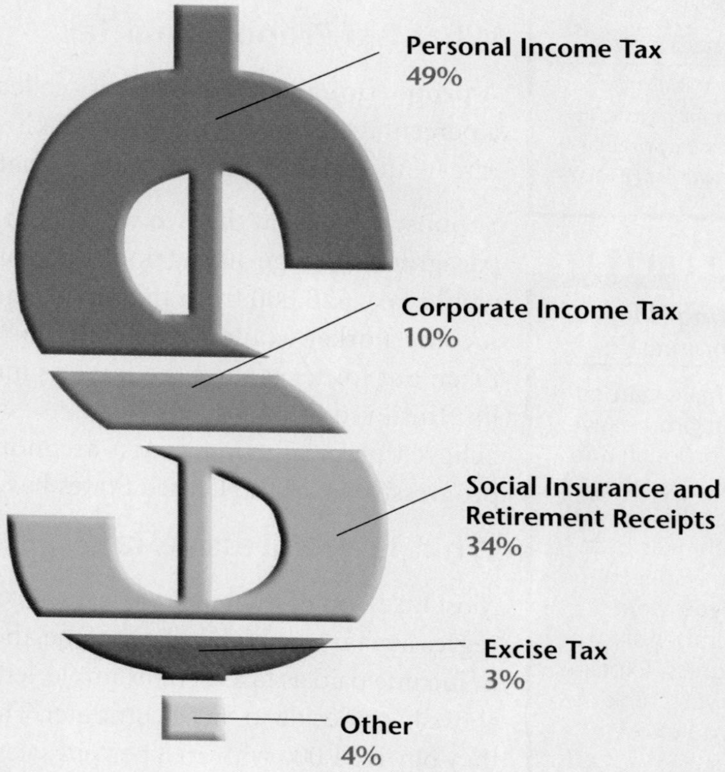

Personal Income Tax
49%

Corporate Income Tax
10%

Social Insurance and Retirement Receipts
34%

Excise Tax
3%

Other
4%

Corporations pay taxes too. **Corporate income tax** is the amount of money a corporation pays the government on money it earns each year.

People and corporations pay taxes based on "taxable income." It is the income after **deductions**, **adjustments**, and **exemptions** from the total or gross income. Deductions are expenses like medical expenses and interest on loans. Adjustments may be parts of income that are not taxed, such as all or part of Social Security benefits. An exemption is an exact dollar amount that is not taxed. Taxpayers can claim an exemption for each child who depends on his or her parents.

Anyone who works knows that take-home pay is much less than gross pay. A certain amount is taken out for federal and state income taxes. Some money also is taken out for Social Security tax. The Social Security tax is shown as FICA on the paychecks that workers receive. FICA stands for Federal Insurance Contribution Act. Everybody has to pay this tax no matter how little they earn. Social Security is money the government pays to retired and disabled workers. More than 50 million Americans receive Social Security payments each month.

An **excise tax** is a tax on certain goods made in the country. The goods taxed are often luxuries, but not always. There are excise taxes on perfume, alcohol, and tobacco. Sometimes an excise tax helps pay for services for the people who buy an item. For example, the excise tax on gasoline helps pay for roads. Businesses sometimes pay excise taxes too. For example, businesses that process natural resources like lumber and natural gas pay excise taxes. Gas and electric companies also pay them.

A **customs tax** was the first tax Congress passed. The customs tax, or tariff, is a tax placed on goods imported from another country.

When a person dies, that person can leave property and money to family and friends. An **estate tax** is a tax on the property that was left. The person receiving money from the person who died may have to pay taxes. This tax is called an **inheritance tax**. People are allowed to give gifts of money or property before they die. Whether a tax has to be paid depends on the total value of the money or property. If the value is less than $1,000,000, no estate taxes have to be paid.

The Internal Revenue Service is the federal agency that collects tax money. It is commonly known by its initials, IRS.

What Kinds of Taxes Do States and Local Governments Collect?

States and local governments also collect a variety of taxes. Local taxes are paid to towns, cities, and counties. The taxes are computed and collected in the same way as federal taxes. The rates, however, are not as high. Therefore, people or corporations pay less to state and local governments than to the federal government. Income taxes are the major source of income for most state and local governments.

Many state and local governments collect **sales taxes**. A sales tax is a tax that is paid on the price of goods or services. Sales taxes are not paid on every product. For example, some states do not collect sales taxes on food or medicine. There is not a sales tax on home sales. Sales taxes differ from state to state.

Economics in Your Life

Identity Theft

Identity theft happens when someone uses another person's name to commit a crime, usually for financial gain. The thief may take money from bank accounts, make credit purchases, or run up large phone card bills. Sometimes the identity thief opens new accounts in the victim's name. Recovering from identify theft can be a very long, difficult process. In 1998, the U.S. Congress passed laws making identity theft a federal crime.

Identity thieves may look through trash to find banking or credit card account numbers. At times, they gain personal information by telephone or during Internet sessions. You can decrease the likelihood of identity theft in many ways.

- Destroy old credit cards and banking materials before throwing them into the trash.

- Never give out personal information over the telephone unless you know the other person well.

- Make Internet purchases only through secure payment sites and pay by credit card.

- Review monthly credit card and bank statements to check on all charges.

Property tax

A tax that people who own buildings, land, and other property must pay

A big source of money for state and local governments is **property tax**. This is a tax that people who own buildings, land, and other property must pay. The amount of tax collected depends on the estimated value of the property. The money collected from property taxes often pays for such things as police and fire protection. It also helps pay for road building and repair. Much of the property taxes collected pay for the cost of building and maintaining public schools.

Word Bank

finds harmful

customs taxes

imports

Internal Revenue Service

regressive taxes

Lesson 4 Review On a separate sheet of paper, write the word from the Word Bank to complete each sentence.

1. A protective tariff is a tax on _____.

2. A sin tax is placed on something the government _____.

3. _____ are a higher percentage of a smaller income.

4. The first taxes used in the United States were _____.

5. The agency that collects U.S. taxes is the _____.

What do you think

6. Most states have both state income taxes and sales taxes. In the states with no state taxes, sales taxes are usually much higher than in states with income taxes. Which kind of state would you prefer to live or work in? Explain using what you learned in this lesson.

7. Taxes are used for many purposes. What might happen if there were no taxes at all? Explain.

Document-Based Reading

Tax Relief Plan

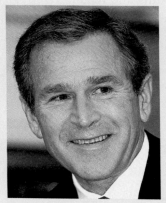

When United States President George W. Bush took office, one thing he wanted to do was reduce taxes. He believed a tax cut would help create jobs and boost the economy. Below is an excerpt from Radio Address by the President to the Nation *from February 2001.*

Today many Americans are feeling squeezed. They work 40, 50, 60 hours a week, and still have trouble paying the electric bill and the grocery bill at the same time. At the end of a long week, they collect their paycheck, and what the federal government takes is often unfair. . . .

My plan does some important things for America. It reduces taxes for everyone who pays taxes. It lowers the lowest income tax rate from 15 percent to 10 percent. It cuts the highest rate to 33 percent, because I believe no one should pay more than a third of their income to the federal government. The average family of four will get about $1,600 of their own money returned back to them.

There's a lot of talk in Washington about paying down the national debt, and that's good, and that's important. And my budget will do that. But American families have debts to pay, as well. A tax cut now will stimulate our economy and create jobs. . . .

My plan will keep all Social Security money in the Social Security system, where it belongs. We will eliminate the death tax [estate tax], saving family farms and family-owned businesses. We'll reduce the maximum rate on small business income to 33 percent, so they can help create the jobs we need. Above all, my plan unlocks the door to the middle class for millions of hardworking Americans.

Despite much criticism from Democrats, Congress approved a $330 billion 10-year tax cut. The Senate approved the bill by a 51–50 vote with Vice President Dick Cheney casting the deciding vote. The bill passed in the House by a 231–200 vote. President Bush signed the bill into law on May 28, 2003.

Document-Based Questions

1. Why did President Bush want to reduce taxes?

2. According to Bush, how would his plan affect income tax rates?

3. What are two other ways Bush said his plan would help Americans?

4. Why do you think Democrats criticized the tax plan?

5. Do you think it is more important to reduce taxes or to pay down the national debt? Explain.

- During the late 1800s and early 1900s, the U.S. government grew. After the Great Depression of the 1930s, the government's role in the economy grew even more.

- To deal with issues affecting many people, the government creates public policy. This occurs when all of the laws and rules about people's behavior are brought together.

- The large group of people who work for the government is the federal bureaucracy. Because the bureaucracy is so large, it is sometimes called the fourth branch of government.

- The three main parts of the federal bureaucracy are Cabinet departments and independent executive agencies, independent regulatory commissions, and government corporations.

- The president directly controls independent executive agencies. The Small Business Administration (SBA) and the Social Security Administration (SSA) are examples.

- Independent regulatory commissions watch over areas of the U.S. economy. Some examples are the Federal Trade Commission (FTC), Federal Communications Commission (FCC), and the National Labor Relations Board (NLRB).

- A general manager and board of directors chosen by the president run government corporations. The United States Postal Service (USPS) and the Federal Deposit Insurance Corporation (FDIC) are two government corporations.

- Fiscal policy is the use of spending and taxing to create a strong economy. Fiscal policy can be either expansionary or contractionary.

- Taxes serve many purposes. They may pay for government services. They protect certain businesses. Protective tariffs increase the cost of imports. Sin taxes may be used to get people to stop harmful activities. Other taxes encourage helpful activities.

- The three kinds of taxes are progressive, regressive, and proportional, or flat, taxes. Some federal tax examples are income, Social Security, excise, customs, and estate taxes.

- The Internal Revenue Service (IRS) collects tax money in the United States.

- Besides federal taxes, states and other local governments collect taxes. Some examples are sales and property taxes.

Chapter 15 REVIEW

On a separate sheet of paper, write the word from the Word Bank to complete each sentence.

Word Bank

bureaucracy

Cabinet

Constitution

deficit

excise

progressive tax

tax cuts

1. The _____ gives the U.S. government the power to control trade.

2. The _____ is a group of people who advise the president.

3. The federal _____ is a group of workers who work for the federal government.

4. Sometimes the government uses _____ to make the economy grow.

5. The _____ is the difference between the money the government takes in and the money it spends.

6. A(n) _____ tax is a tax on goods made in a country.

7. With a _____, a person pays a greater percentage of taxes by earning more money.

On a separate sheet of paper, write the letter of the answer that correctly completes each sentence.

8. Government decision making is called public _____.

   A affairs   **C** policy

   B good   **D** voting

9. _____ are agencies in the executive branch under the president's direct control.

   A Independent executive agencies   **C** Public corporations

   B Nonprofit corporations   **D** Public agencies

10. The government, rather than private shareholders, owns a _____.

   A government corporation   **C** private business

   B government lobby   **D** public office

11. To have a strong, healthy economy, the government uses
_____.

   A competition   **C** increased taxation

   B fiscal policy   **D** excise taxes

12. A tax that protects certain businesses is a(n) _____.

   A enterprise   **C** protective tariff

   B progressive tax   **D** tax cut

13. Another name for a proportional tax is a(n) _____.

   A flat tax   **C** steep tax

   B regressive tax   **D** tariff

On a separate sheet of paper, write answers to the following questions. Use complete sentences.

14. What does laissez-faire mean?

15. Which department was created to enforce laws against unfair labor practices?

16. Which economic point of view wants to increase the economy by increasing the supply of goods and services?

17. List the three basic types of taxes. Explain each.

On a separate sheet of paper, write your opinion to each question. Use complete sentences.

18. Why do you think the government has grown as huge businesses developed?

19. Many people complain about government bureaucracy. What do you think might happen if no bureaucracy existed?

20. Where do you think higher taxes are needed? Where do you think lower taxes might be needed?

Test-Taking Tip

When taking a short-answer test, first answer the questions you know. Then go back to spend time on the questions that you are less sure about.

16 The Federal Budget

We know that government has a large income. It collects trillions of dollars in taxes. Government also is a big spender. Every year, the United States government creates a budget. This budget has an important influence on all Americans.

This chapter will discuss the federal budget and the debt the United States owes.

Goals for Learning

◆ To describe the federal budget process

◆ To discuss how the government spends its money

◆ To explain the national debt and its impact on the economy

Federal budget

An estimate of how much money the federal government will take in and how much it will spend in a year

Fiscal year

The government's spending period from October 1 to September 30 of the next year

Priority

Something that receives attention before anything else; the thing that is most important

Compromise

To give up a part of what one wants in order to settle differences and reach agreement

In Chapter 13, you learned how important it is to create a budget for yourself. You learned that a budget is a plan for spending and saving money. The **federal budget** is an estimate of how much money the government will take in and how much it will spend in a year. The budget covers 12 months starting on October 1 and ending September 30 of the next year. This period is the government's **fiscal year**.

Why Is the Budget Important?

The federal budget tells us the national **priorities**. Priorities are things that receive attention before anything else. In other words, they are what is most important. For example, finishing school has a higher priority than getting married for most high school students. Likewise, if the government decides to spend more on education, that means that the government thinks good schools are important. Cutting spending does not mean that the areas of cuts are not important. It means that they have a lower priority, at least in the government's opinion at the time.

Work begins on the federal budget more than a year before the money is spent. Both the president and the Congress look at the budget carefully. Deciding which programs to fund and which to cut is very hard. Rarely is everyone happy with the final budget. Some groups become upset because the budget leaves out things that are important to them. The final budget is always a **compromise**. This means that to settle differences and reach agreement, all groups have to give up a part of what they want.

What Is the Budget Process?

The president proposes the budget to Congress, but Congress must approve it. The proposed budget reflects the president's priorities. For example, the president may have to decide on a new weapons system or a program to help senior citizens, or both. Of course, the president does not have time to make every minor budget decision. Most details are left to the budget director and the White House staff. Congress then draws up its own version of the budget. It can expand some programs and cut others.

What Is the Job of the Office of Management and Budget?

The budget director heads the Office of Management and Budget (OMB). It is in charge of preparing the president's budget. It begins work more than a year and a half before the beginning of the fiscal year. The OMB reports to the president on the state of the economy. The budget director may suggest to the president what fiscal policies the government should follow.

What Is the President's Role in the Budget?

The president adjusts the size of the federal budget based on information from the OMB. The president suggests general spending targets for each of the Cabinet departments. After the president has set the targets, the many parts of the federal bureaucracy begin planning their budgets. OMB leaders meet with each department and agency to work out budget details. The president reviews each department's plans and makes the final changes. In January of each year, the president sends the proposed budget to Congress.

What Is the Role of Congress in the Budget?

Congress and the president do not always agree on spending priorities. There often is conflict over the budget. Both the Senate and the House of Representatives have budget committees. These committees look at the president's budget

The president of the United States proposes the budget, but Congress must approve it.

and make changes. The Congressional Budget Office (CBO) helps Congress look at the budget. Congress approves the final budget by passing a set of **appropriation bills**. These bills give each government agency the money it needs for the year.

Veto

To reject

What Happens After Congress Approves the Budget?

Like all bills, appropriation bills are sent to the president. If the president signs them, they become law. The president may **veto**, or reject, any appropriation bills. In 1996, Congress gave the president the power to reject certain budget items. Before then, the president had to accept or reject the budget as a whole. A bill can still become law even if the president vetoes it. This happens only if two-thirds of Congress votes for the bill.

Why Does the Budget Have to Be Changed?

Just like a personal budget, the federal budget has to be flexible. It is based on estimated income and spending. For many reasons, the amount of money the government collects in taxes can be lower than expected. Likewise, there can be unexpected expenses. For example, after the September 11, 2001 attacks, the government spent billions of dollars defending the country against similar attacks. The government also has spent billions of dollars fighting in Iraq and Afghanistan. These events forced Congress to adjust the budget.

Biography

John Maynard Keynes: 1883–1946

British economist John Maynard Keynes is an important person in the history of economics. During World War I, Keynes created a plan for paying for Britain's war effort. He did so well that he was asked to take part in the peace conference at the end of the war. At the conference, he felt that damage payments asked of Germany were too harsh. Keynes resigned from the conference and wrote *Economic Consequences of Peace*. This book criticized the Treaty of Versailles, the peace treaty that ended World War I.

In 1936, Keynes published a book called *The General Theory of Employment, Interest, and Money*. Many economists believe that this book is the most important economics writing of the 20th century. It changed the way the world looked at how the role of government affects the economy.

Keynes also taught at Cambridge University. His talks and writings brought him into debates on public policy. He believed that monetary policy of governments could control the economy. Many of his ideas were used during World War II, including controlling supply and demand of consumer goods through a system of rationing.

Lesson 1 Review On a separate sheet of paper, write the letter of the answer that correctly completes each sentence.

1. The 12 months from October 1 to September 30 of the next year is the government's _____ year.

   A calendar
   B fiscal
   C governing
   D planning

2. The final budget for any year is a _____ because all groups have had to give up something.

   A compromise
   B failure
   C necessity
   D success

3. During the _____, the president proposes a budget, and Congress must approve it.

   A budget process
   B coming year
   C compromise process
   D fiscal year

4. The president sends the budget to Congress every _____.

   A month
   B July
   C January
   D two years

5. The president can _____, or reject, Congress's appropriation bills.

   A increase
   B decrease
   C lower
   D veto

What do you think ?

6. Why do you think Congress has to approve the president's budget?

7. Why do you think the government must start working on the federal budget so far in advance? Give examples from the lesson to support your ideas.

What Are Private and Public Sectors?

Private sector

Consumers buying goods and services

Public sector

Federal, state, and local governments buying goods and services

Human resources

The benefits paid directly to people, including Social Security, income security, Medicare, health, education, and veterans' benefits

Income security

The benefits paid to retired workers who are not covered by Social Security

Consumer spending is called the **private sector**. Governments are important consumers too. Federal, state, and local governments spend nearly three trillion dollars a year. This spending is called the **public sector**.

On What Does the U.S. Government Spend Money?

The United States government spent over two trillion dollars in 2002. Where did the money go? To better understand government spending, the government breaks down its spending into several large categories. (See Figure 16.1.)

Human Resources

The largest category of government spending is **human resources**. It includes all benefits paid directly to the people: Social Security, **income security**, Medicare, health, education, and benefits and services for those who have served in the military.

The Social Security program is the largest category of government spending on human resources. Benefits are paid mostly to retired or disabled workers. Children and spouses dependent on workers who have become too sick to work or who have died also may get money.

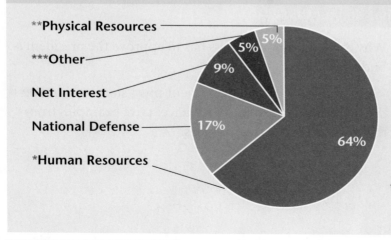

Figure 16.1 **Federal Spending for 2002**

**Physical Resources
***Other
Net Interest
National Defense — 17%
*Human Resources — 64%

5% 5%
9%

*Human Resources includes: education, training, employment, and social services; health; Medicare; income security; Social Security; and veterans' benefits and services.

**Physical Resources includes: energy; natural resources and environment; commerce and housing credit; transportation; and community and regional development.

***Other includes: international affairs, agriculture, administration of justice, and general government.

Medicaid

A government program that gives medical insurance to low-income people

Veteran

A man or woman who has served in the armed forces

Entitlement

A benefit such as Social Security, income security, or Medicare to which people feel they have a right

Writing About Economics

Find a newspaper, magazine, or Internet article about government spending. Read the article and summarize it in a paragraph. Include where the money is being spent and how much it will cost. Share your article and paragraph with your class.

Income security includes benefits paid to retired workers who are not covered by Social Security. They include retired military persons, government workers, and railroad workers. This category also includes such things as food programs to help low-income families.

Medicare, as you learned in Chapter 14, is a government program that provides medical services to people over age 65. The largest part of the health category is **Medicaid**. This is a program that gives medical insurance to people with low income. Drug treatment and mental health programs, as well as cancer research, fall under health spending. The Occupational, Safety, and Health Administration (OSHA) does too.

The federal government spends a lot of money on education. It funds schools at every level, programs for daycare, foster care, and summer employment for students. Children who are homeless, neglected, or handicapped also receive help.

Veterans are men and women who have served in the armed forces. They receive education and training benefits from the government. Veterans who want to buy a home can get special mortgages that charge a lower interest rate than regular mortgages.

Social Security, income security, Medicare, and similar programs are **entitlements**. Many people believe they are entitled, or have a right to, these benefits. As a result, the president and Congress are not likely to cut these benefits. Entitlements are the fastest growing part of the federal budget.

National Defense

Until the late 1990s, national defense was the largest category of federal spending. Some of the money goes to pay the men and women in the armed forces. Much of the money is spent developing new weapons and buying equipment for the military.

Net Interest

The government often spends more money than it takes in. When this happens, it has to borrow money. Much of the federal budget goes to paying the interest on the money owed. This is called net interest. In 2002, the government paid an estimated $178.4 billion in interest. As the amount of money owed continues to grow, so does the net interest.

Physical Resources

Physical resources include money spent on natural resources and the environment. The costs of pollution control and buying land for new national parks also fall into this group. Transportation is part of physical resources. This includes spending for new highways, airports, and certain forms of mass transit, such as buses and trains.

Economics at Work

Sociologist

A sociologist studies the ways in which groups of people interact. Sociologists complete research, field work, and written reports about human behavior. They study many different groups, including social classes, minorities, women, children, political groups, and religious groups.

There are many other career fields in which a sociologist may work. Sociologists may teach or write about social issues. They often work as experts for leaders dealing with social problems. In some cases, sociologists work for change on behalf of a certain group. Sometimes sociologists work in social services, such as family planning or job training.

Sociology is a very large field. Many sociologists choose to specialize in certain areas. They may study crime prevention. They may work to solve problems within certain businesses. Some sociologists study the effects of technology in rural areas. Others look at the positive and negative outcomes of city development.

Lesson 2 Review On a separate sheet of paper, write answers to the following questions. Use complete sentences.

1. What is the largest category of government spending?

2. Who receives Social Security benefits?

3. What is an entitlement?

4. What is net interest?

5. How is money in the physical resources category spent?

What do you think ?

6. What do you think might happen if not enough money was available to pay for entitlement programs?

7. The government collects billions of dollars in taxes. Why do you think it must borrow money in addition to that?

Surplus

A budget in which more money is collected than is spent

National debt

All of the money the federal government owes to lenders

Crowding-out effect

The higher interest rates on borrowed money that result after the government has borrowed what it needs

If taxes equal government spending, the budget is balanced. However, it is unusual for a government to have an exactly balanced budget. Most of the time, budgets are either in deficit or **surplus**. If the government spends less than it collects, the budget has a surplus. More often, the government spends more than it collects. Such a budget has a deficit. Many people worry about a string of deficit budgets. The government has to borrow money to pay for the extra spending. The borrowed money must be paid back with interest. The money the government owes to all lenders is called the **national debt**.

How Long Has the United States Had a National Debt?

The United States first went into debt in 1790. The government decided to take over the Revolutionary War debts of the Continental Congress. By the end of 1790, the debt was just over $75 million. Because of World War II, there was a huge increase in the national debt. It rose from $40 billion to $279 billion. Wars like the Korean War and the Vietnam War made the debt even greater. In 2003, the government was spending nearly $4 billion a month on the war in Iraq. The Office of Management and Budget projected that the budget deficit will grow to $455 billion. This increased the national debt to nearly $7 trillion for 2003.

What Are Some Problems with Having a Large National Debt?

Many people have concerns about the growing national debt. One concern is higher interest rates. There is only so much money available for borrowing. The government has to borrow even if the interest rate is high. It results in what is called the **crowding-out effect**. Government borrowing "crowds out" other people and businesses that need to borrow. After the government takes what it needs, other borrowers must pay higher rates to borrow money. Some economists believe that if government borrowing increases, then economic growth will slow down. Productivity no longer will grow and the economy will slow down.

Another concern is the effect of the rising debt on future Americans who must pay back the debt. Some people are afraid of so much money being used to pay interest on the debt. They fear that the government will have to reduce its spending on other important goods and services. There may not be enough money to provide some of the programs Americans take for granted, such as Social Security. Businesses may not have enough capital to invest. America will lose its competitive edge.

Are There Any Advantages to the High Debt?

It is important to remember that government spending helped lift the economy out of depression and recession many times. The government continues to provide Americans with many necessary goods and services. If the government was forced to balance the budget, the quality of life for many Americans might get worse.

How Can the Government Spend Money It Does Not Have?

We know that the government owes trillions of dollars. Where does it borrow that much money? The government raises money by selling bonds and securities. There are four main types of bonds and securities that the United States Treasury sells: treasury bills, **treasury notes**, **treasury bonds**, and savings bonds. Treasury bills are short-term securities. They mature, or come due, in one year or less. The minimum amount is $1,000. Treasury notes mature in one to ten years. Notes range from $1,000 to $5,000. They earn a little higher interest rate than treasury bills. Treasury bonds are issued in units of $1,000. They are long-term investments whose maturity ranges from 10 to 30 years. Savings bonds can be bought for as little as $25. If you own a savings bond, you own part of the national debt.

Some government agencies hold the national debt. For example, the Social Security Administration holds about $2 trillion. It uses some of its surplus to buy government bonds and securities. People, businesses, banks, and even foreigners hold much of the debt. In fact, people in other countries and their governments own about one-fourth of the debt. Savers view government bonds and securities as good investments.

They know that their money is safe. The federal government always pays investors back with interest. For this reason, the government has little trouble selling its bonds and securities.

Economics in Your Life

The National Debt—Just How Big Is It?

The national debt is the total amount of money that the United States government owes. As of September 2003, the national debt was about $6.7 trillion. Written out, this number is $6,700,000,000,000. It is rising at a rate of more than $1 billion per day. The amount of the debt has risen steadily since 1983.

Just how much money is $6.7 trillion? Think about these examples.

- If your take-home pay was $20,000 per year, it would take you about 335 million years to earn this much money.
- You could buy 1,340,000 personal jets.
- You could buy 13,400 professional football teams.
- The richest person in America is worth about $50 billion. It would take the combined wealth of about 130 people like this to pay off the debt.

People sometimes confuse the national debt with the federal budget deficit. The national debt is the total amount the government owes. The deficit is the difference between the amount the government takes in and the amount it spends each year.

Word Bank

crowding-out effect

interest

national debt

savings bond

treasury bond

Lesson 3 Review On a separate sheet of paper, write the word from the Word Bank to complete each sentence.

1. The money the government owes to all lenders is the _____.

2. The _____ is when borrowers pay higher interest rates for money after the government takes what it needs.

3. One way people loan the government money is by purchasing a(n) _____.

4. The type of security with the longest maturity is the _____.

5. The government has little trouble selling bonds and securities because it always repays investors with _____.

What do you think?

6. Why might government debt be good? Explain.

7. If you had extra money, would you buy a shorter-term or longer-term government security? Why?

Savings Bonds

One way the United States government raises money is by selling savings bonds. During World War II, Americans bought bonds to help finance the war effort. They felt that by purchasing bonds, they were doing their part to help the United States win the war. Since World War II, savings bonds have continued to be an important way to help pay for the national debt. After the September 11, 2001 terrorist attacks, many Americans again felt the need to help. Because of this, the government issued a new savings bond called the Patriot Bond.

Secretary of the Treasury Paul H. O'Neill and U.S. Treasurer Rosario Marin . . . unveiled Series EE savings bonds designated as "Patriot Bonds" on the three-month anniversary of the September 11, 2001 terrorists attacks. . . .

"Since September 11, everywhere I go, Americans of every age come up to me and say they want to help," said Secretary O'Neill.

"We've seen an amazing outpouring of charity from across the nation, and an increase in the number of people who want to do public service," he said. "These are all healthy trends for our nation and our government. The Patriot Bond is an opportunity for all Americans to contribute to the government's war effort and save for their futures as well."

Series EE savings bonds sold through financial institutions will be specially inscribed with the legend "Patriot Bond." . . .

Series EE savings bonds, earn 90 percent of 5-year Treasury securities yields. . . . The bonds sell as half face value and are available in denominations of $50, $75, $100, $200, $500, $1,000, $5,000 and $10,000. *(For example, a $100 Patriot Bond costs $50.)*

Series EE bonds increase in value monthly and interest is compounded semiannually. Interest is exempt from state and local income taxes and federal tax can be deferred until the bond is redeemed or it stops earning interest at 30 years.

The money raised from the sale of Patriot Bonds is deposited in the general fund and spent according to law. While the funds are not used only for the War on Terrorism, they do help support America's anti-terrorism effort.

Document-Based Questions

1. Why does the United States government sell savings bonds?

2. Why did many Americans buy bonds during World War II?

3. What is a Patriot Bond?

4. How much would a $500 Patriot Bond cost?

5. Do you think savings bonds are a good investment for Americans? Explain.

- Work on the federal budget starts more than a year before the money is spent. The White House staff and the Office of Management and Budget (OMB) draw up the president's budget.

- The president suggests spending targets. OMB officials work out the details. The president presents the budget to Congress each January.

- Congress looks at the budget with help from the Congressional Budget Office (CBO). Congress passes appropriation bills and returns the budget to the president. The president may either sign the bills into law or veto them.

- Consumer spending is called the private sector. Government spending is called the public sector.

- Human resources is the largest category of government spending. Entitlements are programs that people feel they have a right to receive.

- Social Security pays benefits to retired or disabled workers and people dependent on workers who have become too sick to work or have died.

- Retired workers not covered by Social Security receive income security. These people include retired military, government, and railroad workers.

- Medicare provides medical services to people older than age 65. Medicaid provides health insurance to low-income people.

- Schools in every state and at every level receive education funds. This money also funds daycare programs and foster care.

- Veterans' benefits include education and training benefits and special mortgage rates.

- Other government expenses include national defense, interest payments on the national debt, and physical resources.

- The national debt is money the government owes all lenders. The United States has had a national debt since 1790.

- One concern with having a large national debt is that government spending will create a crowding-out effect and push interest rates higher. A second concern is that the government spends too much on paying back the debt. People worry that not enough money will remain to pay for other necessary goods and services.

- Many times, government spending has helped lift the country out of a depression or recession.

- The four main types of government bonds and securities are treasury bills, treasury notes, treasury bonds, and savings bonds.

- Government agencies, businesses, banks, and people and governments from other countries hold much of the national debt in bonds.

Chapter 16 REVIEW

On a separate sheet of paper, write the word from the Word Bank to complete each sentence.

1. Things that receive attention before other things have high _____.

Word Bank

Congress

Medicare

national debt

priority

public

savings

veterans

2. The president does not always agree with _____ on budget priorities.

3. Spending by local, state, and federal government occurs in the _____ sector.

4. _____ is a government program that provides medical services to people over age 65.

5. Men and women who have served in the armed forces are _____.

6. Someone who owns a _____ bond owns part of the national debt.

7. People and governments in other countries own about one-fourth of the _____.

On a separate sheet of paper, write the letter of the answer that correctly completes each sentence.

8. The _____ heads the Office of Management and Budget.

   A budget director   **C** secretary of the treasury

   B president   **D** speaker of the house

9. The Congressional _____ helps Congress judge the president's budget.

   A Accountant   **C** Budget Office

   B Balancing Office   **D** Office of Budgetary Commitment

10. The _____ involves consumers buying goods and services.

   A federal budget   **C** private sector

   B national defense   **D** public sector

11. _____ pays benefits to workers not covered by Social Security.

   A Medicaid   **C** Net interest

   B Income security   **D** Physical resources

12. By increasing spending, the government has lifted the country out of _____.

   A budgetary restrictions   **C** war

   B communism   **D** depression

13. The government security with the shortest maturity period is a _____.

   A treasury dollar   **C** treasury bill

   B treasury bond   **D** treasury note

On a separate sheet of paper, write answers to the following questions. Use complete sentences.

14. What is the federal government's fiscal year?

15. Briefly describe the budget process.

16. How is part of the budget spent for veterans?

17. Why are some people concerned about the effect of the national debt on future Americans?

On a separate sheet of paper, write your opinion to each question. Use complete sentences.

18. Why must the budget go back and forth between Congress and the president so many times?

19. If you had to do away with one of the entitlements mentioned in the text, which would you choose? Explain your choice.

20. Do you think the federal government should be forced to have a balanced budget every year? Explain.

Test-Taking Tip

In a matching test, each item should be used just once. Check your answers. If you repeated an item, then another item was left out. Find the best spot for the item you left out.

17 Checking the Economy

Imagine you are not feeling well. You go to a doctor. The first thing the doctor does is take some measurements of your health. He or she checks your temperature, pulse, and blood pressure. The doctor uses these and other measurements to help determine what the problem is and how to fix it. In a way, economists are like doctors. They take measurements to check the health of the economy. They want to know how big the economy is and if it is growing. If they find a problem, they try to fix it.

This chapter discusses the many ways to measure an economy. It also talks about the four phases of the business cycle and economic growth.

Goals for Learning

◆ To define the gross domestic product (GDP)

◆ To explain how GDP is measured

◆ To list the four phases of the business cycle

◆ To explain why economic growth is important

Gross domestic product (GDP)	The most important measure of the economy is the **gross domestic product (GDP)**. The GDP is the total value of all final goods and services produced in a country in one year.

Gross domestic product (GDP)

The total value of all final goods and services produced in a country in one year

Export

A good or service sold to other countries

The most important measure of the economy is the **gross domestic product (GDP)**. The GDP is the total value of all final goods and services produced in a country in one year.

Suppose we looked at a very small economy that produced only five goods. It made 100 cars, 100 telephones, 100 computers, 100 pencils, and 100 guitars. The GDP of this economy would be the value of all of these items combined. Here is how the total is calculated:

100 cars $\times$ \$20,000 = \$2,000,000

100 telephones $\times$ \$50 = \$5,000

100 computers $\times$ \$1,000 = \$100,000

100 pencils $\times$ \$1 = \$100

100 guitars $\times$ \$1,500 = \$150,000

In this example, the GDP—the total value of all goods and services produced—is \$2,255,100.

How Is the GDP Determined?

Calculating the GDP is the job of the Commerce Department. It measures GDP by adding up spending in four areas:

• Consumer spending (C)

• Investment, or spending by businesses (I)

• Purchases of goods and services by the government (G)

• **Exports** minus imports $(X - M)$; Exports are goods and services sold to other countries. Imports are goods and services brought into a country to be sold.

The formula used to measure GDP is $C + I + G + (X - M) = GDP$.

Why Does GDP Include Only Final Goods and Services?

Look at our definition of GDP again. It is the value of *final* goods and services. Final goods and services are the goods and services sold to the final user. This can be confusing. Let's use a car as an example. The carmaker has to buy steel, plastic, glass, and other things that go into its cars. These are not figured in the GDP because they are **intermediate goods**. Intermediate goods are goods that have not reached the final user. They are goods used to make final goods. The final user in our example is the person who buys the car. By using only the value of final goods and services, economists avoid counting products more than once.

Only goods and services sold to the final user are figured in the GDP.

What Are Some Problems with GDP?

Using GDP as the measurement of how well a country is doing creates some problems. GDP leaves out some economic activity. For example, it does not count illegal goods and services. In some places, making and selling illegal drugs is a big business. Because there is no record of this activity, it does not count in the GDP.

The GDP also does not count legal business for which there is no record. Let's say a plumber agrees to fix your leaky sink if you agree to wash and wax his car. No money is involved. It is not included in the GDP. Used goods are not included either. If you buy a used car, it would not be part of this year's GDP. It was part of the GDP of the year it was first sold.

Think of the many services that people produce and use themselves but never sell. These include things like taking care of children, cleaning the house, doing laundry, and fixing the family car. None of these activities is included in the GDP.

Another problem with GDP is that it does not measure "well-being." Well-being refers to health and happiness. Does a country with a GDP twice the size of another mean that its people are healthier and happier?

Let's look at an example. A typical American family might have a bigger home and more cars than a typical family living in Mexico. This might be because both American parents work and then spend their money buying many goods. They may eat many of their meals in restaurants. Maybe in the Mexican home, only the father works. The mother has more time to spend with the children. She prepares meals at home. Is the American family healthier and happier? Not always.

What Is the Difference Between Nominal GDP and Real GDP?

The United States GDP today is many times higher than what it was in 1980. Does this mean that the economy is really that much greater? The answer depends on whether the increased GDP is the result of increased production or just an increase in prices.

An increase in GDP due to an increase in prices alone does not mean that the economy is growing. **Nominal GDP**, or current GDP, can give us information about current production and current prices. However, to compare this year's GDP with last year's, we need to remove the effects of price increases. **Real GDP** is GDP adjusted for price changes. A rise in the real GDP shows economic growth. A fall in the real GDP shows the economy is not growing.

For example, if the price of a car increased by 10 percent, the nominal GDP would show the price increase. However, that does not mean that more cars were produced, so economic growth is not shown. Real GDP would adjust the price increase so economic growth can be shown.

Why Are Changes in the Real GDP Important?

The real GDP is one of the most important ways to measure the economy's health. Real GDP is used to form fiscal and monetary policies.

Economics in Your Life

E-Commerce

The growth of computers has created a new way of buying and selling called e-commerce. It is the buying and selling of items electronically through use of the Internet. Although e-commerce has been a common practice for only a few years, it has become a multimillion dollar part of the world economy.

Sellers set up Web sites to provide buyers with an online catalog of products. Customers visit the Web sites, look at listings and photos of products, and make their purchases. Customers most often pay using a credit card or an online check. Then the seller ships the customer's purchases.

E-commerce sellers spend far less money on overhead such as buildings and insurance. Buyers benefit because they do not have to travel to stores and stand in lines for their purchases. However, Internet theft of credit information is a risk. Internet agencies are working to provide an even greater security for Internet credit purchases.

Word Bank

consumer
  spending

economic growth

gross domestic
  product

illegal activity

real GDP

Lesson 1 Review On a separate sheet of paper, write the word from the Word Bank to complete each sentence.

1. The total value of final goods and services a country produces in a year is the _____.

2. One of the four areas used to measure GDP is _____.

3. One problem with GDP is that it does not count _____.

4. The _____ is adjusted for price changes.

5. _____ happens when there is a rise in the real GDP.

What do you think ?

6. Why do economists not want to count products more than once to figure GDP?

7. Should economists try to measure a country's health and happiness? Explain your answer.

The economy is always changing. Figure 17.1 shows that real GDP follows a pattern of ups and downs. Sometimes it grows. Sometimes it shrinks. The swings up and down in the real GDP are called the **business cycle**.

Business cycle

The swings up and down in the real GDP

Peak

The highest point in the business cycle when the economy is booming

Recession

Six months (two quarters) of declining GDP

Trough

The lowest point in the business cycle

Expansion

The final stage of the business cycle when the economy begins to grow again

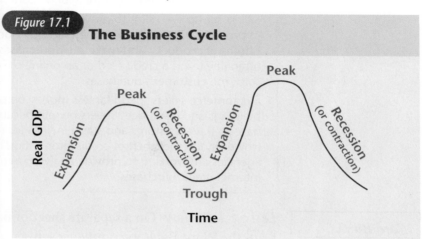

Figure 17.1 **The Business Cycle**

What Are the Four Phases of the Business Cycle?

The business cycle usually is divided into four phases, or stages. Look at Figure 17.1 again. It shows the four stages. They are **peak**, **recession**, **trough**, and **expansion**.

The highest point in the cycle is the peak. At the peak of the business cycle, the economy is booming. Everyone looking for work usually can find it. People and businesses have money to spend. Consumer spending is high. Business is producing as much as it can. Investment is high, and new workers are being hired. Demand is high, so prices are increasing.

When GDP stops growing, the cycle begins the recession phase. (This is also called the contraction phase.) A recession is six months (two quarters) of declining GDP. Consumers begin to spend less. Businesses may lay off workers. Investment in new buildings and equipment slows. Production is cut. Economists predict that the economy is slowing down. This causes some consumers and businesses to reduce their spending even more.

Writing About Economics

Which phase of the business cycle do you think the United States is in right now? Use examples from class discussions and the media for support. Write a paragraph explaining your choice.

The lowest point in the business cycle is the trough. In this stage, production of goods and services is at its lowest point. Consumer demand is very low. Unemployment is at its highest level. Times are tough. Many businesses fail, and jobs are hard to find.

The final stage is recovery or expansion. During an expansion, the economy begins to grow again. Business and consumer spending begin to increase. Businesses begin to increase production. New workers are hired. This causes consumer spending to increase. As spending goes up, production again increases, and new jobs are created. At some point, the economy reaches a peak once again.

What Is a Depression?

A very long and severe recession is called a depression. The United States has had several depressions in its history. The largest depression in the 20th century was the Great Depression. It lasted from 1930 to 1940. In 1933, the worst year, nearly one out of every four workers was out of work. Many businesses failed. More than 4,000 banks closed. Many people lost their life savings.

How Long Does Each Phase Last?

Business cycles are very irregular. The ups and downs can last from several months to several years. Since World War II, recessions have lasted between six and eighteen months. The longest peacetime expansion in U.S. history was between November 1982 and June 1990.

Economics at Work

Civil Engineer

Civil engineers design and oversee the building of roads, bridges, tunnels, harbors, airports, buildings, and dams. Other projects include water and sewage systems. Civil engineers work closely with utility companies, government leaders, and business leaders during the course of their work. Engineers often review and change plans based on the advice of these people. Many civil engineers are involved in the budgeting process to get funds for their projects.

Most projects need detailed planning and flexibility during construction. Civil engineers must be skilled at dealing with complaints and working out problems. In some cases, civil engineers specialize in areas such as structural engineering, environmental impacts, water resources, transportation, or geology. Some civil engineers manage other engineers and workers. Others may work in research or teaching.

Lesson 2 Review On a separate sheet of paper, write the letter of the answer that correctly completes each sentence.

1. The up-and-down swings in a country's GDP are its _____ .
    A booms
    B business cycle
    C busts
    D economics

2. A business cycle usually is divided into _____ .
    A real GDP and time
    B recessions and depressions
    C four stages
    D years

3. A _____ is defined as six months of falling GDP.
    A depression
    B trough
    C peak
    D recession

4. The lowest point of a business cycle is called a(n) _____ .
    A bankruptcy
    B expansion
    C peak
    D trough

5. The economy is booming in the _____ stage of the business cycle.
    A recession
    B peak
    C trough
    D expansion

What do you think ?

6. Do you think it is best for the economy to be at the peak stage or the expansion stage? Explain.

7. During the early 2000s, the United States went through a recession. How did it affect you and your family?

Real economic growth

An increase from one year to the next in real GDP

Real per capita GDP

The real GDP for each person in a country from one year to the next; it is determined by dividing real GDP by the number of people in a country

Standard of living

The way of living that is usual for a person, community, or country

What Is Economic Growth?

Real economic growth is an increase (in real GDP) from one year to the next. Remember that the figures for real GDP can be misleading. They may not look at the effect of rising prices or increases in population. Many economists believe that **real per capita GDP** is a more useful figure. Real per capita GDP is the real GDP for each person in a country from one year to the next. It is figured by dividing the real GDP by the number of people in the country. It gives a better idea of how well off the "average" person is.

For example, let's look at two countries. India is a large country with over one billion people. Ireland is a small country with fewer than four million people. India's GDP is much larger than that of Ireland. Yet the real per capita GDP of Ireland is much higher than India's. We probably can say that the average person in Ireland is better off than the average person in India.

Why Is Economic Growth Important?

Every country wants its economy to grow. Economic growth means there is an increase in goods and services. Economic growth results in an improved **standard of living**. The standard of living is the way of living that is usual for a person, community, or country. The standard of living includes what people have to eat, as well as their housing and clothing. The things people own like cars, television sets, computers, and telephones also are included.

Every society aims to improve the standard of living for its people. People with a high standard of living have more money to spend. They have more goods and services to choose from. They do not have to work all the time just to feed and clothe themselves and their families. They have more time to spend with family and to enjoy themselves.

How Is Economic Growth Achieved?

Several factors are important in achieving economic growth. A richness of natural resources helps increase production. Human resources in the form of well-educated and well-trained workers are important. Production grows as capital goods increase. As countries get more machines, factories, and technology, their economies grow. Another factor is a society's laws. Economic growth occurs best in countries where laws encourage people to take risks like starting a new business or investing in existing ones.

Why Do Most People Believe That Economic Growth Is Good?

Economic growth means that a country produces more goods and services from one year to the next. Growth usually creates jobs. Most people believe that economic growth creates wealth. Governments are able to raise more money in taxes. The tax money is used to support education and health programs. Taxes can help support people who are poor, disabled, or ill. More money also is available for things like sports, music, and art.

Why Might Economic Growth Not Always Be Good?

Some people disagree that economic growth is good. They point out that there are trade-offs to economic growth. For example, let's say a country begins to industrialize. Factories begin to replace farms. Air and water pollution levels increase. Traditional skills may be forgotten. Traditional values—what people think is useful and important—may be lost. They may be replaced by a push to get ahead and to have things like cars, computers, and televisions. People move to crowded cities to find work. Crowding can cause problems like crime and disease. The people who disagree with economic growth believe that the well-being of most people goes down rather than up.

Others are against economic growth because of its effect on the land, air, and water. They point out that economic growth uses up limited natural resources. According to these people, a time will come when we will run out of resources. There will not be enough food for all of the world's people. Air and water will be polluted. The quality of life will go down for everyone. They want governments to slow down economic growth.

Biography

Gary Becker: 1930–

Gary Stanley Becker is an American economist and Nobel Prize winner. He teaches at the University of Chicago. He also writes a column for a business magazine. He has become well-known for his economic studies of social changes in America.

Becker said that people make economic choices each day. A family, he believed, can be compared to a small factory. The family produces shelter, meals, and entertainment for its members. He is credited with joining many other areas of study to economics. Becker's main focus of study is on how family issues—marriage, divorce, and family size—affect economic growth. His writings also relate sociology, criminology, and demography to economics.

Lesson 3 Review On a separate sheet of paper, write answers to the following questions. Use complete sentences.

1. What is real per capita GDP?

2. How is real per capita GDP figured?

3. Why do most people think economic growth is good?

4. List some examples of economic trade-offs in an industrialized country.

5. Why might a society want to increase its people's standard of living?

What do you think ?

6. Do you agree with people who believe economic growth is good? Or do you agree with those who believe it is not always good? Explain.

7. Why do you think economists are so interested in measuring economic growth?

Encouraging Economic Growth

The Federal Reserve (Fed) began in 1913. The Federal Reserve Act says that the Fed should "promote effectively the goals of maximum employment, stable prices, and moderate long-term interest rates." Because of this, the Fed encourages economic growth by raising and lowering interest rates. Interest rates are lowered to help stimulate a weak economy. Rates are increased to prevent inflation.

The following article from CNN Money *discusses recent interest rate cuts.*

The Federal Reserve cut its key short-term interest rate [on June 25, 2003] by a quarter percentage point to the lowest level in 45 years, expressing worry that the economy still isn't strong enough to fight off deflation. . . .

In the statement accompanying its decision . . . the Fed said it expects economic growth to strengthen in the near future, but that the risks to the economy were weighted toward weak inflation.

"The economy . . . has yet to exhibit sustainable growth," the [Fed] statement said. . . .

U.S. stocks were mixed after the news, while Treasury bond prices fell and the dollar recovered some ground. Markets were widely expecting a rate cut but were uncertain about the size of the cut or the language of the Fed's statement.

The Fed's statement, combined with a less-aggressive rate cut, was likely designed to keep markets from panicking about the state of the economy, while also leaving the door open for future rate cuts. . . .

Many banks use the fed funds rate as a basis for their prime lending rates and were expected to announce cuts in those rates. . . .

The Fed cuts rates to lower the cost of borrowing, pumping more money into the economy when it thinks activity is too slow. . . .

Most economists—including Fed Chairman Alan Greenspan—believe the economy will strengthen in the second half of [2003]. But some Fed officials have expressed concern that the economy might not grow fast enough to cause inflation to rise. . . .

Document-Based Questions

1. When was the Federal Reserve created?

2. How does the Federal Reserve encourage economic growth?

3. What was important about the interest rate decrease on June 25, 2003?

4. What happened to the stock market after the Fed lowered interest rates?

5. How do you think economists can tell when the economy is getting better?

Chapter 17 SUMMARY

- The gross domestic product (GDP) is the total value of all goods and services produced in a country in one year. GDP includes only final goods and services.

- Economists use this formula to determine GDP: C + I + G + (X − M) = GDP. The C is consumer spending. I is business investing. G is all the goods and services a government buys. X − M is total exports minus total imports.

- GDP does not measure illegal goods and services, legal business without any records, used goods, or services people use and produce themselves but do not sell. GDP also does not measure well-being.

- Real GDP is GDP adjusted for price changes. It allows one year's GDP to be compared with another year's GDP. When there is a decrease in real GDP, the economy is not growing.

- The four phases of the business cycle are peak, recession, trough, and expansion. A long, severe recession is a depression. The ups and downs of a business cycle can last a few months to several years.

- Real economic growth is an increase in GDP from one year to the next. Real per capita GDP is an increase in real GDP per person.

- Economic growth is important to improve a society's standard of living. Growth increases as the number of goods and services increase. When laws encourage people to take business risks, economies are more likely to grow.

- Most people believe economic growth creates wealth. Governments can raise more money with taxes. This money supports education and health programs. Tax money also helps poor, disabled, or ill people. Everyone's quality of life rises.

- Some people believe economic growth is not always good. It may lower people's well-being or use up resources. Factories replace farms, pollution increases, and traditional skills and values may be lost. As cities become crowded, crime and disease increase.

Chapter 17 REVIEW

On a separate sheet of paper, write the word from the Word Bank to complete each sentence.

1. GDP is the total value of _____ goods and services.

2. GDP does not measure people's _____.

3. A rise in real GDP shows _____ growth.

4. The highest point of a business cycle is called its _____.

5. Business cycles are very _____.

6. Economic growth results in a higher _____.

7. When an economy grows, a government can raise _____ to help support people and programs.

Word Bank

economic
final
irregular
peak
standard of living
taxes
well-being

On a separate sheet of paper, write the letter of the answer that correctly completes each sentence.

8. In the formula C + I + G + (X − M), the letter X stands for _____.

   A expenses   **C** imports
   B exports   **D** economics

9. Intermediate goods do not count toward GDP because they have not reached the _____.

   A economists   **C** final user
   B factory   **D** government

10. When GDP stops growing, the _____ stage of the business cycle begins.

    A backward   **C** recession
    B depression   **D** trough

11. The growth stage of the business cycle is _____.

    A expansion   **C** recession
    B peak   **D** trough

12. _____ shows an increase in real GDP from one year to the next.

   A Standard of living

   B Real economic growth

   C Expansion

   D An import

13. Negative results of economic growth do not include _____.

   A having more money to spend

   B increasing air pollution

   C the loss of traditional skills

   D using up natural resources

On a separate sheet of paper, write answers to the following questions. Use complete sentences.

14. What are exports?

15. List two problems some economists have with using GDP to measure growth.

16. List and describe the four phases of a business cycle.

17. List three factors that encourage economic growth.

On a separate sheet of paper, write your opinion to each question. Use complete sentences.

18. How might measuring illegal drug sales affect the U.S. GDP?

19. Which phase of the business cycle do you think is most important for the development of the economy? Why?

20. Many people consider the United States to be the richest country in the world. If that is true, how do you explain the large numbers of U.S. citizens who are poor?

Test-Taking Tip

After you have completed a test, reread each question and answer. Ask yourself: Have I answered the question that was asked? Have I answered it completely?

18

Economic Challenges

The economy of the United States is the largest in the world. People in many other countries admire the high standard of living in the United States. They admire all the goods and services available. Yet even the United States economy has some problems.

This chapter discusses some of these economic problems. Unemployment, inflation, deflation, poverty, and the environment affect all Americans.

Goals for Learning

◆ To list the causes of unemployment

◆ To compare and contrast inflation and deflation

◆ To list the causes of poverty

◆ To identify the economic impact of human activity on the environment

What Does It Mean to Be Unemployed?

Unemployed

A person who wants to work but cannot find a job

Unemployment rate

The percentage of all unemployed workers

Most students assume that they will find a job once they are finished with their schooling. Jobs give us wages. With our wages we can buy some of the goods and services we need and want. However, not everyone who wants a job will find one. The people who want work but cannot find jobs are the **unemployed**. The percentage of all unemployed workers is the **unemployment rate**. (This does not include members of the military.)

Why Are Some People Out of Work?

People leave their jobs for many reasons. Some people lose their jobs because of layoffs. Workers are laid off when they are put out of work for a time. The reasons for the layoffs are varied. Sometimes the employer may go out of business. If a factory closes, the workers lose their jobs even if they are very good workers. Businesses lay off workers to cut costs when they have more goods and services than they can sell.

Another reason for layoffs is changes in technology. New ways of production may put some people out of work. For example, a robot may complete a task better and faster than any human can. Robots can work 24 hours a day. They do not get sick, take breaks, or demand benefits. The use of computers also has cut down on the number of workers needed. The workers who are no longer needed might be laid off.

Some jobs are needed for only certain seasons. In other seasons, the workers are laid off. Farming is a good example. Many people are needed to harvest crops such as grapes, lettuce, and cherries. When the harvest is over, the workers are laid off. Other examples include carpenters, bricklayers, and construction workers.

Seasonal work, such as harvesting strawberries, can cause workers to be laid off when the season is over.

Strikes may be another reason why people are out of work. People go on strike for many reasons. Strikers often want better pay and better working conditions. When the strike ends, people usually go back to work. A strike can last days or many months, or even years.

Sometimes people lose their jobs because they are disabled. A disabled person is one who is sick or hurt and cannot continue working. For example, a firefighter could not continue working if his or her back were hurt. It would be impossible to do the heavy lifting that sometimes is required. Disabilities can last a long time or a short time.

Finally, some people lose their jobs because they are fired. Workers can be fired for things like being late, not doing a good job, or not getting along with other workers. Many businesses have strict drug and alcohol policies. Workers who use drugs may be fired.

Economics at Work

Restaurant Manager

Restaurant managers have many duties. These vary depending upon the size of the restaurant. The manager of a large restaurant may oversee many employees, including cooks, servers, and hosts. In most settings, restaurant managers hire all staff members. Managers make adjustments in hiring and scheduling according to the flow of customers.

People who go to a restaurant expect good food, a clean and pleasant place to eat, and a friendly wait staff. The restaurant manager must watch all of these factors and make any necessary changes. Return customers are essential to the success of a restaurant.

A profitable restaurant must have a large margin between money paid out and money received. Good restaurant managers regularly compare costs of food products to menu prices. Part of this review may include paying close attention to purchases of food or service products. Those people directly responsible for buying supplies may need to make changes. In some cases, menu prices may need to be changed. Because of all of their responsibilities, restaurant managers should be organized and should have good communication and leadership skills.

Word Bank
disabled
fired
seasons
strike
unemployed

Lesson 1 Review On a separate sheet of paper, write the word from the Word Bank to complete each sentence.

1. People who want work but cannot find it are _____.

2. Someone who cannot work because of sickness or injury is _____.

3. Some workers are needed only for certain _____.

4. Workers may go on _____ because they want better pay or better working conditions.

5. Being late, using drugs, or not doing a good job may cause a worker to be _____.

What do you think ?

6. Do you believe businesses should have the right to test their employees for alcohol or drug use? Why or why not?

7. List some ways computers might reduce the number of human workers a business needs.

What Are Inflation and Deflation?

Inflation happens when the buying power of money goes down. Prices go up. Let's say the inflation rate is 5 percent. This means an item that cost $10 last year costs $10.50 this year. **Deflation** is the opposite of inflation. Changes in the buying power of money affect the economy in many ways.

How Does Inflation Affect Consumers?

Suppose a worker earns $500 a week. She spends it on things she wants and needs. If the prices of these items go up to $550 a week, her wages will no longer buy as much. Buying power has been lost. The worker might have to get a raise to keep up with inflated prices. She might need a second job. She might have to do without something.

What Causes Inflation?

Higher prices may result from an increase in the cost of raw materials. Prices will go up if businesses have to pay their workers higher wages. Increases in the cost of raw materials or wages can be caused by several factors. If there is less competition, the remaining suppliers can raise prices. Unexpected shortages can cause prices of raw materials to rise too. This kind of inflation is called **cost-push inflation**. The higher cost of resources pushes prices higher even if demand has not increased. Cost-push inflation may occur in farming. Suppose there is a long period without rain. This cuts agricultural production. The smaller supply pushes prices up.

A second kind of inflation is **demand-pull inflation**. Demand-pull inflation follows the law of supply and demand. Prices are pulled up because demand is greater than supply. This may happen when governments print too much money. Economists call this "too much money chasing too few goods."

An extreme example of demand-pull inflation occurred in Germany in the 1920s. The German government printed so much money, called marks, that the country was flooded with it. The supply of food and other goods available to buy stayed the same. Soon people were spending millions of marks just to buy a loaf of bread. Prices soared daily. Inflation caused the entire economic system to collapse.

What Is an Inflationary Cycle?

Remember that inflation results in a loss of buying power. When the prices for goods and services go up, workers need higher wages to keep up with the rising prices. If businesses give workers more money, businesses may be forced to raise their prices in order to earn a profit. The higher prices lead to more inflation and then to another round of higher wages. The process continues with wages and prices constantly going up. Because the pattern repeats itself in the same way over and over, the process is called an **inflationary cycle**.

How Is Inflation Measured?

Economists use two scales or indexes to measure inflation. The **consumer price index (CPI)** measures how much the prices of necessary items are changing. The Bureau of Labor Statistics (BLS) calculates the CPI every month. The sample of items includes food, housing, clothing, transportation, medical care, personal care, and entertainment. Let's say the total price of this fixed group of products increases by 3 percent over a year's time. This would make the official rate of inflation 3 percent for that year.

The **producer price index (PPI)** measures how the price of goods and services bought by producers has changed over time. The BLS figures the PPI by looking at the prices of over 3,000 products to see how they have changed.

What Are Some Effects of Inflation?

The most noticeable effect of inflation is the loss of buying power. Money does not go as far as it used to. This loss hurts people who are on a **fixed income** the most. A fixed income is an income that does not change. For example, retired people

Retired people have a fixed income—their income does not change. When prices go up, people with a fixed income are unable to afford as many goods and services.

usually are on a fixed income. They may receive money based on the average wage they earned while working. Unless this amount is adjusted for inflation, they will not be able to buy as many goods and services over time.

Another effect is an increase in interest rates. As prices increase, so does the cost of borrowing money. High interest rates may discourage consumers from buying goods that are usually bought with credit. For example, most people have to borrow money to buy homes and cars. Inflation pushes the interest rates higher and makes it hard for some people to buy. Inflation also affects the interest rate on credit cards. Consumers may find that they have to pay high interest rates on balances that are carried over from month to month.

Inflation also lowers the value of savings and investments. Let's say you put $100 into a savings account 10 years ago. Suppose the inflation rate was 5 percent for each of the 10 years. You would have earned interest on your money, but the principal, the original $100, would be worth half as much. You still would have $100, but you would be able to buy less with it. Because of this, high inflation encourages consumers to spend their money now rather than save for the future.

Why Might Deflation Be a Problem?

In deflation, prices go down. This sounds like a good thing, but it can be a problem. During deflation there is too much of everything for sale. There are not enough people who want or can afford to buy the items for sale. During the Great Depression, prices went down for four years in a row from 1929 to 1933. The prices farmers got for their crops plunged. Farmers were unable to pay their mortgages, and many lost their farms. Banks closed, wiping out people's savings. This left people with little money to buy anything, no matter how cheap it was.

 **Biography**

Wilma Mankiller: 1945–

Wilma Mankiller's last name is a term of respect for the person who protects a village. Mankiller was born in Oklahoma, but a serious drought forced her to move to California in 1956. Indian protests in California in 1969 prompted her to become involved in the American Indian struggle. She focused on education programs, jobs, and securing grant money for important agricultural programs.

In 1983, after her return to Oklahoma, Mankiller was elected deputy chief of the Cherokee Nation. In 1985, she became chief. She was the first woman in modern history to lead a major tribe. As chief, Mankiller's task was to lead a tribe of 140,000 Cherokees and manage a yearly budget of over $75 million.

Mankiller was made a member of the Oklahoma Women's Hall of Fame in 1986. She was recognized for the things she did to help Oklahoma and the Indian Nation. She won many other awards and honorary degrees, many for her work with women and the Indian Nation. Mankiller served as Cherokee chief until 1995.

Lesson 2 Review On a separate sheet of paper, write the letter of the answer that correctly completes each sentence.

1. A decrease in the buying power of money is called _____.
   A cost-push
   B deflation
   C inflation
   D demand-pull

2. The _____ measures how much the prices of necessary items change.
   A inflationary cycle
   B consumer price index
   C producer price index
   D poverty line

3. The Bureau of _____ calculates the consumer price index every month.
   A Engraving
   B Government Spending
   C Labor Statistics
   D Inflation

4. Falling prices because of too much supply and not enough demand is called _____.
   A cost-push
   B deflation
   C inflation
   D demand-pull

5. Inflation hurts people on a(n)_____ most.
   A fixed income
   B government program
   C interest-free account
   D transportation system

What do you think ?

6. How do you think inflation affects you each day?

7. What might happen if people think their money may be worth less tomorrow than it is today? Explain.

What Is Poverty?

Poverty

Being poor

Poverty line

A measure used to define which people are poor; three times the amount it costs to buy healthy food for a family

Poverty means being poor. During the last 30 years, the number of people living in poverty in the United States has risen. According to one expert, about one-sixth of people living in rural America are poor. The same expert believes about one-fifth of people living in cities are poor. In 2002, the poverty rate rose to 12.1 percent. There are many reasons for poverty, but one of the main causes is a change in the American economy.

What Is the Poverty Line?

In the 1960s, economist Mollie Orshansky came up with a way of defining which people are poor. She created a formula that still is used today. She figured out that families spend about one-third of their income on food. Therefore, the official **poverty line** was defined as three times the amount it costs to buy healthy food for a family. The poverty line is adjusted each year based on changes in the CPI. Figure 18.1 shows the poverty line in the U.S.

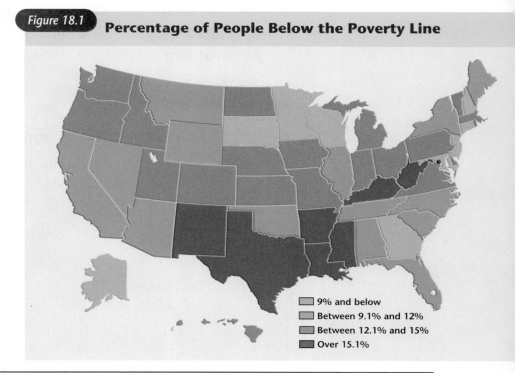

Figure 18.1   **Percentage of People Below the Poverty Line**

☐ 9% and below
☐ Between 9.1% and 12%
☐ Between 12.1% and 15%
■ Over 15.1%

Child support

Money a divorced person pays for family expenses

Who Are the Poor?

In 2002, the United States had 34.6 million poor people. This included 12.1 million children. There are poor people in every state. Some live in cities, and others live in rural America. They represent every ethnic group in the United States.

Why Is the Number of Poor People Increasing?

One reason is the loss of manufacturing jobs. Many manufacturers have moved production to countries where workers earn less money than in the United States. Generally, unskilled jobs are the first to go. Some of these displaced workers have found jobs in the service sector. Many of these jobs pay much less than the lost manufacturing jobs.

Another reason is rapid changes in technology. There are fewer jobs for lower skilled workers because of new machines and equipment. Today, there are very few jobs for workers with no skills. At the same time, technology has increased the need for highly skilled, well-trained, and educated workers. These workers earn high wages. Young people with computer skills and a willingness to learn new technology are in high demand.

Many people have been pushed into poverty because of the breakdown of the traditional family. Today more than half of all marriages in America end in divorce. Young children often stay with their mothers. The fathers are expected to pay **child support**—money to help care for the family. However, almost one-third of divorced fathers pay nothing or very little. The U.S. Census Bureau reports that single women head about half of the families living in poverty today.

Writing About Economics

Draw a diagram showing the cycle of poverty. Below the diagram, write a description of the cycle in your own words.

What Is the "Cycle of Poverty"?

The poor often live in poor living conditions. There may not be enough food. As a result, children may miss school often. When they go to school, they may have trouble paying attention. Often they fall behind in school. Sometimes they drop out. Students who drop out have no real job skills, so they have little chance of finding good jobs. Without a job, they cannot improve their living conditions. This is the cycle of poverty.

What Is the Income Gap?

Some people make more money than others. This is not too surprising. People have different skills and talents. Some are well educated, and some have very little education. In a market economy, people with skills and talents that are in high demand make a lot of money. People who have few skills for which there is little demand earn much less.

The difference between what the richest and the poorest Americans earn is called the **income gap**. Over the last 20 years, the income gap in the United States has been growing larger.

Lesson 3 Review On a separate sheet of paper, write answers to the following questions. Use complete sentences.

1. What is the poverty line?

2. Where do poor people live in the United States?

3. List three reasons why the number of poor people is increasing.

4. Explain the income gap.

5. How does divorce affect poverty?

What do you think ?

6. How do you think the U.S. income gap might be narrowed?

7. How do you think the cycle of poverty might be broken?

What Is the Environment?

People care about the quality of the air they breathe, the water they drink, and the soil in which they grow crops. This is the **environment**. People depend on their environment for water, air, and food needed to survive. Certain economic activities affect the environment in harmful ways.

How Does Mining Affect the Environment?

Mining is the taking of minerals from the earth for human use. People have mined since prehistoric times. Mining provides us with many of the things we need. Almost every item we use is made of metal, stone, or minerals that have been mined. Even our food is grown with the help of these minerals.

Mining provides many jobs, but like all economic activities, there are trade-offs. The way minerals are mined may harm the environment. In open-pit mining, huge holes are dug in the land, and the minerals are removed. In strip-mining, large strips of land are dug up and laid aside. The minerals are removed, and the land is put back. Valuable minerals are then separated from the rock by chemicals. The chemicals sometimes pollute water sources. Silt, fine particles of soil, sometimes is washed away into rivers and lakes. Often, the mined area is badly damaged. Plants are dead. Animals are gone. The soil is open to **erosion**. This is the wearing away and moving of rock and soil by weather.

How Do Farming and Industry Harm the Environment?

Learning how to raise animals and grow food were two of the most important developments in human history. To do this, humans had to change their environment. Forests were removed. Ditches were dug to bring water to the crops. Today, farmers use all sorts of technology to produce more goods. Some use chemicals to grow more crops and to control harmful insects. These chemicals may be harmful to people.

Industrialization needs huge amounts of resources. Water and energy are needed. Land has to be cleared to build the factories that produce the products consumers want. Roads, railroad lines, and airports may have to be built. Developing industries can create problems. Garbage, air and water pollution, and hazardous wastes are by-products of industrialization.

Why Are Fossil Fuels Important to the Economy?

The energy we use to light, heat, and cool our homes and to run our cars comes from **fossil fuels**. Fossil fuels are products of decayed plants and animals. They are preserved in the earth's crust. Liquid fossil fuel is called petroleum, or oil. Oil is found in huge pools in underground rocks. It can be reached by drilling, both on land and in lake or ocean water. Natural gas is another type of fossil fuel. It is usually found with petroleum. Coal is a solid fossil fuel. Coal, petroleum, and natural gas are the main sources of energy for industry, transportation, and homes.

Energy use in the world is growing. The United States alone uses nearly one-third of all the fossil fuel energy produced in the world. Oil and gas **reserves** in the world are limited. Reserves are the unused fossil fuel deposits left in the earth. To satisfy growing needs, new fuel sources must be found. Scientists always are looking for new energy sources.

What Are the Economic Trade-Offs?

Thousands of people work in the mining industry and in other industries. Factories are a major consumer of fossil fuels. As you have learned, energy resources are scarce. This forces people to make difficult choices. How can humans protect the environment and still conserve resources for the future? What are the costs of protecting the environment? Do the benefits of environmental protection outweigh the costs?

As future voters, you will have to answer these questions. You already know that the United States has limited economic resources. There is only a limited amount of money to protect the environment. Future voters like you must decide what issues have the highest need. You will have to try to balance the desire to preserve and improve America's standard of living with the desire to preserve the planet for the future.

Life After Hurricane Mitch

Sometimes nature also destroys the environment. Natural disasters can be especially harmful to countries in poverty. Hurricane Mitch ruined much of Honduras, Nicaragua, El Salvador, Guatemala, and Costa Rica in October 1998. About 11,000 people died in these Central American countries. More than one million others were injured. Three million people were left homeless. Honduras and Nicaragua had the highest death tolls and damage. Hurricane Mitch was the deadliest storm in the Western Hemisphere in the last two centuries.

Homes, businesses, and entire communities were destroyed in Central America. Roads and bridges were damaged, mostly by severe flooding. In many cases, farming was entirely ruined. The estimated cost of repairs has been over $6 billion.

The World Bank and the International Monetary Fund donated many millions of dollars for food, relief supplies, and reconstruction. The U.S. Agency for International Development provided $92 million in food, supplies, and temporary housing for people who had lost their homes. The U.S. Departments of Defense and Agriculture gave over $210 million to help the people of Central America rebuild after the damaging storm.

Lesson 4 Review On a separate sheet of paper, write the word from the Word Bank to complete each sentence.

Word Bank

environment

fossil fuels

industrialization

mining

reserves

1. Taking minerals from the earth is called _____.

2. Products made from decayed plants and animals are _____.

3. The air, water, and soil people use to survive is the _____.

4. Garbage, pollution, and hazardous wastes are often by-products of _____.

5. Unused fossil fuel deposits left in the earth are called _____.

What do you think

6. Why do you think the United States uses so much of the world's energy?

7. How could agriculture and industrialization be made less harmful to the environment?

Rachel Carson's *Silent Spring*

Rachel Carson was one of the first environmentalists. In the 1930s, she began studying ocean life and wrote many articles about marine biology. After World War II, Carson turned her focus to the use of pesticides. These were becoming common as industry continued to develop. Carson wrote her most famous book, Silent Spring, *in 1962 to warn people about the deadly effects of these pesticides. The book was controversial, but it made many people think about the environment for the first time. Carson died of breast cancer in 1964, but her fight to protect the earth continues today. Read the excerpt from* Silent Spring *below.*

For the first time in the history of the world, every human being is now subjected to contact with dangerous chemicals from the moment of conception until death. . . . They have been recovered from most of the major river systems and even from streams of groundwater flowing unseen through the earth. Residues of these chemicals linger in soil to which they may have been applied a dozen years before. They have entered and lodged in the bodies of fish, birds, reptiles, and domestic and wild animals so universally

that scientists carrying on animal experiments find it almost impossible to locate subjects free from such contamination. They have been found in fish in remote mountain lakes, in earthworms burrowing in soil, in the eggs of birds—and in man himself. . . .

All this has come about because of the sudden rise and prodigious [huge] growth of an industry for the production of man-made or synthetic chemicals with insecticidal properties. . . .

If a huge skull and crossbones were suspended above the insecticide department the customer might at least enter it with the respect normally accorded death-dealing materials. But instead the display is homey and cheerful. . . .

Document-Based Questions

1. Who was Rachel Carson?

2. Why did Carson write the book *Silent Spring?*

3. According to Carson, where were the dangerous chemicals found?

4. What event caused the increase in contamination of people and animals?

5. Do you think people have become more concerned today with the environment since Carson's book was written? Explain.

- Layoffs, changes in technology, seasonal jobs, strikes, disabilities, or being fired all cause unemployment.

- Inflation occurs when money's buying power decreases. Deflation occurs when there is too much for sale.

- Causes of inflation include rising costs of raw materials, rising wages, or shortages of resources. Cost-push inflation happens when higher costs of resources push prices higher even if demand does not rise. Demand-pull inflation raises prices when demand is greater than supply.

- The inflationary cycle begins when prices rise. Workers need higher wages to keep up. If businesses raise wages, they may have to raise prices. This action continues the cycle.

- Two indexes that measure inflation are the consumer price index (CPI) and the producer price index (PPI).

- The most noticeable effect of inflation is the loss of buying power. This most hurts people on fixed incomes. Inflation also raises interest rates and lowers savings and investment values.

- Deflation is a problem when supply exceeds the number of people who need or want a good or service.

- The poverty line is defined as three times the cost of buying healthy food for a family. In 2002, the United States had nearly 35 million poor people.

- The number of poor people is increasing because of a loss of manufacturing jobs, rapid changes in technology, and the breakdown of traditional families.

- The cycle of poverty occurs when people live in poor conditions and cannot afford enough food. Children may miss school or have trouble paying attention. They may drop out. Without job skills, they may not find a good job and cannot improve their living conditions.

- The income gap is the difference between the richest and poorest people. The U.S. income gap has widened over the last 20 years.

- The environment is made up of the air, water, and soil. People depend on the environment to live. Mining, agriculture, and industrialization may harm the environment.

- Fossil fuels such as oil, natural gas, and coal are created from decayed plants and animals. World use of fossil fuels is increasing. The United States uses about one-third of all the fossil fuels produced in the world.

- Industries employ many people but also may harm the environment. Sometimes people must choose between the benefits of industrialization and protecting the environment.

On a separate sheet of paper, write the word from the Word Bank to complete each sentence.

1. Many people lose their jobs because of _____.

2. Someone who is _____ cannot work because of illness or injury.

3. Buying power is lost when _____ occurs.

4. _____ is a decrease in prices because there is too much for sale.

5. When a shortage of resources pushes prices higher, _____ occurs.

6. One main cause of _____ is changes in the economy.

7. In _____, huge holes are dug into the earth so minerals can be removed.

Word Bank

cost-push inflation
deflation
disabled
inflation
layoffs
open-pit mining
poverty

On a separate sheet of paper, write the letter of the answer that correctly completes each sentence.

8. People sometimes _____ to gain better wages or working conditions.

   A get fired   **C** go on strike

   B file a lawsuit   **D** work harder

9. When the price of goods and services rises, workers need higher _____ to keep up.

   A goals   **C** productivity

   B inflation   **D** wages

10. The _____ measures how prices of goods and services change.

   A inflationary cycle   **C** unemployment rate

   B consumer price index **D** producer price index

11. The poverty line is defined as _____ times the cost of healthy food for a family.

   A two   **C** four

   B three   **D** five

12. Usually, the first kinds of jobs lost in a poor economy are _____ jobs.

   A skilled   **C** unskilled

   B technological   **D** white-collar

13. Two examples of fossil fuels are _____.

   A air and water   **C** coal and oil

   B silt and minerals   **D** metal and rock

On a separate sheet of paper, write answers to the following questions. Use complete sentences.

14. List six reasons why people may lose their jobs.

15. Explain three effects of inflation.

16. Describe the cycle of poverty.

17. What are some problems with industrialization?

On a separate sheet of paper, write your opinion to each question. Use complete sentences.

18. What do you think could be done to lower unemployment? Explain at least three things.

19. If you were president, how would you try to end poverty? Explain.

20. If you had to choose between having enough energy but damaging parts of the environment, or not having enough energy but leaving the environment alone, which would you choose? Why?

Test-Taking Tip

When a test item asks you to write a paragraph, make a plan first. Jot down the main idea of your paragraph. List the supporting details you can include. Then write the paragraph.

Unit 5

Skill Builder

Income Tax

The Internal Revenue Service (IRS) requires American citizens to file an income tax return. A tax return is a tool used to figure out how much income tax a person owes. Every year by April 15, people under age 65 who earn at least $7,700 per year must file a tax return.

The basic tax form is the Form 1040. Instructions tell taxpayers how to fill out the form. Taxpayers fill in their name, address, and Social Security number. This is followed by the taxpayer's number of personal exemptions. Single people usually have one exemption. Married people have two. Any children are listed as extra exemptions.

The math of a tax return begins with the amount of money earned during the past year. This is called gross income. The taxpayer may subtract costs such as college expenses, moving expenses, interest on home loans, and some medical expenses paid during the year. Some work-related expenses also may be subtracted. Things subtracted from gross income are called deductions. After all deductions have been taken from the gross income, the remainder is called taxable income. The amount of taxes owed is found on an IRS tax table. (See Figure U5.1—Sample Tax Table—on this page.)

Most people have taxes taken from their paychecks during the year. The employer sends this money to the IRS for the employees. The employer supplies a W-2 form to the employee. This lists the employee's yearly gross income and the amount of taxes already paid. Employees must send a copy of the W-2 form along with their completed Form 1040.

The taxpayer subtracts the amount of taxes already paid from the amount owed. If more taxes were paid than are owed, the taxpayer

will be given back the difference. If less taxes were paid than were owed, the taxpayer must send payment of the difference with the completed tax return.

Figure U5.1 Sample Tax Table

If line 41 (taxable income) is—		And you are—			
At least	But less than	Single	Married filing jointly	Married filing separately	Head of a house-hold
23,000		Your tax is—			
23,000	23,050	3,154	2,854	3,154	2,954
23,050	23,100	3,161	2,861	3,161	2,961
23,100	23,150	3,169	2,869	3,169	2,969
23,150	23,200	3,176	2,876	3,176	2,976
23,200	23,250	3,184	2,884	3,184	2,984
23,250	23,300	3,191	2,891	3,191	2,991
23,300	23,350	3,199	2,899	3,199	2,999
23,350	23,400	3,206	2,906	3,209	3,006
23,400	23,450	3,214	2,914	3,223	3,014
23,450	23,500	3,221	2,921	3,236	3,021
23,500	23,550	3,229	2,929	3,250	3,029
23,550	23,600	3,236	2,936	3,263	3,036
23,600	23,650	3,244	2,944	3,277	3,044
23,650	23,700	3,251	2,951	3,290	3,051
23,700	23,750	3,259	2,959	3,304	3,059
23,750	23,800	3,266	2,966	3,317	3,066
23,800	23,850	3,274	2,974	3,331	3,074
23,850	23,900	3,281	2,981	3,344	3,081
23,900	23,950	3,289	2,989	3,358	3,089
23,950	24,000	3,296	2,996	3,371	3,096

1. What is the difference between gross income and taxable income?

2. Ed is single. He had a gross income of $30,000. He deducted a total of $8,000. What is Ed's taxable income?

3. Mr. and Mrs. Brown have two children. How many exemptions can they take?

4. Look at Figure U5.1 on this page. What is the amount of taxes owed by a married couple filing jointly who earned $23,720?

5. What is the amount of taxes owed by a head of household who earned $23,959?

Unit 5 SUMMARY

- Laissez-faire means the government should keep out of economic matters.

- The United States Constitution gives the government the right to be involved in the economy.

- Public policy is the process of government decision making that addresses problems affecting many people.

- The federal bureaucracy has Cabinet departments and independent executive agencies; independent regulatory commissions; and government corporations.

- Fiscal policy is the government's use of taxes and spending to achieve a healthy economy.

- Three kinds of taxes are progressive, regressive, and proportional (flat).

- Federal taxes include income, excise, customs, and estate taxes. States, counties, and other political bodies also collect taxes.

- Congress and the president must compromise to reach a final federal budget.

- Government spending includes Social Security, income security, Medicare, health, education, and veterans' benefits. Other federal payments are for national defense, interest on the national debt, and physical resources.

- The money the government owes is the national debt. The government raises money by selling bonds and securities.

- Gross domestic product is all final goods and services a country produces in one year. GDP does not include illegal business, legal business without records, used goods, or services people produce but do not sell.

- A business cycle has peaks, recessions, troughs, and expansions.

- Real economic growth is a yearly increase in real GDP.

- People are jobless because of layoffs, loss of jobs to new technology, seasonal work, striking, disabilities, or being fired.

- Inflation causes a loss of buying power. Inflation occurs in a cycle. It may cause rising interest rates and lowered savings and investments.

- In deflation, too much of everything is for sale. Not enough people can or will buy the items for sale.

- The number of American poor is rising because of loss of manufacturing jobs, rapid technology changes, and the breakdown of the traditional family. Many people are stuck in a cycle of poverty.

- Mining disturbs the land. Some mining chemicals pollute the soil or water. Farming chemicals may harm the environment. Industrialization uses large amounts of resources and creates harmful by-products. On the other hand, all of these industries provide people with jobs and wages.

"We face tremendous challenges as populations soar, mostly in the poorer nations, and as consumption increases in the industrialized world. . . . The decisions we make in the decades to come will affect not only all of human civilization but also the fate of thousands of species representing millions of years of evolution."

—Former President Jimmy Carter, "Challenges for Humanity: A Beginning," *National Geographic Magazine*, 2002

6 A Global Economy

The world has always been a place where countries work together and where countries compete with each other economically. Even 2,000 years ago, people in one place traded with people in far away places. For example, silk was once a very valuable export because it was used to make fine clothing. It was produced in East Asia, then carried across much of southern Asia to the Middle East. This route became known as the Silk Road.

In today's world, economics is a global issue more than ever before. Countries are working to increase trade and to grow their economies. This is not always an easy task, especially for poorer nations that have more disadvantages than richer nations.

This unit will discuss the state of trade in the world today. It also will discuss less developed countries and how these nations are trying to improve economically.

19

International Trade

I n 2003, goods worth nearly $2 trillion were shipped into and out of the United States. People in other countries bought American goods worth about $700 billion. Americans spent over $1 trillion to buy goods produced in other countries. The chief trading partners of the United States are Canada, Mexico, Japan, China, the United Kingdom, and other European countries.

This chapter discusses the importance of international trade. The balance of trade, specialization, and trade restrictions affect goods and services that are available for people to buy. You also will read about different organizations that help promote trade around the world.

Goals for Learning

◆ To explain the benefits and costs of trade

◆ To explain how trade and specialization are related

◆ To explain why countries create trade barriers

◆ To identify key international trade organizations

Capital good

A good such as machinery or farm tractors that is used to produce other things

Look around your home, school, and community, and you will soon discover that we live in a global economy. You may be driving a car designed in Japan, but built in Canada, Mexico, or the United States. You might heat up your breakfast in a microwave oven made in Asia. The backpack you use to carry your things to school is likely to have been made overseas. How about the clothes you are wearing? They, too, often are made in other countries. Trade is an exchange of goods. It is the process of buying and selling. It has both a good side and one that is not so good.

Why Do Countries Trade with Each Other?

Trade is needed because people want or need things they cannot get in their own country. Not all countries have the same resources. Some countries have a lot of oil, but other countries have none at all. Some countries have a climate that allows them to grow many different kinds of food. Other countries have a harsh climate that allows them to grow only a few crops. It makes sense that a country with a harsh climate but lots of oil would sell its oil. A country with a good climate for raising crops should sell its food to get the oil it needs. By trading, both countries benefit.

What Are Exports?

Exports are goods and services sold to foreign countries. The most important American exports are **capital goods**, or goods that are used to produce other things. Capital goods include things like machinery, farm tractors, and construction equipment. The United States also exports airplanes, coal, scientific equipment, plastics, and farm products. The major U.S. farm exports are corn, wheat, and soybeans. Other important exports are industrial supplies and raw materials. In addition, foreign countries buy a lot of U.S. consumer products like soap, beauty products, and clothes. Americans who travel overseas sometimes are surprised to see some of the same shop names and restaurants they have at home.

What Are Imports?

Imports are goods and services bought from foreign countries. The most important goods imported by the United States include oil, machinery, and automobiles. The United States also buys many consumer products from other countries. For example, all diamonds and most shoes are made in other countries. The United States buys a lot of industrial raw materials from foreign countries too. It buys iron, steel, aluminum, gold, and other valuable minerals. Fish, cheese, and olives are among imported food items.

What Is the Balance of Trade?

The difference between the value of a country's imports and its exports is its **balance of trade**. A country that sells more than it buys from other countries has a favorable balance of trade. A country that buys more than it sells has an unfavorable balance of trade. Figure 19.1 shows the balance of trade in the United States. It shows that the United States has an unfavorable balance of trade because it imports more than it exports.

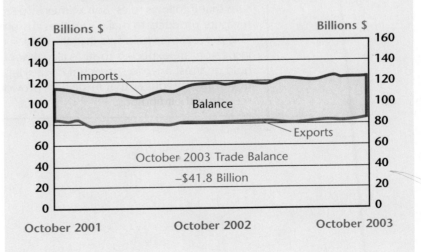

Figure 19.1 **United States International Trade in Goods and Services**

Billions $

October 2003 Trade Balance
−$41.8 Billion

Imports

Balance

Exports

October 2001   October 2002   October 2003

The unfavorable balance of trade in the United States is a recent trend. The United States has a **trade deficit** with Canada, Mexico, China, and Japan. This means these countries sell a lot more to the United States than they buy. For example, the United States spends six dollars in China for every one dollar China spends in the United States.

Still, there are many countries with which the United States has a **trade surplus**. It sells more to these countries than it buys from them. The countries with which the United States has the largest trade surpluses are Australia, the Netherlands, Belgium, Egypt, and the United Arab Emirates.

Economics at Work

Customs Inspector

Customs inspectors enforce laws related to people and cargo entering a country. Inspectors often inspect baggage of passengers arriving from foreign countries. Inspectors are looking for illegal or undeclared materials that the people may be carrying. Inspectors may search passengers or crew members and may question anyone who looks suspicious. Inspectors also explain rules to tourists and others who are unfamiliar with them.

At times, customs inspectors may board ships, planes, and other vessels. They do this to check the type and amount of the cargo. They may oversee the loading and unloading of cargo to make sure that it follows rules. Sometimes inspectors must weigh or measure products to make sure that customs reports are correct. This process may help find illegally hidden goods. Customs inspectors are expected to seize illegal goods. They also must hold or arrest anyone suspected of carrying those goods. The government requires that inspectors provide detailed written reports of their findings.

Lesson 1 Review On a separate sheet of paper, write the letter of the answer that correctly completes each sentence.

1. The process of buying and selling is called _____.

   A barter   **C** importing

   B exporting   **D** trade

2. Countries need to trade because they do not have the same _____.

   A geography   **C** people

   B governments   **D** resources

3. _____ are a major American export.

   A Capital goods   **C** Oil supplies

   B Olives   **D** Minerals

4. Goods and services bought from foreign countries are called _____.

   A capital goods   **C** imports

   B exports   **D** raw materials

5. If a country imports more than it exports, the country has a _____.

   A trade surplus   **C** balance of trade

   B trade deficit   **D** trade compromise

What do you think ?

6. If one country needs a resource that another country has but will not trade, what should the country that wants the resource do to solve the problem? Explain.

7. Why do you think American clothing, beauty products, and other consumer products are so popular in foreign countries?

What Are the Benefits of Trade?

Trade is good for both partners. When the United States buys foreign goods, it puts dollars into the hands of people in other countries. Countries then use these dollars to buy goods from the United States. Trade improves the standard of living in both countries. It gives people a greater choice of products and services. Competition keeps prices low and quality high. Trade may affect the work you do. It allows you to specialize in what you do best.

What Is the Link Between Trade and Specialization?

Let's say that there was no trade among countries. People only could use goods and services they produced. Some countries like the United States have a lot of resources. Even so, the resources might not be able to provide Americans with all of the products available today. For example, maybe you enjoy bananas with your breakfast. Can bananas be grown in the United States? Maybe, but it would be difficult and costly to grow them. It makes more sense for the United States to grow the crops that grow best there. The United States can import the products like bananas that grow best elsewhere. Trade allows a country to specialize in the production of certain goods and services. These goods and services then can be traded for another country's specialties.

You already know that resources are not evenly divided around the world. Trade allows countries to buy the resources they do not have. They do this by selling their own goods and services. For example, some countries like Saudi Arabia and the United Arab Emirates have a lot of oil but few factories. Japan has almost no oil. Japan sells its goods and services to the Arab countries for the oil they produce.

How Does a Country Decide What to Specialize in?

Every economy has to decide what to specialize in. Because it has limited resources, a country has to decide how best to use those resources. Let's say a country could make both airplanes and ships. Both require a large place to put together all of the

Absolute advantage

The ability to produce an item more easily and less expensively than a trading partner using the same resources

Comparative advantage

The ability to produce a product or service at a lower cost and more efficiently than another country; the ability to produce an item at a lower opportunity cost

parts. Both also require skilled laborers and materials. Suppose the country is not located on a body of water large enough for ships. Therefore, it would make more sense for the country to make airplanes rather than ships.

Farmers often make similar decisions. They know the kinds of crops that grow best in their climate and with their type of soil. A farmer in Canada, for example, might specialize in growing wheat. A farmer in Colombia knows that his land is better suited for growing flowers, so he might specialize in flowers.

What Is Absolute Advantage?

Let's say you are a 7-foot-tall basketball player. You certainly have an advantage over a 6-foot-tall player. No matter how good the shorter player is, the taller player always has an advantage. It requires less effort for the tall player to make a basket. This same idea can be applied to trade. Such an advantage is called an **absolute advantage**. A country has an absolute advantage if it can produce something more easily and less expensively using the same resources than a trading partner can.

For example, the United States and Canada have an absolute advantage over Mexico in producing wheat and corn. They have a lot of rich, flat farmland. It is easy to use large farm machinery on that kind of land. Growing wheat and corn in Canada and the United States uses fewer resources than it would to grow the same crops in Mexico. Mexico has an absolute advantage over Canada and the United States in growing coffee. Its landforms and climate are better suited for growing coffee than for growing wheat or corn.

Countries that grow bananas have an absolute advantage because bananas grow best in certain climates.

What Is Comparative Advantage?

Some countries have a **comparative advantage** over others. A country has a comparative advantage if it can produce a product or service at a lower cost and more efficiently than another country. Comparative advantage is the ability to produce an item at a lower opportunity cost. Remember, opportunity cost is what is given up when a decision is made to produce a good or service.

The United States and China both are able to make shoes and airplanes, but their resources are limited. If they each decide to make shoes, they cannot make as many airplanes. Making shoes requires a lot of human resources. China is rich in human resources. Making airplanes requires technology that the United States has. It costs the United States a lot more to make shoes than it costs China. Therefore, China has a comparative advantage and specializes in shoes. The United States can make airplanes more quickly and less expensively than China can. Therefore, the United States is better off making airplanes with the same resources.

Based on their comparative advantages, China and the United States will trade with one another. The United States gets shoes, and China gets airplanes. Workers in both countries are using their resources in the most effective way.

Lesson 2 Review On a separate sheet of paper, write answers to the following questions. Use complete sentences.

1. List three reasons why trade is good for both partners.

2. Why might a farmer in Canada specialize in growing wheat rather than flowers?

3. Give an economic example of absolute advantage.

4. What is comparative advantage?

5. Why is opportunity cost important to a country with a comparative advantage?

What do you think ?

6. Think of an activity you are good at, like singing, sports, or mathematics. How is specializing in what you are good at similar to the way a country specializes in a product?

7. Do you think it is better to be rich in human resources, like China, or in technology resources, like the United States? Explain.

What Are Trade Barriers?

Trade barrier
Something that restricts or limits trade between countries

Tariff
A tax on imports

Revenue tariff
A tax added to the cost of imported goods and used to raise money for the government

In Lesson 2, we discussed the shoe industry in the United States and China. What happened to the shoe industry in the United States when China used its comparative advantage to make shoes? American shoemakers had to lay off workers, and many shoemakers went out of business.

It is not surprising, then, that some people do not favor trade with other countries. Businesses want to be protected from foreign competition. Workers are very concerned about their jobs. They want to keep their jobs even if workers in other countries can make the same products more easily and at a lower cost. Political leaders often are pressured by voters and businesses to create **trade barriers**. A trade barrier restricts or limits trade between countries.

How Do Tariffs Restrict Trade?

A **tariff** is a tax on imports. There are two types of tariffs. The **revenue tariff** is used to raise money for the government. It is a tax added to the cost of imported goods. Revenue tariffs were the main source of money for the government until 1910. The protective tariff is used to protect an industry from foreign competition. It raises money, but this is not its main goal. It protects an industry by making similar imported goods more expensive.

For example, let's say the United States wants to protect its carmakers by putting a tariff on cars made in other countries. If the tariff were high enough, the foreign cars would be more expensive than those made in America. Americans would likely buy the less expensive American cars. Of course, the United States is not the only country to have tariffs. Every country wants to protect its economy by limiting imports.

How Do Import Quotas and Voluntary Trade Restrictions Limit Trade?

Import quota

A restriction on the number of specific goods that can enter a country

Voluntary trade restriction

An offer made by a foreign country to limit the sale of their goods in another country

Embargo

The act of cutting off all trade with another country

Countries sometimes use **import quotas** and **voluntary trade restrictions** to cut down on the number of imports. Restrictions on the number of specific goods that can enter a country are called import quotas. Suppose the United States had an import quota on MP3 players made in China. If the quota were small, the number of Chinese MP3 players allowed into the country would be small. This would allow American makers of MP3 players to sell more, even though they might be more expensive.

Sometimes foreign countries offer to limit the sale of their goods in another country. This is called a voluntary trade restriction. Countries do this to keep good relations and to stay friendly. They know that if they did not limit trade, bad feelings might develop.

What Are Embargoes?

Sometimes a country cuts off all trade with another country. This is called an **embargo**. The reason for the embargo usually is more political than economic. For example, the United States and several other countries have an embargo against Cuba. It is intended to pressure Cuba's leader, Fidel Castro, to end his dictatorship.

Why Do Countries Disagree About Subsidies?

Countries try to control imports to protect the nation's economy.

In Chapter 5, you learned that subsidies are grants of money made by the government. The governments of many developed countries subsidize certain industries. For example, the United States gives over $3 billion in subsidies to American cotton farmers. These allow growers to sell their cotton at a lower price. The price is so low that cotton farmers in West Africa cannot compete. The Africans argue that world cotton prices are so low that many of their cotton farmers are becoming even

Free trade

Trade without barriers

Trade war

An act in which a country places tariffs on foreign goods and, in return, finds that tariffs are placed on their own goods

poorer, and some are starving. The U.S. government argues that ending the subsidies would drive American farmers out of business. It argues that it is unfair to force the United States to end subsidies unless other countries also agree to end theirs.

What Arguments Are Made in Favor of Free Trade?

Many countries restrict trade but oppose trade restrictions made by other countries. Every country wants to protect its industries and jobs. But countries still want a variety of goods and services available to their people. The answer, according to some people, is **free trade**. Free trade is trade without barriers.

Those who favor free trade say that countries with the lowest trade barriers have the highest standard of living. Their people enjoy a higher quality of goods and a greater variety. The prices they pay for goods are lower.

No country allows completely free trade. The United States and Canada are two countries with few trade barriers. Consumers in both countries benefit from the goods that flow in from many other countries. Keep in mind that trade barriers can backfire. Countries that place tariffs on foreign goods often find that tariffs are placed on their own goods. The result is sometimes a **trade war** that hurts both economies.

What Arguments Are Made in Favor of Restricting Trade?

It seems that restrictions on trade would give consumers fewer choices. There would be no imports. All goods and services would have to be made within the country. The quality of life would go down. What arguments, then, could be made to support trade restrictions?

One argument is that restrictions protect important industries needed for a nation's defense. For example, oil is an important resource. In wartime, a large supply is needed. The United States might want to restrict oil imports so that most imported oil is saved for defense. This might encourage American companies to find a substitute for oil or to hunt for new oil sources within the United States.

Diversify

To vary

Another argument is that restrictions protect new industries. Developing countries sometimes set trade restrictions on goods made elsewhere. They know their new industries cannot compete with industries in more developed countries. Early in U.S. history, this argument was used to support protective tariffs for the young United States.

Some people argue that restrictions encourage countries to **diversify**, or vary, their economies. Some developing countries rely on just one product or crop. If it fails, terrible results follow. To prevent this from happening, people argue that governments should encourage new products and crops. While these new products are being introduced, the government needs to provide help. The government could help keep out foreign products by placing tariffs and other trade restrictions.

In countries like the United States, some argue that restrictions are needed because of cheap labor in other countries. Other countries pay their workers much less than U.S. workers are paid. This gives them a big advantage. These countries can sell their goods for much less. American producers argue that without trade restrictions, they will be forced out of business.

Word Bank

defense

embargo

free trade

import quota

tariff

Lesson 3 Review On a separate sheet of paper, write the word from the Word Bank to complete each sentence.

1. A tax on imports is a(n) _____.

2. A(n) _____ usually is placed for reasons that are political rather than economic.

3. Trade without barriers is _____.

4. A(n) _____ cuts down on imports into a country.

5. Trade restrictions might help support a nation's _____.

What do you think ❓

6. Should the U.S. government give subsidies to their own farmers even if those subsidies hurt farmers in less developed countries? Explain.

7. Do you agree with the arguments in favor of free trade or in favor of trade restrictions? Explain.

What Is Globalization?

Have you heard people saying that the world is getting smaller every day? What they mean is that the world is becoming more **interdependent**. This means countries are depending more on each other for economic success.

International trade has increased. Many businesses now have branches in many countries. The world's economies are becoming more closely tied together. Economists call this trend **globalization**.

How Do Countries Cooperate Economically?

Almost all of the world's countries believe that trade is a way to improve the quality of life for their people. For this reason, it makes sense that countries want to promote trade. There are many ways that countries can promote trade.

What Are Reciprocal Trade Agreements?

United States President Franklin Roosevelt believed that high tariffs were one of the causes of the Great Depression. He urged Congress to do something to increase trade. Congress gave the president the power to lower American tariffs by as much as 50 percent. The president can reduce a tariff if the trading partners reduce their tariff on American goods by the same percentage. This is called a **reciprocal trade agreement**. It means that both sides agree to the same terms of trade.

Congress can give **most favored nation (MFN)** status to a trading partner. Any country that is a most favored nation gets the same lowered tariff that the United States gets with another country. For example, if the United States agrees to lower the tariff on imported cheese from one MFN, the tariff for cheese would be lowered for all other MFNs.

Interdependent

When countries depend on each other for economic success

Globalization

The act of bringing world economies closer together through international business and trade

Reciprocal trade agreement

An agreement that allows the United States to reduce a tariff if the trading partner reduces their tariff on American goods by the same percentage

Most favored nation (MFN)

A country that receives the same lowered tariff that the United States negotiates with another country

What Are GATT and the WTO?

General Agreement on Tariffs and Trade (GATT)

An agreement signed by 23 countries at the end of World War II to promote international trade as a way to stop future wars

World Trade Organization (WTO)

An organization created in 1995 to replace GATT; member countries agree to cut tariffs on capital goods, end import quotas on textiles and clothing, and loosen other trade barriers

At the end of World War II, 23 countries signed the **General Agreement on Tariffs and Trade (GATT)**. They thought the way to stop future wars was by promoting international trade. Through a series of trade meetings since 1947, tariffs have been cut. Other trade barriers have been reduced.

In 1994, after talking for nearly eight years, the now 123 nations of GATT reached a new agreement. They agreed to cut tariffs on capital goods and products like prescription drugs and computer chips. Import quotas on textiles and clothing would end over a period of time. Fewer restrictions would be placed on farm products. Trade barriers on such services as computer software and accounting programs would be loosened. All countries that signed the agreement said they would protect patents, copyrights, and trademarks. Those countries created the **World Trade Organization (WTO)** in 1995 to enforce the agreement and eventually replace GATT.

Economics in Your Life

World Trade Organization Riots in Seattle

Representatives of the World Trade Organization (WTO) gathered at Seattle's Washington State Convention Center in late November 1999. The main goal of the WTO was to remove trade barriers so that all nations of the world could trade freely.

About 50,000 environmentalists, trade unionists, and others went to Seattle to protest the WTO convention. These protesters did not agree with the WTO's goals. They thought that removing trade barriers would allow U.S. companies to use cheaper foreign labor instead of American workers. Other protesters were concerned about ongoing abuse of the environment by many large members of the WTO.

The protest started out peacefully. However, it soon became one of the worst riots Seattle had ever seen. Widespread damage of property took place. Rioters looted stores and started fires. The mayor declared a state of emergency. The governor called in the Washington National Guard to help control the protesters. Despite the protests, the WTO members continue their work to improve trade.

How Are Free-Trade Associations and Customs Unions Different?

Both **free-trade associations** and **customs unions** are trade agreements between trading countries. In a free-trade association, members reduce trade barriers among themselves. Each member, however, can set its own tariffs on goods from non-member countries it trades with. In a customs union, members agree to remove all trade barriers among themselves. However, they place the same tariff on goods imported from non-member countries.

What Is NAFTA?

The **North American Free Trade Agreement (NAFTA)** is a trade agreement signed by Mexico, Canada, and the United States. It took effect in 1994. It created one large free-trade area in North America. The three countries removed many trade barriers and agreed to phase out the rest. Now products from the three members of NAFTA cross international borders as easily as they cross state borders. The agreement has made it easier for each country to sell its goods and services. Exports and imports have increased for all three NAFTA members. Investments also have increased, especially in Mexico. Mexico and Canada have become the two most important U.S. trading partners.

Leaders signed the North American Free Trade Agreement to remove many trade barriers among Mexico, Canada, and the United States.

What Is the European Union?

European Union (EU)

An organization that links European countries both economically and politically and promotes cooperation among its members

Regional trade organization

An organization that works toward lowering or removing trade barriers among its members, which are located in the same region of the world

The **European Union (EU)** is an organization linking European countries both economically and politically. It is an example of a **regional trade organization**. These organizations work toward lowering or removing trade barriers among their members. The members are located in the same general region of the world. The EU grew out of a customs union created after World War II in some western European countries. Currently, 15 countries are member states, but in May 2004, the number will grow to 25. The goal of the EU is to promote cooperation among its members, especially in trade. All trade barriers among the members of the European Union have been dropped. Since 2000, most members use the same form of currency called the euro.

What Other Regional Trade Organizations Exist?

The EU is the largest regional trade organization. However, there are trade organizations in other regions. The Caribbean Community and Common Market (CARICOM) includes many small nations in the Caribbean region. The Association of Southeast Asian Nations (ASEAN) promotes economic cooperation among 10 countries in the region. The Central American Common Market dropped trade barriers among its five Central American members. The Southern Common Market (MERCOSUR) does the same for four countries in the southern part of South America.

Biography

Javier Solana: 1942–

As a young man, Javier Solana studied as a Fulbright scholar at some American universities. He worked toward his degree in physics. Afterwards, he became a professor of physics at Madrid University. Solana was also a member of the Spanish parliament from 1977 to 1995. He served as Minister of Culture, Minister of Education and Science, and finally as Minister of Foreign Affairs. Solana was then appointed Secretary General of NATO in 1995.

In 1999, Solana became the European Union's High Representative for Common Foreign and Security Policy. The EU works to support agriculture and promote trade among its member nations. It also tries to create closer cooperation in the areas of justice, domestic affairs, and social policy. As High Representative, Solana presents ideas and studies policy choices to help other EU leaders make good decisions.

Lesson 4 Review On a separate sheet of paper, write the letter of the answer that correctly completes each sentence.

1. The trend of world economies becoming more closely tied together is _____.

    A globalization   **C** protectionism

    B unionism   **D** trade

2. The World Trade Organization *does not* _____.

    A cut tariffs on capital goods

    B prevent trade in the European Union

    C end import quotas

    D loosen trade barriers

3. Countries that belong to a customs union use the same _____.

    A currency   **C** tariffs

    B government   **D** resources

4. NAFTA created a free-trade area in _____.

    A Canada   **C** Europe

    B Central and   **D** North America
    South America

5. Since 2000, many countries of the European Union have used the _____ as their currency.

    A dollar   **C** franc

    B euro   **D** mark

What do you think ?

6. What do you think are the biggest advantages of European Union members using the same money, the euro? What do you think are the biggest disadvantages?

7. When members of the World Trade Organization meet, people sometimes gather to protest the organization's policies. Why do you think people become upset about the WTO?

Iraqi Embargo

Iraqi leader Saddam Hussein was removed from power in 2003.

Because of increasing tensions between the United States and Iraq, the senior President George Bush issued an embargo on August 3, 1990. This meant that the United States would no longer trade or do business with Iraq.

I, GEORGE BUSH, President of the United States of America, find that the policies and actions of the Government of Iraq constitute [create] an unusual and extraordinary threat to the national security and foreign policy of the United States and hereby declare a national emergency to deal with that threat.

I hereby order:

All property and interests in property of the Government of Iraq, its agencies, instrumentalities and controlled entities [parts] and the Central Bank of Iraq that are in the United States . . . are hereby blocked.

The embargo included imports and exports, business deals, the purchase of Iraqi goods, and credit extensions to the Iraqi government. News journalists were the only Americans allowed to travel to Iraq.

At a May 7, 2003 press conference, the junior President Bush announced the end of the embargo that his father had signed 13 years earlier. The war in Iraq had removed dictator Saddam Hussein from power. Bush believed that ending the embargo would help Iraq rebuild.

Today I removed the sanctions [limits] imposed by the United States against Iraq's old government. First, based on the authority recently given to me by Congress, I am suspending the Iraq Sanctions Act, which restricts the export of certain equipment necessary for Iraq's reconstruction.

Secondly, I am directing Treasury Secretary Snow to relax administrative sanctions on American companies and citizens conducting business in Iraq that contributes to humanitarian relief and reconstruction.

Soon, at the U.N. Security Council, the United States, Great Britain, and Spain will introduce a new resolution to lift the sanctions imposed by the United Nations. The regime that the sanctions were directed against no longer rules Iraq. And no country in good conscience can support using sanctions to hold back the hopes of the Iraqi people.

The U.N. lifted its sanctions on May 22, 2003.

Document-Based Questions

1. Why did the senior President Bush place an embargo on Iraq?

2. What were three things the embargo restricted?

3. How long did the embargo last?

4. Why did the junior President Bush remove the embargo?

5. Do you think it is good or bad for the United States to place embargoes on other countries? Explain.

■ Trade allows countries to get goods and services they cannot produce or grow themselves.

■ Exports are goods and services sold to foreign countries. Imports are goods and services bought from a foreign country.

■ A balance of trade is the difference between the value of a country's imports and exports. Countries may have a trade deficit or trade surplus.

■ Specialization allows countries to do what they do best and trade for other countries' specialties.

■ An absolute advantage is producing something less expensively and more easily than a trading partner with the same resources. A comparative advantage is the ability to produce an item at a lower opportunity cost than another country.

■ Tariffs tax imports and restrict trade. Revenue tariffs raise money for a government. Protective tariffs protect certain industries.

■ Import quotas limit imports. Countries sometimes limit the sale of goods in another country with voluntary trade restrictions.

■ Embargoes cut off all trade with another country for political reasons.

■ Government subsidies support an industry. Subsidies may hurt foreign competitors who cannot compete with the low prices of goods.

■ Free trade is trade free of all barriers. Those who support free trade say it raises the living standards of a country.

■ Some people think trade restrictions protect industries important for a nation's defense, protect new industries, diversify a country's economy, or offset other countries' cheap labor.

■ Globalization brings world economies closer together.

■ Reciprocal trade agreements allow two countries to lower tariffs for each other. Most favored nation (MFN) status gives the MFN the same lowered tariff as other trading partners.

■ The General Agreement on Tariffs and Trade (GATT) began in 1947 to promote international trade and stop future wars. The World Trade Organization (WTO) has replaced GATT.

■ Members of free-trade associations reduce trade barriers among themselves but set their own tariffs toward non-members. Members of customs unions remove trade barriers among themselves and have a common tariff on goods with non-members.

■ The North American Free Trade Agreement (NAFTA) set up a free-trade area between the United States, Mexico, and Canada.

■ The European Union is the world's largest regional trade organization.

■ Other regional trade organizations exist around the world.

Chapter 19 REVIEW

On a separate sheet of paper, write the word from the Word Bank to complete each sentence.

1. The most important _____ of the United States include oil, machinery, and automobiles.

2. Trade among countries allows countries to specialize in producing certain _____.

3. Restrictions on the amount of a good that can enter a country are _____.

4. Most favored _____ receive the same lowered tariff that the United States has with another country.

5. Countries in _____ reduce trade barriers among themselves but can set their own tariffs toward other countries.

6. A country with a(n) _____ advantage can produce a good at a lower opportunity cost.

7. Governments in many countries subsidize certain _____.

Word Bank

comparative

free-trade associations

goods or services

import quotas

imports

industries

nations

On a separate sheet of paper, write the letter of the answer that correctly completes each sentence.

8. The difference between a country's imports and its exports is its _____.

   A balance of imports   **C** trade deficit

   B balance of trade   **D** trade surplus

9. When a country has a _____, it imports more than it exports.

   A balance of imports   **C** trade deficit

   B balance of trade   **D** trade surplus

10. Trade allows countries to buy _____ they do not have.

   A advantages   **C** resources

   B protection   **D** tariffs

11. Placing _____ on goods sometimes results in trade wars.

   A freedom   **C** trade agreements

   B low prices   **D** tariffs

12. After NAFTA took effect in 1994, exports and imports have _____ for the United States, Canada, and Mexico.

   A stopped   **C** increased

   B decreased   **D** stayed the same

13. In a _____, members remove all trade barriers and place the same tariffs on goods from non-member countries.

   A customs union   **C** globalized economy

   B free-trade association **D** reciprocal trade agreement

On a separate sheet of paper, write answers to the following questions. Use complete sentences.

14. What is a trade surplus?

15. What is an absolute advantage?

16. What are the two types of tariffs? Explain what each does.

17. Briefly describe the European Union.

On a separate sheet of paper, write your opinion to each question. Use complete sentences.

18. If a trading partner of the United States used dangerous chemicals to help grow crops, how might U.S. citizens be affected?

19. The text discusses friendly and unfriendly relations between countries. Why are countries so concerned with how they get along with others?

20. Do you think closer economic and political ties among countries decreases the possibility of war? Why or why not?

Test-Taking Tip

Review your corrected homework and tests to learn from your mistakes. Make a list of your mistakes to use as a study guide.

20 Less Developed Countries

Have you ever thought about how people in other countries live? The photo to the left shows a family in Ghana, Africa. Ghana is like many countries in the world today—it is still developing.

Mexico is another less developed country. In many parts of Mexico, people make a living by farming on less than an acre of land. The per capita GDP in Mexico is less than $9,000. Many people find it difficult to feed themselves and their family. Some people move to the cities in hopes of finding better paying jobs. Some try to find jobs in the United States. They often are forced to accept low wages and poor living conditions. Unfortunately, Mexico is not unusual. In fact, Mexicans are better off than millions of people living in other parts of Latin America, Africa, and Asia.

This chapter discusses the challenges facing people who live in less developed countries. It also looks at organizations that help poor countries.

Goals for Learning

◆ To identify the characteristics of a less developed country

◆ To describe some of the challenges facing less developed countries

◆ To explain the work of international organizations in less developed countries

What Is a Less Developed Country?

Less developed country (LDC)

A country with an economy that is still developing

The South

The name given by economists to the poorer countries in the southern hemisphere of the world

The North

The name given by economists to the richer countries in the northern hemisphere of the world

Countries of the world have different levels of economic development. Today, the United States, Canada, Japan, Australia, and most European countries are considered developed countries. Poorer countries in the world are called **less developed countries (LDC)**. A less developed country is a country with an economy that is still developing and growing.

Most of the LDCs are located in the southern hemisphere, or the southern half of the earth. Most of the developed countries are located in the northern hemisphere. For this reason, economists sometimes refer to the poorer countries as **the South**. The richer countries are called **the North**.

What Features Do Less Developed Countries Share?

LDCs are very different from one another. The people speak different languages. They practice different religions. Their history, culture, and traditions are different. But they also have much in common.

LDCs have a low GDP and limited economic development. They usually are much poorer than developed countries. For example, the North has only about 25 percent of the world's people, but it uses almost 80 percent of the world's energy. Americans make up 6 percent of the world's population but use about one-third of the world's resources.

People in LDCs often do not live as long as people in developed countries. Many babies die before their first

Figure 20.1

Life Expectancy of Selected Nations

Country	Expectation of Life at Birth (years)	
	2001	**2010** (projected)
Afghanistan	46.2	49.6
Angola	38.6	41.3
Argentina	75.3	77.1
Australia	79.9	81.0
Brazil	63.2	66.3
Canada	79.6	80.7
Chile	75.9	77.7
China	71.6	73.9
Colombia	70.6	73.1
Cuba	76.4	78.1
Ethiopia	44.7	42.1
Ghana	57.2	55.5
India	62.9	66.1
Iraq	67.0	70.3
Italy	79.1	80.2
Japan	80.8	81.7
Malawi	37.1	35.8
Mexico	71.8	74.1
Mozambique	36.5	31.4
Russia	67.3	68.8
Saudi Arabia	68.1	70.9
South Africa	48.1	35.5
United Kingdom	77.8	79.3
United States	77.3	78.5
Vietnam	69.6	72.2

birthday. Figure 20.1 compares the **life expectancy** of people living in different countries. Life expectancy is the average number of years a person will live.

In many rural areas, children have to work. If they go to school, it usually is for only two or three years. Many people cannot read or write. In urban areas, many of the people barely survive. They live in run-down areas called **slums** with no electricity or indoor plumbing. They drink polluted water and often do not have enough to eat.

In some countries, medical care has gotten better. As a result, the population is growing. Less developed countries often have high **birthrates**. The birthrate is the ratio of births to the total population of an area in one year. The population may double every 25 years. (Figure 20.2 compares birthrates in several countries.) In many countries, the population is growing at a faster rate than the rate of food production. Many people face starvation and hunger.

In less developed countries, many people cannot find work. Most people work in **subsistence farming**. This means they grow crops mainly for their own use. To earn money for economic development, some countries have encouraged farmers to grow **cash crops**. Cash crops are grown and sold for money. Common cash crops in LDCs are tea, cotton, and vegetables. Sometimes it is hard for farmers in LDCs to sell their products. This is

Figure 20.2 **Birthrates of Selected Nations**

Country	Birthrates (during one year per 1,000 persons)	
	2001	2010 (projected)
Afghanistan	41.1	37.3
Angola	46.5	42.9
Argentina	18.4	16.6
Australia	12.9	11.7
Brazil	18.5	15.6
Canada	11.2	10.7
Chile	16.8	14.5
China	16.0	13.1
Colombia	22.4	19.3
Cuba	12.4	11.0
Ethiopia	44.7	41.6
Ghana	29.0	23.3
India	24.3	20.7
Iraq	34.6	29.4
Italy	9.1	7.5
Japan	10.0	8.9
Malawi	37.8	31.8
Mexico	22.8	19.3
Mozambique	37.2	31.1
Russia	9.4	12.1
Saudi Arabia	37.3	37.1
South Africa	21.1	17.8
United Kingdom	11.5	10.6
United States	14.2	14.3
Vietnam	21.2	18.3

because the governments of developed countries subsidize many crops. Another problem with the move toward cash crops is a drop in food production.

Transportation and communication also are often limited in LDCs. Less developed countries have few manufacturing and service industries to provide jobs. People who are poor, hungry, and desperate do not want to wait to improve their lives. Often they turn to political leaders who promise a brighter future. Sometimes these leaders become dictators. The dictators usually do not help the poor very much. Political unrest is common in LDCs.

Word Bank

cash crops

communication

economy

slums

subsistence
  farming

Lesson 1 Review On a separate sheet of paper, write the word from the Word Bank to complete each sentence.

1. In a less developed country, the _____ is still developing.

2. In urban areas of less developed countries, people often live in _____.

3. Growing crops for a family's own use is _____.

4. Transportation and _____ are often limited in LDCs.

5. Tea, cotton, and vegetables are commonly grown as _____.

What do you think ?

6. Why do you think poorer countries tend to be in the south and richer countries tend to be in the north? List some possible reasons.

7. This lesson describes some causes of poverty in less developed countries. What do you think could be done to prevent some of the poverty?

Family planning
*An effort to slow
population increases by
controlling and spacing
the number of births*

Less developed countries face many problems. How they respond to these challenges will affect all of us.

How Are Less Developed Countries Dealing with High Birthrates?

LDCs know that they have to deal with their high birthrates. About half of the people in many LDCs are children. Even if the LDCs make progress in economic growth, the progress can be stopped if the population continues to grow. Many countries have used some of their scarce resources to pay for **family planning**. Workers travel from village to village showing the people how to control and space the number of births. Men and women are encouraged to marry later. Even if these efforts are successful, it may take a while before the birthrate drops.

What Are Less Developed Countries Doing to Promote Economic Growth?

Some LDCs have rich natural resources such as oil or natural gas. Developing these resources can promote growth. The income from these resources can be used for education and improving communication and transportation.

Many LDCs believe that industrialization will create jobs and wealth. But as we have learned, every economic decision has trade-offs. Forests are being cut down to make land for raising cattle and farming. This has led to widespread damage of the rain forests in South America and Asia. Farmers use chemicals to try to control plant disease and to increase production. Some of these chemicals spoil the drinking water and create health problems.

Development takes money, but most of the LDCs are poor. Many countries try to borrow money from developed countries. Like all loans, these must be repaid with interest. Often the less developed countries do not have the resources to pay back the loans. They continue to borrow and fall further into debt.

Over time, more and more of the country's resources go to paying off just the interest. For example, in the 1970s and 1980s, Mexico borrowed a lot of money to pay for industrial development. Soon Mexico owed about $100 billion. Because of this, the government had to cut back on imports, medical care, education, and care for the elderly. Some developed countries have cancelled the debt because they know there is no way the LDCs can ever repay it.

Why Should People Care About LDCs?

The best reason for helping the people of less developed countries is that they are fellow human beings. Another reason is that we all share the same planet. We should help others for **humanitarian** reasons, not political or economic ones. Humanitarians are people who are devoted to helping all human beings no matter where they live.

The developed countries have helped the LDCs with **foreign aid**. This is money, medicine, machinery, and food to help less developed countries. Developed countries give foreign aid to promote political and economic stability. They also give aid for humanitarian reasons.

Helping the developing countries is good for business. Poor countries cannot buy the many things they want and need. Helping LDCs develop increases their wealth. With more money, they have the ability to buy more goods and services from developed countries.

Economics in Your Life

The International Red Cross

The International Committee of the Red Cross was founded in 1863. It started after a Swiss man named Jean Henry Dunant pleaded for aid to wounded soldiers. Today, the Red Cross is based in Geneva, Switzerland. With over 178 member countries, it is the largest network of humanitarian relief in the world. More than 115 million volunteers are a part of the organization around the world.

The Red Cross gives medicine and food to people who are victims of war. It also helps with relief actions after natural disasters. A third job of the Red Cross is to make sure nations follow the rules of international humanitarian law. This includes volunteer visits to prisoners of war camps. These Red Cross volunteers make sure that people are being treated well.

In less developed countries, Red Cross volunteers provide health care training to people. Volunteers place a special focus on the diseases of children. They work to make it easier for people to get medicine and medical treatment. During each year of the past decade, the Red Cross has delivered food to about one million people in many countries.

Lesson 2 Review On a separate sheet of paper, write the letter of the answer that correctly completes each sentence.

1. To promote _____, some LDCs develop their natural resources.
   A economic growth   **C** foreign aid
   B family planning   **D** humanitarian programs

2. Many LDCs believe industrialization will create _____.
   A economic recessions   **C** jobs and wealth
   B interest payments   **D** trade-offs

3. Workers try to slow population growth in LDCs with _____.
   A birthrates   **C** natural resources
   B family planning   **D** industrialization

4. People who try to help others just because they are humans are called _____.
   A developers   **C** government workers
   B educators   **D** humanitarians

5. Developing countries sometimes give LDCs money, medicine, food, and other _____.
   A economic incentives   **C** industrial development
   B foreign aid   **D** natural resources

What do you think ?

6. What are some ways that you could help someone at your school, in your neighborhood, in your state or country, or in another country?

7. All less developed countries have their own problems. How do you think a developed country should balance solving its own problems with helping out less developed countries?

What Is the United Nations?

There are many international groups that are working toward improving the quality of life in LDCs. The **United Nations (UN)** was organized in 1945. Its members try to promote higher standards of living for all people. International organizations like the UN are a major source of help to developing countries.

How Does the UN Promote Economic Development?

The **Economic and Social Council (ECOSOC)** is the part of the UN that promotes economic development. It tries to stop wars by improving the way people live. ECOSOC works through its many **agencies**, or groups that provide special services.

• The United Nations Educational, Scientific, and Cultural Organization (UNESCO) gives advice to LDCs in Africa, Asia, and Latin America. One of its main goals is to teach people how to read. It trains teachers and provides books to people in developing countries.

• The United Nations Children's Fund (UNICEF) cares for sick, starving, and homeless children in LDCs. It provides health care, food, and education.

• The Food and Agricultural Organization (FAO) fights hunger in LDCs. Farm experts from the FAO teach modern farming methods. This helps farmers in less developed countries grow more food. The FAO is concerned with protecting the soil, proper use of fertilizers, and controlling and treating animal diseases.

• The World Health Organization (WHO) tries to improve peoples' health. One of its greatest successes was getting rid of two terrible diseases, polio and smallpox. These diseases affected many people in less developed countries.

• The International Labor Organization (ILO) is working toward improving working conditions and living standards around the world. One of its main goals is to get rid of child labor.

What Is the UN Development Program?

In 1965, the UN Development Program (UNDP) was created. It controls most of the UN development projects around the world. These projects involve almost all of the agencies already discussed in this lesson. They affect farming, mining, fishing, forestry, and manufacturing.

The UNDP also runs all projects in transportation, communication, housing, electrical power, trade, and tourism. It manages health, **sanitation** (keeping things clean and removing trash), education, and environmental protection programs too.

What Is the World Bank?

The **World Bank** is an agency of the UN that started in 1945. It is really a group of many banks that specialize in certain areas. Its focus today is to direct money from developed countries to less developed countries. Since its founding, the World Bank has loaned out billions of dollars to developing countries.

The largest part of the World Bank is the International Bank for Reconstruction and Development. It loans money to build dams, mines, roads, ports, and bridges. Other groups include the International Development Association, the International Finance Corporation, and the Multilateral Investment Guarantee Agency.

Biography

Carol Bellamy: 1942–

Carol Bellamy has a long history of helping others. In 1995, she was named Executive Director of UNICEF. As director, she challenges world leaders to use national resources for the benefit of children.

Before joining UNICEF, Bellamy was the director of the Peace Corps, another group that helps developing countries. She was the first former Peace Corps volunteer to head the organization. She has worked as a banker and a lawyer on Wall Street and was the first woman elected as head of the New York City Council. Bellamy also served in the New York State Senate from 1973 to 1977.

What Is the International Monetary Fund?

International Monetary Fund (IMF)

An agency of the UN that gives money and economic advice to countries when they have economic problems

The **International Monetary Fund (IMF)** is another UN agency founded in 1945. It works closely with the World Bank. The IMF gives money and economic advice to countries when they have economic problems. The problem may be inflation, an unfavorable balance of trade, a huge budget deficit, or something else. When these problems arise, the country may ask for help from the IMF. The country usually is given a list of steps it must take before the emergency loans are granted. The steps might include cutting government spending or adopting free market policies.

The United Nations supports many efforts to raise standards of living for all people. These UN workers are helping people in the war-torn Jenin refugee camp in the West Bank.

Why Do People Disagree with Some World Bank and IMF Policies?

Both the World Bank and the IMF have had some success. Some people, however, believe that the policies of these agencies actually hurt the people they are trying to help. The World Bank and IMF push the less developed countries to adopt free market economies. To solve the countries' economic problems, the World Bank and the IMF may ask them to lower trade barriers and get rid of subsidies. To control the money supply, countries are told to raise interest rates or to lower the value of currencies. To cut budget deficits, LDCs are forced to cut spending on education, health, and welfare. The result may be economic progress, but it comes at a great cost to the poor people of the LDCs.

The IMF and the World Bank understand the problem. They believe that if their policies are followed, the standard of living in LDCs will improve over time.

Economics at Work

Urban/Regional Planner

Urban planners study the best use of land and buildings for a city, downtown area, or other urban region. Their work usually involves collecting data on social, economic, and physical aspects of land use. Urban planners often help government and business leaders with development or redevelopment projects. Such projects might include changes in housing, business sites, or industry. Goals may include keeping a high standard of living, improving the economy, or aiding community growth.

The area's geography, population changes, public utilities, and transportation are some of the things that planners study. The environmental problems that a new development might cause also must be studied and carefully explained.

Much of the work of urban planners involves meeting with community leaders. Urban planners often must create reports showing present conditions. They also must suggest ideas for change. At times, urban planners have to join many different viewpoints together into a single plan. A good planner needs solid communication skills to help city leaders reach a compromise. While many urban planners work for local governments, others work for private companies.

Lesson 3 Review On a separate sheet of paper, write answers to the following questions. Use complete sentences.

1. What are the goals of UNESCO?

2. How does UNICEF try to care for children in LDCs?

3. What is the purpose of the FAO?

4. What are the goals of the ILO?

5. What are some ways the IMF works with LDCs?

What do you think

6. Some nations give large amounts of money to UN organizations. Should these nations be able to control what these organizations do? Explain.

7. Why might an LDC not want to agree when the IMF says the country must cut spending on education or welfare?

Population Explosion

The world population has continued to increase since humans have lived on the earth. However, in the 20th century, there was a rapid increase in the world's population. The world had never seen such a large increase before. This was mostly because more babies were surviving at birth and people were living longer. In 1998, the Census Bureau released a report about the future increases in world population.

According to Census Bureau projections, world population will increase to a level of nearly 8 billion persons by the end of the next quarter century, and will reach 9.3 billion persons—a number more than half again as large as today's total—by 2050. . . .

Today, more than half the world's population lives in Asia, with China and India accounting for nearly 2 of every 5 persons on earth. More developed countries as a group make up just 20 percent of world population, and the United States constitutes [makes up] less than 5 percent of the global total. . . .

[F]uture additions to world population will be concentrated in the world's less-affluent regions. Ninety-eight percent of the increase

in human numbers during the next quarter century will take place in the less developed countries of Africa, Asia, and Latin America. . . .

[B]ecause the growth rates of today's more developed countries are slower than the global average, the share of world population living in today's more-affluent [wealthy] nations will continue to shrink. . . .

Of the 79 million persons to be added to world population [in 1998], over 16 million will live in India, about 11 million will be in China, 34 million more will live in the rest of Asia and Oceania. Over 15 million will be added in Sub-Saharan Africa, nearly 8 million in Latin America and the Caribbean, and 7 million in the Near East and North Africa.

In early 2003, the United Nations decreased its population estimates for 2050 from 9.3 billion to 8.9 billion. The UN believes more deaths from the AIDS virus and a declining world birthrate will cause the decrease in population growth.

Document-Based Questions

1. Why did the world population increase so much in the 20th century?

2. Where did more than half of the world's population live in 1998?

3. Why is the population decreasing in wealthy nations?

4. Why did the United Nations decrease its population estimates for 2050?

5. What do you think are some problems caused by an increase in population?

■ A less developed country (LDC) is a country with an economy that is developing. Most developed countries are in the North (northern hemisphere). Most LDCs are in the South (southern hemisphere).

■ LDCs have limited economic development and a low GDP. People in LDCs do not live as long as people in developed countries. Children often have to work, and many people cannot read or write. People who live in urban areas often live in slums.

■ Medical care has improved in some LDCs. This has caused the birthrates to rise, which has led to starvation.

■ Work is hard to find in LDCs. Many people work in subsistence farming. Farmers often grow tea, cotton, vegetables, or other cash crops. One problem with cash crop farming is a drop in food production.

■ LDCs face many other challenges. Transportation and communication are often limited. Few manufacturing or service jobs exist. Leaders often become dictators, and political unrest is common.

■ Some LDCs have natural resources to develop. LDCs believe industrializing will help their country, but industrialization has trade-offs. Forests may be cut down for raising

cattle and farming. This leads to the destruction of rain forests. Chemicals used in farming may spoil water and cause health problems.

■ Economic development takes money. LDCs often have to borrow from developed countries. Sometimes so much money goes to repay the debt that there is little money left for medical care, education, or imports.

■ People often care about LDCs for humanitarian reasons. Developed countries help LDCs with foreign aid.

■ The United Nations was organized in 1945. It tries to promote higher standards of living of all people. One part of the UN is ECOSOC, or the Economic and Social Council. Its agencies include UNESCO, UNICEF, the FAO, the WHO, and the ILO.

■ The UN Development Program organizes UN projects around the world.

■ The World Bank is a group of banks that loans money to LDCs for development. The International Monetary Fund (IMF) gives economic advice. It also may give money to LDCs if they meet certain conditions. Some people disagree with some World Bank and IMF policies. They think certain economic policies may hurt poor people in LDCs.

On a separate sheet of paper, write the word from the Word Bank to complete each sentence.

1. Cash crops are grown and sold for _____.

2. Most LDCs are located in the _____ hemisphere.

3. _____ farming means growing crops for a family's own use.

4. A high _____ may cause starvation for LDCs.

5. _____ is money, medicine, machinery, and food that a developed country gives to a less developed country.

6. The World Bank is a(n) _____ of the United Nations.

7. Economic progress in LDCs often comes at great cost to their _____.

Word Bank

agency
birthrate
foreign aid
money
poor
southern
subsistence

On a separate sheet of paper, write the letter of the answer that correctly completes each sentence.

8. Sometimes leaders in LDCs become _____ and may not help the poor people.

   A dictators   **C** farmers

   B economists   **D** poor

9. People in LDCs often do not live as long as those in _____.

   A Asia   **C** poor urban areas

   B developed countries   **D** rural areas

10. One way countries try to reduce birthrates is to pay for _____.

   A family planning   **C** hospitals

   B farms   **D** marriages

11. _____ has led to damaged rain forests in large areas of South America and Asia.

   A Education   **C** Industrialization

   B Humanitarian aid **D** Income

12. The UN tries to promote higher _____ for all people.

    A birthrates   **C** industrialization

    B child labor rates   **D** standards of living

13. The UN _____ runs projects in transportation, housing, and tourism.

    A Food and Agricultural   **C** International Labor
        Organization   Organization

    B Development Program **D** World Health Organization

On a separate sheet of paper, write answers to the following questions. Use complete sentences.

14. What are some characteristics of less developed countries?

15. What are two trade-offs of industrialization?

16. Why do people disagree with some World Bank and IMF policies?

17. What is the job of the UN Development Program?

On a separate sheet of paper, write your opinion to each question. Use complete sentences.

18. Why do you think there is a difference in economic development around the world?

19. How might helping LDCs with economic development also help the United States or other developed countries?

20. If you were able to start your own humanitarian group, what kind of group would you start? What things would your group try to do to help others? Why? (Think about how your own interests might help you form this group.)

Test-Taking Tip

When finished with a test, read over all written answers. As you read, imagine that you are someone reading the test for the first time. Ask yourself if the ideas and information make sense. Revise and rewrite to make the answers as clear as you can.

Compare and Contrast

To compare and contrast is to show how things are alike and how they are different. To compare is to show how things are alike. To contrast is to show how things are different. Sometimes when reading you will notice that people, ideas, and events are compared and contrasted. As you read, ask questions to see if you are reading a comparison or a contrast.

> **Remember:**
>
> To compare, ask: "How are these things alike?"
>
> To contrast, ask: "How are these things different?"

• To decide if things are being compared, look for words such as

> also   both   like   similar
>
> **Example:**
>
> The United States and China <u>both</u> are able to make shoes and airplanes.

• To decide if the things are being contrasted, look for words such as

> but   however   instead
>
> not   only   while
>
> **Example:**
>
> The United States makes airplanes, <u>but</u> China makes shoes.

Decide whether each sentence compares or contrasts.

1. Both the World Bank and the IMF have had some success.

2. Some countries have a lot of oil, but other countries have none at all.

3. Transportation and communication also are often limited in LDCs.

4. While many urban planners work for local governments, others work for private companies.

5. Farmers and businesses must make similar decisions.

Compare and contrast developed and less developed countries by writing a sentence for each word below. (Look back at Chapter 20 for ideas.) Write a comparing sentence or a contrasting sentence for each word. Be sure to use words that compare and contrast.

6. economy

7. poverty

8. life expectancy

9. cash crops

10. foreign aid

Unit 6 SUMMARY

■ Countries trade with each other because not all countries have the same resources. Exports are goods and services sold to other countries. Imports are goods and services bought from foreign countries. A favorable balance of trade is a trade surplus. A negative balance is a trade deficit.

■ Absolute advantage allows a country to produce a good less expensively and more easily than a trading partner with the same resources. Comparative advantage allows a country to produce a good at a lower opportunity cost.

■ Revenue tariffs raise money for a government. Protective tariffs protect certain industries in a country. Import quotas and voluntary trade restrictions reduce the number of imports. Embargoes cut off all trade with another country. Government subsidies sometimes hurt foreign competitors.

■ Free trade is trade free of all barriers. It may increase a country's standard of living or provide more goods and services. Trade may be restricted to protect national defense, protect new industries, encourage economic diversity, or to offset cheap labor costs of other countries.

■ Globalization has caused countries to depend more on each other. Reciprocal trade agreements and most favored nation status help reduce tariffs on goods. GATT was created to encourage international trade. The WTO later replaced GATT.

■ Members of free-trade associations trade without barriers among themselves. They place their own tariffs on other countries. Customs unions remove trade barriers among members and have the same tariff on imports from non-members.

■ Free trade associations such as NAFTA and the European Union promote trade among members. Other regional trade organizations exist in the Caribbean, Asia, and Central and South America.

■ A country whose economy is developing is a less developed country (LDC). LDCs have limited economic development and a low GDP. Medical care has improved in some LDCs, which has caused birthrates to rise. Many people in LDCs work in subsistence farming. There often is political unrest in LDCs.

■ LDCs often have to borrow money for economic development. Paying debts may leave little money for medical care, education, or imports. LDCs often receive foreign and humanitarian aid from developed countries.

■ The United Nations promotes higher standards of living. The UN Development Program controls UN projects around the world.

■ The World Bank loans money to LDCs for development. The International Monetary Fund (IMF) gives money and economic advice to countries in need. Some people do not agree with policies of the World Bank and IMF.

United States Economics Timeline

1776
- Adam Smith writes *Wealth of Nations*
- The Declaration of Independence is written

1787
- The United States Constitution is ratified

1790
- The first U.S. census takes place; the population of the new country is 3,929,214
- The Industrial Revolution begins in the United States with the first cotton mill by Samuel Slater
- The first United States Patent is issued to Samuel Hopkins for making potash and pearl ash

1791
- Amendment 4—Search and Arrest Warrants—is ratified
- Amendment 5—Rights in Criminal Trial—is ratified
- Congress establishes the first Bank of the United States as a private business

1792
- The U.S. Mint opens
- Twenty-four brokers sign an agreement on May 17 to trade under a Buttonwood tree at 68 Wall Street; Bank of New York stock is the first corporate stock traded

1848
- Gold is discovered in California

1859
- Edwin Drake drills the first petroleum oil well at Titusville, PA

1863
- The national banking system is established

1869
- The transcontinental railroad is completed at Promontory Point, UT
- Knights of Labor is founded in Philadelphia

1877
- The railroad workers' strike is the first nationwide strike in the United States

1886
- The AFL is founded by Samuel Gompers

1887
- The Interstate Commerce Commission Act establishes the ICC

1890
- The Sherman Antitrust Act is passed to prohibit trusts

1894
- Labor Day is made a federal holiday

1911
- The Standard Oil Company (Ohio) is declared a monopoly
- Upton Sinclair publishes *The Jungle,* a book about the meatpacking industry

1913
- The Federal Reserve System is created
- The U.S. Department of Labor is established
- Ford uses the assembly line
- Amendment 16—Federal Income Tax—is ratified

1914
- President Wilson creates the Federal Trade Commission
- The Clayton Antitrust Act is passed to prohibit price setting and price discrimination

1920
- Women gain the right to vote

1929
- The stock market crashes on Oct. 29, starting the Great Depression

1933
- FDR becomes president and establishes the New Deal for recovery

1934	• The Gold Reserve Act eliminates the gold standard in the United States
1935	• The Banking Act of 1935 makes the FDIC permanent • The National Labor Relations Act (Wagner Act) is passed; it permits collective bargaining
1936	• The Robinson-Patman Act outlaws the favoring of certain customers over others
1938	• The Fair Labor Standards Act establishes a 40-hour workweek, minimum wage, and bans child labor • The CIO is founded with John L. Lewis as president
1947	• The Taft-Hartley Act is passed and gives government the power to regulate relations between labor and management
1955	• The AFL-CIO merges • Ray Kroc opens his first fast-food restaurant in the United States
1964	• Title VII of Civil Rights Act outlaws discrimination and establishes the Equal Employment Opportunities Commission
1969	• The first ATM appears
1971	• President Nixon sets price and wage controls; the value of a dollar decreases • The New York Stock Exchange (NYSE) is incorporated
1979	• Inflation reaches 13.3%
1981	• President Reagan supports supply-side economics; Reaganomics
1987	• The world stock market crashes; Congress sets computer blocks to avoid future crashes
1990	• Sam Walton's discount-store company becomes the nation's number one retailer • The Americans with Disabilities Act prohibits workplace discrimination of persons with a disability
1994	• NAFTA creates one large free-trade area between Mexico, Canada, and the United States
1995	• The World Trade Organization is founded
1999	• E-commerce becomes a major trend in the United States • The world population reaches six billion
2000	• The Dow closes at a record high; the value is 11,722.8
2001	• The September 11 attacks rock the U.S. and world markets
2002	• The Euro becomes the common, single currency of 12 European countries • The highest volume day of trade on NYSE occurs on July 24; 2.81 billion shares are traded
2003	• Congress approves a $330 billion tax cut

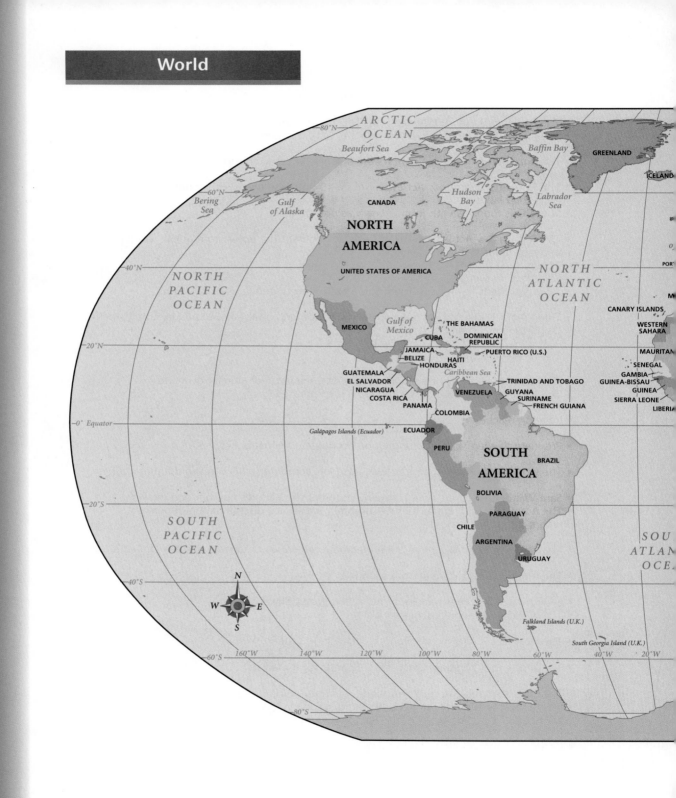

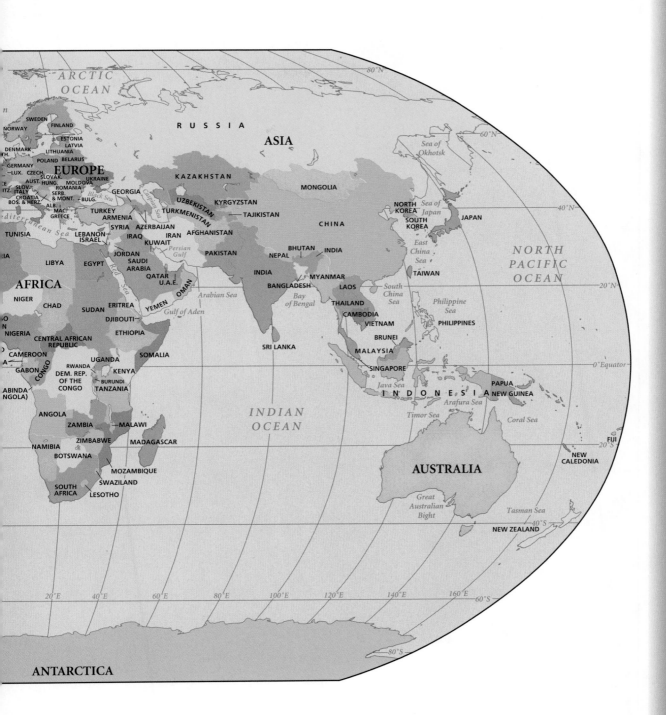

ARCTIC
OCEAN

SWEDEN
FINLAND
NORWAY
DENMARK
TH.
LITHUANIA
GERMANY
POLAND BELARUS
LUX. CZECH
EUROPE
AUST. HUNG. UKRAINE
ITZ. ITALY SLOV.
CROATIA ROMANIA
BOS. & HERZ. SERB.
ALB. & MONT. BULG.
MAC.
GREECE
TURKEY ARMENIA
TUNISIA
LEBANON SYRIA AZERBAIJAN
ISRAEL IRAQ IRAN
KUWAIT
JORDAN
LIBYA EGYPT SAUDI
ARABIA
QATAR
U.A.E.
AFRICA
NIGER CHAD SUDAN ERITREA
YEMEN
DJIBOUTI
NIGERIA ETHIOPIA
CENTRAL AFRICAN
REPUBLIC
CAMEROON UGANDA
GABON RWANDA
DEM. REP. KENYA
OF THE BURUNDI
CONGO TANZANIA
ABINDA
NGOLA)
ANGOLA
ZAMBIA MALAWI
NAMIBIA ZIMBABWE
BOTSWANA MADAGASCAR
MOZAMBIQUE
SOUTH SWAZILAND
AFRICA LESOTHO

RUSSIA

ASIA

KAZAKHSTAN

MONGOLIA

GEORGIA
UZBEKISTAN KYRGYZSTAN
TURKMENISTAN TAJIKISTAN
CHINA

NORTH
KOREA Sea of
Japan
SOUTH
KOREA JAPAN

AFGHANISTAN
PAKISTAN
BHUTAN
NEPAL INDIA
East
China
Sea
MYANMAR TAIWAN

INDIA
BANGLADESH
LAOS South
China
THAILAND Sea
CAMBODIA
VIETNAM
BRUNEI
MALAYSIA
SINGAPORE

SRI LANKA

INDONESIA PAPUA
NEW GUINEA

AUSTRALIA

Mediterranean Sea

Black Sea

Caspian Sea

Red Sea

Persian
Gulf

OMAN

Arabian Sea

Gulf of Aden

SOMALIA

Bay
of Bengal

Philippine
Sea

PHILIPPINES

Java Sea
Arafura Sea

Timor Sea
Coral Sea

Sea of
Okhotsk

NORTH
PACIFIC
OCEAN

80°N

60°N

40°N

20°N

0° Equator

INDIAN
OCEAN

Great
Australian
Bight

Tasman Sea

NEW ZEALAND

FIJI

NEW
CALEDONIA

20°S

40°S

60°S

80°S

ANTARCTICA

20°E 40°E 60°E 80°E 100°E 120°E 140°E 160°E

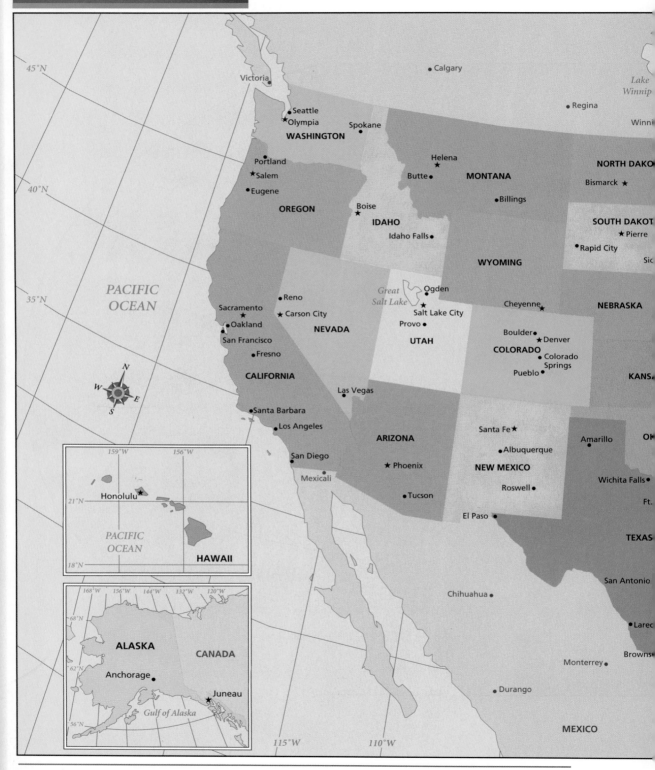

Victoria

• Calgary

Lake Winnip

• Regina

Winni

★ Seattle
★ Olympia
Spokane

WASHINGTON

Helena
★

NORTH DAKO

Portland
★ Salem

Butte •

MONTANA

Bismarck ★

• Eugene

OREGON

Boise
★

• Billings

SOUTH DAKOT

IDAHO

★ Pierre

Idaho Falls •

• Rapid City

WYOMING

Sic

PACIFIC OCEAN

Great
Salt Lake

Ogden •

Cheyenne
★

NEBRASKA

• Reno

Salt Lake City ★

Sacramento
★

★ Carson City

Provo •

Boulder •
★ Denver

• Oakland
San Francisco

NEVADA

UTAH

COLORADO

• Colorado
Springs

Pueblo •

KANS

• Fresno

CALIFORNIA

Las Vegas
•

Santa Fe ★

Amarillo
•

O

• Santa Barbara

ARIZONA

• Albuquerque

• Los Angeles

★ Phoenix

NEW MEXICO

Wichita Falls •

San Diego
•

Roswell •

Ft.

Mexicali •

TEXAS

• Tucson

159°W   156°W

El Paso •

San Antonio

Honolulu ★

PACIFIC OCEAN

HAWAII

Chihuahua •

• Lared

Brownsv

168°W 156°W 144°W 132°W 120°W

Monterrey •

ALASKA

CANADA

Anchorage •

• Durango

★ Juneau

Gulf of Alaska

MEXICO

115°W   110°W

CANADA

Ft. Albany

Sept-Iles

Gulf of St. Lawrence

NOVA SCOTIA

Quebec

Fredericton

Halifax

Thunder Bay

Lake Superior

Sault Ste. Marie

Montreal

MAINE

Augusta ★

Duluth

MINNESOTA

St. Paul

Minneapolis ★

WISCONSIN

Lake Michigan

Lake Huron

MICHIGAN

Lansing ★

Ottawa ✪

Montpelier ★

VT

NH

Concord ★

Augusta ★

Madison ★

Milwaukee

Detroit

Toronto

L. Ontario

Albany ★

Boston ★

NEW YORK

Hartford ★

Providence ★

Buffalo

CT

RI

MA

Waterloo

IOWA

Davenport

Des Moines ★

Chicago

Gary

ILLINOIS

Ft. Wayne

Peoria

OHIO

Cleveland

PENNSYLVANIA

Newark

New York City

Lake Erie

Columbus ★

Pittsburgh

Harrisburg ★

Philadelphia

Trenton ★

NJ

Atlantic City

Indianapolis ★

INDIANA

Cincinnati

MD

Dover ★

ATLANTIC OCEAN

Springfield ★

Washington, D.C. ✪ ★

WEST VIRGINIA

Annapolis ★

DE

Kansas City

St. Louis

Frankfort ★

Charleston ★

Richmond ★

Jefferson City ★

MISSOURI

Louisville

VIRGINIA

Norfolk

KENTUCKY

Springfield

Durham

Raleigh ★

Knoxville

NORTH CAROLINA

Nashville ★

Charlotte

TENNESSEE

Greenville

Fort Smith

ARKANSAS

Memphis

Wilmington

Little Rock ★

Birmingham

Columbia ★

SOUTH CAROLINA

Greenville

Atlanta ★

Augusta

Charleston

MISSISSIPPI

ALABAMA

Montgomery ★

GEORGIA

Savannah

Shreveport

Jackson ★

Albany

LOUISIANA

Mobile

Tallahassee ★

Jacksonville

Baton Rouge ★

New Orleans

FLORIDA

Tampa

Miami

Gulf of Mexico

THE BAHAMAS

Havana ★

CUBA

60°W

65°W

70°W

75°W

80°W

85°W

90°W

95°W

United States of America

✪ National Capital

★ State Capital

• City

0   400 km

0   400 Miles

World Employment and GDP

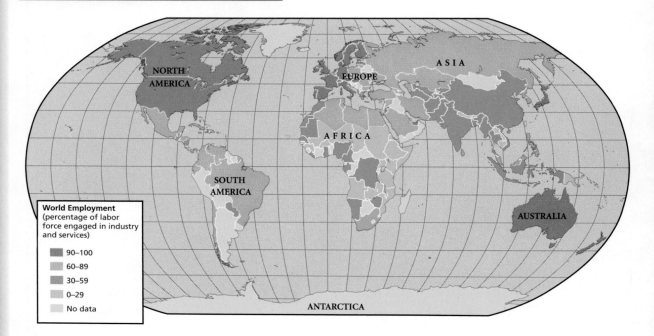

World Employment
(percentage of labor force engaged in industry and services)

- 90–100
- 60–89
- 30–59
- 0–29
- No data

NORTH AMERICA
SOUTH AMERICA
EUROPE
AFRICA
ASIA
AUSTRALIA
ANTARCTICA

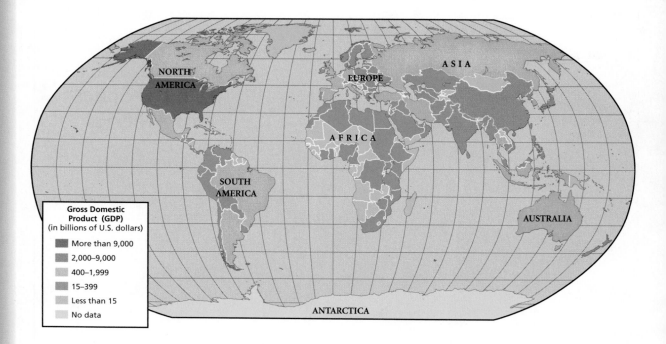

Gross Domestic Product (GDP)
(in billions of U.S. dollars)

- More than 9,000
- 2,000–9,000
- 400–1,999
- 15–399
- Less than 15
- No data

NORTH AMERICA
SOUTH AMERICA
EUROPE
AFRICA
ASIA
AUSTRALIA
ANTARCTICA

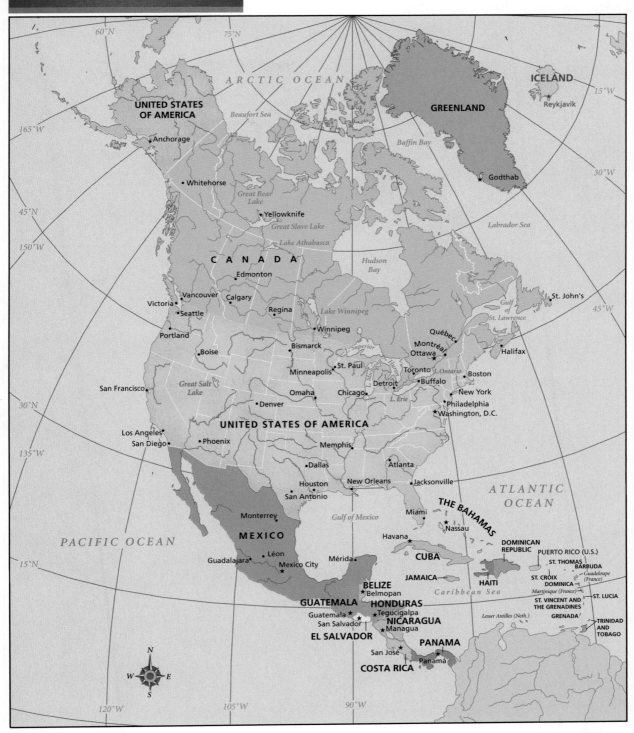

ARCTIC OCEAN

ICELAND

Reykjavík

15°W

GREENLAND

Baffin Bay

30°W

UNITED STATES
OF AMERICA

Beaufort Sea

Godthab

165°W

Anchorage

Labrador Sea

45°W

Whitehorse

Great Bear
Lake

45°N

150°W

Yellowknife

Great Slave Lake

Hudson
Bay

Gulf
of
St. Lawrence

St. John's

Lake Athabasca

C A N A D A

Edmonton

Lake Winnipeg

Québec

Vancouver
Victoria
Seattle

Calgary
Regina

Winnipeg

Montréal
Ottawa

Halifax

Portland

Bismarck

Superior

Toronto
L. Ontario
Buffalo

Boston

30°N

135°W

San Francisco

Great Salt
Lake

Minneapolis
St. Paul

Minneapolis
Omaha
Denver

Chicago

Detroit

L. Erie

New York
Philadelphia
Washington, D.C.

UNITED STATES OF AMERICA

Los Angeles
San Diego

Phoenix

Memphis

Dallas

Atlanta

ATLANTIC
OCEAN

Houston
San Antonio

New Orleans

Jacksonville

Miami

THE BAHAMAS

15°N

PACIFIC OCEAN

Monterrey

Gulf of Mexico

Nassau

DOMINICAN
REPUBLIC

PUERTO RICO (U.S.)

MEXICO

Havana

CUBA

ST. THOMAS
BARBUDA

Guadeloupe
(France)

Guadalajara

Léon
Mexico City

Mérida

JAMAICA

HAITI

ST. CROIX
DOMINICA

Martinique (France)

ST. LUCIA

BELIZE
Belmopan

Caribbean Sea

ST. VINCENT AND
THE GRENADINES

GUATEMALA

HONDURAS

Lesser Antilles (Neth.)

GRENADA

Guatemala
San Salvador

Tegucigalpa
NICARAGUA
Managua

TRINIDAD
AND
TOBAGO

EL SALVADOR

PANAMA

San José

Panamá

COSTA RICA

N
W   E
S

120°W

105°W

90°W

60°N   75°W

South America

Caribbean Sea

Managua ★

San José ★

Panama ★

Barranquilla ★

Cúcuta ●

Medellín ●

Bogotá ★

COLOMBIA

Mitú ●

Quito ★

ECUADOR

Guayaquil ●

Galápagos
Islands
(Ecuador)

Talara ●

PERU

Trujillo ●

Huánuco ●

Lima ●

Ica ●

Cuzco ●

Iquique ●

Antofagasta ●

CHILE

Valencia ●

Caracas ★

VENEZUELA

TRINIDAD AND TOBAGO

Georgetown ★

GUYANA

Paramaribo ★

SURINAME

Cayenne ●

FRENCH
GUIANA

Manaus ●

Belém ●

Fortaleza ●

Recife ●

Pôrto Velho ●

BRAZIL

Salvador ●

BOLIVIA

La Paz ★

Santa Cruz ●

Sucre ★

Brásília ★

Goiânia ●

PARAGUAY

Asunción ★

Rio de Janeiro ●

São Paulo ●

PACIFIC OCEAN

Córdoba ●

Rosario ●

Santiago ★

Buenos Aires ★

URUGUAY

Montevideo ★

Concepción ●

ARGENTINA

ATLANTIC OCEAN

Valdivia ●

Puerto Montt ●

N
W E
S

Comodoro Rivadavia ●

Falkland Islands
(U.K.)

South Georgia Island
(U.K.)

10°N

0°

10°S

20°S

30°S

40°S

50°S

90°W   80°W   70°W   60°W   50°W   40°W

15°W   0°   15°E   45°E

Norwegian Sea

60°N

NORTH
ATLANTIC
OCEAN

Reykjavik ★ **ICELAND**

*Faroe
Islands*

FINLAND

SWEDEN

RUSSIA

*Gulf
of
Bothnia* Helsinki ★

NORWAY

Oslo ★

North Sea

Stockholm ★

★ Tallinn
ESTONIA

Moscow ★

Riga ★ **LATVIA**

Baltic Sea

DENMARK

Belfast ★
IRELAND Dublin ★

LITHUANIA

Vilnius ★

Minsk ★

**UNITED
KINGDOM**

London ★

★ Copenhagen

NETHERLANDS

Amsterdam ★

BELARUS

Berlin ★

Warsaw ★

POLAND

★ Kiev

UKRAINE

English Channel

Brussels ★
BELGIUM

GERMANY

Prague ★

**CZECH
REP.**

SLOVAKIA

Paris ★
LUXEMBOURG

Vienna ★ ★ Bratislava

MOLDOVA

Chisinau ★

45°N

LIECHTENSTEIN
Bern ★

AUSTRIA

Budapest ★

FRANCE

SWITZERLAND

Ljubljana ★ **HUNGARY**

ROMANIA

Bay of Biscay

SLOVENIA ★

★ Zagreb

Belgrade ★

Bucharest ★

Black Sea

ITALY

**BOSNIA AND
HERZEGOVINA**

**SERBIA
AND
MONTENEGRO**

BULGARIA

MONACO

CROATIA

Sarajevo ★

PORTUGAL

ANDORRA

Corsica

★ Rome

*Adriatic
Sea*

Tirana ★

Sofia ★

★ Skopje

Ankara ★

Lisbon ★

Madrid ★

SPAIN

*Balearic
Islands*

Sardinia

Algiers

ALBANIA

MACEDONIA

*Aegean
Sea*

★ Gibraltar (U.K.)

Tyrrhenian Sea

Sicily

GREECE

★ Athens

Rabat ★

Tunis ★

★ Valletta

MALTA

Ionian Sea

Crete

Tripoli ★

Mediterranean Sea

Alexandria ★

N
W ★ E
S

*Red
Sea*

Africa

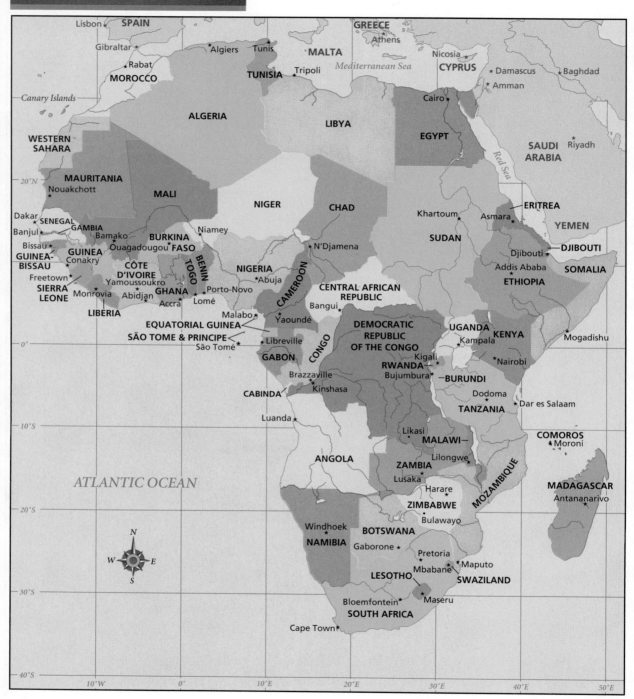

Lisbon ★ **SPAIN**

GREECE
Athens ★

Gibraltar ★ Algiers ★ Tunis ★

MALTA

Rabat ★ **TUNISIA** Tripoli ★ *Mediterranean Sea* Nicosia ★ **CYPRUS** ★ Damascus ★ Baghdad

MOROCCO ★ Amman

Canary Islands

Cairo ★

ALGERIA **LIBYA** **EGYPT** **SAUDI ARABIA** ★ Riyadh

WESTERN SAHARA *Red Sea*

20°N **MAURITANIA** **ERITREA** **YEMEN**
Nouakchott Khartoum ★ Asmara ★
Dakar ★ **MALI** **NIGER** **CHAD** Djibouti ★ **DJIBOUTI**
★ **SENEGAL** **SUDAN** Addis Ababa ★ **SOMALIA**
Banjul ★ **GAMBIA** Bamako Niamey N'Djamena ★ **ETHIOPIA**
Bissau ★ **BURKINA** **GUINEA-** Ouagadougou ★ **FASO**
BISSAU **GUINEA** **NIGERIA** **CENTRAL AFRICAN**
Conakry **CÔTE** **TOGO** *Abuja **REPUBLIC**
Freetown ★ **D'IVOIRE** **GHANA** Porto-Novo **CAMEROON** Bangui ★ **UGANDA** **KENYA**
SIERRA Yamoussoukro **BENIN** **DEMOCRATIC** Kampala ★ Mogadishu ★
LEONE Monrovia ★ Abidjan ★ Accra Lomé Yaoundé ★ **REPUBLIC** Kigali ★ Nairobi ★
LIBERIA Malabo ★ **OF THE CONGO** **RWANDA** —
EQUATORIAL GUINEA Libreville ★ **CONGO** Bujumbura ★ — **BURUNDI**
0° **SÃO TOMÉ & PRINCIPE** São Tomé ★ **GABON** Dodoma ★ Dar es Salaam
Brazzaville ★ **TANZANIA**
CABINDA ★ Kinshasa
Luanda ★ Likasi ★ **COMOROS** ★ Moroni
10°S **MALAWI** —
ANGOLA **ZAMBIA** Lilongwe ★
MADAGASCAR
Lusaka ★ Harare ★ **MOZAMBIQUE** Antananarivo ★
ATLANTIC OCEAN **ZIMBABWE**
20°S Bulawayo ★
Windhoek ★ **BOTSWANA**
NAMIBIA Gaborone ★ Pretoria ★
Mbabane ★ Maputo
LESOTHO ★ ★ **SWAZILAND**
30°S **SOUTH AFRICA** Maseru
Bloemfontein ★
Cape Town ★

N
W ⊕ E
S

10°W 0° 10°E 20°E 30°E 40°E 50°E

40°S

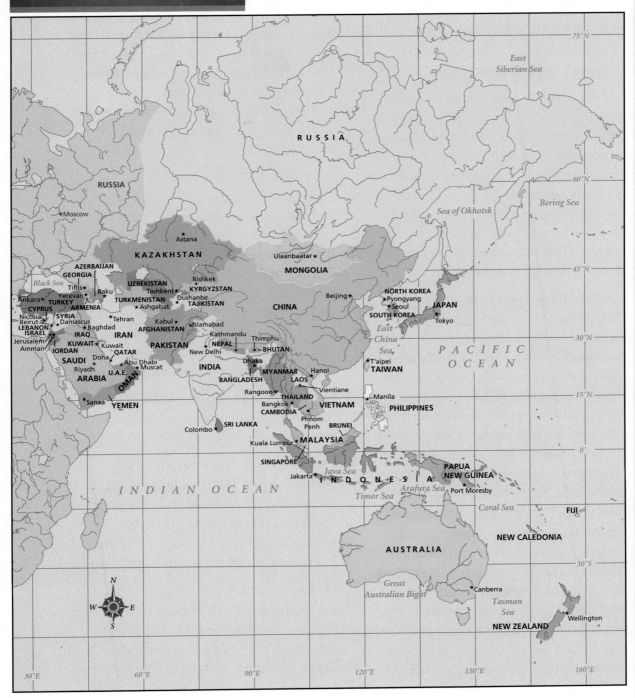

Asia and Australia

East Siberian Sea

75°N

RUSSIA

60°N

Bering Sea

RUSSIA

★Moscow

Sea of Okhotsk

★Astana

KAZAKHSTAN

Ulaanbaatar★

45°N

MONGOLIA

AZERBAIJAN

GEORGIA

Bishkek

Black Sea

Tiflis★

UZBEKISTAN

KYRGYZSTAN

NORTH KOREA

JAPAN

Ankara★

Yerevan★

Baku★

Tashkent★

Beijing★

Pyongyang

TURKEY

ARMENIA

TURKMENISTAN

Dushanbe★

★Seoul

CYPRUS

Ashgabat★

TAJIKISTAN

CHINA

SOUTH KOREA

Nicosia

SYRIA

Tehran★

Tokyo★

Beirut

Damascus★

Kabul★

Islamabad★

East China Sea

LEBANON

Baghdad★

AFGHANISTAN

Kathmandu

PACIFIC OCEAN

ISRAEL

IRAQ

IRAN

Thimphu

30°N

Jerusalem★

KUWAIT

Kuwait

New Delhi★

BHUTAN

Amman★

Kuwait★

PAKISTAN

NEPAL

★T'aipei

JORDAN

Doha★

Dhaka★

SAUDI

QATAR

Abu Dhabi★

INDIA

MYANMAR

TAIWAN

Riyadh★

U.A.E.

★Muscat

BANGLADESH

Hanoi★

ARABIA

OMAN

LAOS

15°N

Rangoon★

Vientiane★

Manila★

★Sanaa

THAILAND

VIETNAM

YEMEN

Bangkok★

PHILIPPINES

CAMBODIA

Phnom

Colombo★

SRI LANKA

Penh★

BRUNEI

0°

Kuala Lumpur★

MALAYSIA

SINGAPORE★

Java Sea

INDIAN OCEAN

Jakarta★

INDONESIA

PAPUA

NEW GUINEA

Arafura Sea

Port Moresby★

Timor Sea

Coral Sea

FIJI

NEW CALEDONIA

AUSTRALIA

30°S

Great
Australian Bight

★Canberra

Tasman Sea

★Wellington

NEW ZEALAND

30°E

60°E

90°E

120°E

150°E

180°E

N
W E
S

The Declaration of Independence

Adopted in Congress July 4, 1776
The Unanimous Declaration of the
Thirteen United States of America

When, in the course of human events, it becomes necessary for one people to dissolve the political bands which have connected them with another, and to assume among the powers of the earth, the separate and equal station to which the laws of nature and of nature's God entitle them, a decent respect to the opinions of mankind requires that they should declare the causes which impel them to the separation.

We hold these truths to be self-evident, that all men are created equal, that they are endowed by their Creator with certain unalienable rights, that among these are life, liberty, and the pursuit of happiness. That to secure these rights, governments are instituted among men, deriving their just powers from the consent of the governed. That whenever any form of government becomes destructive of these ends, it is the right of the people to alter or to abolish it, and to institute new government, laying its foundation on such principles and organizing its powers in such form, as to them shall seem most likely to effect their safety and happiness. Prudence, indeed, will dictate that governments long established should not be changed for light and transient causes; and accordingly all experience hath shown that mankind are more disposed to suffer, while evils are sufferable, than to right themselves by abolishing the forms to which they are accustomed. But when a long train of abuses and usurpations, pursuing invariably the same object evinces a design to reduce them under absolute despotism, it is their right, it is their duty, to throw off such government, and to provide new guards for their future security.

Such has been the patient sufferance of these colonies; and such is now the necessity which constrains them to alter their former systems of government. The history of the present King of Great Britain is a history of repeated injuries and usurpations, all having in direct object the establishment of an absolute tyranny over these states. To prove this, let facts be submitted to a candid world.

He has refused his assent to laws, the most wholesome and necessary for the public good.

He has forbidden his governors to pass laws of immediate and pressing importance, unless suspended in their operation till his assent should be obtained; and when so suspended, he has utterly neglected to attend to them.

He has refused to pass other laws for the accommodation of large districts of people, unless those people would relinquish the right of representation in the legislature, a right inestimable to them and formidable to tyrants only.

He has called together legislative bodies at places unusual, uncomfortable, and distant from the depository of their public records, for the sole purpose of fatiguing them into compliance with his measures.

He has dissolved representative houses repeatedly, for opposing with manly firmness his invasions on the rights of the people.

He has refused for a long time, after such dissolutions, to cause others to be elected; whereby the legislative powers, incapable of annihilation, have returned to the people at large for their exercise; the state remaining in the mean time exposed to all the dangers of invasion from without, and convulsions within.

He has endeavored to prevent the population of these states; for that purpose obstructing the laws for naturalization of foreigners; refusing to pass others to encourage their migrations hither, and raising the conditions of new appropriations of lands.

He has obstructed the administration of justice, by refusing his assent to laws for establishing judiciary powers.

He has made judges dependent on his will alone, for the tenure of their offices, and the amount and payment of their salaries.

He has erected a multitude of new offices, and sent hither swarms of officers to harass our people, and eat out their substance.

He has kept among us, in times of peace, standing armies without the consent of our legislatures.

He has affected to render the military independent of and superior to the civil power.

He has combined with others to subject us to a jurisdiction foreign to our constitution, and unacknowledged by our laws; giving his assent to their acts of pretended legislation:

For quartering large bodies of armed troops among us:

For protecting them, by a mock trial, from punishment for any murders which they should commit on the inhabitants of these states:

For cutting off our trade with all parts of the world:

For imposing taxes on us without our consent:

For depriving us in many cases, of the benefits of trial by jury:

For transporting us beyond seas to be tried for pretended offenses:

For abolishing the free system of English laws in a neighboring province, establishing therein an arbitrary government, and enlarging its boundaries so as to render it at once an example and fit instrument for introducing the same absolute rule into these colonies:

For taking away our charters, abolishing our most valuable laws, and altering fundamentally the forms of our governments:

For suspending our own legislatures, and declaring themselves invested with power to legislate for us in all cases whatsoever.

He has abdicated government here, by declaring us out of his protection and waging war against us.

He has plundered our seas, ravaged our coasts, burned our towns, and destroyed the lives of our people.

He is at this time transporting large armies of foreign mercenaries to complete the works of death, desolation and tyranny, already begun with circumstances of cruelty and perfidy scarcely paralleled in the most barbarous ages, and totally unworthy the head of a civilized nation.

He has constrained our fellow citizens taken captive on the high seas to bear arms against their country, to become the executioners of their friends and brethren, or to fall themselves by their hands.

He has excited domestic insurrections amongst us, and has endeavored to bring on the inhabitants of our frontiers, the merciless Indian savages, whose known rule of warfare, is an undistinguished destruction of all ages, sexes, and conditions.

In every stage of these oppressions we have petitioned for redress in the most humble terms: our repeated petitions have been answered only by repeated injury. A prince, whose character is thus marked by every act which may define a tyrant, is unfit to be the ruler of a free people.

Nor have we been wanting in attentions to our British brethren. We have warned them from time to time of attempts by their legislature to extend an unwarrantable jurisdiction over us. We have reminded them of the circumstances of our emigration and settlement here. We have appealed to their native justice and magnanimity, and we have conjured them by the ties of our common kindred to disavow these usurpations, which would inevitably interrupt our connections and correspondence. They too have been deaf to the voice of justice and of consanguinity. We must, therefore, acquiesce in the necessity, which denounces our separation, and hold them, as we hold the rest of mankind, enemies in war, in peace friends.

We, therefore, the representatives of the United States of America, in General Congress, assembled, appealing to the Supreme Judge of the world for the rectitude of our intentions, do, in the name, and by authority of the good people of these colonies, solemnly publish and declare, that these united colonies are, and of right ought to be free and independent states; that they are absolved from all allegiance to the British Crown, and that all political connection between them and the state of Great Britain, is and ought to be totally dissolved; and that as free and independent states, they have full power to levy war, conclude peace, contract alliances, establish commerce, and to do all other acts and things which independent states may of right do. And for the support of this declaration, with a firm reliance on the protection of Divine Providence, we mutually pledge to each other our lives, our fortunes, and our sacred honor.

Signed by John Hancock of Massachusetts as President of the Congress and by the fifty-five other Representatives of the thirteen United States of America:

New Hampshire

Josiah Bartlett
William Whipple
Matthew Thornton

Connecticut

Roger Sherman
Samuel Huntington
William Williams
Oliver Wolcott

Massachusetts Bay

Samuel Adams
John Adams
Robert Treat Paine
Elbridge Gerry

Rhode Island

Stephen Hopkins
William Ellery

Pennsylvania

Robert Morris
Benjamin Rush
Benjamin Franklin
John Morton
George Clymer
James Smith
George Taylor
James Wilson
George Ross

Delaware

Caesar Rodney
George Read
Thomas M'Kean

New York

William Floyd
Philip Livingston
Francis Lewis
Lewis Morris

Virginia

George Wythe
Richard Henry Lee
Thomas Jefferson
Benjamin Harrison
Thomas Nelson, Jr.
Francis Lightfoot Lee
Carter Braxton

North Carolina

William Hooper
Joseph Hewes
John Penn

South Carolina

Edward Rutledge
Thomas Heyward, Jr.
Thomas Lynch, Jr.
Arthur Middleton

Georgia

Button Gwinnett
Lyman Hall
George Walton

Maryland

Samuel Chase
William Paca
Thomas Stone
Charles Carroll of
    Carrollton

New Jersey

Richard Stockton
John Witherspoon
Francis Hopkinson
John Hart
Abraham Clark

The Constitution of the United States

Preamble

We the people of the United States, in order to form a more perfect Union, establish justice, insure domestic tranquility, provide for the common defense, promote the general welfare, and secure the blessings of liberty to ourselves and our posterity, do ordain and establish this Constitution for the United States of America.

Article I
The Legislative Branch*

Congress

Section 1

All legislative powers herein granted shall be vested in a Congress of the United States, which shall consist of a Senate and House of Representatives.

The House of Representatives

Section 2

1 The House of Representatives shall be composed of members chosen every second year by the people of the several states, and the electors in each state shall have the qualifications requisite for electors of the most numerous branch of the state legislature.

2 No person shall be a representative who shall not have attained to the age of twenty-five years, and been seven years a citizen of the United States, and who shall not, when elected, be an inhabitant of that state in which he shall be chosen.

3 Representatives and direct taxes shall be apportioned among the several states which may be included within this Union, according to their respective numbers, [which shall be determined by adding to the whole number of free persons, including those bound to service for a term of years, and excluding Indians not taxed, three-fifths of all other persons]. The actual enumeration shall be made within three years after the first meeting of the Congress of the United States, and within every subsequent term of ten years, in such manner as they shall by law direct. The number of representatives shall not exceed one for every thirty thousand, but each state shall have at least one representative; [and until such enumeration shall be made, the state of New Hampshire shall be entitled to choose 3, Massachusetts 8, Rhode Island and Providence Plantations 1, Connecticut 5, New York 6, New Jersey 4, Pennsylvania 8, Delaware 1, Maryland 6, Virginia 10, North Carolina 5, South Carolina 5, and Georgia 3].

Headings and paragraph numbers have been added to help the reader. The original Constitution has only the article and section numbers.

4 When vacancies happen in the representation from any state, the executive authority thereof shall issue writs of election to fill such vacancies.

5 The House of Representatives shall choose their speaker and other officers; and shall have the sole power of impeachment.

The Senate

Section 3

1 The Senate of the United States shall be composed of two senators from each state, [chosen by the legislature thereof,] for six years; and each senator shall have one vote.

2 Immediately after they shall be assembled in consequence of the first election, they shall be divided as equally as may be into three classes. The seats of the senators of the first class shall be vacated at the expiration of the second year, of the second class at the expiration of the fourth year, and of the third class at the expiration of the sixth year, so that one-third may be chosen every second year; [and if vacancies happen by resignation, or otherwise, during the recess of the legislature of any state, the executive thereof may make temporary appointments until the next meeting of the legislature, which shall then fill such vacancies].

3 No person shall be a senator who shall not have attained to the age of thirty years, and been nine years a citizen of the United States, and who shall not, when elected, be an inhabitant of that state for which he shall be chosen.

4 The Vice President of the United States shall be president of the Senate, but shall have no vote, unless they be equally divided.

5 The Senate shall choose their other officers, and also a president pro tempore, in the absence of the Vice President, or when he shall exercise the office of President of the United States.

6 The Senate shall have the sole power to try all impeachments. When sitting for that purpose, they shall be on oath or affirmation. When the President of the United States is tried, the Chief Justice shall preside: and no person shall be convicted without the concurrence of two-thirds of the members present.

7 Judgment in cases of impeachment shall not extend further than to removal from office, and disqualification to hold and enjoy any office of honor, trust, or profit under the United States: but the party convicted shall nevertheless be liable and subject to indictment, trial, judgment, and punishment, according to law.

Organization of Congress

Section 4

1 The times, places, and manner of holding elections for senators and representatives, shall be prescribed in each state by the legislature thereof; but the Congress may at any time by law make or alter such regulations, [except as to the places of choosing senators].

2 The Congress shall assemble at least once in every year, [and such meeting shall be on the first Monday in December,] unless they shall by law appoint a different day.

Rules and Procedures

Section 5

1 Each house shall be the judge of the elections, returns and qualifications of its own members, and a majority of each shall constitute a quorum to do business; but a smaller number may adjourn from day to day, and may be authorized to compel the attendance of absent members, in such manner, and under such penalties as each house may provide.

2 Each house may determine the rules of its proceedings, punish its members for disorderly behavior, and, with the concurrence of two-thirds, expel a member.

3 Each house shall keep a journal of its proceedings, and from time to time publish the same, excepting such parts as may in their judgment require secrecy; and the yeas and nays of the members of either house on any question shall, at the desire of one-fifth of those present, be entered on the journal.

4 Neither house, during the session of Congress, shall, without the consent of the other, adjourn for more than three days, nor to any other place than that in which the two houses shall be sitting.

Payment and Privileges

Section 6

1 The senators and representatives shall receive a compensation for their services, to be ascertained by law, and paid out of the treasury of the United States. They shall in all cases, except treason, felony, and breach of the peace, be privileged from arrest during their attendance at the session of their respective houses, and in going to and returning from the same; and for any speech or debate in either house, they shall not be questioned in any other place.

2 No senator or representative shall, during the time for which he was elected, be appointed to any civil office under the authority of the United States, which shall have been created, or the emoluments whereof shall have been increased during such time; and no person holding any office under the United States, shall be a member of either house during his continuance in office.

How a Bill Becomes a Law

Section 7

1 All bills for raising revenue shall originate in the House of Representatives; but the Senate may propose or concur with amendments as on other bills.

2 Every bill which shall have passed the House of Representatives and the Senate, shall, before it becomes a law, be presented to the President of the United States; if he approve he shall sign it, but if not he shall return it, with his objections to that house in which it shall have originated, who shall enter the objections at large on their journal, and proceed to reconsider it. If after such reconsideration two-thirds of that house shall agree to pass the bill, it shall be sent, together with the objections, to the other house, by which it shall likewise be reconsidered, and if approved by two-thirds of that house, it shall become a law. But in all such cases the votes of both houses shall be determined by yeas and nays, and the names of the persons voting for and against the bill shall be entered on the journal of each house, respectively. If any bill shall not be returned by the President within ten days (Sundays excepted) after it shall have been presented to him, the same shall be a law, in like manner as if he had signed it, unless the Congress by their adjournment prevent its return, in which case it shall not be a law.

3 Every order, resolution, or vote to which the concurrence of the Senate and House of Representatives may be necessary (except on a question of adjournment) shall be presented to the President of the United States; and before the same shall take effect, shall be approved by him, or being disapproved by him, shall be repassed by two-thirds of the Senate and House of Representatives, according to the rules and limitations prescribed in the case of a bill.

Powers Granted to Congress

Section 8

The Congress shall have power:

1 To lay and collect taxes, duties, imposts, and excises, to pay the debts and provide for the common defense and general welfare of the United States; but all duties, imposts, and excises shall be uniform throughout the United States;

2 To borrow money on the credit of the United States;

3 To regulate commerce with foreign nations, and among the several states, and with the Indian tribes;

4 To establish a uniform rule of naturalization, and uniform laws on the subject of bankruptcies throughout the United States;

5 To coin money, regulate the value thereof, and of foreign coin, and fix the standard of weights and measures;

6 To provide for the punishment of counterfeiting the securities and current coin of the United States;

7 To establish post offices and post roads;

8 To promote the progress of science and useful arts, by securing for limited times to authors and inventors the exclusive right to their respective writings and discoveries;

9 To constitute tribunals inferior to the Supreme Court;

10 To define and punish piracies and felonies committed on the high seas, and offenses against the law of nations;

11 To declare war, grant letters of marque and reprisal, and make rules concerning captures on land and water;

12 To raise and support armies, but no appropriation of money to that use shall be for a longer term than two years;

13 To provide and maintain a navy;

14 To make rules for the government and regulation of the land and naval forces;

15 To provide for calling forth the militia to execute the laws of the Union, suppress insurrections and repel invasions;

16 To provide for organizing, arming, and disciplining, the militia, and for governing such part of them as may be employed in the service of the United States, reserving to the states respectively, the appointment of the officers, and the authority of training the militia according to the discipline prescribed by Congress;

17 To exercise exclusive legislation in all cases whatsoever, over such district (not exceeding ten miles square) as may, by cession of particular states, and the acceptance of Congress, become the seat of the government of the United States, and to exercise like authority over all places purchased by the consent of the legislature of the state in which the same shall be, for the erection of forts, magazines, arsenals, dockyards, and other needful buildings; —And

18 To make all laws which shall be necessary and proper for carrying into execution the foregoing powers, and all other powers vested by this Constitution in the government of the United States, or in any department or officer thereof.

Powers Denied Congress

Section 9

1 The migration or importation of such persons as any of the states now existing shall think proper to admit, shall not be prohibited by the Congress prior to the year one thousand eight hundred and eight, but a tax or duty may be imposed on such importation, not exceeding ten dollars for each person.

2 The privilege of the writ of habeas corpus shall not be suspended, unless when in cases of rebellion or invasion the public safety may require it.

3 No bill of attainder or ex post facto law shall be passed.

4 No capitation, [or other direct,] tax shall be laid, unless in proportion to the census or enumeration herein before directed to be taken.

5 No tax or duty shall be laid on articles exported from any state.

6 No preference shall be given by any regulation of commerce or revenue to the ports of one state over those of another: nor shall vessels bound to, or from, one state, be obliged to enter, clear, or pay duties in another.

7 No money shall be drawn from the treasury, but in consequence of appropriations made by law; and a regular statement and account of the receipts and expenditures of all public money shall be published from time to time.

8 No title of nobility shall be granted by the United States: And no person holding any office of profit or trust under them, shall, without the consent of the Congress, accept of any present, emolument, office, or title, of any kind whatever, from any king, prince, or foreign state.

Powers Denied the States

Section 10

1 No state shall enter into any treaty, alliance, or confederation; grant letters of marque and reprisal; coin money; emit bills of credit; make anything but gold and silver coin a tender in payment of debts; pass any bill of attainder, ex post facto law, or law impairing the obligation of contracts, or grant any title of nobility.

2 No state shall, without the consent of the Congress, lay any imposts or duties on imports or exports, except what may be absolutely necessary for executing its inspection laws: and the net produce of all duties and imposts, laid by any state on imports or exports, shall be for the use of the treasury of the United States; and all such laws shall be subject to the revision and control of the Congress.

3 No state shall, without the consent of Congress, lay any duty of tonnage, keep troops, or ships of war in time of peace, enter into any agreement or compact with another state, or with a foreign power, or engage in war, unless actually invaded, or in such imminent danger as will not admit of delay.

ARTICLE II
The Executive Branch

The President

Section 1

1 The executive power shall be vested in a President of the United States of America. He shall hold his office during the term of four years, and, together with the Vice President, chosen for the same term, be elected, as follows:

2 Each state shall appoint, in such manner as the legislature thereof may direct, a number of electors, equal to the whole number of senators and representatives to which the state may be entitled in the Congress: but no senator or representative, or person holding an office of trust or profit under the United States, shall be appointed an elector.

[The electors shall meet in their respective states, and vote by ballot for two persons, of whom one at least shall not be an inhabitant of the same state with themselves. And they shall make a list of all the persons voted for, and of the number of votes for each; which list they shall sign and certify, and transmit sealed to the seat of the government of the United States, directed to the president of the Senate. The president of the Senate shall, in the presence of the Senate and House of Representatives, open all the certificates, and the votes shall then be counted. The person having the greatest number of votes shall be the President, if such number be a majority of the whole number of electors appointed; and if there be more than one who have such majority, and have an equal number of votes, then the House of Representatives shall immediately choose by ballot one of them for President; and if no person have a majority, then from the five highest on the list the said House shall in like manner choose the President. But in choosing the President, the votes shall be taken by states, the representation from each state having one vote; a quorum for this purpose shall consist of a member or members from two-thirds of the states, and a majority of all the states shall be necessary to a choice. In every case, after the choice of the President, the person having the greatest number of votes of the electors shall be the Vice President. But if there should remain two or more who have equal votes, the Senate shall choose from them by ballot the Vice President.]

3 The Congress may determine the time of choosing the electors, and the day on which they shall give their votes; which day shall be the same throughout the United States.

4 No person except a natural-born citizen, or a citizen of the United States at the time of the adoption of this Constitution, shall be eligible to the office of President; neither shall any person be eligible to that office who

shall not have attained to the age of thirty-five years, and been fourteen years a resident within the United States.

5 In case of the removal of the President from office, or of his death, resignation, or inability to discharge the powers and duties of the said office, the same shall devolve on the Vice President, and the Congress may by law provide for the case of removal, death, or resignation or inability, both of the President and Vice President, declaring what officer shall then act as President, and such officer shall act accordingly, until the disability be removed, or a President shall be elected.

6 The President shall, at stated times, receive for his services, a compensation, which shall neither be increased or diminished during the period for which he shall have been elected, and he shall not receive within that period any other emolument from the United States, or any of them.

7 Before he enter on the execution of his office, he shall take the following oath or affirmation: —"I do solemnly swear (or affirm) that I will faithfully execute the office of President of the United States, and will to the best of my ability, preserve, protect, and defend the Constitution of the United States."

Powers of the President
Section 2

1 The President shall be commander in chief of the Army and Navy of the United States, and of the militia of the several states, when called into the actual service of the United States; he may require the opinion, in writing, of the principal officer in each of the executive departments, upon any subject relating to the duties of their respective offices, and he shall have power to grant reprieves and pardons for offenses against the United States, except in cases of impeachment.

2 He shall have power, by and with the advice and consent of the Senate, to make treaties, provided two-thirds of the senators present concur; and he shall nominate, and by and with the advice and consent of the Senate, shall appoint ambassadors, other public ministers and consuls, judges of the Supreme Court, and all other officers of the United States, whose appointments are not herein otherwise provided for, and which shall be established by law: but the Congress may by law vest the appointment of such inferior officers, as they think proper, in the President alone, in the courts of law, or in the heads of departments.

3 The President shall have power to fill up all vacancies that may happen during the recess of the Senate, by granting commissions which shall expire at the end of their next session.

Duties of the President
Section 3

He shall from time to time give to the Congress information of the state of the Union, and recommend to their consideration such measures as he shall judge necessary and expedient; he may, on extraordinary occasions, convene both houses, or either of them, and in case of disagreement between them, with respect to the time of adjournment, he may adjourn them to such time as he shall think proper; he shall receive ambassadors and other public ministers; he shall take care that the laws be faithfully executed, and shall commission all the officers of the United States.

Impeachment
Section 4

The President, Vice President, and all civil officers of the United States, shall be removed from office on impeachment for, and conviction of, treason, bribery, or other high crimes and misdemeanors.

ARTICLE III
The Judicial Branch

Federal Courts and Judges
Section 1

The judicial power of the United States, shall be vested in one Supreme Court, and in such inferior courts as the Congress may from time to time ordain and establish. The judges, both of the Supreme and inferior courts, shall hold their offices during good behavior, and shall, at stated times, receive for their services, a compensation, which shall not be diminished during their continuance in office.

Jurisdiction of United States Courts
Section 2

1 The judicial power shall extend to all cases, in law and equity, arising under this Constitution, the laws of the United States, and treaties made, or which shall be made, under their authority; — to all cases affecting ambassadors, other public ministers and consuls; — to all cases of admiralty and maritime jurisdiction; —to controversies to which the United States shall be a party; — to controversies between two or more states; — [between a state and citizens of another state;] — between citizens of different states; — between citizens of the same state claiming lands under grants of different states, and between a state, or the citizens thereof, and foreign states, [citizens or subjects].

2 In all cases affecting ambassadors, other public ministers and consuls, and those in which a state shall be party, the Supreme Court shall have original jurisdiction. In all the other cases before mentioned, the Supreme Court shall have appellate jurisdiction, both as to law and fact, with such exceptions, and under such regulations as the Congress shall make.

3 The trial of all crimes, except in cases of impeachment, shall be by jury; and such trial shall be held in the state where the said crimes shall have been committed; but when not committed within any state, the trial shall be at such place or places as the Congress may by law have directed.

Treason

Section 3

1 Treason against the United States, shall consist only in levying war against them, or in adhering to their enemies, giving them aid and comfort. No person shall be convicted of treason unless on the testimony of two witnesses to the same overt act, or on confession in open court.

2 The Congress shall have power to declare the punishment of treason, but no attainder of treason shall work corruption of blood, or forfeiture except during the life of the person attainted.

ARTICLE IV
The States and the Federal Government

State Acts and Records

Section 1

Full faith and credit shall be given in each state to the public acts, records, and judicial proceedings of every other state. And the Congress may by general laws prescribe the manner in which such acts, records, and proceedings shall be proved, and the effect thereof.

Rights of Citizens

Section 2

1 The citizens of each state shall be entitled to all privileges and immunities of citizens in the several states.

2 A person charged in any state with treason, felony, or other crime, who shall flee from justice, and be found in another state, shall on demand of the executive authority of the state from which he fled, be delivered up, to be removed to the state having jurisdiction of the crime.

3 [No person held to service or labor in one state, under the laws thereof, escaping into another, shall, in consequence of any law or regulation therein, be discharged from such service or labor, but shall be delivered up on claim of the party to whom such service or labor may be due.]

New States and Territories

Section 3

1 New states may be admitted by the Congress into this Union; but no new state shall be formed or erected within the jurisdiction of any other state; nor any state be formed by the junction of two or more states, or parts of states, without the consent of the legislatures of the states concerned as well as of the Congress.

2 The Congress shall have power to dispose of and make all needful rules and regulations respecting the territory or other property belonging to the United States; and nothing in this Constitution shall be so construed as to prejudice any claims of the United States, or of any particular state.

Protection of States Guaranteed

Section 4

The United States shall guarantee to every state in this Union a republican form of government, and shall protect each of them against invasion; and on application of the legislature, or of the executive (when the legislature cannot be convened) against domestic violence.

ARTICLE V
Amending the Constitution

The Congress, whenever two-thirds of both houses shall deem it necessary, shall propose amendments to this Constitution, or, on the application of the legislatures of two-thirds of the several states, shall call a convention for proposing amendments, which, in either case, shall be valid to all intents and purposes, as part of this Constitution, when ratified by the legislatures of three-fourths of the several states, or by conventions in three-fourths thereof, as the one or the other mode of ratification may be proposed by the Congress; provided [that no amendment which may be made prior to the year one thousand eight hundred and eight shall in any manner affect the first and fourth clauses in the ninth section of the first article; and] that no state, without its consent, shall be deprived of its equal suffrage in the Senate.

ARTICLE VI
General Provisions

1 All debts contracted and engagements entered into, before the adoption of this Constitution, shall be as valid against the United States under this Constitution, as under the Confederation.

2 This Constitution, and the laws of the United States which shall be made in pursuance thereof; and all treaties made, or which shall be made, under the authority of the United States, shall be the supreme law of the land; and the judges in every state shall be bound thereby, anything in the constitution or laws of any state to the contrary notwithstanding.

3 The senators and representatives before mentioned, and the members of the several state legislatures, and all executive and judicial officers, both of the United States and of the several states, shall be bound by oath or affirmation, to support this Constitution; but no religious test shall ever be required as a qualification to any office or public trust under the United States.

ARTICLE VII
Ratifying the Constitution

The ratification of the conventions of nine states shall be sufficient for the establishment of this Constitution between the states so ratifying the same.

Done in convention by the unanimous consent of the states present the seventeenth day of September in the year of our Lord one thousand seven hundred and eighty-seven and of the independence of the United States of America the twelfth. In witness thereof we have hereunto subscribed our names.

George Washington,
  President and deputy
  from Virginia

Delaware

George Read
Gunning Bedford, Jr.
John Dickinson
Richard Bassett
Jacob Broom

Maryland

James McHenry
Dan of St. Thomas Jenifer
Daniel Carroll

Virginia

John Blair
James Madison, Jr.

North Carolina

William Blount
Richard Dobbs
  Spaight
Hugh Williamson

South Carolina

John Rutledge
Charles Cotesworth
  Pinckney
Charles Pinckney
Pierce Butler

Georgia

William Few
Abraham Baldwin

New Hampshire

John Langdon
Nicholas Gilman

Massachusetts

Nathaniel Gorham
Rufus King

Connecticut

William Samuel
  Johnson
Roger Sherman

New York

Alexander Hamilton

New Jersey

William Livingston
David Brearley
William Paterson
Jonathan Dayton

Pennsylvania

Benjamin Franklin
Thomas Mifflin
Robert Morris
George Clymer
Thomas FitzSimons
Jared Ingersoll
James Wilson
Gouverneur Morris

Attest:

William Jackson, Secretary

Amendments to the Constitution

The Bill of Rights

Amendment 1
Religious and Political Freedoms (1791)

Congress shall make no law respecting an establishment of religion, or prohibiting the free exercise thereof; or abridging the freedom of speech, or of the press; or the right of the people peaceably to assemble, and to petition the government for a redress of grievances.

Amendment 2
Right to Bear Arms (1791)

A well-regulated militia, being necessary to the security of a free state, the right of the people to keep and bear arms shall not be infringed.

Amendment 3
Housing of Soldiers (1791)

No soldier shall, in time of peace be quartered in any house, without the consent of the owner, nor in time of war, but in a manner to be prescribed by law.

Amendment 4
Search and Arrest Warrants (1791)

The right of the people to be secure in their persons, houses, papers, and effects, against unreasonable searches and seizures, shall not be violated, and no warrants shall issue, but upon probable cause, supported by oath or affirmation, and particularly describing the place to be searched, and the persons or things to be seized.

Amendment 5
Rights in Criminal Cases (1791)

No person shall be held to answer for a capital, or otherwise infamous crime, unless on a presentment or indictment of a grand jury, except in cases arising in the land or naval forces, or in the militia, when in actual service in time of war or public danger; nor shall any person be subject for the same offense to be twice put in jeopardy of life or limb; nor shall be compelled in any criminal case to be a witness against himself, nor be deprived of life, liberty, or property, without due process of law; nor shall private property be taken for public use, without just compensation.

Amendment 6
Rights to a Fair Trial (1791)

In all criminal prosecutions, the accused shall enjoy the right to a speedy and public trial, by an impartial jury of the state and district wherein the crime shall have been committed, which district shall have been previously ascertained by law, and to be informed of the nature and cause of the accusation; to be confronted with the witnesses against him; to have compulsory process for obtaining witnesses in his favor, and to have the assistance of counsel for his defense.

Amendment 7
Rights in Civil Cases (1791)

In suits at common law, where the value in controversy shall exceed twenty dollars, the right of trial by jury shall be preserved, and no fact tried by a jury, shall be otherwise re-examined in any court of the United States, than according to the rules of the common law.

Amendment 8
Bails, Fines, and Punishments (1791)

Excessive bail shall not be required, nor excessive fines imposed, nor cruel and unusual punishments inflicted.

Amendment 9
Rights Retained by the People (1791)

The enumeration in the Constitution, of certain rights, shall not be construed to deny or disparage others retained by the people.

Amendment 10
Powers Retained by the States and the People (1791)

The powers not delegated to the United States by the Constitution, nor prohibited by it to the states, are reserved to the states respectively, or to the people.

Amendment 11
Lawsuits Against States (1795)

The judicial power of the United States shall not be construed to extend to any suit in law or equity, commenced or prosecuted against one of the United States by citizens of another state, or by citizens or subjects of any foreign state.

Amendment 12
Election of the President and Vice President (1804)

The electors shall meet in their respective states and vote by ballot for President and Vice President, one of whom, at least, shall not be an inhabitant of the same state with themselves; they shall name in their ballots the person voted for as President, and in distinct ballots the person voted for as Vice President, and they shall make distinct lists of all persons voted for as President, and of all persons voted for as Vice President, and of the number of votes for each, which lists they shall sign and certify, and transmit sealed to the seat of the government of the United States, directed to the president of the Senate; — the president of the Senate shall, in the presence of the Senate and House of Representatives, open all the certificates and the votes shall then be counted; — the person having the greatest number of votes for President, shall be the President, if such number be a majority of the whole number of electors appointed; and if no person have such majority, then from the persons having the highest numbers not exceeding three on the list of those voted for as President, the House of Representatives shall choose immediately, by ballot, the President. But in choosing the President, the votes shall be taken by states, the representation from each state having one vote; a quorum for this purpose shall consist of a member or members from two-thirds of the states, and a majority of all the states shall be necessary to a choice. And if the House of

Representatives shall not choose a President whenever the right of choice shall devolve upon them, [before the fourth day of March next following,] then the Vice President shall act as President, as in the case of the death or other constitutional disability of the President.

The person having the greatest number of votes as Vice President, shall be the Vice President, if such number be a majority of the whole number of electors appointed, and if no person have a majority, then from the two highest numbers on the list, the Senate shall choose the Vice President; a quorum for the purpose shall consist of two-thirds of the whole number of senators, and a majority of the whole number shall be necessary to a choice. But no person constitutionally ineligible to the office of President shall be eligible to that of Vice President of the United States.

Amendment 13
Abolition of Slavery (1865)

Section 1

Neither slavery nor involuntary servitude, except as a punishment for crime whereof the party shall have been duly convicted, shall exist within the United States, or any place subject to their jurisdiction.

Section 2

Congress shall have power to enforce this article by appropriate legislation.

Amendment 14
Civil Rights (1868)

Section 1

All persons born or naturalized in the United States, and subject to the jurisdiction thereof, are citizens of the United States and of the state wherein they reside. No state shall make or enforce any law which shall abridge the privileges or immunities of citizens of the United States; nor shall any state deprive any person of life, liberty, or property, without due process of law; nor deny to any person within its jurisdiction the equal protection of the laws.

Section 2

Representatives shall be apportioned among the several states according to their respective numbers, counting the whole number of persons in each state, [excluding Indians not taxed]. But when the right to vote at any election for the choice of electors for President and Vice President of the United States, representatives in Congress, the executive and judicial officers of a state, or the members of the legislature thereof, is denied to any of the male inhabitants of such state, being twenty-one years of age, and citizens of the United States, or in any way abridged, except for participation in rebellion, or other crime, the basis of representation therein shall be reduced in the proportion which the number of such male citizens shall bear to the whole number of male citizens twenty-one years of age in such state.

Section 3

No person shall be a senator or representative in Congress, or elector of President and Vice President, or hold any office, civil or military, under the United States, or under any state, who, having previously taken an oath, as a member of Congress, or as an officer of the United States, or as a member of any state legislature, or as an executive or judicial officer of any state, to support the Constitution of the United States, shall have engaged in insurrection or rebellion against the same, or given aid or comfort to the enemies thereof. But Congress may by a vote of two-thirds of each House, remove such disability.

Section 4

The validity of the public debt of the United States, authorized by law, including debts incurred for payment of pensions and bounties for services in suppressing insurrection or rebellion, shall not be questioned. But neither the United States nor any state shall assume or pay any debt or obligation incurred in aid of insurrection or rebellion against the United States, or any claim for the loss or emancipation of any slave; but all such debts, obligations, and claims shall be held illegal and void.

Section 5

The Congress shall have power to enforce, by appropriate legislation, the provisions of this article.

Amendment 15
Right to Vote (1870)

Section 1

The right of citizens of the United States to vote shall not be denied or abridged by the United States or by any state on account of race, color, or previous condition of servitude.

Section 2

The Congress shall have power to enforce this article by appropriate legislation.

Amendment 16
Income Taxes (1913)

The Congress shall have power to lay and collect taxes on incomes, from whatever source derived, without apportionment among the several states, and without regard to any census or enumeration.

Amendment 17
Direct Election of Senators (1913)

Section 1

The Senate of the United States shall be composed of two senators from each state, elected by the people thereof for six years; and each senator shall have one vote. The electors in each state shall have the qualifications requisite for electors of the most numerous branch of the state legislatures.

Section 2

When vacancies happen in the representation of any state in the Senate, the executive authority of such state shall issue writs of election to fill such vacancies: provided, that the legislature of any state may empower the executive thereof to make temporary appointments until the people fill the vacancies by election as the legislature may direct.

Section 3

This amendment shall not be so construed as to affect the election or term of any senator chosen before it becomes valid as part of the Constitution.

Amendment 18
Prohibition of Liquor (1919)

Section 1

After one year from the ratification of this article the manufacture, sale, or transportation of intoxicating liquors within, the importation thereof into, or the exportation thereof from the United States and all territory subject to the jurisdiction thereof for beverage purposes is hereby prohibited.

Section 2

The Congress and the several states shall have concurrent power to enforce this article by appropriate legislation.

Section 3

This article shall be inoperative unless it shall have been ratified as an amendment to the Constitution by the legislatures of the several states, as provided in the Constitution, within seven years from the date of the submission hereof to the states by the Congress.

Amendment 19
Women's Suffrage (1920)

Section 1

The right of citizens of the United States to vote shall not be denied or abridged by the United States or by any state on account of sex.

Section 2

Congress shall have power to enforce this article by appropriate legislation.

Amendment 20
Terms of the President and Congress (1933)

Section 1

The terms of the President and Vice President shall end at noon on the 20th day of January, and the terms of senators and representatives at noon on the third day of January, of the years in which such terms would have ended if this article had not been ratified; and the terms of their successors shall then begin.

Section 2

The Congress shall assemble at least once in every year, and such meeting shall begin at noon on the third day of January, unless they shall by law appoint a different day.

Section 3

If, at the time fixed for the beginning of the term of the President, the President elect shall have died, the Vice President elect shall become President. If a President shall not have been chosen before the time fixed for the beginning of his term, or if the President elect shall have failed to qualify, then the Vice President elect shall act as President until a President shall have qualified; and the Congress may by law provide for the case wherein neither a President elect nor a Vice President elect shall have qualified, declaring who shall then act as President, or the manner in which one who is to act shall be selected, and such person shall act accordingly until a President or Vice President shall have qualified.

Section 4

The Congress may by law provide for the case of the death of any of the persons from whom the House of Representatives may choose a President whenever the right of choice shall have devolved upon them, and for the case of the death of any of the persons from whom the Senate may choose a Vice President whenever the right of choice shall have devolved upon them.

Section 5

Sections 1 and 2 shall take effect on the 15th day of October following the ratification of this article.

Section 6

This article shall be inoperative unless it shall have been ratified as an amendment to the Constitution by the legislatures of three-fourths of the several states within seven years from the date of its submission.

Amendment 21
Repeal of Prohibition (1933)

Section 1

The eighteenth article of amendment to the Constitution of the United States is hereby repealed.

Section 2

The transportation or importation into any state, territory, or possession of the United States for delivery or use therein of intoxicating liquors, in violation of the laws thereof, is hereby prohibited.

Section 3

This article shall be inoperative unless it shall have been ratified as an amendment to the Constitution by conventions in the several states, as provided in the Constitution, within seven years from the date of the submission hereof to the states by the Congress.

Amendment 22
Limitation on Presidential Terms (1951)

Section 1

No person shall be elected to the office of the President more than twice, and no person who has held the office of President, or acted as President, for more than two years of a term to which some other person was elected President shall be elected to the office of the President more than once. But this article shall not apply to any person holding the office of President when this article was proposed by the Congress, and shall not prevent any person who may be holding the office of President, or acting as President, during the term within which this article becomes operative from holding the office of President or acting as President during the remainder of such term.

Section 2

This article shall be inoperative unless it shall have been ratified as an amendment to the Constitution by the legislatures of three-fourths of the several states within seven years from the date of its submission to the states by the Congress.

Amendment 23
Suffrage in the District of Columbia (1961)

Section 1

The district constituting the seat of government of the United States shall appoint in such manner as the Congress may direct: A number of electors of President and Vice President equal to the whole number of senators and representatives in Congress to which the district would be entitled if it were a state, but in no event more than the least populous state; they shall be in addition to those appointed by the states, but they shall be considered, for the purposes of the election of President and Vice President, to be electors appointed by a state; and they shall meet in the district and perform such duties as provided by the twelfth article of amendment.

Section 2

The Congress shall have power to enforce this article by appropriate legislation.

Amendment 24
Poll Taxes (1964)

Section 1

The right of citizens of the United States to vote in any primary or other election for President or Vice President, for electors for President or Vice President, or for senator or representative in Congress, shall not be denied or abridged by the United States or any state by reason of failure to pay any poll tax or other tax.

Section 2

The Congress shall have power to enforce this article by appropriate legislation.

Amendment 25
Presidential Disability and Succession (1967)

Section 1

In case of the removal of the President from office or of his death or resignation, the Vice President shall become President.

Section 2

Whenever there is a vacancy in the office of the Vice President, the President shall nominate a Vice President who shall take office upon confirmation by a majority vote of both houses of Congress.

Section 3

Whenever the President transmits to the president *pro tempore* of the Senate and the Speaker of the House of Representatives his written declaration that he is unable to discharge the powers and duties of his office, and until he transmits to them a written declaration to the contrary, such powers and duties shall be discharged by the Vice President as acting President.

Section 4

Whenever the Vice President and a majority of either the principal officers of the executive departments or of such other body as Congress may by law provide, transmit to the president pro tempore of the Senate and the Speaker of the House of Representatives their written declaration that the President is unable to discharge the powers and duties of his office, the Vice President shall immediately assume the powers and duties of the office as acting President.

Thereafter, when the President transmits to the president pro tempore of the Senate and the speaker of the House of Representatives his written declaration that no inability exists, he shall resume the powers and duties of his office unless the Vice President and a majority of either the principal officers of the executive department or of such other body as Congress may by law provide, transmit within four days to the president pro tempore of the Senate and the Speaker of the House of Representatives their written declaration that the President is unable to discharge the powers and duties of his office. Thereupon Congress shall decide the issue, assembling within forty-eight hours for that purpose if not in session. If the Congress, within twenty-one days after receipt of the latter written declaration, or, if Congress is not in session, within twenty-one days after Congress is required to assemble, determines by two-thirds vote of both houses that the President is unable to discharge the powers and duties of his office, the Vice President shall continue to discharge the same as acting President; otherwise, the President shall resume the powers and duties of his office.

Amendment 26
Suffrage for 18-Year-Olds (1971)

Section 1

The right of citizens of the United States, who are eighteen years of age or older, to vote shall not be denied or abridged by the United States or by any state on account of age.

Section 2

The Congress shall have power to enforce this article by appropriate legislation.

Amendment 27
Congressional Pay (1992)

No law, varying the compensation for the services of the senators and representatives, shall take effect, until an election of representatives shall have intervened.

Glossary

A

Absolute advantage (ab′ sə lüt ad van′ tij) the ability to produce an item more easily and less expensively than a trading partner using the same resources (p. 379)

Adjustment (ə just′ ment) a part of income that is not taxed, such as all or part of Social Security benefits (p. 308)

AFL-CIO (ā ef el sē ī ō) the largest group of independent labor unions; stands for the American Federation of Labor and Congress of Industrial Organizations (p. 185)

Agency (ā′ jən sē) a group that provides a special service (p. 402)

Agriculture (ag′ rə kul chər) farming (p. 28)

Amendment (ə mend′ mənt) a formal change to the Constitution (p. 47)

Americans with Disabilities Act (ADA) (ə mer′ ə kans wiŧʜ dis ə bil′ ə tēz akt) a law that outlaws discrimination against persons with physical or mental handicaps (p. 171)

Ancestor (an′ ses tər) a person who lives before your time (p. 27)

Annual percentage rate (APR) (an′ yü əl pər sən′ tij rāt) the amount of money earned if left deposited in a savings account for one year (p. 269); the yearly percentage paid for money borrowed on credit (p. 280)

Appropriation bill (ə prō prē ā′ shən bil) a bill that gives a government agency the money it needs for the year (p. 319)

Arbitration (är bə trā′ shən) when both sides agree to have a mediator who will decide how to solve a disagreement (p. 188)

Assembly line (ə sem′ blē līn) a system in which a product moves from worker to worker so it can be assembled faster (p. 14)

Automated teller machine (ATM) (ô′ tə mā tid tel′ ər mə shēn′) an electronic terminal where customers can do their banking (p. 282)

B

Bait and switch (bāt and swich) the illegal act of advertising a product at a low price and then discouraging customers to buy the item in order to get them to buy a more expensive item (p. 254)

Balance of trade (bal′ əns ov trād) the difference between the value of a country's imports and its exports (p. 375)

Barter (bär′ tər) the trading of goods and services (p. 208)

Bear market (ber mär′ kit) a term used to describe the stock market when the prices of most stocks are falling (p. 278)

Benefits (ben′ ə fitz) anything extra provided to workers besides wages, such as paid vacations, retirement plans, and medical insurance (p. 169)

Bill of Rights (bil ov rītz) the first ten amendments to the American Constitution (p. 47)

Birthrate (bėrth′ rāt) the ratio of births to the total population of an area in one year (p. 397)

Black market (blak mär′ kit) an illegal market in which goods and services are sold above their legal price (p. 104)

Blue-collar (blü′ kol′ ər) a name used to describe unskilled or semiskilled workers (p. 161)

Bond (bond) a type of loan that an investor buys from a company or from the government; the company or government promises to pay the investor back their money plus a profit at a later date (p. 146)

Bottom line (bot′ əm līn) how much profit a business makes (p. 68)

Boycott (boi′ kot) a refusal to buy something in hopes that it pressures a company to give in to worker demands (p. 190)

Brand name (brand nām) the name of a product used to identify the product quickly, often through use of a logo (p. 126)

Bread and butter unionism (bred and but´ ər yü´ nyə niz əm) the belief that unions should focus on improving working conditions and pay for skilled workers rather than political reform (p. 185)

Budget (buj´ it) a plan for spending and saving money (p. 248)

Bull market (bůl mär´ kit) a term used to describe the stock market when the prices of most stocks are going up (p. 278)

Business cycle (biz´ nis sī´ kəl) the swings up and down in the real GDP (p. 338)

C

Cabinet (kab´ ə nit) a group of executive department leaders who advise the president (p. 297)

Capacity (kə pas´ ə tē) the ability to pay a loan back (p. 281)

Capital (kap´ ə təl) things of worth: machines, buildings, tools, and money (p. 4); savings and assets used to gain credit (p. 281)

Capital good (kap´ ə təl gůd) a good such as machinery or farm tractors that is used to produce other things (p. 374)

Capitalism (kap´ ə tə liz əm) a system in which individuals and private businesses own and control production (also called market economy) (p. 32)

Cash crop (kash krop) crops such as tea, cotton, and vegetables that are grown and sold for money (p. 397)

Certificate of deposit (CD) (sər tif´ ə kit ov di poz´ it) a certificate stating that a person has made a deposit for a fixed period of time at a fixed interest rate (p. 270)

Character (kar´ ik tər) how trustworthy a person seems to a lender (p. 281)

Charter (chär´ tər) an official document issued by state governments that gives the right to create a corporation (p. 146)

Check clearing (chek klir´ ing) the act of processing a check that transfers money (p. 234)

Child support (chīld sə pôrt´) money a divorced person pays for family expenses (p. 359)

Choice (chois) the act of deciding on and selecting what is wanted most (p. 4)

Circular flow (sėr´ kyə lər flō) a model that shows the process of exchange among consumers (also called households), businesses, and government (p. 149)

Citizenship (sit´ ə zən ship) the act of being a member of a country (p. 47)

Closed shop (klōzd shop) a business closed to nonunion workers (p. 190)

Collateral (kə lat´ ər əl) something of value that is offered as a guarantee of repayment (p. 282)

Collective bargaining (kə lək´ tiv bär´ gən ing) when representatives of labor and management sit down together to try to reach an agreement on something (p. 188)

Collusion (kə lü´ zhən) a secret agreement between competing firms to cooperate with each other (p. 124)

Command economy (kə mand´ i kon´ ə mē) an economy in which government leaders give the answers to the three economic questions (p. 28)

Commercial bank (kə mėr´ shəl bangk) a bank whose main function is to receive deposits and make short-term loans (p. 217)

Committee (kə mit´ ē) a group that gathers regularly for a certain purpose or goal (p. 189)

Common stock (kom´ ən stok) a share in the ownership of a corporation (p. 273)

Communism (kom´ yə niz əm) a government in which the government owns all property (p. 29)

Comparative advantage (kəm par´ ə tiv ad van´ tij) the ability to produce a product or service at a lower cost and more efficiently than another country; the ability to produce an item at a lower opportunity cost (p. 379)

Comparison shopping (kəm par´ ə sən shop´ ing) looking at many brands of the same item to find the best buy (p. 253)

a	hat	e	let	ī	ice	ȯ	order	ů	put	sh	she	ə	a	in about
ā	age	ē	equal	o	hot	oi	oil	ü	rule	th	thin		e	in taken
ä	far	ėr	term	ō	open	ou	out	ch	child	ᵺ	then		i	in pencil
â	care	i	it	ȯ	saw	u	cup	ng	long	zh	measure		o	in lemon
													u	in circus

Competition (kom pə tish´ ən) a contest between businesses or individuals to sell a product or service (p. 31)

Compromise (kom´ prə mīz) when both sides of a disagreement give and take (p. 188); to give up a part of what one wants in order to settle differences and reach agreement (p. 318)

Congress (kong´ gris) the lawmaking branch of the American government (p. 47)

Constitution (kon stə tü´ shən) a plan of government (p. 46)

Consumer (kən sü´ mer) one who buys and uses products (p. 49)

Consumer fraud (kən sü´ mer frôd) when an uninformed consumer is tricked into buying something that falls short of what the seller claimed (p. 254)

Consumer goods (kən sü´ mer gùdz) everyday items that people purchase (p. 28)

Consumer price index (CPI) (kən sü´ mer prīs in´ deks) a measure of how much the prices of necessary items are changing (p. 354)

Contract (kon´ trakt) a legal agreement between two or more people (p. 144)

Contractionary fiscal policy (kən trak´ shə ner ē fis´ kəl pol´ ə sē) a government financial policy in which decreased government spending or an increase in taxes hopes to get the economy to slow down (p. 302)

Copyright (kop´ ē rīt) the sole right given to writers and artists to sell or make copies of their works (p. 121)

Corporate income tax (kôr´ pər it in´ kum taks) the amount of money a corporation pays the government on money it earns each year (p. 308)

Corporation (kôr pə rā´ shən) a business that can be made up of many owners, but the law allows it to act like a single person (p. 145)

Cost-push inflation (kôst push in flā´ shən) a rise in prices due to unexpected shortages of raw materials (p. 353)

Craft union (kraft yü´ nyən) a union that represents skilled workers in a certain craft (p. 185)

Credit (kred´ it) a loan of money to be paid back over a period of time (p. 280)

Credit rating (kred´ it rā´ ting) a report that shows how well someone can manage their money and pay off debts and bills (p. 218)

Credit union (kred´ it yü´ nyən) a company that provides low-cost loans and savings accounts; members own and run the credit union (p. 217)

Creditworthy (kred´ it wər´ ᴛʜē) having the capacity, capital, and character to pay back borrowed money (p. 281)

Crisis (krī´ sis) an event that threatens people's well-being (p. 103)

Crossing the picket line (krôs´ ing ᴛʜə pik´ it līn) when a worker takes the job of another worker who is on strike (p. 190)

Crowding-out effect (krou´ ding out ə fekt´) the higher interest rates on borrowed money that result after the government has borrowed what it needs (p. 325)

Currency (kėr´ ən sē) money, either coins or bills (p. 214)

Customer services (kus´ tə mər ser´ vi sez) a way a company attracts buyers by providing services to those who have bought products (p. 125)

Customs tax (kus´ təmz taks) a tax placed on goods imported from another country, such as perfume, alcohol, and tobacco (p. 309)

Customs union (kus´ təmz yü´ nyən) a trade agreement in which members remove all trade barriers among themselves but place the same tariff on goods from non-member countries (p. 387)

D

Database (dā´ tə bās) a large collection of information stored on a computer (p. 16)

Debit card (deb´ it kärd) a card used as payment like a credit card, but the money comes from a person's checking account (p. 282)

Decentralize (dē sen´ trə līz) to spread out power (p. 229)

Declaration of Independence (dek lə rā´ shən ov in di pen´ dens) document written by American colonists explaining why the American colonies should no longer be ruled by Great Britain (p. 46)

Deduction (di duk´ shən) an expense like medical expenses and interest on loans that can be subtracted from income taxes (p. 308)

Deficit (def´ ə sit) the difference between how much money the government takes in and how much it spends (p. 302)

Deflation (di flā´ shən) the opposite of inflation; a decrease in prices because there is too much for sale and not enough people to buy the items for sale (p. 353)

Demand (di mand´) the amount of a good or service that consumers are willing and able to buy at a given price (p. 62)

Demand curve (di mand´ kėrv) a way to explain the law of demand in a picture; the picture shows prices and units demanded at each price (p. 63)

Demand-pull inflation (di mand´ pùl in flā´ shən) a rise in prices that happens when demand is greater than supply (p. 353)

Demand-side economics (di mand´ sīd ek ə nom´ iks) the belief that the government's policies can increase the total amount of goods and services consumers want to buy (p. 303)

Democracy (di mok´ rə sē) a government in which citizens take part (p. 29)

Democratic socialism (dem ə krat´ ik sō´ shə liz əm) a government in which the people have a say in government but in which the government owns the major industries (p. 29)

Deposit (di poz´ it) to put money into a bank (p. 214)

Depression (di presh´ ən) a period of economic hard times (p. 170)

Dictatorship (dik´ tā tər ship) a government in which the people have no rights; one person or a small group of people rule the country by force and make all the laws (p. 29)

Differentiate (dif ə rən´ shē āt) a way a company attracts buyers by showing the differences between their product and their competitors' (p. 125)

Diminishing marginal utility (də min´ ish ing mär´ jə nəl yü til´ ə tē) a decrease in need because enough units are being produced to meet demand (p. 72)

Diminishing returns (də min´ ish ing ri tėrnz´) when adding resources is not always a good thing; it can cause production to slow down slightly (p. 90)

Disabled (dis ā bəld´) having a physical or mental handicap (p. 158)

Discount rate (dis´ kount rāt) the price that banks must pay to borrow money from the Federal Reserve (p. 239)

Discretionary expense (dis kresh´ ə ner ē ek spens´) an expense that people decide for themselves whether to spend or not, often for entertainment (p. 250)

Discrimination (dis krim ə nā´ shən) unfair treatment because of a person's race, sex, religion, age, or physical condition (p. 51)

Diversify (də vėr´ sə fī) to purchase stock in several companies to reduce the risk of loss (p. 273); to vary (p. 384)

Dividend (div´ ə dend) the investor's share of a company's profit (p. 147)

Divisibility (də viz ə bil´ ə tē) the ability of money to be divided up evenly into exact change (p. 210)

Division of labor (də vizh´ ən ov lā´ bər) dividing up workers so that each worker completes one job, which is one part of a larger job (p. 14)

Dow Jones Industrial Average (DJIA) (dou jōnz in dus´ trē əl av´ ər ij) a measure of stock market performance; the average selling price of 30 top stocks (p. 277)

Due process (dü pros´ es) the act of following clear rules in court and treating everyone fairly (p. 47)

Durable (dùr´ ə bəl) the ability of money to last a long time and withstand wear and decay (p. 211)

a	hat	e	let	ī	ice	ô	order	ù	put	sh	she	ə	a	in about
ā	age	ē	equal	o	hot	oi	oil	ü	rule	th	thin		e	in taken
ä	far	ėr	term	ō	open	ou	out	ch	child	ᴛʜ	then		i	in pencil
â	care	i	it	ȯ	saw	u	cup	ng	long	zh	measure		o	in lemon
													u	in circus

E

Economic and Social Council (ECOSOC) (ek ə nom´ ik and sō´ shəl koun´ səl) the part of the UN that promotes economic development (p. 402)

Economics (ek ə nom´ iks) the study of how people and countries make decisions about how to use their scarce resources in the most efficient way (p. 4)

Elastic demand (i las´ tik di mand´) the state in which a price increase causes a large change in demand (p. 65)

Elastic supply (i las´ tik sə plī´) when a change in price has a big effect on the quantity supplied (p. 82)

Elasticity of supply (ē las tis´ ə tē ov sə plī´) the measure of how changes in price affect the quantity of supply (p. 82)

Electronic money transfer (i lek tron´ ik mun´ ē tran´ sfèr) the process in which money changes hands through the use of computers (p. 234)

Embargo (em bär´ gō) the act of cutting off all trade with another country (p. 382)

Entitlement (en tī´ tl mənt) a benefit such as Social Security, income security, or Medicare to which people feel they have a right (p. 323)

Entrepreneurship (än trə prə nèr´ ship) when someone starts a new business or improves an old one (p. 12)

Environment (en vi´ rən mənt) the air, water, and soil people depend on to survive (p. 361)

Equilibrium point (ē kwə lib´ rē əm point) the point at which the quantity demanded equals the quantity supplied (p. 106)

Equilibrium price (ē kwə lib´ rē əm prīs) the price that both buyers and sellers will accept (p. 106)

Equilibrium wage rate (ē kwə lib´ rē əm wāj rāt) the point at which the quantity of labor demanded is equal to the quantity of labor supplied (p. 167)

Erosion (i rō´ zhən) the wearing away and moving of weathered rock and soil by weather (p. 361)

Estate tax (e stāt´ taks) a tax on the property that was left by someone who has died (p. 309)

European Union (EU) (yùr ə pē´ ən yü´ nyən) an organization that links European countries both economically and politically and promotes cooperation among its members (p. 388)

Exchange (eks chānj´) the act of giving another person something and getting something back (p. 51)

Excise tax (ek´ sīz taks) a tax on certain goods made in that country (p. 309)

Executive agencies (eg zek´ yə tiv ā´ jən sēz) agencies within the executive branch of government under the direct control of the president (p. 297)

Executive branch (eg zek´ yə tiv branch) the branch of the U.S. government that makes sure the laws are carried out; the president and the federal bureaucracy (p. 297)

Exemption (eg zemp´ shən) an exact dollar amount that is not taxed, such as a claim for each child who depends on his or her parents (p. 308)

Expansion (ek span´ shən) the final stage of the business cycle when the economy begins to grow again (p. 338)

Expansionary fiscal policy (ek span´ shə ner ē fis´ kəl pol´ ə sē) a government financial policy in which an increase in government spending or a decrease in taxes hopes to get the economy to grow (p. 301)

Expense (ek spens´) a good or service that costs money (p. 248)

Experience (ek spir´ ē əns) knowledge and skill gained from being on the job (p. 160)

Explorer (ek splôr´ ər) one who searches around a new place (p. 212)

Export (ek´ spôrt) a good or service sold to other countries (p. 334)

Externalities (ek stər na´ lə tēz) side effects of an economic situation; they can be either helpful or harmful (p. 101)

F

Factors of production (fak´ tərz ov prə duk´ shən) resources that are used to make goods and services (p. 11)

Family planning (fam´ ə lē pla´ ning) an effort to slow population increases by controlling and spacing the number of births (p. 399)

Federal budget (fed′ ər əl buj′ it) an estimate of how much money the federal government will take in and how much it will spend in a year (p. 318)

Federal bureaucracy (fed′ ər əl byù rok′ rə sē) the large group of people who work for the federal government, mostly for the executive branch (p. 297)

Federal Open Market Committee (FOMC) (fed′ ər əl ō′ pən mär′ kit kə mit′ ē) a committee that meets to review the state of the U.S. economy (p. 237)

Finance charge (fī′ nans chärj) the interest, service charges, and other fees charged on borrowed money (p. 281)

Fiscal policy (fis′ kəl pol′ ə sē) the government's use of spending and taxes to achieve a strong, stable economy (p. 301)

Fiscal year (fis′ kəl yir) the government's spending period from October 1 to September 30 of the next year (p. 318)

Fixed cost (fikst kôst) a cost that stays the same no matter how much business is done (p. 53)

Fixed expense (fikst ek spens′) an expense that does not change from month to month (p. 250)

Fixed income (fikst in′ kum) an income that does not change (p. 354)

Foreign aid (fôr′ ən ād) money, medicine, machinery, and food given by developed countries to help LDCs (p. 400)

Fossil fuel (fos′ əl fyü′ əl) a product of decayed plants or animals; energy sources such as oil, natural gas, and coal (p. 362)

Free enterprise (frē en′ tər prīz) a name for the American style of economy; same as capitalist or market economy (p. 49)

Free trade (frē trād) trade without barriers (p. 383)

Free-trade association (frē trād a sō sē ā′ shən) a trade agreement in which members reduce trade barriers among themselves but set their own tariffs on goods from non-member countries (p. 387)

G

General Agreement on Tariffs and Trade (GATT) (jen′ ər əl ə grē′ mənt ôn tar′ ifz and trād) an agreement signed by 23 countries at the end of World War II to promote international trade as a way to stop future wars (p. 386)

Generic (je nər′ ik) a store-brand product rather than a name brand (p. 253)

Glass ceiling (glas sē′ ling) the belief that women were being prevented from rising to a position of leadership in corporations because they were women (p. 164)

Globalization (glō bə lə zā′ shən) the act of bringing world economies closer together through international business and trade (p. 385)

Good (gùd) an item people buy, such as a car, television, or bed (p. 5)

Greenback (grēn′ bak) the name given to Union money, which was black on one side and green on the other (p. 214)

Grievance (grē′ vəns) a worker complaint (p. 189)

Gross domestic product (GDP) (grōs də mes′ tik prod′ əkt) the total value of all final goods and services produced in a country in one year (p. 334)

Gross income (grōs in′ kum) money earned before taxes and other expenses are taken out (p. 250)

H

Heavy industry (hev′ ē in′ də strē) large-scale production of basic items (p. 28)

Homemaker (hōm′ mā kər) one who takes care of the home and children without pay (p. 158)

Human resources (hyü′ mən rē′ sôr sez) the benefits paid directly to people, including Social Security, income security, Medicare, health, education, and veterans' benefits (p. 322)

a	hat	e	let	ī	ice	ô	order	ù	put	sh	she		a	in about
ā	age	ē	equal	o	hot	oi	oil	ü	rule	th	thin	ə	e	in taken
ä	far	ėr	term	ō	open	ou	out	ch	child	ᵺ	then		i	in pencil
â	care	i	it	ò	saw	u	cup	ng	long	zh	measure		o	in lemon
													u	in circus

Humanitarian (hyü man ə ter´ ē ən) a person devoted to helping all human beings no matter where they live (p. 400)

I

Import (im´ pôrt) a good entering the country from another country (p. 306)

Import quota (im´ pôrt kwō´ tə) a restriction on the number of specific goods that can enter a country (p. 382)

Impulse shopping (im´ puls shop´ ing) buying something you did not intend to buy (p. 254)

Incentive (in sen´ tiv) something that makes a person take an action (p. 32)

Income (in´ kum) the amount of money a person makes (p. 62)

Income gap (in´ kum gap) the difference between what the richest and the poorest Americans earn (p. 360)

Income security (in´ kum si kyûr´ ə tē) the benefits paid to retired workers who are not covered by Social Security (p. 322)

Income tax (in´ kum taks) a tax people pay on money earned (p. 306)

Increasing returns (in krē´ sing ri tėrnz´) when adding resources increases production (p. 90)

Industrial union (in dus´ trē əl yü´ nyən) a union that brings together all workers, skilled and unskilled (p. 185)

Inelastic demand (in i las´ tik di mand´) the state in which a price increase has little effect on demand (p. 66)

Inelastic supply (in i las´ tik sə plī´) when a change in price has very little effect on the quantity supplied (p. 82)

Inflation (in flā´ shən) a steady rise in the price of goods and services (p. 237)

Inflationary cycle (in flā´ shə ner ē sī´ kəl) a pattern that occurs when prices go up; workers need higher wages to keep up with rising prices, and businesses have to raise prices in order to pay workers more money (p. 354)

Information technology (IT) (in fər mā´ shən tek nol´ ə jē) a service job that involves the processing of information by computer (p. 160)

Inheritance tax (in her´ ə təns taks) a tax a person receiving money from a person who died must pay (p. 309)

Injunction (in jungk´ shən) a court order preventing some activity (p. 183)

Integration (in tə grā´ shən) a process in the 1960s in which African-American students were allowed to attend schools with white students (p. 171)

Interdependent (in tər di pen´ dənt) when countries depend on each other for economic success (p. 385)

Interest (in´ tər ist) a percentage of money paid for a loan or debt (p. 234); money earned back from investing money (p. 249)

Interest rate (in´ tər ist rāt) the percentage of interest charged for borrowing money (p. 239)

Intermediate good (in tər mē´ dē it gùd) a good that has not reached the final user; it is combined with other goods to make a final product for sale (p. 335)

International Monetary Fund (IMF) (in tər nash´ ə nəl mon´ ə ter ē fund) an agency of the UN that gives money and economic advice to countries when they have economic problems (p. 404)

Internet banking (in´ tər net bang´ king) banking by computer (p. 220)

Interstate trade (in´ tər stāt´ trād) trade among the states (p. 295)

Investment (in vest´ mənt) something bought for future financial benefit (p. 249)

Investor (in vest´ tər) one who spends money to buy stock in the hope of gaining money back (p. 146)

Invisible hand (in viz´ ə bəl hand) Adam Smith's idea that competition acts like an invisible hand; it pushes people to do what is best for themselves (p. 31)

J

Job security (job si kyûr´ ə tē) a guarantee that the workers will not lose their jobs (p. 189)

Judicial branch (jü dish´ əl branch) the branch of the U.S. government that interprets the laws; the courts (p. 297)

L

Labor (lā´ bər) work (p. 4)

Labor force (lā´ bər fôrs) people who work for pay or who are looking for work (p. 158)

Labor union (lā´ bər yü´ nyən) a group that makes sure workers are treated fairly (p. 170)

Laissez-faire (les ā fer´) the French phrase that means "leave us alone;" it refers to the belief that the government should not get involved in economic matters (p. 294)

Law of supply (lô ov sə plī´) the belief that as the price of a good rises, the quantity supplied will rise (p. 80)

Law of variable proportions (lô ov ver´ ē ə bəl prə pôr´ shənz) the belief that in the short run, changing one of the inputs changes the output (p. 88)

Lay off (lā ôf) to release a worker because there is no longer work or no longer money to pay the worker (p. 54)

Legal tender (lē´ gəl ten´ dər) legal currency that must be accepted in payment of a debt (p. 214)

Legislative branch (lej´ ə slā tiv branch) the branch of the U.S. government that makes the laws; Congress (p. 297)

Legislature (lej´ ə slā chər) a lawmaking branch of government (p. 47)

Less developed country (LDC) (les di vel´ əpd kun´ trē) a country with an economy that is still developing (p. 396)

Life expectancy (līf ek spek´ tən sē) the average life span of a person (p. 397)

Limited capital (lim´ ə tid kap´ ə təl) the limit on the amount of money to grow the business (p. 144)

Limited liability (lim´ ə tid lī a bil´ ə tē) when investors can only lose as much money as they have invested (p. 146)

Liquidity (li kwid´ ə tē) the ability to withdraw funds from a savings account (p. 269)

Lockout (lok´ out) when management closes the doors to the place of work and keeps the workers from entering until an agreement is reached (p. 190)

Logo (lō´ gō) a symbol that everyone knows, which is used to identify a product (p. 126)

Loss (lôs) the event in which money is lost because the total cost of doing business is greater than the total revenue (p. 54)

Luxury (luk´ shər ē) a thing that gives us pleasure but that we really do not need (p. 67)

M

M1 (em wun) a measure of the money supply that includes only the money actually in use, such as currency, checking accounts, and traveler's checks (p. 240)

M2 (em tü) a measure of the money supply that includes all M1 money and other monies worth less than $100,000 (p. 240)

M3 (em thrē) a measure of the money supply that includes all the money in M1 and M2 as well as all large time deposits over $100,000 (p. 240)

Majority (mə jôr´ ə tē) the quality or state of being greater (p. 127)

Manager (man´ ə jər) the person who runs a business or some part of it (p. 12)

Manufacture (man yə fak´ chər) to turn materials into products people use every day (p. 5)

Marginal cost (mär´ jə nəl kôst) the additional cost of producing one more unit (p. 92)

Marginal product (mär´ jə nəl prod´ əkt) the extra amount produced by adding one resource to production (p. 89)

Market (mär´ kit) a place where people come together to buy and sell (p. 31)

Market economy (mär´ kit i kon´ ə mē) a system in which individuals and private businesses own and control production (also called capitalism) (p. 32)

Market failure (mär´ kit fā´ lyər) market problems caused when buyers and sellers are not well informed, resources are not free to shift to where they can be better used, or prices are not set reasonably (p. 101)

a	hat	e	let	ī	ice	ô	order	ů	put	sh	she		a	in about
ā	age	ē	equal	o	hot	oi	oil	ü	rule	th	thin	ə	e	in taken
ä	far	ėr	term	ō	open	ou	out	ch	child	ᵮH	then		i	in pencil
â	care	i	it	ȯ	saw	u	cup	ng	long	zh	measure		o	in lemon
													u	in circus

Measure of prices (mezh´ ər ov prī´ sez) the way money helps to determine how much something is worth (p. 208)

Mediator (mē´ dē ā tər) a neutral third party who listens to arguments from both sides and suggests ways agreements can be reached (p. 188)

Medicaid (med´ ə kād) a government program that gives medical insurance to low-income people (p. 323)

Medicare (med´ ə ker) the program that provides medical care for the elderly (p. 299)

Medium of exchange (mē´ dē əm ov eks chānj´) the way money serves as something that both buyers and sellers will accept (p. 208)

Merger (mėr´ jər) when one business buys another (p. 129)

Minimum wage (min´ ə məm wāg) the lowest wage an employer can pay an employee (p. 108)

Minority (mə nôr´ ə tē) a person who belongs to a smaller group of people within a larger group (p. 163)

Mint (mint) a place that makes coins (p. 212)

Mixed economy (mikst i kon´ ə mē) an economy in which there is a blend of economic systems; individuals and the government share in the decision-making process (p. 34)

Monetary policy (mon´ ə ter ē pol´ ə sē) the decisions the Fed makes about money and banking (p. 237)

Money market account (mun´ ē mär´ kit ə kount´) a type of savings account that usually requires a minimum deposit of $500 or $1,000 but that earns a higher interest rate than a simple savings account (p. 269)

Monopolistic competition (mə nop ə lis´ tik kom pə tish´ ən) a type of market where there are many buyers and sellers, there is some product variation, and entry into the market is easy (p. 124)

Monopoly (mə nop´ ə lē) a market in which there is no competition; one company controls the market (p. 119)

Mortgage (môr´ gij) a home loan (p. 248)

Most favored nation (MFN) (mōst fā´ vərd nā´ shən) a country that receives the same lowered tariff that the United States negotiates with another country (p. 385)

Mutual fund (myü´ chü əl fund) a special fund in which people pool their money to buy a variety of investments (p. 273)

Mutual savings bank (myü´ chü əl sā´ vingz bangk) a bank that accepts smaller deposits than commercial banks (p. 217)

N

National debt (nash´ ə nəl det) all of the money the federal government owes to lenders (p. 325)

Nationality (nash ə nal´ ə tē) the nation one belongs to or comes from (p. 140)

Natural monopoly (nach´ ər əl mə nop´ ə lē) a monopoly that is allowed to exist because competition is not needed (p. 120)

Natural resource (nach´ ər əl rē´ sôrs) a raw material found on Earth, such as water, minerals, land, and forests (p. 4)

Natural right (nach´ ər əl rīt) a right given by God (p. 46)

Necessity (nə ses´ ə tē) a thing we need to live (p. 67)

Need (nēd) something that is necessary to remain alive (p. 4)

Negative externality (neg´ ə tiv ek stər nal´ ə tē) a harmful side effect of an economic situation (p. 101)

Negative returns (neg´ ə tiv ri tėrnz´) when adding resources causes production to be less than before (p. 90)

Net income (net in´ kum) money left over after all expenses are taken out (p. 250)

New Deal (nü dēl) the name of President Roosevelt's program for getting the United States out of the depression (p. 170)

New York Stock Exchange (NYSE) (nü yôrk stok eks chānj´) the largest stock exchange in the world, located on Wall Street in New York City (p. 275)

Nominal GDP (nom´ ə nəl jē dē pē) the current GDP, not adjusted for price changes (p. 336)

North American Free Trade Agreement (NAFTA) (nôrth ə mer´ ə kən frē trād ə grē´ mənt) a trade agreement signed by Mexico, Canada, and the United States that created one large free-trade area in North America (p. 387)

O

Occupational Safety and Health Administration (OSHA) (ok yə pā´ shə nəl sāf´ tē and helth ad min ə strā´ shən) a U.S. government agency that protects workers by setting and enforcing health and safety standards (p. 171)

Oligopoly (ol ə gop´ ə lē) a type of market where there only are a few sellers, there is a nearly standardized product, and entry into the market is difficult (p. 123)

Open shop (ō´ pən shop) workers can work for a company even if they do not join the union (p. 190)

Open-market operations (ō´ pən mär´ kit op ə rā´ shənz) the Fed's buying and selling of U.S. government securities (p. 237)

Opportunity (op ər tü´ nə tē) each possible use of a resource (p. 8)

Opportunity cost (op ər tü´ nə tē kôst) the cost of choosing one choice over another (p. 8)

Outsource (out´ sôrs) sending work to an outside source, such as another country, to cut costs (p. 195)

Overdraft (o´ vər draft) the act of returning a check to the bank when there are not funds to cover the check; also called "bouncing" a check (p. 218)

Overhead (o´ vər hed) the costs of doing business (p. 53)

Overtime (o´ vər tīm) extra money paid to employees for work beyond 40 hours per week or on weekends or holidays (p. 189)

P

Panic (pan´ ik) a widespread fear of financial loss (p. 228)

Partnership (pärt´ nər ship) a business that two or more people own (p. 144)

Patent (pat´ nt) right of sole ownership of an invention given to the inventor of an item (p. 121)

Peak (pēk) the highest point in the business cycle when the economy is booming (p. 338)

Picketing (pik´ i ting) a way of informing the public about worker grievances; workers carry signs explaining why their employer is unfair or why they are on strike (p. 190)

Portable (pôr´ tə bəl) the ability of money to be small, light, and easy to carry (p. 210)

Positive externality (poz´ ə tiv ek stər na´ lə tē) a helpful side effect of an economic situation (p. 101)

Poverty (pov´ ər tē) being poor (p. 358)

Poverty line (pov´ ər tē līn) a measure used to define which people are poor; three times the amount it costs to buy healthy food for a family (p. 358)

Price ceiling (prīs sē´ ling) a maximum price for some goods and services (p. 108)

Price discrimination (prīs dis krim ə nā´ shən) the practice of selling different buyers the same product for different prices (p. 128)

Price-fixing (prīs fik´ sing) an agreement to sell products for the same or similar prices (p. 124)

Price floor (prīs flôr) a minimum price for some goods and services (p. 108)

Price support (prīs sə pôrt´) a government-guaranteed minimum price farmers receive for their products (p. 86)

Price system (prīs sis´ təm) communication between buyers and sellers through the use of prices (p. 100)

Price war (prīs wôr) a series of price cuts to price below the competition (p. 124)

Prime rate (prīm rāt) the interest rate banks charge their best customers (p. 240)

Principal (prin´ sə pəl) the amount of money borrowed (p. 280)

Priority (prī ôr´ ə tē) something that receives attention before anything else; the thing that is most important (p. 318)

Private sector (prī´ vit sek´ tər) people buying goods and services (p. 322)

a	hat	e	let	ī	ice	ȯ	order	u̇	put	sh	she	ə	a in about
ā	age	ē	equal	o	hot	oi	oil	ü	rule	th	thin		e in taken
ä	far	ėr	term	ō	open	ou	out	ch	child	ᴛʜ	then		i in pencil
â	care	i	it	ȯ	saw	u	cup	ng	long	zh	measure		o in lemon
													u in circus

Producer price index (PPI) (prə dü′ sər prīs in′ deks) a measure of how the price of goods and services bought by producers has changed over time (p. 354)

Production possibilities (prə duk′ shən pos ə bil′ ə tēz) all combinations of goods and services that can be produced from a fixed amount of resources in a given period of time (p. 9)

Production schedule (prə duk′ shən skej′ ûl) a table that shows how the number of workers affects productivity and marginal product (p. 88)

Productivity (prō duk′ tiv ə tē) the amount of goods and services workers can produce in a given time (p. 14)

Professional (prə fesh′ ə nəl) a type of worker who has a college degree and special training (p. 160)

Profit (prof′ it) money left over after all the costs of production have been paid (p. 31)

Progressive tax (prə gres′ iv taks) a tax in which the more money a person makes, the greater the percentage paid in taxes (p. 306)

Progressives (prə gres′ ivz) reformers in the 1900s who tried to improve the lives of working people (p. 170)

Property tax (prop′ ər tē taks) a tax that people who own buildings, land, and other property must pay (p. 311)

Proportional tax (prə pôr′ shə nəl taks) a tax that is stated as a percentage; also called flat tax (p. 307)

Protective tariff (prə tek′ tiv tar′ if) a tax used to protect certain businesses; it is a tax on imports (p. 306)

Public goods (pub′ lik gûdz) products or services available to everyone (p. 101)

Public policy (pub′ lik pol′ ə sē) the process of government decision making that addresses problems affecting many people (p. 295)

Public sector (pub′ lik sek′ tər) federal, state, and local governments buying goods and services (p. 322)

Pure competition (pyûr kom pə tish′ ən) competition in which there are many buyers and sellers, there is a standardized product, the buyers and sellers are well informed, and there is easy entry into and out of the market (p. 116)

Pure monopoly (pyûr mə nop′ ə lē) a monopoly in which there is only one seller, there are no substitutes for a product or service, getting into and out of the market is difficult, and there is almost complete control over prices (p. 119)

Pyramid scheme (pir′ ə mid skēm) a kind of fraud where people invest money but the investment falls through, and the investors lose their money (p. 256)

R

Radical (rad′ ə kəl) something that is extreme (p. 180)

Ration coupon (rash′ ən kü′ pon) a piece of paper that can be exchanged for goods during rationing (p. 103)

Rationing (rash′ ə ning) a system in which the government provides a fixed amount of limited supplies to each person (p. 103)

Real economic growth (rē′ əl ek ə nom′ ik grōth) an increase from one year to the next in real GDP (p. 341)

Real estate (rē′ əl e stāt′) a type of investment that includes land and the buildings on it (p. 273)

Real GDP (rē′ əl jē dē pē) the GDP adjusted for price changes; a rise shows economic growth, a fall shows no economic growth (p. 336)

Real per capita GDP (rē′ əl pər kap′ ə tə jē dē pē) the real GDP for each person in a country from one year to the next; it is determined by dividing real GDP by the number of people in a country (p. 341)

Recall (rē′ kôl) when a company asks consumers to return a product for repair because the product has a safety problem (p. 259)

Recession (ri sesh′ ən) six months (two quarters) of declining GDP (p. 338)

Reciprocal trade agreement (ri sip′ rə kəl trād ə grē′mənt) an agreement that allows the United States to reduce a tariff if the trading partner reduces their tariff on American goods by the same percentage (p. 385)

Reform (ri fôrm′) change to make things work better (p. 127)

Regional trade organization (rē´ jə nəl trād ôr gə nə zā´ shən) an organization that works toward lowering or removing trade barriers among its members, which are located in the same region of the world (p. 388)

Regressive tax (ri gres´ iv taks) a tax in which the higher the income, the smaller the percentage of income paid as taxes (p. 307)

Regulatory commissions (reg´ yə lə tôr ē kə mish´ ənz) government agencies that watch over some part of the U.S. economy (p. 297)

Relative worth (rel´ ə tiv wėrth) the value that most people would place on a good (p. 100)

Representative (rep ri zen´ tə tiv) an elected leader who makes and carries out laws (p. 29)

Reserve (ri zėrv´) a percentage of money from deposits that a bank must keep around in case the money is needed (p. 220); an unused fossil fuel deposit left in the earth (p. 362)

Resource (rē´ sôrs) anything that people use to make things or do work (p. 4)

Retired (ri tīrd´) past the working age (p. 151)

Return (ri tėrn´) the amount investors receive as a payment for use of their money (p. 272)

Revenue (rev´ ə nü) all the money taken in by a business (p. 53)

Revenue tariff (rev´ ə nü tar´ if) a tax added to the cost of imported goods and used to raise money for the government (p. 381)

Right-to-work law (rīt tü wėrk lô) a law that is against forcing a worker to join a union (p. 193)

Rural (rür´ əl) away from the city (p. 27)

S

Sales tax (sālz taks) a tax that is paid on the price of goods or services (p. 310)

Sanitation (san ə tā´ shən) keeping things clean and removing trash (p. 403)

Savings and loan company (sā´ vingz and lōn kum´ pə nē) a company that allows people to put money in an account and to borrow money, often to buy a home (p. 217)

Scab (skab) another name for strikebreakers or replacement workers (p. 190)

Scarcity (skar´ sə tē) a problem in which wants are greater than what is available (p. 7)

Search warrant (sėrch wôr´ ənt) a document issued by a judge that says exactly who and what will be searched (p. 47)

Sector (sek´ tər) any of the three groupings of workers: agriculture, manufacturing/construction, and service (p. 159)

Securities (si kyür´ ə tēz) things that show ownership of something or proof of debt; examples are bonds, gold certificates, notes, drafts, and bills of exchange (p. 215)

Segregation (seg rə gā´ shən) the separation of people of different races (p. 171)

Semiskilled worker (sem i skild´ wėr´ kər) a type of worker who works in a job that requires some training, but not as much training as skilled workers (p. 161)

Service (sėr´ vis) work done for other people for a fee (p. 5)

Share (sher) a unit of stock in a company (p. 146)

Shortage (shôr´ tij) when the number of goods needed is greater than the number producers are willing to sell (p. 107)

Sin tax (sin taks) a tax that can be used to get people to stop doing certain things that the government finds harmful (p. 306)

Skilled worker (skild wėr´ kər) a type of worker who is well trained and experienced with a certain skill (p. 160)

Slum (slum) a run-down, urban area often without electricity or indoor plumbing (p. 397)

Socialism (so´ shə liz əm) the belief that governments rather than individuals should own a country's major industries (p. 28)

Social Security (so´ shəl si kyür´ ə tē) a government program of retirement and disability benefits (p. 250)

a	hat	e	let	ī	ice	ô	order	ů	put	sh	she	ə {	a	in about
ā	age	ē	equal	o	hot	oi	oil	ü	rule	th	thin		e	in taken
ä	far	ėr	term	ō	open	ou	out	ch	child	ᴛʜ	then		i	in pencil
â	care	i	it	ȯ	saw	u	cup	ng	long	zh	measure		o	in lemon
													u	in circus

Sole proprietorship (sōl prə prī´ ə tər ship) a business that one person owns (p. 143)

Spam (spam) e-mail messages offering goods or services to purchase (p. 255)

Specialization (spesh ə lə zā´ shən) when a person, country, or region works on making one part of an item good (p. 14)

Stable (stā´ bəl) the ability of money to maintain a certain value over a period of time (p. 210)

Standard of living (stan´ dərd ov liv´ ing) the way of living that is usual for a person, community, or country (p. 341)

Standardized product (stan´ dər dizd prod´ əkt) a product group in which competing products are nearly the same (p. 116)

Statement (stāt´ mənt) a document that shows details about an account (p. 218)

Stock (stok) a sign of ownership in a corporation (p. 146)

Stockbroker (stok´ brō kər) one who is licensed to buy and sell stocks (p. 276)

Stockholder (stok´ hōl dər) someone owning shares (or stock) of a company (p. 146)

Stock market (stok mär´ kit) the activity of buying and selling stocks (p. 275)

Store of value (stôr ov val´ yü) the way money serves as something that can be exchanged for the value of something else (p. 208)

Strike (strīk) the act of stopping work to get better pay and working conditions (p. 180)

Strikebreaker (strīk´ brā kər) a worker who works in place of a worker who is on strike (p. 181)

Subsidy (sub´ sə dē) a government grant (p. 85)

Subsistence farming (səb sis´ təns fär´ ming) growing crops mainly for personal use and not for sale (p. 397)

Substitute (sub´ stə tüt) a product that can be used in place of another product (p. 67)

Supply (sə plī´) the ability and willingness of sellers to make things available for sale (p. 80)

Supply curve (sə plī´ kėrv) a graph showing that suppliers are more willing to sell at higher prices than lower prices (p. 81)

Supply schedule (sə plī´ skej´ ül) a way to show the law of supply using a chart; it shows the quantity of a good offered at each possible market price (p. 81)

Supply-side economics (sə plī´ sīd ek ə nom´ iks) the belief that the best way to get a stable and growing economy is to increase the supply of goods and services (p. 303)

Surplus (sėr´ pləs) a budget in which more money is collected than is spent (p. 107); extra goods caused by the difference between what a seller is willing to supply and what buyers are willing to pay at that price (p. 325)

T

Tactic (tak´ tik) a way to achieve change or a goal (p. 190)

Tariff (tar´ if) a tax on imports (p. 381)

Tax (taks) money that people and businesses pay to help pay the cost of government (p. 85)

Technical know-how (tek´ nə kəl nō´ hou) the knowledge or skill to do something (p. 140)

Technology (tek nol´ ə jē) the use of science to create new products or make old ones better (p. 15)

Telemarketing (tel ə mär´ kə ting) the business of selling things over the telephone (p. 255)

Telemarketing fraud (tel ə mär´ kə ting frôd) any attempt over the phone to cheat consumers (p. 255)

Textile (tek´ stīl) an industry that is in the business of making cloth (p. 182)

The North (ŦHə nôrth) the name given by economists to the richer countries in the northern hemisphere of the world (p. 396)

The South (ŦHə south) the name given by economists to the poorer countries in the southern hemisphere of the world (p. 396)

Theory (thē´ ər ē) a possible explanation (p. 150)

Thrift institution (thrift in stə tü´ shən) a loan company, mutual savings bank, or credit union (p. 217)

Time deposit (tīm di poz´ it) a type of savings account that requires money to be kept in the account for a certain period of time (p. 270)

Time-and-a-half (tīm and a haf) money earned for working more than 40 hours per week; the hourly wage, plus half of the hourly wage (p. 193)

Total cost (tō´ tl kôst) all costs involved in making something to sell (p. 53)

Total revenue (tō´ tl rev´ ə nü) all money received by selling something; this amount is reached by multiplying the number of units sold by the average price of a unit (p. 53)

Trade barrier (trād bar´ ē ər) something that restricts or limits trade between countries (p. 381)

Trade deficit (trād def´ ə sit) an unfavorable balance of trade that occurs when a country's imports are greater than its exports (p. 376)

Trade-off (trād ôf) the act of giving up one thing for another (p. 8)

Trade surplus (trād sėr´ pləs) a favorable balance of trade that occurs when a country's exports are greater than its imports (p. 376)

Trade war (trād wôr) an act in which a country places tariffs on foreign goods and, in return, finds that tariffs are placed on their own goods (p. 383)

Tradition (trə dish´ ən) something that is passed down from one group to another (p. 27)

Traditional economy (trə dish´ ən nəl i kon´ ə mē) an economy that does things as they were done in the past; custom and tradition determine answers to the three economic questions (p. 27)

Traveler's check (trav´ ə lərz chek) a kind of check purchased from a bank that people often use on trips (p. 240)

Treasury bill (trezh´ ər ē bil) a security in which buyers pay money to the U.S. Treasury for the bill and receive more money in return later (p. 237)

Treasury bond (trezh´ ər ē bond) a long-term security issued in units of $1,000 that matures in 10 to 30 years (p. 326)

Treasury note (trezh´ ər ē nōt) a security with a value of $1,000 to $5,000 that matures in one to ten years (p. 326)

Trough (trôf) the lowest point in the business cycle (p. 338)

Trust (trust) when a few giant companies control important industries (p. 127)

U

Unemployed (un em ploid´) a person who wants to work but cannot find a job (p. 350)

Unemployment rate (un em ploi´ mənt rāt) the percentage of all unemployed workers (p. 350)

Uniform (yü´ nə fôrm) the ability of money to have the same size, weight, appearance, and value as money of the same kind (p. 210)

Union shop (yü´ nyən shop) a company that allows nonunion workers to be hired if they join the union (p. 193)

United Nations (UN) (yü nī´ tid nā´ shənz) an international organization started in 1945 to promote higher standards of living for all people (p. 402)

Unlimited liability (un lim´ ə tid lī ə bil´ ə tē) when the owner of a business is responsible for paying all of the money the business owes (p. 144)

Unlimited life (un lim´ ə tid līf) the ability of a corporation to go on, even if there is a change in ownership, management, or labor (p. 146)

Unskilled worker (un skild wėr´ kər) a type of worker who works in a job that requires very little training (p. 161)

Utilities (yü til´ ə tēz) items such as electricity, water, or gas (p. 28)

Utility (yü til´ ə tē) the usefulness or satisfaction a consumer gets from a product (p. 72)

V

Variable cost (ver´ ē ə bəl kôst) a cost that changes (p. 54)

Variable expense (ver´ ē ə bəl ek spens´) an expense that changes from month to month (p. 250)

Venture capitalist (ven´ chər kap´ ə tə list) an investor who backs an entrepreneur in return for part of the profits (p. 141)

Veteran (vet´ ər ən) a man or woman who has served in the armed forces (p. 323)

Veto (vē´ tō) to reject (p. 320)

a	hat	e	let	ī	ice	ô	order	ù	put	sh	she		ə	a	in about
ā	age	ē	equal	o	hot	oi	oil	ü	rule	th	thin			e	in taken
ä	far	ėr	term	ō	open	ou	out	ch	child	ᴛʜ	then			i	in pencil
â	care	i	it	ò	saw	u	cup	ng	long	zh	measure			o	in lemon
														u	in circus

Voluntary exchange (vol′ ən ter ē eks chānj′) an exchange someone makes on purpose (p. 51)

Voluntary trade restriction (vol′ ən ter ē trād ri strik′ shən) an offer made by a foreign country to limit the sale of their goods in another country (p. 382)

Volunteer (vol ən tir′) to choose to do work for no pay (p. 166)

W

Wage (wāj) the money a worker gets in exchange for labor (p. 166)

Want (wont) a thing that is not needed to survive but that makes life better (p. 4)

Warranty (wôr′ ən tē) a promise to fix something if it does not work (p. 125)

Welfare (wel′ far) aid (money or goods) for those in need (p. 28)

White-collar (hwīt′ kol ər) a name used to describe office workers and professionals (p. 161)

Workers' compensation (wėr′ kərz kom pən sā′ shən) payments made to workers who are injured or disabled while working (p. 185)

World Bank (wėrld bangk) an agency of the UN that directs money from developed countries to less developed countries (p. 403)

World Trade Organization (WTO) (wėrld trād ôr gə nə zā′ shən) an organization created in 1995 to replace GATT; member countries agree to cut tariffs on capital goods, end import quotas on textiles and clothing, and loosen other trade barriers (p. 386)

Y

Yellow dog contract (yel′ ō dog′ kon′ trakt) contracts some employers forced workers to sign that made the workers promise not to join a union (p. 192)

Index

Acknowledgments and Photo Credits

Acknowledgments

Acknowledgment is made for permission to reprint and record the following copyrighted material.

Page 74: From "Construction Delays Resulting from Shortage of Wallboard," by Edmond Conchas from *San Antonio Business Journal*, July 5, 1999. Reprinted with permission of the San Antonio Business Journal.

Page 94: From "Captain Sutter's account of the first discovery of the Gold," www.sfmuseum.org. Used by permission of www.sfmuseum.org.

Page 152: From *Titan: The Life of John D. Rockefeller, Sr.* by Ron Chernow, New York: Random House, Inc., 1998.

Page 262: From *Barnes & Noble Basics: Saving Money* by Barbara Loos, New York: Silver Lining Books, © 2003. Used by permission.

Page 284: Excerpt from *The New York Times* taken from www.nytimes.com. Copyright 1929 by The New York Times Co. Reprinted with permission.

Page 344: From "Fed Cuts A Quarter" from *CNNMoney,* June 25, 2003 taken from money.cnn.com. Copyright (2003) CNNMoney, Inc. Reprinted with the permission of CNNMoney.

Page 364: Excerpt from *Silent Spring* by Rachel Carson. Copyright © 1962 by Rachel L. Carson, renewed 1990 by Roger Christie. Reprinted by permission of Houghton Mifflin Company. All rights reserved.

Photo Credits

Cover images: (background) © Peter Sherrard/Getty Images, (inset) © Royalty-Free/Corbis; page xxii, © ThinkStock LLC/Index Stock Imagery; page 2, © Adalberto Rios Szalay/Sexto Sol/PhotoDisc; page 5, © David R. Frazier PhotoLibrary; page 8, © Patti McConville/Rainbow; page 12, © Michael Newman/PhotoEdit; page 13, © The Granger Collection; page 18, © Stock Montage; page 22, © Steve Dunwell/Image Bank/Getty Images; page 25, © David Young-Wolff/PhotoEdit; page 26, © Eli Reichman/Time Life Pictures/Getty Images; page 29, © Peter Christopher/Masterfile; page 31, © The Granger Collection; page 36, © The Granger Collection; page 42, © Anthony Boccaccio/Image Bank/Getty Images; page 44, © Gary Randall/Taxi/Getty Images; page 46, © The Granger Collection; page 52, © The Granger Collection; page 53, © Omni Photo Communications Inc./Index Stock Imagery; page 56, © Aaron Haupt/David R. Frazier PhotoLibrary; page 60, © Tom Stewart Photography/Corbis; page 62, © Getty Images News Services; page 65, © Ryan McVay/PhotoDisc; page 69, © Getty Images News Services; page 74, © Michael S. Yamashita/Corbis; page 78, © Don Tremain/PhotoDisc; page 86, © Syracuse Newspapers/The Image Works, Inc.; page 89, © AP/Wide World Photos; page 94, © The Granger Collection; page 98, © Mark E. Gibson/Gibson Stock Photography; page 101, © Rommel/Masterfile; page 102, © AP/Wide World Photos; page 104, © Bettmann/Corbis; page 110, © The Granger Collection; page 114, © Dennis MacDonald/PhotoEdit; page 117, © George Glod/SuperStock; page 120, © Robert Llewellyn/ImageState; page 128, © Robert Sorbo/Corbis/Sygma; page 134, Courtesy of Florence Fang, Publisher, San Francisco Examiner; page 136, © Charles Orrico/SuperStock; page 138, © Charles Gupton/Stone/Getty Images; page 141, © Gibson Stock Photography; page 144, © Eric R. Berndt/Unicorn Stock Photos; page 152, © Hulton Archive/Getty Images; page 156, © Spencer Grant/PhotoEdit; page 160, © Aneal Vohra/Unicorn Stock Photos; page 161, © Bob Daemmrich Photography; page 165, Courtesy/Walter E. Williams; page 171, © Bob Daemmrich Photography; page 174, © SuperStock; page 178, © Mark Richards/PhotoEdit; page 181, © North Wind Picture Archives; page 182, © The Granger Collection; page 188, © Michael Newman/PhotoEdit; page 198, © Bettmann/Corbis; page 204, © David Young-Wolff/PhotoEdit; page 206, © Spencer Grant/PhotoEdit; page 213, © North Wind Picture Archives; page 215, © Bettmann/Corbis; page 218, © Bob Daemmrich/Stone/Getty Images; page 222, © Stock Montage; page 226, © Rob Crandall/The Image Works, Inc.; page 228, © Corbis; page 233, © Jo MacMillan/Folio Inc.; page 235, © Getty Images/Getty Images Editorial; page 238, © Dennis Brack/IPN/Aurora Photos; page 242 (both images), © Getty Images Editorial; page 246, © David Young-Wolff/Stone/Getty Images; page 248, © Brian Pieters/Masterfile; page 255, © RANDY BISH reprinted by permission of United Feature Syndicate, Inc./Newspaper Enterprise Association, United Media (United Features Syndicate); page 259, © Royalty-Free/Corbis; page 260, © Getty Images Editorial; page 262, © Getty Images Editorial; page 266, © Dallas and John Heaton/Corbis; page 269, © David Young-Wolff/PhotoEdit; page 274, © Rob Crandall/The Image Works, Inc.; page 276, © Gail Mooney/Corbis; page 278, © Rob Crandall/Folio Inc.; page 284, © Topham/The Image Works, Inc.; page 290, © Greg Pease/Stone/Getty Images; page 292, © JFPI Studios, Inc./Corbis; page 294, © The Granger Collection; page 299, © Mark Richards/PhotoEdit; page 302, © Hulton Archive/Getty Images; page 312, © Getty Images Editorial; page 316, © Thomas Del Bras/Stone/Getty Images; page 319, © Wally McNamee/Corbis; page 320, © Bettmann/Corbis; page 328, © Susan Van Etten/PhotoEdit; page 332, © Jiang Jin/SuperStock; page 335, © James A. Sugar Photography/Corbis; page 343, © Ralf-Finn Hestoft/Corbis/SABA; page 348, © Jim McGuire/Index Stock Imagery; page 351, © David Butow/Corbis/SABA; page 355, © David Young-Wolff/PhotoEdit; page 356, © Peter Turnley/Corbis; page 364, © AP/Wide World Photos; page 370, © Don Mason Photography/Corbis; page 372, © Keren Su/Corbis; page 379, © Jon Mitchell/Lightroom Photos/Alamy.com; page 382, © Paul Chesley/Stone/Getty Images; page 387, © AP/Wide World Photos; page 388, © Getty Images Editorial; page 390, © Sygma Collection/Corbis; page 394, © Betty Press/Woodfin Camp & Associates; page 403, © AFP/Corbis; page 404, © Getty Images Editorial; page 406, © Christopher Arnesen/Stone/Getty Images